THE Rose & THE Briar

Death, Love and Liberty in the American Ballad

Edited by **Sean Wilentz** and **Greil Marcus**

W. W. NORTON & COMPANY

NEW YORK • LONDON

Manufacturing by The Maple-Vail Book Manufacturing Group
Book design by Rubina Yeh
Production manager: Amanda Morrison

Library of Congress Cataloging-in-Publication Data

The rose & the briar : death, love and liberty in the American ballad / edited by Sean Wilentz and Greil Marcus.— 1st ed.
    p. cm.
Includes bibliographical references and index.
Discography: p.
ISBN 0-393-05954-5 (hardcover)
1. Ballads, English—United States—History and criticism. 2. Death in music. 3. Love songs—United States—History and criticism. 4. Liberty—Songs and music—History and criticism. I. Title: Rose and the briar. II. Wilentz, Sean. III. Marcus, Greil.
    ML3551.R67 2005
    782.4'3—dc22

                                                                            2004014811

ISBN 0-393-32825-2 pbk.

W. W. Norton & Company, Inc., 500 Fifth Avenue, New York, N.Y. 10110
www.wwnorton.com

W. W. Norton & Company Ltd., Castle House, 75/76 Wells Street, London W1T 3QT

1 2 3 4 5 6 7 8 9 0

Praise for *The Rose & the Briar*

"Open up *The Rose & the Briar*, begin reading the real and imagined stories that make up its investigation of American ballads, and you will believe that the air itself has become a radio. Songs are all around you, with their inevitable tales of lost love, or love turned to murder or other forms of death, swirling through the air, not so much raising the dead as reminding you that those people and places you thought of as dead were always with us, waiting for their moment to reclaim their hold on you."   —Charles Taylor, *Salon*

"Not only is *The Rose & the Briar* a guide to how the ballad has shaped American music, but—thanks to the powerful and often eccentric essayists enlisted in this effort to identify and explicate the signal and variegated songs that make the case—it's a heartfelt, cock-eyed, be-plumed and dark-cornered history of the country herself, a clipper ship ripe for mutiny, full of violence, vanity and big-ass dreams, just like America today."   —Barry Gifford

"I love *The Rose & the Briar* as I have few other music books of the past few years. It's a total original—two terrific writer/editors asking critics and daring writers to investigate the entire history of the American ballad. . . . Absolutely nothing about *The Rose & the Briar* is ordinary, including Columbia/Legacy's separate anthology of the songs discussed. It's impossible not to learn or be utterly delighted with something within."
—Jeff Simon, *Buffalo News*

"Great stuff about music and about America."   —Randy Newman

"As an author who has devoted more care and thought than most to the question of just what shadowy forces lurk behind the enduring myths, Greil Marcus is the right man to edit this splendid processional, an eccentric mélange of fanciful speculation and academic research, criticism and mash notes. . . . Ballads are everywhere. They're mixed into the water supply of popular culture but still retain a wraithlike ability to shape-shift and elude fixed meanings. *The Rose & the Briar* is a frequently superb and generous Baedeker into the crevices of the ballad's half-lit history."
—Marc Weingarten, *San Francisco Chronicle*

In Memory of
Dave "Snaker" Ray
1943–2002

Contents

Introduction
Sean Wilentz and Greil Marcus 1

I

1. "Barbara Allen"
Dave Marsh 7

2. "The Water Is Wide"
Ann Powers 19

3. "Pretty Polly"
Rennie Sparks 35

4. Music, When Soft Voices Die
Sharyn McCrumb 51

5. Naomi Wise, 1807
Anna Domino 69

6. John Brown's Body
Sarah Vowell 81

II

7. "When You Go A Courtin'"
R. Crumb 93

8. Little Maggie—A Mystery
Joyce Carol Oates 99

9. We Did Them Wrong: The Ballad of Frankie and Albert
Cecil Brown 123

10. The Sad Song of Delia Green and Cooney Houston
Sean Wilentz 147

11. Destiny in My Right Hand: "The Wreck of Old 97"
and "Dead Man's Curve"
David Thomas 159

12. I Thought I Heard Buddy Bolden Say
   Luc Sante 175

13. "See Willy Fly By" and "The Cuckoo"
   Jon Langford 187

III

14. Mariachi Reverie
   Paul Berman 201

15. "The Foggy, Foggy Dew"
   John Rockwell 229

16. "Come Sunday"
   Stanley Crouch 241

17. "El Paso"
   James Miller 259

18. "Trial of Mary Maguire"
   Ed Ward 273

19. Love, Lore, Celebrity, and Dead Babies:
   Dolly Parton's "Down from Dover"
   Eric Weisbard 287

20. "Sail Away" and "Louisiana 1927"
   Steve Erickson 305

21. Dancing with Dylan
   Wendy Lesser 315

22. "Nebraska"
   Howard Hampton 327

23. "Blackwatertown"
   Paul Muldoon 345

Envoi
Greil Marcus 349

Notes, Books and Recordings 355

Contributors 383

Acknowledgments 391

Index 395

THE Rose & THE Briar

Death, Love and Liberty in the American Ballad

SEAN WILENTZ AND GREIL MARCUS

Introduction

What does the American ballad say about America? That it's a place of great stories and storytellers, for one thing. For another, that the sardonic bard, the sly salesman, the trusting soul, the blank-faced or charming killer, the hopeless fool, the heedless lover are all of a piece: all in some way talk the same slow, deliberate language; all call out to each other, and to the country at large. And if the work collected here is any clue, it says that our nation—dedicated to the proposition that liberty is real—is obsessed with death: the death of actors in the ballads; the death of the nation itself as a field of liberty. No matter what form the ballad takes—traditional or modern, handed down or composed, national epic or local story, tale of love or true-crime report—more than one life is always at stake.

Printed broadside ballads first appeared in sixteenth-century England and on the Continent shortly after the earliest European landings in the New World. Sometimes known as "slips" or "slip songs," and sold cheaply, they were the dim forerunners of modern commercial popular music. They related folklore about aristocrats and Bible characters and Robin Hood. They chronicled fourteenth-century wars and told current stories of murder and heartbreak. Exported to America (and then sent back, altered, to the Old World), they evolved with the Western Hemisphere and assumed a singular place in the life and art of what would become the United States.

Ballads became a major form—musically, perhaps, the major form—through which Americans told each other about themselves and the country they inhabited. Ancient songs from the Scots Highlands assumed new life and meaning in the Appalachian mountains. Polyglot traditions mingled, from Maine to the

Mississippi Delta, from Texas to Oregon, to produce ballads about floods, flights (of outlaws and fledgling airmen), presidents, and every other imaginable theme. After World War II, amid the explosion of a musical mass culture, the ballad persisted and even proliferated, not simply as a folksy throwback but as a resource for telling new kinds of stories in old ways with a shifting sound and style, from the car crash in Mark Dinning's "Teen Angel" to the changing seasons of Frank Sinatra's "It Was a Very Good Year."

This book takes up the American ballad from the past to the present: the music the ballad made and the culture it both drew from and transformed. It is based on a number of certainties, and one big hunch. Several generations of great folklorists—from Francis Child to John and Alan Lomax to their numerous scholarly progeny—have tracked the arcs that hundreds of ballads have traveled in time and place. Their research makes it possible to speak with some assurance about how specific songs, chiefly in the Anglo-American tradition, originated and evolved. The earliest folklorists' work usually involved the search for an authentic popular culture without formal literary or commercial influence, in the Romantic vein that arose in the early nineteenth century. Yet their findings, and those of their successors, actually revealed how snarled the origins and development of American balladry were and are. Quite distinct musical and storytelling forms from across the British Isles, as well as from the European continent, Africa, the Caribbean, and Latin America, twisted branches from many trees into single songs that then, sometimes, broke away to take new, separate shapes. The folklorists have also shown—and our own listening has confirmed—that commerce and American ballads have enjoyed fruitful and complex connections that stretch from Tin Pan Alley back to Stephen Foster and the pre–Civil War blackface minstrel shows all the way to the slip songs—and, even earlier, to the paid minstrels of medieval times. Following these tangles convinced us that there was still more to find out about specific songs we loved, as well as about the plethora of American ballad traditions—and, most of all, about the versions and visions of America they describe.

Our big hunch was that the best way to learn more would be to invite a wide range of novelists, short-story writers, artists, poets, songwriters, and performers, as well as critics, to create something new about an American ballad of their own choosing. The folklorists' work, invaluable as it is in establishing provenances and cultural connections, can take us only so far in understanding the life of any song. Something ineffable is always missing about the emotional or historical or visual or aural experience of singing or hearing a ballad. We became convinced that the American ballad made a language; today that language may be partly forgotten, but it also remains unlearned. By setting up something like a stage, and asking people we admire to get up and perform any ballad they liked, however they saw fit, we hoped to unlock some of the deeper mysteries of these songs and help create some new works of art.

The problem we faced at the outset was coming up with a working definition of "ballad" for contributors to follow. The word seems to derive from the Old Provençal *balada*, meaning a piece sung while dancing. There are references to a poetic form, the *ballata*, dating back to the late thirteenth century, but the French *balada* came into its own as the *ballade* over the two ensuing centuries, most powerfully in the poems of François Villon. As poetry, the *ballade* became, like the sonnet, a fixed form, one that consisted of three eight-line stanzas followed by a four-line envoi, which addressed a particular person and summarized the poem's message. At the same time, in Britain, narrative songs began appearing, invented and sung by minstrels as well as by ordinary rural folk. By the time Europeans arrived in America, these anonymously composed sagas had become identified as ballads. Today, the word connotes any narrative song, no matter its stanza structure—a promiscuous definition we were happy to adopt.

More vexing was the question of balladry and authorship. For a long time, experts treated the ballad strictly as a popular form of singing and writing that emerged from the mist of the experience of country commoners, passed down through folkways that eventually crossed oceans and continents. According to the once-definitive *Cambridge History of English and American Literature* of eighty years ago, the "weight of authority, as well as numbers, inclines to the side of those who refuse to obliterate the line between popular ballads and lettered verse, and who are unable to accept writers like Villon in France and [William] Dunbar in Scotland as responsible for songs which, by this convenient hypothesis, have simply come down to us without the writers' names."

We decided differently. In their preface to *Lyrical Ballads* (1798), Samuel Taylor Coleridge and William Wordsworth wrote of the poems that followed as "experiments" that they had composed "chiefly with a view to ascertain how far the language of conversation in the middle and lower classes of society is adapted to the purposes of poetic pleasure." We were interested in conducting similar experiments with the help of modern writers and artists. And it seemed to us absurd to have them take as their starting points only traditional folk compositions. Whatever sense it once might have made to separate lettered verse from ballads—a proposition that is not, to us, self-evident—the distinction seemed to have collapsed utterly in twentieth-century America. Marty Robbins's "El Paso" or Randy Newman's "Louisiana 1927" are as interesting as "Barbara Allen" or "Pretty Polly." To adopt the more restrictive folklorish definition would be to pronounce the ballad tradition over and done with—extinguished in the last pockets of cultural isolation that did not survive the coming of rural electrification and the radio—when in fact the form is very much alive.

As the pieces here appear in roughly the order in which their songs appeared in the historical record—from Dave Marsh's dive into the fable of "Barbara Allen" to Rennie Sparks's map of the travels of "Pretty Polly"; from Anna Domino's re-imagining of the story inside "Omie Wise" to Sarah Vowell's account of "John Brown's Body" (sometimes the story a storytelling song tells is the story of its own making); from Luc Sante's journey back to the night someone first sang "I thought I heard Buddy Bolden say . . ." to Howard Hampton staring down Bruce Springsteen's "Nebraska"—the reader can perhaps hear the tradition call its own tune. As our collaborators sent in their work, they forced us to think in new ways about what a ballad really is—and what an American ballad can be. Through dogged historical research, fiction, radical fantasy, memoir, comic strip, cartooning, poetry, and critical freebooting, they covered material that ran from the distant past to the almost-here-and-now. If we set up a stage for them, they sang their hearts out. Now we are proud to lift the curtain.

I

"Barbara Allen"

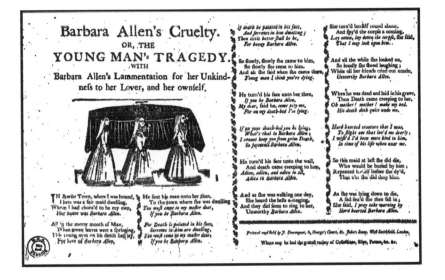

"Barbara Allen's Cruelty. Or the Young Man's
Tragedy." Broadside, J. Davenport, London,
between 1800 and 1802. Courtesy the Bodleian
Library, University of Oxford. Reference
Harding B 3(49).

DAVE MARSH

"Barbara Allen"

The problem began on January 2, 1666. In his diary entry for that day, Samuel Pepys wrote, "In perfect pleasure I was to hear her [an actress named Mrs. Knipp] sing, and especially her little Scotch song of Barbary Allen." At that moment, "Barbary Allen" ("Barbara Allen," "Barbry Ellen," or any of the several other variations by which it's known) passed out of the dim recesses of folklore and into an even more shadowy existence as a literary reference point.

"Barbara Allen" already was an old song, sung for a century or more before it made its backdoor entry as a footnote in the canon. Scholars now consider "Barbara Allen" (the most common contemporary title) the most widespread folk song in the English language, with more variant versions than any other song and the greatest geographic spread. From Scotland, where it probably originated some time in the medieval period, through the rest of the British Isles and on into the North American Appalachian mountains, where the English transplanted that curious breed, the Scots-Irish, the song was very well known from pioneer days—Abraham Lincoln is said to have sung it as a child—until deep into the twentieth century. Francis Child listed it as number 84 in his collection, but Child's system took into account neither the numbers of people who might know or sing the song nor the number of versions in existence. Child presented three texts, all to the same tune. There seem to be at least four basic tunes (one source cites twelve altogether), and God knows

9

how many different versions of the lyrics. Folklorist Bertrand Harris Bronson listed 198 and included two variants in his addenda.

Discussion of "Barbara Allen" takes two forms—one about accounting, the other about poetry. The accountants enumerate and sometimes describe the minor variations among versions—in fact, there are few versions with any major changes and many alter only a few images. The other discussion of "Barbara Allen" takes place in secondary school, where it has entered the curriculum as the model of the ballad form. It's not the only folk song taught in this fashion but it seems to be the main one.

Virtually no one discusses "Barbara Allen" in terms of the emotion its music conveys, or what its lyric has to say. Absolutely no one, as far as I can tell, discusses the song as a whole, the way in which the words and music interact to construct a meaning that (this is written sotto voce, lest the students find out) cannot be conveyed on paper, with or without a G clef. Most curiously of all, no one mentions that the song's survival may be a result of that meaning.

The literary value of "Barbara Allen," that is, lies in the Pepys diary reference and in its exemplification of a certain form of poetry. That it is not a poem in the first place occurs to no one—but it isn't, no song lyric is, if by poem we understand "something we can read and understand without performing."

The Ballad Book of John Jacob Niles (1960) devotes four pages to "Barbry Allen," including two different versions of the lyric. The version that Niles, one of the earlier ballad collectors and folk-song performers, sang onstage has sixteen verses; the version he gathered from an Appalachian teenager smitten with it had but thirteen. "As performance material," he calls "Barbara Allen" "absolutely foolproof." Nevertheless, as far as Niles and the other folksingers and scholars of his era (which stretches from the 1930s to the 1960s) were concerned, there was little to say about "Barbara Allen."

Niles makes the point explicitly: "It is simply boy meets girl, boy falls in love with girl, girl rejects boy, boy dies of love, girl follows, dying of sorrow, both are buried close to one another, and, in the fullness of time, a love knot is tied by a rose and a briar."

Everything Niles says is in the song is in it, sort of. The boy meeting the girl nowhere comes into it, but other than that, the account contains no inaccuracy. What distinguishes his description is what it leaves out.

At the start of the song, in the inevitably merry month of May, often as not in a place called Scarlet Town, the boy, who goes under an assortment of names (Sweet William, Poor William, William Green, Willie Grove, Jimmy—Jemmy or Jemmye—Grove; in Scotland, apparently, it is always John Graeme), lies on his deathbed. Why is he dying? Because he loves Barbara Allen and she does not love him. This already makes the song something other than standard boy-meets-girl stuff because dying of a broken heart is, to say the least, quite uncommon.

He sends his servants to bring Barbara to him. They do not recognize her, which is odd, if Sweet William had been courting her. Nevertheless, she comes along—but slowly, slowly. The next events occur in different sequences depending on who's singing, but always he pledges his devotion, and always she spurns him, cruelly commenting, "Young man, I think you're dying." I've seen this line printed with an exclamation point, but I've never heard it sung that way—what makes the cruelty so painful is her indifference.

But Barbara is not indifferent; she is steamed, in a huff. In many versions, she tells him that she doesn't believe his love is real because, in a tavern some night previously, he had toasted all the ladies fair but did not toast Barbara Allen. To which William replies that he did intend to give all the girls a shout, but to Barbara Allen alone he gave his heart.

All that we are told—and not always even this much—is that William then turns his face to the wall, says adieu to his friends, and (most of the time) bids them be kind to Barbara Allen.

Barbara learns that William has died through various means. While walking home, sometimes she hears the church bells toll and every stroke seems to say, "Hard-hearted Barbara Allen." Sometimes, she looks east and she looks west and sees "his pale corpse comin'" (which does not mean she sees a ghost but only a funeral procession). Sometimes, she goes right up to the hearse and asks to see the corpse; in one East Kentucky rendition, "She says 'Come round you nice young man/And let me look upon you.'"

At this point, Barbara changes. Most commonly, she asks her mother to make her grave: "Make it both long and narrow/Sweet William died on yesterday/And I shall die tomorrow." Die she does, and she is buried in the same churchyard as William. Then the red rose and the briar grow—the red rose of love from his heart, the prickly, lonely briar from hers. And after they reach a certain height—in one version, after they reach above the church's tower—they entwine in a lovers' knot.

It's that last image that drives the whole song, for me. It's not quite a punch line, but when you hear the song sung well, this mystical occurrence feels entirely of a piece with reality, which is to say, it feels not mystical at all but right and necessary. It tells us why we have paid attention through all these improbabilities, and why we are not alone in doing so.

If there is a reason that people have sung "Barbara Allen" for half a millennium, it lies right here. We want to know that rose and thorn are still joined and we hope, someday, that we will understand why.

∿↟↡∿

John Jacob Niles, born in 1892, grew up around Louisville, Kentucky, where his father farmed and worked as a carpenter. His mother played classical piano. His father had a reputation as one of the area's finest singers of folk songs and gave his son a three-stringed dulcimer, telling John Jacob he'd be expected to make his own instruments from then on. He made the first when he was twelve. In 1909, Niles graduated from high school and, taking a job as a surveyor, went through the mountainous regions of the state, collecting songs from the locals in his spare time. After World War I, he studied music in France and Cincinnati. His genial performances are similar to the best-known early recording of "Barbara Allen," made in 1928 by Bradley Kincaid, the Kentucky Mountain Boy with his Houn' Dog Guitar, who became a star of the WLS Radio *National Barn Dance* (and who named Marshall Jones "Grandpa"). Kincaid gave "Barbara Allen" and similar songs a Prohibition-era vogue, primarily through a series of songbooks. (It wasn't until after World War II that music became the pure spectator sport it is today.)

Niles and Kincaid do their best to stay out of the story's way. They play the melody with a moderate rhythm, and their vocals do not dwell upon any of its odd emotional corners. The version by the great Merle Travis, another native Kentuckian, manages to make the tune seem almost jolly, the story no more sad than "I Gave My Love a Cherry." In a way, they prepare listeners well for the folk-revival version by Joan Baez, which appeared on a 1961 album, *Volume Two.* In the liner notes to the Baez record, producer Maynard Solomon describes "Barbara Allen" as "the classic ballad of a repentant virgin," which is one way to look at it. Baez plunges further into the song. Her vocal, for all its arty flourishes, contains a breath of wonder, and she's accompanied by a repetitive guitar figure that adds some dramatic tension.

All of these versions, however, are separate from the recorded one by Jean Ritchie, yet another Kentucky singer, who, also in 1961, included the song on her Folkways album *Ballads.* Ritchie sings "Barbara Allen" without any accompaniment, in a full, pure voice with just a hint of vibrato and a strong Southern twang. To her, the song clearly is something more than an odd story. It is a tragedy and a warning and a mystery, a way of taking the measure of things for which there is no easy accounting. Her Barbara is the cruelest imaginable. When William tells her he is very low and death is on him dwelling, she agrees and adds, "No better, no better you never will be/For you can't get Barbry Allen." Ritchie, arguably the greatest of all American traditional ballad singers, makes this feel as cold as it reads, and yet, somehow, her singing retains compassion—there is no sense that Barbara gets what she deserves and there is nothing matter-of-fact about any of the events. In the world where Jean Ritchie lived, perhaps, the consequences of an emotional misstep could be just this steep. The stillness when the recording finishes is a haunting thing.

Perhaps the difference is between the way a man approaches the song and the way a woman tells the story. At least Sweet William, Poor William, dies after having made a positive decision and trying to reach out to his beloved. And it's true, nowhere does the song suggest that his hearty toast that seemed to embrace every girl around might *reasonably* have been interpreted as threatening and insulting by the girl who was—perhaps—already his lover (whether or not she remained a virgin, but the more so if not). On the other side of it, perhaps it's Barbara dying because there is no chance for redemption from her error that haunts the Ritchie and even the Baez performances. And isn't the great modern version of "Barbara Allen" the one Dolly Parton made in 1994, with an introduction that made it an integral part of the web of her life growing up in the Smoky Mountains in the 1950s, where the poor Scots-Irish still claim "Barbara Allen" as their own? Or if not that, then the fragment of the very ancient-sounding version by the actress Emmy Rossum, playing a teenage mountain singer, that we get to hear on the soundtrack of the film *Songcatcher*? (Of the clueless rendition by Emmylou Harris on the same soundtrack, we need not speak.)

Except that the only version I know that comes anywhere near Jean Ritchie's is by a man.

Traditional folksingers never liked Bob Dylan's approach to their material much. He put into it more exuberant affection than sober respect, and some of the things he did with his voice fouled up trying to understand the lyrics. Such folksingers are almost as obsessed with clarity of enunciation, even at the expense of emotional clarity, as show-tune singers. Dylan did not have any of this to offer.

Dylan loved the old ballads, and "Barbara Allen" in particular. In "For Dave Glover," a poem that appeared in the program for the 1963 Newport Folk Festival, Dylan wrote:

> The folk songs showed me the way
> They showed me that songs can say somethin human
> Without "Barbara Allen" there'd be no "Girl From the North Country"

Dylan understood the songs completely differently from someone like John Jacob Niles. "[A]ll the authorities who write about what it is and what it should be, when they say keep things simple, they should be easily understood . . . folk music is the only music where it isn't simple," Dylan told Nora Ephron and Susan Edmiston in 1965. "It's never been simple. It's weird, man, full of legend, myth, Bible and ghosts. I've never written anything hard to understand, not in my head anyway, and nothing as far out as some of the old songs. They were out of sight."

What songs? ask Ephron and Edmiston. "Little Brown Dog," replies Dylan, where a man flies to Turkey on a bottle, and "Nottemun Town," where a herd of ghosts passes through on the way to Tangier. "'Lord Edward,' 'Barbara Allen,' they're full of myth." Elsewhere, he refers to the rose and the briar as one of the strangest images he knows.

On what's now known as the "Second Gaslight Tape," from 1962, Dylan takes a little over eight minutes to get through the story. (It took Ritchie about five and a half, Joan Baez four and a quarter, Merle Travis four on the dot, Bradley Kincaid 3:08.)

A musical magpie, Dylan undoubtedly knew what both Baez and Ritchie had recently done with "Barbara Allen." He took his guitar figure, an endless cycle of strumming, from Baez, but he took his aim squarely from Ritchie, reaching down into her stockpile of implications and dredging them up, bit by bit. He aimed less for a story than for an atmosphere, and the atmosphere, judging from the Gaslight show, mostly spoke of death. The most clearly articulated couplet he delivers is, "Cryin' put him down and leave him there/So I might gaze upon him."

His guitar-playing stumbles, his pitch wavers—these are not surprises. What's amazing is that he starts at the place Ritchie leaves us—a place where the improbabilities of Barbara Allen's story represent a grave lesson of mortal peril.

In a sense, this claustrophobic rendition prefigures some of the songs Dylan sang on the second side of his 1965 album *Bringing It All Back Home*, where, after a tear-ass trip through a set of rock 'n' roll songs on the first side, he returns with just a guitar and drones through "Mr. Tambourine Man," "Gates of Eden," "It's All Right Ma (I'm Only Bleeding)," and "It's All Over Now, Baby Blue." The music has that same sense of living in an ill-fated world, that air of helplessness that is not quite hopelessness. Dylan wanted to update the fatalistic world that people like Jean Ritchie and Dolly Parton inhabited; he wanted to find a way to show modern people how their world connected to that one. In this sense, his "Barbara Allen" is truly his beginning.

Yet he does not stray a bit from the common tale. The only meaningful variation he makes, as far as I can tell, is to repeat the last verse at the very end—which he clearly does so he can draw out that last "Barbara Allen" for what feels like a heartbroken eternity. Yes, he sings "Charlotte Town," instead of "Scarlet Town," but that's meaningless. He's not looking to use "Barbara Allen" to comment on the civil rights movement in North Carolina. To the contrary: Dylan's whole point— unlike Jean Ritchie, he is a modern artist and needs to have one—is that the song requires no such alterations to have this music speak of the contemporary world. What it uniquely contains was beyond the understanding of medieval man; it is also beyond the reckoning of people today. Why do people do these things to one another? Why must they, and who pays the price, and why is life a thing of grace and beauty anyway? What is it that roses and briars have in common?

The answer is not blowing in the wind. The answer is that we will never find the answer, and never stop seeking it. And so we sing the song.

⁕

"Barbara Allen" has been my favorite song for a very long time—since I heard Ritchie sing it, and a wild instrumental version, "Barbara Allen Blues," by Roscoe Holcomb.

I do not know very much about why. I do know that, when my daughter died—from something much more concrete and just as little understood as heartbreak—my only thought for her headstone was a red rose and a briar. (She has a plain rose in concrete and a quote from a Bob Dylan song that her mother chose.) But I know, from having concentrated on the song, that you can hear its echoes in places where no one ever thought to put them. In Paul McCartney's "Silly Love Songs" and Bruce Springsteen's "Hungry Heart," and, much more faintly, in every teen-tragedy tune there ever was, but especially in Pearl Jam's remodeling of J. Frank Wilson and the Cavaliers' "Last Kiss."

As my friend Danny Alexander recently wrote, after I asked what he made of it:

> What got me about that story all day long was how it struck a chord with my most recent, and devastating, heartbreak. The fact that he

would give anything and yet something he did sent the wrong message, the fact that he lies on his deathbed regretting his missteps, that another life might have been possible, resonates with the essence of the anguish of heartache in my ears, and the essence of a million love songs. It reminds me of my favorite moment in "Yesterday"—I said something wrong, now she's gone.

And that briar, that hard heart that Barbara Allen feels tragically burdened with, her own regret for turning him away that ultimately kills her, perhaps the fact that she judges too quickly, that she didn't give him the benefit of the doubt and is now responsible for ending his life, makes me think of the other side of the anguish of the breakup. What if the hard choices you are making are not the right ones? What if, as Warren Zevon asks in "Empty-Handed Heart," you've "thrown down diamonds in the sand"?

Humans invent songs and stories so that they can be repeated. Their endless variation should surprise us no more than the endless variation of each face we see. The fact that the good songs and stories are spread far and wide and kept and cherished is not an amazement, although it is a blessing. What amazes me is that people—educated people and, for that matter, people who educate—can gaze so long at such a beautiful mystery and instead see nothing but a perfectly formed shell containing interesting things to count.

What's amazing is our ability to ignore the lesson that "Barbara Allen" has to teach, which is the peril of denying the complicated mysteries that throb within our hardened hearts and the equal peril of horsing around instead of acknowledging our love for one another. This is not a lesson you can squeeze onto a tombstone, or, for that matter, our current conception of a curriculum, but it is one to carry through this life.

"The Water Is Wide"

Edward Hopper (1882–1967), Room in Brooklyn, *1932, oil on canvas. Museum of Fine Arts, Boston. The Hayden Collection—Charles Henry Hayden Fund. Photograph © 2004 Museum of Fine Arts, Boston.*

ANN POWERS

"The Water Is Wide"

I n this part of the story, nothing happens. A woman walks through a garden, as she does every morning. A lover remembers taking a risk that ended in disappointment. A match misses by inches. A young girl might or might not be pregnant. A marriage drifts. A sailor can't decide on a route by which to return from the sea. A lady waits. A lady always waits at this point in the story. It is her nature to surface in the spaces between.

> The water is wide
> I cannot get o'er
> And neither have
> I wings to fly

Music for times like this is known as "floating." It's everywhere but can't claim a permanent location. Animate, shape-shifting, it does not respond well to its history's being traced. Perhaps for that reason, it's not taken that seriously. Like a woman sitting quietly on a bench in a garden, its presence is expected and it pretties up the landscape, so in large part it may be tactfully ignored.

> I leaned my back
> Up against an oak
> I thought it was
> A trusty tree

"What was your name again?" That's a question that women who frequent public places come to expect. The folk song that best captures the part of the story where nothing happens might be called "The Water Is Wide," "O Waly Waly," "O Love Is Teasing," or "Come All You Fair and Tender Ladies," depending on which verses appear or dissipate. The song is related to sea shanties like "When Cockle Shells Turn Silver Bells" and cautionary ballads like "The Butcher Boy." Carl Sandburg shoved it in his *American Songbag* as "Waillie, Waillie"; Alan Lomax found a trace of it in a blues he called "Dink's Song." Its oldest connection seems to be to Child Ballad 204, "Jamie Douglas," first collected by poet and wig-maker Allan Ramsay in his 1727 *Tea-Table Miscellany*—a chronicle of a woman's punishment for an act of adultery that she claims never occurred. That story is absent, hardly even implied, in the lament that singers favor now. Everyone who really explores the song agrees it's lost a lot of layers since the days when it qualified as a real ballad. Yet it's more popular than ever. It has a different purpose now.

> For love grows old
> And waxes cold

In what plot does accrue to this lovely bit of lyrical inertia, wishing gives way to regret and, finally, resignation. The action is entirely internal. Musically, there's a similar sense of choices unmade. The version most familiar to contemporary ears has a melody that's tidal, moving inconclusively up and down the major scale and finally ending on the same note that followed the first. It could easily transform into a never-ending round. Stuck in your brain, it nags, like the memory of that time when you listened to her talking for so long into your answering machine, the moment when he leaned in to kiss you and you turned your head.

> And fades away
> Like morning dew

❧

Debra Allbery's long poem of 1990, "The Reservoir," depicts a woman who has returned to her hometown of Enterprise, Ohio, to figure out how to tie up some loose ends in her life. She gets stuck for a while. Every day she jogs around the local man-made lake.

> She's outside of Enterprise, running the reservoir,
> singing to herself, *The water is wide,*
> looking past the south and east edges
> of town, at the reach of August sky
> and black clouds moving quickly
> from the west, and she's thinking
> *Sometimes if I open my eyes very wide*
> *there's this space which is like*
> *room for error. And I see limits,*
> *I see things that can change my mind.*
> It's what she'll remember most
> from this long wedded summer—her orbits
> around a five-sided body of water
> with usually a storm of some kind in the distance.

In Allbery's beautifully modulated rendering of the mundane side of crisis, her protagonist acts out the ageless stalled narrative of the folk song she idly hums. But how did that song end up on her lips in the first place? She first hears her brother crooning it on the porch of their family house, and she senses listeners sitting in the seemingly quiet playground across the street, as if the song couldn't be sung without someone receiving it. Allbery uses the lyric emblematically, assuming that readers will remember that expanding and contracting tune and feel the deep longing it conveys. Otherwise the lyric fragment is just a metaphor, and a fairly banal one, not up to Allbery's standards. She understands how embedded in our consciousness these sound-images are. The couplets that comprise "The Water Is Wide" are like so many stones washed up on the shore of a shared history, smoothed over by time, marked with the traces of countless real and imagined occurrences. They are as empty as a summer spent sleeping in your childhood bedroom, and as full of uncertainty, hope, and loss.

According to the folk detectives, this nonballad (its official classification in the *Traditional Ballad Index*) claimed more weight in the first hundred years of its life, which Cecil Sharp found began sometime around the middle of the sixteenth century. A Scottish lament about unreliable love, it had a chicken-and-egg relationship to the ballad of the wronged Lady Douglas. That now-obscure chronicle is a fine illustration of how little credence was given a woman's claims in the age of gentility. Accused by a manservant of having taken up with a dashing newcomer (who, in an interesting symbolic stroke, shares her husband's first name and bears the trusty last name "Lockhart"), she fails to charm her way back into her husband's graces and must depart, without her three children, for her father's land. In most versions, she vows fidelity to the man who judged her incapable of it, and never remarries. In one or two, he accepts her back. More often, she simply pines away, lamenting her decision to wed Douglas in the first place, and her inability to be unfaithful even in her banishment.

"Lord Jamie Douglas" warns women of the consequences of becoming open to accusations of infidelity. It's a powerful injunction to avoid even seeming to act. By the nineteenth century, verses associated with this ballad had become attached to the vastly popular array of songs about women who refuse or are unable to move forward: those awaiting their lovers' return, from the war or the sea or some other adventure, and those abandoned to the social and psychological limbo of defiled honor, with or without the physical consequence of unwanted pregnancy.

> A ship there is
> And it sails the sea
> It's loaded deep
> As deep can be

"Women in nineteenth-century culture were supposed to be passive, compliant, and patient, but the women in sea songs wait longer and better than most," writes folklorist Caroline Moseley in her account of women's images in sailors' shanties. The homosocial environment of the maritime industry exacerbated the ideal of the "True Woman" in sailors' lore; popular verses about abandoned sweethearts highlight their willingness to wait almost endlessly and be completely available once their man blows into town. While a few daring maidens venture forth in songs like "The Female Solder," most haunt the rocks oceanside, angelically wishing for boats or wings. In the choruses that helped seamen get through the working day, idylls involving these bonny lasses alternated with bawdy songs about barroom "flash packets." Fidelity—though not their own—mattered much to the wandering breadwinners. The cost of easy virtue is one theme that haunts "The Water Is Wide"; the torpor the song captures afflicts a heart and body that may have been too hastily given in the first place.

The most popular sung variants on the theme of fidelity present its preservation as an adventure unto itself. "Broken-token" ballads outnumber all others concerning romance; the sociologist Robert M. Rennick counted 160 versions in America alone. Most begin with that well-worn portrait of the lady in a garden, and apparently stem from a single broadside, "The Sailors' Return, or the Broken Token," published around 1750. The encounter detailed in that lyric and its antecedents involves a vigorous suitor approaching our heroine not only with offers of affection but also with whispers that the betrothed to whom she clings will never return. "His face you'll never see again. . . ." Perhaps he's drowned, or been slain by an enemy, or stolen off with another girl. These cruel intimations can't sway our stalwart maid, of course, and the disguised lover finally reveals himself by producing half a trinket they'd divided long ago, at which point she falls at his feet in a puddle of happiness, undisturbed that the face she adored has changed so much that it's unrecognizable, simply relieved that her waiting has come to an end.

"Broken token" tales are magical, recalling such fairy stories as "Beauty and the Beast," in which illusions that stir troubling desires clarify themselves to reveal the stability of true love. It's hardly surprising that these songs were widespread at a time when immigration and itinerant work often forced couples apart. Yet it's the psychological side of these ballads that strikes more deeply than their historical relevance. Writing in 1964, Rennick expressed admiration for the broken-token theme's "exemplary effect upon the folk morality," postulating that its depiction of erotic desire as naturally steadfast helped those who shared the song maintain their bonds in their own lives. Such ballads make the consequences of a woman's choice internal. In "Jamie Douglas," the outcome of even perceived female infidelity—banishment—offered a fright. By all appearances, the fair maid in a broken-token song would actually gain by relinquishing her promise in favor of her "new" suitor. It's not her place in society that her virtue preserves, but her soul.

The happy endings of broken-token stories granted some inspiration for lovers tested by time and space. But as any moralist knows, a threat often works better than a promise. As the current that leads to "The Water Is Wide" speeds on, a new strain emerges that leaves our waiting lady alone. The songs linked by the phrase "come all you fair and tender ladies" (or "pretty maids" or "tender maidens") offer moral entreaties to young women to keep waiting for their princes, despite the temptations that rogues present; sung in the voice of a sadder-but-wiser girl, they tell of a false love that will entrap the heart. Folklorists link these songs to that primordial "O Waly Waly," and therefore back to the dark "Jamie Douglas." They also share phrases with songs like "O Love Is Teasing" and "Careless Love." Jean Ritchie, who claimed to have learned "O Love Is Teasing" at her uncle Jason's knee, recorded it in her book *Folk Songs from the Southern Appalachians*, in 1965. Her lyrics read, in part:

Come all you fair and tender ladies
Take warning how you court young men
They're like a bright star on a cloudy morning
They will first appear and then they're gone

I wish I was some little sparrow
That I had wings and I could fly
I would fly away to my false truelover
And while they'd talk I'd sit and cry

But I am not no little sparrow
I have no wings and I can't fly
I'll sit right here in my grief and sorrow
And pass my troubles by and by

It's only a step from the Fair Maiden songs to "The Water Is Wide." The difference is that the warning to others, stressed in songs like the one Ritchie relates, becomes almost an afterthought. Instead, what dominates is an almost luxuriant sorrow, which some might interpret as a sign of a masochistic heart.

> I put my hand into some soft bush,
> Thinking the sweetest flower to find.
> I pricked my finger to the bone,
> And left the sweetest flower alone

The middle verses of the song we sing today, which employ the metaphors of the rotten tree and the prickly bush, reveal its roots in the history of female abandonment. Most singers, affecting an air of solemnity, don't fully tap the eroticism of the metaphors: the blood that trickles from the hand that grabs for a blossom and the oak whose wood proves so soft that the singer collapses into it. Some lore collectors say that the latter reference hints at an antiquated abortion method, perhaps the taking of herbs found in the woods to "quicken" menses. A woman would lean back, woozy, as this often-fatal folk "cure" sickened her. But it seems more likely that the lyric refers to an earlier surrender, the sensual surrender that led to such trouble in the first place.

> But first it swayed
> And then it broke
> And so my false love
> Proved unto me

In such a song, we are shoved into the midst of irresolution. No hero appears, proffering a ring; only time may provide any peace. The lover is trapped in a state of regret, betrayed, unable to stop loving. In the "Careless Love" versions, time, hard pressing, may also cause her further confinement, for the sign of her apron rising heralds the child that will result from her willingness. She did not wait, in the virginal sense, for her love to prove true, and now she waits, perhaps forever, for her sorrow to abate.

These stories come from the last century of true darkness, we career women and serial monogamists tell ourselves. There were no women's clinics then, no morning-after pills. Now, a healthy professional life and drinks on Fridays with the girls is a viable alternative to the hellish isolation of those romanticized Fair Maidens. Feminists have even dug out the history that gives the lie to such songs, celebrating the achievements of women who toiled in factories, wrote novels, dressed as men and fought in battle, founded religious orders, or gave abortions to needy girls, instead of hanging around in some bower to be rescued by a patriarch.

And yet we women still sing these songs, as if they have something to teach us. "The Water Is Wide" actually became more popular after Pete Seeger introduced it to the folk revival in 1961. Myriad musical icons have recorded it, from Joan Baez to Barbra Streisand to the Indigo Girls and Charlotte Church. It gave the women of the pop-feminist Lilith Fair a proper sing-along for its all-star finale. Men like the song, too, not worrying at all about its vestigial aura of sexism. It's performed, regularly and very inappropriately, at weddings; it also shows up, a more likely candidate, at funerals. Something keeps its melancholy ebb and flow pertinent, even in an era when everything is always happening and no one can bear to wait.

> I know not if
> I sink or swim

⁂

"Lovers are always waiting," writes Anne Carson in *Eros the Bittersweet*, her inquiry into the structures of passion. "They hate to wait; they love to wait. Wedged between these two feelings, lovers come to think a great deal about time, and to understand it very well, in their perverse way."

When a lover falls in love, she tends to make time, carving out minutes on end to manufacture conversations, reflect upon encounters, and ponder whether what she's sensing is real or not. Her love is definitely real in these stolen moments, when no one—most of all, the beloved—is around to dispute it. One reason so much popular music revolves around romance is that music has the same power to set time aside, making a little private space within the day where the singer or the listener can build on inner ground. *Give me the beat, boys, and free my soul, I wanna get lost in your rock and roll and drift away . . . give me a boat that can carry two.* Music works like that longed-for vessel, carrying its lover to a place where reality isn't crowding her out.

Humming a half-forgotten melody, the lover can set herself and her beloved within it and navigate a sea of possibility. Similar, though sadder, psychic journeys happen at the end of the affair and can last for years. New-love songs are fine, but heartbreak songs may be more necessary; they help the lover negotiate time in a phase when it may seem about to bury her. Among the things Allbery's reservoir runner treads away from is a ten-year romance; one day, a friend's tactless letter informs her that her once-true love will be marrying soon. She runs into him a while later and feels easily (if painfully) unbound, but waking up to run again, she wonders if she'll ever resolve to fully accept that freedom.

> She has distances she wants to try
> alone. And still, like anyone,
> it's belonging she wants, it's the idea
> of *settled* or *permanent address.*
> And all she's done has been only so much
> rent paid toward that place.

"The Water Is Wide" captures the experience of teetering on that edge between attachment and true solitude. It's not only a cry of abandonment, it's also a reverie of escape. The shore-wandering wife who dreams of a boat that can carry two collides with the bitter innocent who wishes her belly weren't so heavy and she could fly out of her false suitor's reach. "Why must I play such a childish part, and love a girl that will break my heart?" a verse reads in one version of the song to be sung by a male voice. In another rendering, the singer imagines his lover dead and buried—the only situation that will allow him the distance to think comfortably about her. Here, "The Water Is Wide" edges toward the murder-ballad, the subgenre that ruminates on love just too pressing to bear, where the lady is made to wait forever by her suitor, who reckons the only safe place to put his ambivalence is in the ground.

Few variants of the song suggest such aggressive action, however. Let other folk favorites provide rip-roaring escapades, insights into historical events, or details of everyday life in landscapes different from our own. "The Water Is Wide" has been assembled by generations of singers from the connective tissue of those meatier ballads, in order to provide a respite from the external world they portray. Sometimes a lover wants to be left alone, even by the beloved, to shape an idyll from scraps of fantasy, nostalgia, and desire. Songs like "The Water Is Wide" set aside room where that can happen. The psychic remains that the lovers carry in their heads and hearts—the little morality plays, sleeping dreams, anxious visions, revised histories, remorse—must be sorted out before they can move on. "The Water Is Wide," like a good, dark daydream, allows a chance to do that.

"The Water Is Wide" is particularly suited to this role, partly because, like the love it ponders, it can be judged a false construction. Unlike Ivory soap, this song floats because it's impure. Folk music aficionados can be very concerned about issues of authenticity; the problem of "fakesong"—lyrics and tunes passed off as "of the folk," despite their actually being composed by professional writers or cobbled together from various popular sources—has stimulated debate at least since Cecil Sharp and the Lomaxes started their ballad hunting in the early part of the twentieth century. Artists tend to favor what works with the crowd over purism. "A mountaineer singing a pop song to some neighbors in his cabin might have more folk music in it than a concert artist singing to a Carnegie Hall audience an ancient British ballad he learned out of a book," Pete Seeger wrote in his autobiography, *The Incompleat Folksinger*. Yet what about a song made of ancient poetic shards, transformed into a pop hit for modern times by folk preservationists who choose to ignore its dubious past?

Artists and fans have accepted "The Water Is Wide" as part of the American ballad heritage, despite its definitely not being a ballad, probably not being American, and nearly not even being a song. Researchers agree that it is a collection of "floating" verses—snippets of philosophizing, pretty imagery, and moral uplift inserted into musical narratives by broadside writers, printers, individual singers, or collectors to add fiber to the material. Ballad-hunters such as Cecil Sharp, who found pieces of "O Waly Waly" in both England and America at the turn of the twentieth century, were known to cobble together this interstitial stuff to make a palatable song. Phillips Barry, a collector in Maine, recognized some of the remnants of a version he obtained in the 1920s as part of "Jamie Douglas," so he included it in a category he creatively dubbed "Jury Texts"—"because like the jury-mast of a disabled vessel, they take the place of the real mast, lost in a storm, and serve a useful purpose though admittedly a substitute."

Such interpretive leaps bother more stern authenticators no end. "Many editors have been wont to combine traditional versions in a massive conflated text that no singer actually ever sang," writes Malcolm Douglas, one steadfast genealogist who frequently posts comments on the popular folk Internet forum Mudcat. "Unfortunately, conflated texts seem to be more readily available than true traditional versions."

Pete Seeger essentially admitted to performing such a Frankenstein act on "The Water Is Wide" to create his much-referenced version of the song. In the liner notes to his 1961 album *Pete*, he wrote:

I learned it from my sister Peggy. When she was going to Radcliffe in the mid-1950s, I visited Cambridge. I'd seen the song in a book and I'd passed it by as one more of those weepy-waily sentimental songs. I was twenty-eight at the time and impatient with weepy-waily songs. Ten years later, at a party in my sister's house, I heard this version of it. She'd dropped the waily-waily verses and emphasized the poetic verses. It means an awful lot to me now because I keep thinking of the ocean of misunderstanding between human beings. And we can sing all sorts of militant songs, but if we can't bridge that ocean of misunderstanding we are not going to get this world together.

A moral imperative led Seeger to transform "O Waly Waly" into a new fiction, and his agenda is audible in his recorded performances of "The Water Is Wide." He clips the end of each verse, refusing to luxuriate in the spacious endnotes most singers bring to each phrase. The great indulgence of heartbreak doesn't interest him. He's sad about the idea that trusty love can prove rotten; the plainspoken unhappiness he communicates carries little romance. It's a very traditionally masculine reading: let's not dwell on the problem, let's fix it.

Most arrangements don't take the tune in this direction. Instead, they stretch out the song's simple melody to give singers or instrumentalists almost too much breathing room. The lyric's open phonetics encourage vocalists to plunge into each phrase's final notes ("The water is W-I-I-DE . . ."), while its melody easily multiplies into lush harmonies. Get two major personalities vying with each other on this song, as in the Bob Dylan–Joan Baez duet from the Rolling Thunder Revue, as preserved on Dylan's "bootleg series" album *Live 1975*, and it can virtually explode with emotional aggression. But that's a rare reading; most harmonizers use the song as a way to temporarily lose track of their own voices, melding with each other the way lovers dream of and ultimately fear being absorbed by each other.

Performed unthinkingly, "The Water Is Wide" can become one-dimensional—either too mournful or, if the pain of what's expressed is underplayed in favor of prettiness, too romantic. But when a performer shows appreciation for the song's waxing and waning and the iridescence of its lyrical images, the song opens onto emotional terrain that's very tricky to occupy. This is the realm of nothing happening—the nonballad, in which both story and moral matter less than the evocation of an inner life that language can only partially express. Artists who came to typify the modern era, such as Woolf and Beckett, offer models for exploring this elusive area, trying to devise an epistemology of nothing happening. Spirituality can also touch upon it, as in the Buddhist method, increasingly popular in America, of sitting, riding the tide of the breath.

These many paradoxical strivings find their musical counterpart in "The Water Is Wide," a fakesong assembled by no one in particular, telling no real story, ending on an ambiguous note. Accidental as the assembly of verses may have been, the perils in this song pile up— the broken branch and the prickly bush, the heavy-burdened ship and the absent wing. Yet each implied disaster is finally not so devastating.

The lover remains intact, able to reflect. The melody buoys her up on the final note, to yearn again.

> But love grows old
> And waxes cold
> And fades away
> Like morning dew

⚜

What can we learn by dwelling on false starts and unrealized dreams? It's not in the American character to rest in that gray place. The folklorist Edith Fowke once noted that the American folk-song tradition makes scant room for love songs; the uncertainties of erotic longing must have felt distracting on the national march toward the edge of empire. Yet of course, love creeps in, crystallizing like the dew, uncontainable. And in a busy world, the love people find themselves craving most is not the prolific union of man and maid, but self-love— personal regeneration in the face of disappointment, the pause to breathe and to let new notes form that will carry the heart out onto the ebbing tide again.

There is an Edward Hopper painting called *Room in Brooklyn*. For years, a print of it hung in my own room in Brooklyn, my personal picture of Dorian Gray. In it, a woman sits turned away from the viewer in a straight-backed chair, a vaseful of flowers in her peripheral vision. She's looking out onto the street, and Hopper pictures no zooming cars or playing kids, just a quiet view of rooftops and that crisp light that arrives on the verge of fall. It isn't possible to read this woman's feelings. Hopper lets her keep them to herself. But the colors, the browns and yellows of the room, seem ever so slightly to move, as if the fading sun has just begun to unsettle the dust around her feet, and she's finding a moment to remember what she's hoping the next day will bring. The woman is very much alone, but her loneliness is filling up with something, and I imagine her starting to sing.

"Pretty Polly"

The Devil carrying a witch off to Hell. From Olaus Magnus's Historia de gentibus septentrionalibus, *Rome, 1555.*

RENNIE SPARKS

"Pretty Polly"

The first time you hear "Pretty Polly," you giggle nervously. The dark forest flowing with blood, the beautiful girl, the open grave—it makes you dizzy with a strange mix of horror and delight. The flat, vaguely medieval melody circles and drones. The chant rises in fury as the words round their dusky path. Cryptic signifiers flash through your head—red blood, white skin, dark grave.

Pretty Polly is close kin to the Knoxville Girl, Rose Connelly, and all the other beauties with snow-white breasts who shudder and fall in the dim bower of murder ballads. Alternate lyrics and melodies crisscross the lines between one tragic song and the next, but Pretty Polly separates herself from the other lost beauties by two strange things—a grave dug the night before and the call of wild birds.

The song begins with Polly lured away by a shadowy lover. "Come and go with me," he hisses. "I want to show you something in the woods."

He alludes to a far country, vague pleasures, but all the while he's staring at the gold jewelry on her lily-white hands. He promises they'll get married right after this little trip into the trees, but already his calm façade is slipping. He tells her she's wounded his heart. His hands are shaking—but is it love or rage that makes him tremble as he pulls Polly up onto his horse?

Polly seems to know nothing of the dark pleasures that might await a man and a woman in the woods. Does she think they're going on a picnic? To pick wildflowers? Her lover leads her over mountains, through deep valleys. Their path twists in circles as if they're descending the rings of hell. Deep in the forest, Polly begins to get nervous. Dark thoughts enter her head for the first time. Only now, lost under black branches, does she wonder whether her lover is leading her astray.

He sees her growing fear and tells her she's right to be afraid. But it's not sex he's after. He spent all last night digging her grave. There it is now, round the next bend—a freshly dug hole with a spade at the ready. Polly falls to the ground. She weeps and pleads. He pulls out his knife.

In some versions of the song, he stabs her in the heart without saying another word. Sometimes, though, he lingers there with his knife, enjoying her terror. He says he's heard stories. He has suspicions. He's sure that hiding somewhere under Polly's pure, white veils there is a dirty slut who deserves to die.

Who is this snickering psycho? Like so many murder-ballad boyfriends, his name is Willy or Billy or he's nameless. But this boyfriend's hands are ice cold. He's a spider crawling up Polly's pale thigh. He, unlike so many murder-ballad beaus, does not murder the girl "he loved so well." His love for Polly was always rotten with the desire to kill.

He has a strange perfectionism. This is no crime of passion. He stayed up all night to dig her grave ahead of time. You can see him there, measuring the hole, straightening the sides, laying the spade just so. He may be a serial killer. He may be completely insane.

He's the man in the black raincoat who tried to lure me into his car with a lollipop when I was six years old. He's Ted Bundy with a fake cast on his arm asking women to help him load a pile of books into the back of a van. He's Ed Gein, who slaughtered and skinned the women who wounded his heart and then danced around his yard wearing their bloody faces for a mask. How pretty he must have felt, blood-soaked and screaming in the moonlight.

Pretty Polly's boyfriend may want to feel pretty too, but the only way he can think of achieving that is by tearing Polly open and drenching himself in her blood.

He tosses her body into the grave. Sometimes she's still groaning as he covers her with dirt. The song ends with wild birds gathering in the trees to mourn over Polly's unmarked grave. Sometimes there's another verse where we're told the killer will now go to hell, but it always seems like the nervous chatter of a singer uncomfortable with the outcome of his own song. Sometimes the added verse takes the killer off to sea, but out on the ocean, weighed down by guilt, his ship sinks. Sometimes the killer buries Polly, then heads straight to the sheriff and announces, "I just killed Pretty Polly and I'm trying to get away!"

There's an odd logic at work. Why is the killer swallowed by the sea? Why does he beg the sheriff to lock him up? Why do wild birds suddenly appear after Polly dies? Why did Polly's grave have to be dug ahead of time? Why kill harmless Polly in the first place?

In murder ballads, the magic is in the mystery, the parts left unsaid. Like the wordless, unspeakable parts of our own psyche, murder ballads hold secrets that loom larger the farther down they're pushed. The more holes we cut in these songs, the more powerful they become.

To understand how "Pretty Polly" became this dreamy blood mystery, it helps to look backward in time. It's not possible to definitively untangle the history of any traditional song, but the two songs I hear behind "Pretty Polly" are "The Gosport Tragedy" and "Lady Isabel and the Elf Knight." Both songs can be traced back to printed sources in the British Isles that are at least 240 years old, but I suspect both are much older. Songs similar to "Lady Isabel" have been found in Germany dating back to 1550.

"The Gosport Tragedy" follows the same plot as "Pretty Polly," but there are some curious details "Pretty Polly" leaves out. The first clear difference is that Gosport Polly's trouble is obvious—she's pregnant and unmarried. She tries to reason with her boyfriend as he approaches her with the knife.

"I don't want to get married anymore," she says, voice trembling. "I'll leave town with the baby. I won't make trouble. You don't have to kill me!"

Still, her lover is rigid in his determination to get her into the ground. He takes the same sick glee in presenting her grave to her ahead of time. This is brutal and sadistic murder, but, unlike the murder in our "Pretty Polly," the violence in "The Gosport Tragedy" is not without motive. Sometimes men do kill women they get pregnant and don't want to marry.

Polly falls, her blood soaking the forest floor. The lover conceals the grave, heads out to sea. Then "The Gosport Tragedy" gets strange. The killer's ship is well across the ocean when suddenly Polly's ghost appears. The passengers are brought on deck and paraded before her. When she sees her lover, she swoops down on him like a ravenous hawk and tears him to pieces.

In "Lady Isabel and the Elf Knight," birds and magic truly abound. Here, Pretty Polly is, in fact, a bird. She's Lady Isabel's talking parrot. There are many variants, but the song always begins when Isabel hears a harp, a beautiful voice, or an enchanted horn and falls under the spell of a dark lover. He may be a foreign knight, a demonic elf, or just an itinerant killer. He may promise marriage, but often he just orders her to pack her father's gold, steal two horses, and ride away with him. They journey the same twisted path through hill and dale until finally they arrive at the planned murder spot—a cliff by the ocean or a deep well in a shady grove.

Again, the forest transforms lover into killer. The knight proudly announces that here he has already killed a whole mess of girls and is planning to make Isabel his next victim. He orders her to remove her clothing. He doesn't want her medieval finery rotting in the water with her corpse. Isabel tells him to turn his back while she undresses and he agrees—though why he allows this modesty to a woman he plans to kill is inexplicable, except perhaps for the strange notion that he does not want to see her naked.

His fear soon becomes clear. Once Isabel is naked, she develops supernatural strength. One look at her evil boyfriend and his waist shrinks. Naked Isabel grabs him by his tiny torso and effortlessly tosses him into the sea.

In some versions, Isabel uses a magic charm to lull her lover to sleep; then she stabs him. Sometimes she must walk into the water before developing magical power. Often her boyfriend pleads with her as he drowns, holding up his little hands like a child begging to be picked up. She always refuses.

Isabel returns home with her horses at dawn. As she sneaks back into bed, Pretty Polly—her watchful parrot—loudly squawks to distract Isabel's father. In reward, Isabel offers Polly a golden cage.

Who is this Lady Isabel with the sudden strength to toss men into the sea and the ability to make birds do her bidding? Who is the winged, dead Polly of "The Gosport Tragedy," with her bloody claws and screaming fury?

This powerful witching woman surrounded by birds and blood is the dark shadow of the demon goddess who once flew naked through the ancient wilds of Europe and the Middle East.

She is the serpent that coiled out of Eve's mouth to destroy the world. She is the wicked witch who baked children in her oven. She is the great Astarte, once worshipped with human sacrifice and sexual orgies and now remembered only in Easter eggs and bunnies. She is Circe the she-falcon, who turned men into pigs. She is the winged Harpy—the furiously hungry woman with razor-sharp talons. She is Lilith, the original wife of Adam, who sprouted wings and rose into the night as a raging she-demon when Adam tried to make her lie down for sex.

Unclothed in the forest—her horrible hair a twisted mass of snakes, her body dripping with the flood of the womb and the maggots of death—the goddess may kill men with an effortless glance. Like Lady Isabel, the goddess shrinks men to playthings. Like dead Polly with her sharpened claws, the goddess tears men apart with her accusing eye.

Greek logic, the paternal Christian trinity, the great hero-warrior—all the ideals of Western thought—rose in opposition to the swampy stench of the goddess. She is the dark bog trampled under the fortress of the rational Western mind. But she could not be completely silenced.

She was queen at May Day revels that ended with lovemaking in the thickets. She lurked in the sacred oak groves of druids and flew with medieval witches drunk on psychedelic mandrake root. She lives on still in the curving bulk of mountains, the endless mouth of the sea, and the mysterious womb of the Virgin Mary. Her hungry mouth bares its fangs each time a caged parrot squawks, "Polly wants a cracker!"

In folktale and myth, the goddess is every monster ever beheaded by a hero's sword. Behind her raging maw always lies a chained damsel awaiting rescue. But, even in the lily-white breast of the virgin, the goddess lurks, waiting to awaken, just as she does in the third sister of the sinister Grimms' tale "Fitcher's Bird."

In "Fitcher's Bird," a wizard captures two sisters. He demands they care for his spotless white egg and never open one forbidden door in his castle. The girl who can stick to the rules will be his bride. But each sister fails in turn. Each opens the forbidden door, discovers a basin of blood and body parts, and accidentally splashes blood that permanently stains the egg. In punishment, the two sisters are dragged to the forbidden room, hacked to pieces, and thrown into the bloody basin.

The wizard captures a third, naïve sister, but when she peeks into the forbidden room, the sight of all the blood fills her with occult power. She reattaches her sisters' severed limbs and reanimates them. Next she covers herself in feathers and honey, replaces her own head with a skull bedecked in flowers, and on the day she is to be wed to the wizard thus introduces herself to guests as Fitcher's bird. When the wizard arrives, she sets fire to him and the guests and flies away.

This blood, bird, and fire magic is the same sudden power that appears in the end of both "The Gosport Tragedy" and "Lady Isabel and the Elf Knight." Blood and fire, wings and claws, are the veiled memory of the goddesss—she who terrorizes us with the knowledge that life and death, sex and birth, are all forever awash in mystery and gore.

In America, all obvious traces of this vengeful goddess and her sexual sorcery disappear from "Pretty Polly." Our Polly is a mannequin, an empty shell. She wreaks no vengeance. She doesn't even struggle to live. She is limp, weepy, slaughtered without struggle. Her lily-white breast is already corpselike. She is dead before the knife cuts her.

So why does her lover fear her? Why take her so far into the forest to kill her? Why dig her grave ahead of time? Why does he conceal the body, then turn himself in to the sheriff? Why flee to the center of the ocean only to drown in guilt? Again and again, you have to wonder— why bother killing her at all?

Pretty Polly's lover is a man backed into a corner by a beast only he can see. He's driven mad by his trembling desire for blank, weeping Polly. He can't stop wanting her, even though sex with her is impossible. She's too weak to lift her arms in an embrace. Her lips are too slack to kiss. She can only be entered with a knife.

I sometimes wonder if Pretty Polly might have lived if only she had looked at her grave and seen nothing but an innocent hole in the ground. Her lover tests her knowledge of more than sex when he drags her into the woods, just as the wizard tests his girls in "Fitcher's Bird." The knowledge that kills is the knowledge of life and death.

No woman is innocent of this dark knowledge. Even under Polly's snow-white breast lurks the shadowy power to become mother—she who formed us from a squirt of discarded semen and once held us, powerless, in her arms. This hidden magic lives inside all women, but perhaps it is most mysterious and frightening in the young, virginal girl who displays no sexual desire. She is the effortless huntress who snares the unicorn simply with her presence. Who can know the thoughts behind her blank, peaches-and-cream face? Will she stroke the unicorn's mane or will she snap her razor teeth around his horn?

This veiled terror—the cold, bewitching virgin—attacked Salem, Massachusetts, during the long winter of 1691–92. It began when a group of young girls claimed to be tortured by the devilish specters of their neighbors—usually older women and usually accompanied by animal familiars, often little yellow birds.

Susannah Martin transformed herself into an entire flock of birds that mercilessly bit and pinched the tortured girls. Old Martha Cory was spotted sitting up in the rafters of the church, suckling a little bird between her fingers as the girls below were pricked with unseen pins.

The girls flapped their arms, screaming, "Whish! Whish!" as if they believed themselves turned to birds. Little Abigail Parrish tried to fly up a chimney.

It was the winged goddess who held the town in her claws. It was a fight between the immortality of young girls and the world of life and death ruled by childbearing women. The devil played little part in the struggle. He was a small, dark man with a top hat lurking at forest's edge—a middle-management pencil-pusher beckoning people to sign their names in his red book. He was easily ignored.

Not so the goddess. Invisible blood splashed along the floor of the Salem church as if it had become a gigantic womb. Men complained that two of the most attractive of the accused—Susannah Martin and Bridget Bishop (arrested for the crime of wearing scarlet)—had begun appearing at night in spectral form, hopping like birds from windowsills to make sex slaves of the poor men in their own beds. Both women were hung.

Tibetans believe that intense visualization and concentration on an image or idea can bring forth an actual physical entity. Similar suggestions have been made connecting the flying rage of poltergeists and the psychosexual turmoil of pubescent girls. Dr. Nandor Fodor writes of a young girl suffering poltergeist attacks who also suffered from a severe sexual psychosis in which she imagined that her father had assaulted her. Fodor theorizes that the girl's invisible, yet very real, attacker was a paranormal displacement of the girl's own bottled-up anger at her father. Could terrified and angry Puritan girls have formed real demons from their own horrified denial of sex and death?

Sexual frustration alone might have been more easily sublimated, but colonial New England was also terrorized by unspeakable violence. Fighting between colonists and Native Americans led to horrible atrocities on both sides. Hearing that white prisoners had been flayed and roasted to death by Indians (possibly Pequots), English troops captured an Indian at random, tied one leg to a post, and pulled on the other until they tore him apart. In 1637, following the murder of nine whites by Pequots, Connecticut soldiers torched a Pequot fort and shot all who ran from the flames. Six hundred Pequots (many of them women and children) were killed. In the 1670s, during King Philip's native uprising, 2,000 Narragansetts (mostly women and children) were killed in a single attack. King Philip (actually Metacom, leader of the Wampanoags) was killed, and his severed head was mounted on a pike above the entrance to Plymouth.

How could the Puritans explain their own easy slip from righteousness and restraint into lusty brutality unless some poison, some dark magic, had enchanted them from within? Witch after witch was dragged to the gallows, yet the violence and hysteria did not dissipate. As the noose was put around her neck, accused witch Sarah Good stared down defiantly at her judges and screamed, "God will give you blood to drink!"

The lips of the Puritans were already permanently stained red. By 1697, even women and children had developed a taste for blood. When Abnaki Indians attacked Haverhill, Massachusetts, they captured Hannah Duston, her newborn child, and Hannah's nurse, Mary Neff.

When the baby cried, an Indian smashed its head against a tree. For another month, they were marched through the forest. One night, Hannah, Mary, and another captive, ten-year-old Samuel Lennardson, stole hatchets. The two women and little Samuel killed and scalped ten Abnakis (including six children), then walked home.

A new kind of person stalked the New World. This "New American" was a lone hunter, a self-reliant killer. He found freedom in movement and isolation. He was Wild Bill Hickok killing eight men in minutes with a six-shooter and a Bowie knife. He was Meriwether Lewis, with such a passion for solitude that even as he and William Clark traveled up the Missouri River into unknown wilderness, he frequently wandered off alone.

This New American was Paul Bunyan, who made forests fall with one loud whoop of his voice. He was Cannibal Phil, who went off beaver trapping in the Rockies with a companion and returned alone some months later with a half-eaten human leg strapped to his saddle. He was Davy Crockett, who killed Indians and deer with equal abandon and felt no pity for native children with broken bones and seared flesh crawling from buildings he'd ignited.

Killing witches was only the beginning. Again and again, we attacked the wilds around us with a fury that defied rational explanation. The passenger pigeon was once so numerous in North America that flocks darkened the sky as they flew past. Their roosts left layers of dung several inches deep across miles of woodland. They crowded so heavily in trees they often caused huge limbs to crack and fall. We hunted them with such untiring avarice that market gluts often meant thousands of pounds of dead pigeons were dumped into rivers or buried in pits. Even when the monetary incentive to kill these birds dwindled, hunting did not abate. We relentlessly shot, gassed, netted, and burned them. Between 1820 and 1900, they were entirely wiped out. The last surviving passenger pigeon was found dead in its cage at the Cincinnati Zoo in 1914.

Our destruction of the wolf is a similar story. During the nineteenth century, we lured and killed wolves with dead game animals baited with strychnine and cyanide. We laid out so much poison (sometimes lines of poisoned meat stretched solidly for 150 miles!) that we often killed millions of other animals (raccoons, foxes, antelope) that fed either on the baited meat or on the grass poisoned by wolves vomiting in their death throes. The poison found its way into our own water supply. It even killed our children. None of that slowed the hunt.

"Pretty Polly" is so very American. The first American publication in which I've found mention of it is a 1916 collection of Kentucky folk songs, but "Pretty Polly" by then had been passed around the campfires and front porches of rural America for many years. The song was whittled and polished by each singer who touched it. It took on the fear and longing of the American heart. Gone is Lady Isabel's naked, carnal magic. Gone are the pregnancy and sex of "The Gosport Tragedy." Gone is all connection to the forest goddess.

Polly's killer does feel awed by her presence, but he is a hunter breathless with wonder as he sights a graceful deer, raises his gun, and imagines the stuffed trophy hanging over his fireplace. He can't wait to kill her because only by killing Polly can he possess her. Just as Ted Bundy lovingly redid the makeup and shampooed the hair of dead girls he had just clubbed, strangled, and stabbed, for Polly's killer women are impossible to possess and love unless dead.

"The Gosport Tragedy" and "Lady Isabel and the Elf Knight" can easily be read as morality tales in which girls who are sexually active get into trouble. In "Pretty Polly," there is no such clear logic. Our Polly seems utterly unaware of sex. She does, however, know a grave when she sees one. Her only sin is recognizing her grave, having knowledge of death. In America, this may be sin enough.

Who can ever completely explain the cringing terror that made us remove all reference to sex in "Pretty Polly"? In 1927, this same brick wall may have caused the Virginia banjoist Dock Boggs to record a truly vicious version of the song—compassionless, cold as a cockroach—yet still be unable to sing the word *dead*. Boggs's version ends with Polly pleading for her life—and then suddenly "falling asleep." Next he's shoveling dirt over his "sleeping" girlfriend and heading off to sea.

"Pretty Polly" only gained magic as we whittled her down and wrapped her in veils. The song became a series of signifiers, a coded message. The open grave, the mountains and valleys, the spilled blood, the wild birds—all burn with nature's mystery. The spade and knife, the killer and sheriff—all gleam with the cold steel of the manmade. As the knife plunges into Polly's bosom, there is the beautiful shudder of sexual union. The goddess appears and embraces Polly's killer with her bloody arms. But as the corpse falls, he flees. Is he running in guilty horror or from the knowledge that he already wants to kill again? His only happiness may be in piling up beautiful corpses until the world is an ocean of beautiful blood. Only then may he finally swim back inside the dark womb of Mother Nature.

One Chicago night in 1966, Richard Speck forced his way into a dormitory for student nurses. He tied up nine nurses and laid them on the floor around him. They were young, terrified girls. Looking at one of them suspiciously, Speck asked, "Do you know karate?"

One by one, he took them into the next room. He stabbed and strangled them. He punched them in the stomach and raped them. One girl who struggled only slightly was stabbed eighteen times before she was strangled. He killed so many women he lost count, and he left Corazon Amurao alive, hiding under one of the beds.

Why did Speck kill those nurses? One might think he was motivated by a deep hatred for women. But thirty years after his arrest—and five years after his death—a videotape surfaced that told a different story. It showed Speck in a maximum-security prison in the late 1980s. He and two other men had broken into a room containing video equipment meant for staff training. The footage they shot that day shows Speck taking off his prison jumpsuit to reveal a pair of women's panties and huge, hormone-induced breasts. The once-hollow-eyed killer is now fleshy and feminine. He dances like Ed Gein in his bloody party dress—swaying and jiggling, staring at the camera with the dark eyes of the femme fatale. He is the wolf dressed in Grandma's nightie. Why does the wolf want to be Grandma? Just to feel Red Riding Hood cast her loving eyes upon him for that brief moment before she notices Granny's new fangs?

Speck—like Gein, like Polly's killer—may have destroyed beautiful things because he simply wanted to possess beauty, to feel beautiful, to feel alive. These killers are invisible men, desperate for meaning and vision, for beauty and sacredness, but unable to see even their own hands without first drenching them in blood.

I believe "Pretty Polly" is a magic spell written to dispel deadness of the heart. Listen to the song. How does it make you feel? Its savagery may make your hair stand on end—but perhaps this isn't horror you're feeling. It may be reverence. You may feel you're in the presence of something unspeakably sacred, beautiful. "Pretty Polly" is a prayer. It is a cry of pain from a wound so deep we cannot, or will not, acknowledge it.

The nineteenth-century spiritualist Madame Helena Blavatsky was once asked to contact a woman's dead mother. Blavatsky replied that the dead were too busy to bother with the petty needs of the living. Asked her view on the possibility of other life forms in outer space, Blavatsky answered that she did not believe there was any dead matter anywhere in the universe. This idea—that all things have a spirit—led to the gardens of Findhorn, Scotland. Founded by penniless mystics at a garbage dump by the sea, the garden became famous in the 1970s when news spread of forty-pound cabbages and sixty-pound broccoli harvested from the infertile soil along the windy coast of Findhorn Bay. The explanation of such strange wonders was even stranger. The Findhorn gardeners claimed that through deep meditation, and the help of a few talented psychics, they were able to communicate with the actual spirits of the vegetables. The peas told them when they were overwatered. The tomatoes complained when they were cold. Most important, to appease the fairies dancing among the trees, a portion of the garden was left wild.

I think "Pretty Polly" is an attempt to speak to these same nature spirits. It is a ritual of bloodletting, an appeal to invisible forces, a cry to the goddess to come embrace us with her thorny arms. Polly's murder works as Joseph Campbell believed all myth has worked—as a secret opening, a knife slashed in the veil of experience through which deep knowledge may seep. To those not gifted enough to hear the bean plants talk or to see the fairies dancing, myth may be our only access to places outside our conscious perception of reality.

In *Nature and Madness*, Paul Shepard hypothesizes that even our early devotion to the goddess was a step away from the natural world of hunter-gatherers. It was the plea of the farmer to an invisible mother for rain and sunshine. This plea to an all-powerful mother bred deep resentment when crops did not grow. We were, perhaps, doomed to revolt against the mother goddess just as we are doomed to rebel against our real mothers in order to grow up, to be able to accept the uncertainties of life.

In the strange dance of "Pretty Polly," the goddess cannot win; her blood must spill. Why? Because we are holding the knife and we want to use it. We want Polly dead. We plunge our dagger into beautiful Polly, but, as she falls, she smiles and whispers, "I love you, too."

Polly must die. Both she and her killer are performing sacred, necessary actions. This mysterious ritual is nicely exposed in a version of the song by the Kentucky banjoist Pete Steele: he calls Pretty Polly's murderer "Pretty Willy." They are both beautiful—the killer and the killed.

The Cherokee have a dance that tells the story of the green corn woman. She asked her sons to kill her and drag her body around a field. Everywhere her blood touched, corn grew.

A similar story was told in ancient Europe: the story of Attis and Cybele, Aphrodite and Adonis. Attis, the young lover or son of the goddess Cybele, tore off his own genitals in a mysterious sacrifice. Wherever his blood fell, violets grew. When Aphrodite's young lover/son Adonis was attacked by a wild boar, his falling blood turned poppies red. Pretty Polly's forest is also nourished by her falling blood. It fills the trees with singing birds.

Corazon Amurao, the sole survivor of Richard Speck's rampage, waited in terror for hours under her bed. Finally she crept out, but instead of going downstairs to the street, she climbed out a second-floor window onto a narrow ledge and screamed and screamed— "They're all dead! They're all dead!" It was as if a cord had been severed. She had been set adrift into the sky. Corazon, like the young girls of Salem, like Pretty Polly, her spirit incarnated in the birds gathered in the trees above her grave, could no longer bear to touch the ground.

"Pretty Peggy-O"

"The Going."

"I could not love thee, dear, so well
Loved I not honor more."

The Going, *photograph, circa 1917. Courtesy of
the Library of Congress.*

SHARYN McCRUMB

Music, When Soft Voices Die

They that carried us away captive required of us a song....

—PSALM CXXXVII

He had a few seconds to get his bearings while the opening bars of the melody were strummed. Or, in this case, plunked. He saw that he was seated at a round wooden table in a West Texas saloon, straight out of a thousand cheesy Westerns. At the next table, four scruffy-looking cowpokes were playing poker. Aces and eights? No, he didn't think so.

The shot glass in front of him was filled with an amber-colored liquid that was sure to be rye. He had no idea what rye whiskey would taste like—or, rather, what rye would taste like in this current imagining, but he would probably need a slug of it for fortification anyhow. Seizing the glass, he downed its contents in one gulp, and then wished he had not. Cherry cough syrup? He shuddered, and tried to scrape the aftertaste off his tongue. Guy was obviously not a drinker.

Now when was he? From the look of the barroom, 1880s. Sawdust on the plank floor. The Rubenesque nymph-in-the-bulrushes oil painting over the bar. From a back room somewhere came a few notes of a honky-tonk piano tinkling faintly—just for atmosphere, he thought. The other occupants of the saloon wore boots and cowboy hats, and the bartender had a handlebar mustache and an eyeshade.

He wondered what lay outside the saloon and hoped it wasn't the streets of Laredo.

Or worse, the West Texas town of El Paso.

He made a grab for the hat he felt resting on his brow and held it out in front of him. It was a white Stetson. Sort of beige, really. Not a black one, anyhow. That was a relief. He could feel a change in the chords that told him whatever was going to happen would be starting soon.

Long strum on the tonic chord . . . and . . . all eyes gazed expectantly at the swinging doors. He turned slowly in his chair, one hand patting his thigh frantically to see if there was a holster strapped to it. . . . There wasn't. . . . He relaxed a little.

The doors swung open, of their own accord, it seemed, and a beautiful young woman stepped inside, holding the pose for a moment before she entered. She was sloe-eyed and golden-skinned, with gleaming white teeth and the lithe body of a dancer. She was . . . well, she was Halle Berry.

This time, anyhow. But he recognized her as the Dear Little Girl. She walked up to his table and leaned against it, flashing another hundred-watt smile. He eyed her skimpy, off-the-shoulder peasant blouse and her clinging skirt, which he had expected to be yellow, but it wasn't.

He said, "Er—hello. I almost didn't recognize you. Well, I did, but . . ."

She winked. "Hi, Ja-aack. Like what you see?"

"Erm, yes, Dear," he stammered. "It's just that I was expecting an anemic blonde in a yellow-silk ball gown. With a hoop skirt, maybe. Definitely a blonde."

She smiled and shook her head of short, dark curls. "Not this time," she purred. "This time the guy singing it is a music historian."

They winced at a wrong note. *D-7, you fool!* Ah, there it was.

Halle giggled. "You see, this guy really *knows* what a Yellow Rose of Texas is."

Well, there had been worse experiences with that song. Once he had heard the familiar chords and apparated into what he thought would be a fancy-dress ball only to find himself standing on a dusty country road in front of a black carriage driven by a grinning skeleton.

He was able to peer out past the music during an instrumental bridge, and he saw that the listeners were all waving beer mugs and laughing. *(And who the hell was Emily Dickinson, anyway?)*

Sometimes they were together in a place—he thought of it as the "green room," though it really had no discernible color—waiting for their part to come around. Off duty, so to speak, they could talk naturally among themselves. Swap tales about the latest gigs. The Regulars, as he thought of them, numbered six, though occasionally someone else would show up to fill a vacancy. Jack and the Dear Little Girl spent a lot of time together, since one or the other of them was nearly always called for. Dear ended up with Willie a good bit of the time, too, though she always regretted it. Still, what could you do? Narrative constraints and all. It wasn't exactly a life, but it was a living. At other times, Jack was paired with Barbary, whom he secretly found more interesting than the Dear Little Girl. She was more mature, for one thing. Bold and sophisticated. Of course, there was hell to pay in the end, but it was always fun while it lasted.

The other two of the players covered all the supporting roles, necessitating a good many different personas and a great range of temperaments, but nobody ever paid much attention to them. They were pleasant enough, of course: just a couple of conscientious and hard-working avatars, usually one of each sex, but not always. In the green room, they went by The Weasels, Alpha and Beta, though the latter preferred to be called Louise, even when she was incarnated male as the hangman, or the second farmer, or whatever the lyrics required. Their roles in any given song tended to be brief and minor. Well, except for the songs about the bickering old married couple, like "Get Up and Bar the Door," in which the two of them played the fatuous but central parts, while he and Willie appeared in the guise of robbers. Nobody enjoyed that song much, but it paled beside the one in which Beta Weasel tries to convince her husband that the lover's saddle horse was a milk cow. The one about the John B. Stetson chamber pot, etcetera, etcetera, through a dozen excruciating verses. Willie always looked especially morose when he heard the opening bars of that ditty.

They had been together a long time, the six of them. In the early days, there had been fewer changes, fewer surprises when they found themselves on the set of a familiar tune. When a song was just beginning its existence, the place always looked nearly the same, even when the singer changed, and even the faces of the actors were consistent from one rendition to the next. But gradually, the images began to shift and blur, so that no matter how familiar the melody, they could never be quite sure who they would be or what setting they would appear in. The words often stayed the same—but nothing else did.

The sad songs had come first. They had all become experts on dying. They hadn't been as tall or as good-looking in the early days. (Lately, Dear Little Girl and Barbary had become boyishly slender, with teeth so white you could probably use them to read by, and Jack noticed that he and Willie were a good bit taller than they used to be. The Darby Ram didn't seem quite so big any more.) But Jack missed the old days, anyhow. Back then the people out there beyond the firelight had really focused on the singer, as if he were about to impart some great secret of the universe if only they listened carefully enough. Scores of people would sit perfectly still, letting the music wash over them—through them—so that the song hung in the air on their collective belief until it crystallized into . . . into the six of them. They became real. They thought and felt. Sometimes, Jack could even taste the nut-brown ale or the bottle of Burgundy wine as he proceeded through the verses. That didn't often happen anymore. But at least nowadays there was the novelty of never quite knowing where you were going to turn up. The whitewashed Irish cottages of the Wexford Girl or Rose Connelly might be log cabins or frame houses—anything at all, really. Willie swore that he'd once seen his father sit in his cabin door wiping his tear-dimmed eye, and the old man had been on the concrete stoop of an aluminum-sided mobile home!

An American accent was usually an indicator that the images would be slightly awry in an old tune. *Is Little Margaret in the house, or is she in the hall?* He smiled. Even the Dear Little Girl had been annoyed by that one, the first time she found herself in a narrow passage next to a coat rack instead of in the cavernous, tapestry-hung banquet chamber she was accustomed to. They were getting used to it by now, though. Never a dull moment. Gave them something to talk about in the green room. As long as the feelings were genuine, Jack didn't really mind the novelty of a new image, though all of them still complained about one detail or another. Willie could be scathing about the quality of the "burglar's wine" in "Rose Connelly." "I grit my teeth every time I hear the opening chords," he declared.

A G chord summoned Jack into the action.

Jack found himself standing on the dirt track of a rustic village, sword at his side, wearing some sort of military garb, and a few feet away stood Barbary, fetching as ever in a green gown, but surrounded by—chickens?

Chickens?

Dirt road . . . village of whitewashed houses with thatched roofs . . . and soldiers milling about. They weren't shooting or pillaging. Just standing around, as if they weren't sure what they were supposed to do. Well, the road through the village was blocked by all those chickens, so maybe that was the problem. Small, speckled chickens. They were picking in the dirt and strutting around with what appeared to be charm bracelets attached to their legs. Their squawking and tinkling made an interesting counterpoint to the guitar solo. Too bad the audience couldn't hear it as well. Jack shook his head. He couldn't even venture a guess.

He edged his way through the cackling flock, hoping for a quiet word with Barbary between verses. Behind him, the soldiers had formed columns and had begun to march in close-order drill. (*Armed lines of marching men in squadrons passed me by?* No, he didn't think so. Wrong clothing; wrong century. And this wasn't spring in an Irish glen.) As the sergeant on horseback shouted out the commands to the troops, Jack leaned in toward Barbary and whispered, "Where are we?"

Barbary suppressed a smile and shooed away a chicken with her apron. "The Bonnie Streets of Fy-vie-O," she murmured, with a hint of a giggle.

"The Bonnie—" He stepped back to look at her outfit. Usually in that ballad, Barbary was a sight to behold: It depended on the imagination of the singer, of course, but low-cut gowns, gaudy jewelry, and heavy makeup were generally the order of the day.

Not this time. Here Barbary was dressed demurely in what looked like generic eighteenth-century farm-wife attire: ankle-length green gown of linsey-woolsey, white starched cap and apron, and a brown wool cape for good measure. He seldom saw Barbary so covered up.

And her pretty face was innocent of rouge or kohl—another rarity. Barbary looked like a healthy young peasant girl, tending her flock—but in that case, she shouldn't be here at all. Virginal farm lass was Dear Little Girl's role in the ballads, and "The Bonnie Streets of Fy-vie-O" was not a Dear Little Girl sort of song. Not unless they had changed the lyrics.

He listened for a line or two.

No, the words were spot-on. It looked about right, too. There was the requisite troop of Irish dragoons, marching through the village of Fy-vie-O. (Nobody was ever sure where that was, but it was generally imagined as an eighteenth-century village somewhere in Britain. This time a weathered pub sign said Fy-vie-O Arms, just to make sure.) The story was that the captain—a minor character, usually the Alpha Weasel in one of his more personable roles—falls in love with a local lass, a romance that ends in tragedy.

Jack's role in the song was to be the earnest young narrator, a soldier serving under the captain, bitterly disapproving of his commander's choice of lady-love. The events in the song would be filtered through his resentful eye—hence Barbary's playing the role of Pretty Peggy-O, the sluttish local girl, no-better-than-she-should-be, who ensnares the handsome soldier's affections and brings him to his death. She was a woman of negotiable affection, wasn't she? In the narrator's eyes, she certainly was. Jack remembered past performances: Barbary tricked out in everything from feather boas to gypsy costumes, a procession of leering soldiers pressing gold coins into her hands as payment for her favors. But not this time. These soldiers were ignoring the lady completely, so intent were they upon trying to keep up their precision marching without tripping over the milling chickens.

Barbary was doing her best to look demure, as befitted the outfit assigned to her in this rendition, but Jack could tell that she was suppressing a grin.

"Fy-vie-O?" he said. The notes sounded right, but . . . "I don't remember chickens."

Solemnly she intoned, *"What will your mother think when she hears the guineas clink?"*

They looked at the chickens—the guinea fowl, actually—then back at each other, and smiled.

"Ah," said Jack. "Rural American folk singer. Learned it out of a book, I expect. No concept of the word as British currency. Hmmm. . . ."

Barbary patted her golden curls. "Well, it makes for a nice change," she said. "Very restful."

The carriage came to take her away just then, and as it rolled off down the high road, Jack could hear her silvery laughter over the hoofbeats—and, of course, the chickens.

❧

Now they were in a forest clearing.

"It isn't the children I mind," said the Alpha Weasel, pausing for breath. "Bless ye, no. Nice to hear the little ones trying to sing an old song in their piping wee voices. Keeps the world going, I always say. Keeps us in work. Me and Louise gets half our best jobs from the kiddies these days. Many's the Sunday morning I have found myself incarnated in a lovely old church doing a turn as Gladly, the Cross-Eyed Bear, or the Kinky Turtle what's flying a kite 'cause his day of March has come. And never a word of complaint do you hear from me." He got his second wind and sprinted around the bush out of Jack's reach. "But now in this song, I shouldn't be present at all. That's all I'm saying." *(Wheeze.)* Still panting, he called back over his shoulder: "All I'm saying—All I'm saying is . . . This song has come down in the world."

Well, thought Jack, dodging a branch that snapped back in his face, *sometimes in the oldest version you'd be the one to take my hat.* He remembered the jovial Weasel in a green eye-shade and twinkling pince-nez, sliding silver pieces across a wooden counter in the pawnshop.

Sometimes Alpha Weasel *was* the hat. He and Louise took turns with the role. But that hadn't happened for ages.

The Weasel had a point about the song having come down in the world, Jack decided. As if he'd needed convincing about it, anyhow. He plunged on through the underbrush in hot pursuit as the tempo speeded up.

The song had been around for a century and a half, and for the first few decades, it had been a jolly, jaunty tune that Jack had quite enjoyed. He could find himself swathed in an opera cape with a silver-headed cane on the City Road in a bustling London of horse-drawn carriages and hansom cabs. Sometimes, instead of tails, he'd be dressed in his dandified best: frock coat, boiled shirt, diamond tie pin in a silk cravat, and always, *always,* an exquisite beaver top hat. Pockets full of cash, he had. It would be evening, brightly lit by gas lamps swirling in the fog, and loud with music and laughter emanating from the doorways lining the city thoroughfare. He'd join the jostling throng crowding into the Eagle Music Hall, and—if he was lucky—the singer would be very drunk or very silly, and the verse would be sung over and over again, giving him time to stand a round of drinks for everyone in the bar, play a few hands of cards (though he always lost), and see a bit of the show. Sometimes he'd see quite a lot of Barbary in that song, too. *That's the way the money goes.* But well worth it. A corker of a song.

But the tune had fallen on hard times. A century back, people began to forget what the words meant. That was the trouble with slang. And with exporting songs, for that matter. A hundred years or a hundred miles and things began to go fuzzy.

Fuzzy, indeed, he thought wryly, making a lunge for Alpha Weasel with his hairy simian forearms.

People forgot the sense of the song, but they still liked the tune. So they'd thought up new words in order to keep the rinky-dink melody going. The old story was lost to memory, so that now he no longer wore tails. (*Well, in a way he did. Ha.* Jack grimaced at the irony.) Now the city street was a patch of woods, sometimes a playground. And he no longer ended the song by pawning his lovely top hat. Oh, no.

Now he was encased in a hot brown-fur suit, endlessly chasing around in this stupid, overgrown shrubbery. And Barbary was never here anymore, in G-string or otherwise.

"I hate this song," Jack called out through the mulberries.

"You think *you've* got troubles?" said the Weasel. Then he exploded.

Minor annoyances, those. Minor annoyances. It was a bit disorienting to find yourself in a familiar tune, ready to trot through the well-worn paces, only to find that some kink in time has distorted the song into some unrecognizable incarnation, and you must use the opening bars to get your bearings in a frantic scramble for verisimilitude. (Though Louise, for one, had declared herself enormously relieved when The Salty Dog became a Labrador retriever. "Some things improve with forgetfulness," she'd said.)

Jack thought that the songs that made him saddest these days were often the ones that were considered happy tunes by their singers. Raucous, sing-along bar songs, or grindingly familiar ethnic tunes, sung so often (and so badly) that people hardly listened to them anymore, except to note their tiresome familiarity. They had forgotten, but he hadn't.

The odd thing was that sometimes a perfectly innocent, cheerful song could suddenly become unbearably sad, just because of where and when it had been sung. "Wait 'Til the Sun Shines, Nellie." Jack shivered every time he heard it. The images hadn't changed at all, really. A peaceful country lane on a spring afternoon . . . white-blossomed apple trees and flowering hawthorn hedgerows . . . and the Dear Little Girl, often in a long dress and bonnet, strolling along beside him and smiling shyly, as she was called to do more than ninety percent of the time in any song—often right up until Willie throttled the life out of her along the banks of some river. Just seeing a river made the Dear Little Girl begin to twitch. No, the song was happy enough. It was just that little things in the song began to change, making him wonder what was going on.

Jack first began to suspect that something was amiss with "Nellie" when the scenery began to change. The country lane remained a country lane, but suddenly the grass was greener, roses bloomed along the fences, and the trees couldn't seem to decide what season it was. They'd walk past a tree white with apple blossoms and ten paces later, just inside a split-rail fence, there would be another apple tree fully laden with ripe fruit. Then the Dear Little Girl began to change, too. She had always been chocolate-box pretty, and sweet-tempered, capable of discussing the weather until the cows came home, but now in "Nellie" he noticed that she was beginning to look downright ethereal. A golden aura shimmered above her blonder-than-ever hair, and her seraphic expression came straight out of a Christmas carol. She was almost an angel, and their conversations—inconsequential at the best of times—ceased altogether. She would spend the entire song gazing at him with her tragic blue eyes and a smile of infinite pity and love. *Wait 'Til the Sun Shines, Nellie?* The words never changed, though.

Then one day Jack appeared in the song wearing a soldier's uniform. And a time or two after that, he was on crutches, missing a leg, while Dear Little Girl became more angelic and less human with every chorus.

Sometimes if conditions were right and they really concentrated, they could look outside the frame, to see where the music was coming from. Jack started spending his stroll down lovers' lane peering past her into the clouds, trying to catch sight of the singer. Finally his persistence was rewarded with a glimpse of him—the man in the tin helmet singing, "Wait 'til the sun shines, Nellie," in a low, sad voice as if it were a hymn. He was in a trench, and it was dark, except for occasional bursts of shellfire exploding above the field. The song had never felt so real to Jack as it did on that night. He could even taste the apples and smell the rain-soaked leaves. The Dear Little Girl hadn't been a gilt Madonna that time; she had been quite an ordinary-looking young woman in an old cloth coat, but Jack had felt such tenderness for her that he actually stumbled in the road from the shock of that emotion. The singer that night had stopped before the song ended, and Jack had never been able to forget that. He was glad that people hardly ever sang "Nellie" anymore, because nowadays it tended to be crooned by deliberately antiquated barber shop quartets in perfectly pitched harmony but without a smidgen of real feeling, so that he and a bored Dear Little Girl would walk down a generic country lane, exchanging saccharine smiles and holding hands, acting out the perfunctory lyrics, but all the while Jack would be thinking of the man in the tin helmet who never finished the song.

That was the song that changed him, really. Before "Nellie," Jack had been more or less content to act out the songs any way the singer wanted to picture them, and if the images were thunderingly wrong, he never resented it. One version of a song was as good as another, he thought, barring a few discomforts like the monkey suit, which was more of an annoyance than a philosophical objection. After "Nellie," though, Jack began to feel that perhaps there were songs that deserved better than they got. Perhaps the players owed as much to the song as they did to the singer, and perhaps they ought to try to have some voice in how the songs were done.

He began to be aware of tone and feeling in the performances. He began to care how songs were sung. That was when he began to discover that he could shape the singers in much the same way that they shaped him. The connection went both ways. After a bit of concentration and practice, he was able to make a jangly tune circle endlessly in a singer's head—"The Red River Valley," perhaps, or "Sweet Betsy from Pike"—reverberating around the brain cells on an almost-subliminal level until their nerves frayed and they screamed at whoever came near them. It was a pointless exercise, but it did prove that he could reach them.

It was harder to influence the singer's mood, but given the impetus of a strong emotion, he found that he could do it. He confided this new power to Barbary in whispers once while she was leaning over his deathbed in Scarlet Town (wherever that was), chiding him for making the healths go round and round and slighting her.

"Sometimes if I'm angry enough about the way they're treating the song, I can make them sorry for it," he told her.

"But why would you want to?" she whispered back. "What does it matter how somebody imagines a song? I mean, the words are right, aren't they?"

He shrugged. It was hard to explain. It wasn't every song that concerned him. Just the ones that had meant so much to somebody sometime during their existence. The songs that they wept into, or wrapped around themselves as they went into battle, or even the golden-dream tunes that they built into little worlds that were better than where they really lived. Jack himself never had any feelings for a given song unless that emotion had been put there by someone whose heart had gone into the singing of it. One singer couldn't do it all by himself. It had to be many singers, all putting the same feeling into a song, one at a time, day after day or year after year, until finally Jack felt it, too.

The words didn't matter so much, he thought, if the sense stayed straight. Even the melody could change from major to minor, mode to mode. . . . And whether, for instance, the ship was the *Golden Vanity* or the *Gallant Argosy*, whether the enemy was Spanish or Turkish, didn't matter much. Just so the singer still felt the sorrow and the waste of the brave young cabin boy left to drown in the cold sea.

They were back in the green room now, and Jack was still struggling to put his thoughts into words. "I mind when a true song becomes an excuse for noise or a finger-picking exercise, when the feelings get lost," he said. Because feelings were what had made them all real in the first place, and if you lost that, then it was just sounding brass.

Louise, who was playing a hand of cards with Alpha *(Jack o' Diamonds, Jack o' Diamonds)*, looked over at him and shook her head. "Just do your bit," she told him. "It's only a bit of fun for people nowadays. There'll be somebody else along singing your precious tune before you know it, and maybe you'll like that one's version better."

From beyond the boundary they heard the skirl of a fiddle, and Alph stood up to answer the summons. "I believe we're wanted, my dear," he said, offering his arm to Louise. "Know this one? I'll be the bird now, shall I? Yes, I know it's a hen, but I insist, my dear."

My bonnie moorhen, my bonnie moorhen,
Up in the gray hills and doon in the glen . . .

The words were roared, accompanied by laughter and shouts from the crowd. The singer was parodying a woman's voice, and the tinkle of glassware accompanied the music.

Jack remembered this song, too, though he hadn't been summoned to it for a long time.

My bonnie moorhen's gang o'er the faim,
And it will be summer ere she comes again . . .

Jack stood up. "Come on, Barbary," he said. "Let's do this one."
She stared up at him. "But we weren't called."

But when she comes back again some folk will ken,
And drink a toast tae my bonnie moorhen.

"But it was our song once. A long time ago. Remember?"

Barbary listened to the words for a moment and then she nodded. They left the green room and found themselves shivering on a bit of scrub moorland, with a cottage and a barn in the distance, where a red-faced Louise, dressed as a farm wife, a small sack of chick feed tied about her waist, was searching through the bracken, clucking her tongue as she went. "Chick! Chick!" "Go away," said Jack through clenched teeth.

Louise . . . who had been about to catch sight of her errant fowl in the underbrush . . . (*she's red and she's white and she's green and she's gray*) . . . saw the look in Jack's eyes. She dropped the sack of feed and then vanished from the song.

Jack put the drunken fiddler out of his thoughts, remembering other voices singing this same song, long ago. Sad, tired voices . . . with an undercurrent of anger that belied the lightness of the words. And the image that went with the song had nothing to do with a farm wife in search of a hen.

He closed his eyes and became the song.

He was a young man now. Not handsome, but arrogant in his nobility. He wore a white cockade in his cap, and a plaid across his shoulders—it's red, and it's white, and it's green, and it's gray—and over his back lay a great claymore strapped in a leather scabbard. He was making his way through a bleak mountain pass—*up by Glen Duich and doon by Glen Shee*—guarded by shadowy presences, ever alert for the sounds of a distant army. He had the look of a great leader, but he was nearly alone, and he was on the run.

And he would never come back.

The voices who had sung that song in the old days had seen that young man, swathed in the royal tartan, a fugitive in a land he should have ruled. They sang not about the prince but about a bonnie moorhen, because it was more than your life was worth in those times to say the young man's name aloud, to sing openly about him and his cause. But even as they sang their carefully cloaked song with its hidden meanings and its message of rebellion, they knew that all was lost. The young man was not coming back, and the enemy would stay forever.

Jack summoned all the old feelings that had once come into him through the music. The pain from so many muted voices. The sorrow . . . the hunger . . . the despair . . . the knowledge that companions were lost, and that the land would be lost, too. Now or soon, those who sang it would be on distant shores with nothing left of the old world except the memory, and a few scraps of songs to remind them of what was, or what could have been. He felt all that longing and regret, all the helplessness of someone who has lost everything through no fault of his own.

Jack closed his eyes and took in all of those old sorrows. He swelled with the pain and the loss. And then, he . . . pushed.

He had the sensation of throwing a heavy load off his chest and sending it spiraling through the mists to the other side. He imagined the burden hitting the wooden floor of the smoky room and breaking into a thousand pieces and floating upward, like sharp little dust motes, lodging in a listener's ear, in a singer's throat.

The music faltered. The jaunty tune trailed off on a wrong note, and for a moment all was quiet where the singers were. Jack and Barbary stood still in the blurring Scottish bracken, waiting to hear what would happen next.

Then the singer scraped the bow against catgut, and took up the last verse again.

> For Ranald and Donald are out in the fen,
> Tae brak the wing o' my bonnie moorhen.

His voice was somber now, and he sang the words slowly, with the intonation of a man who knows that he is speaking not of bird sport but of armies seeking out one man to kill him, and knowing that many of their neighbors and kinsmen will die in the process. There was a catch in his voice as he sang what it meant this time. What it *meant*.

The crowd was silent now. They looked away and shuffled their feet, caught suddenly in the spell of that distant lament. Someone started to weep, and others began to walk away.

Barbary looked at Jack, princelike now in his red plaid, the pudding face replaced by the countenance of an archangel, glowing with nobility and honor and courage. "Was he really like that?" she whispered. "This prince . . . was he worth such a song?"

Jack shook his head. That wasn't the point. What did it matter if this prince had been noble, or if the soldier's Nellie had been a pretty girl or not? "It's for the singers," he said. "I do it in memory of the singers."

"Omie Wise"

Naomi Wise's family tree. Marion Post Wolcott,
Old Graveyard. North Carolina, *Farm Security*
Administration photograph, 1938. Courtesy of
the Library of Congress.

ANNA DOMINO

Naomi Wise, 1807

Beloved Aunt Esther,

With this letter I beg forgiveness for my long silence and plead your indulgence should it confuse or offend. Some while has passed since I was called to marshal my thoughts into form with such neglected words and I may have lost the more charming terms and fit usage of my book reading days.

Since I left home and Hyde County you have never strayed long from my mind but I did not know what prospects I would face and was truly surprised at the persistence of adversity and how close my little family would run to ruin. Dear Aunt, I can happily say to you that these tribulations are behind us now. A Loving Angel has come forward to rescue and assure our future! This change in fortune allows me to hope for a renewal of our mutual relations and the chance to put before you all that has come to pass since you set me out for this country, some eight years ago.

The getting here took longer than I ever expected it would of course, having no idea the world could become so wild and meandering. We spent days closed in by rain, bogged down in muddy ruts and foggy hollows and always the land was throwing up trees and hillocks for the road to find a way around. This contrary scenery was doubly confounding as the only country I had ever known runs to flat, sandy marshland while the Streets back at home can usually be trusted to follow your aim. Day after day on that long bumpy ride through the farming and the hill country I had plenty of time to think and what I thought was this. I thought once I got out to Randolph County I could make some sense from my life. There would be cause to please everybody that needed a pleasing and to keep my head low and be enough of a help to Old Master Adams and his Missus for them to keep me on once the baby come. Of course I did not tell them right out I was with child. No point asking for fresh trouble at the start. But by and by it come clear enough, no matter how high I tied the apron string, and later that Fall I was delivered of a baby girl. Though with only some fool chatter-mouth maid to help, I am surprised myself and the baby lived beyond it.

Round here they say the country, the weather and the people are each more sharp featured and ornery than the last, which makes every Blessing and Curse count twice over.

Nancy in her infancy was pretty enough, if someways peakish and broody. A silent and inward child for the most part. If I left her with a length of twine or an old planking nail she would still be there worrying it come evening. She kept to our room at back of the Adams house and except for the asthma spells, she kept herself quiet. The Adams are not real fond of infants but as long as we stayed out the way I saw no need to worry. So mostly I was left to my kitchen work and left in peace.

Things had a been fine maybe, if we could have held to it like that but you hold off breathing too long you turn blue and die. So next to come along is Henry, though of course he did not come all of his own. With my Nancy I did not have to name a Father as I was newly arrived in this County and under the protection of Old Adams. That and the bank note you sent along with me provided for the baby's bond and satisfied the Authority. With Baby Henry though, I had to have a name so there would be no talk of Old Adams being the Daddy. That would not have done anybody any good at all. So I fixed an understanding with Ben Sanders who comes out from town now and then peddling sundries, and it got me the money for Baby Henry's bond and a Master for the Certificate.

There were plenty for me to learn of the Law and Regulations I would be bound to abide. As when a child is born to Bastardy you are required to post a bond showing intent to provide support. If you cannot pay then the Father you name must bear the upkeep for the first several years, but without a Father your own baby is an orphan to the Law, and the Authority can take the child and apprentice it out to a trade. They do not say what trade a mere infant is suited for, but the child is indentured to it till coming of age and the Mother is not allowed to see her own babies, thence forth. It is something, you will understand, I would try almost anything to avoid.

As the particulars got squared away with Sanders and we got Missus Adams calmed down, life went on. But from the beginning Baby Henry, though he looked an Angel, was in no way under human control. That right there is where things started to get away from me. The Baby was pretty much on his own at two months, squirming out of his sister's arms and raising High-Hell every waking minute. Nancy was four years older but I swear he was the bigger, he was definitely meaner, and it took us both to hold him down. The Adams noticed I was not getting my chores and churning done, they seen Nancy in the hallway fleeing from one tantrum after another and they could hardly ignore the Infernal caterwauling. It was not just what Baby Henry was up to himself that so disturbed our lives, it was the effect he had on his sister. Nancy had always been a "Perfect itty-bitty Lady" to Missus Adams, having not uttered so much as two words in the Missus' presence. Along come Baby Henry and set the girl off somehow, like she had just been a waiting for him. He started her talking his baby talk, repeating his baby nonsense and before long there is not a Blessed moment of silence between them. Every last gasp of breathable air went to fuel up his bellowing or her babble. Nancy would drag the infant out on the front yard and sit there, in plain sight of the road with Baby Henry huge and a howling in her lap. The Missus finds them like that more than once and she made sure I felt for it. Next thing the boy is up and around and possessed of some wild demonry, I swear it. Henry had a streak of the purely Devilish in him and a boundless creativity for trouble. His sister, acting moony, was wholly enthralled to his spell. There would go Henry, tearing straight along with a look of bitterest determination and Nancy trailing behind him, still in a nightdress, eyes wide as saucers. I would try to stay on my work but soon enough would come a crash or a clatter to spoil the peace and set all teeth on edge.

Worse still was when things fell quiet. As the calm before a thunder gets rolling, I came to dread the ticking of the big clock in the hall. If things hushed enough to where that gentle rhythm could reach me, I learned to drop my labors and round the children up before mayhem ensued. Despite these efforts Henry found his way into the hog pen and the both of them, in the farmhands' heaviest hobnail boots, walked back and forth in the slop and the mire and right on into the house, cross the nice wax polish floor in the vestibule, up the stair into the Master's bedroom and right on across the bed. If nothing else, I continue to hope that I never have to do that much washing with lye soap again in this life. Just getting the stink out of those linens took a week of soaking and airing, soaking and airing. Then, my little Dears brought the best brood hen up on top the roof where the poor creature, in deep confusion, issued an occasional doomed egg until finally fluttering down herself, to the pig trough to drown. Old Adams said if I could not keep them settled, he would let the Authority bound them out to the apprenticeships. As it happened, I was still begging and pleading for Mercy when true disaster struck out for us.

His name was Jonathan Lewis and he was the finest looking young man I had ever seen. Tall and lithesome like a willowy tree and well as strong. He had lots of wavy, shining, near coal black hair and maybe if his ears were a little stuck out to the side, it was all set right by his eyes which were of the purest and deepest blue. Like the sky on a real cold day from on top the Mountain looking straight up sort of blue. I met him at the Randolph County Planter's Fair where he was daring down some of the Town boys in a race. The prize was a handsome bay Mare and Jon went and won her against all that Randleman riffraff. The instant he got hold of his Prize and had himself astride her you could see he was proud as a cock hen. Looked to me like he swelled up some and took on a couple of years right there. Prancing back and forth on that big snorting animal in front of all us lasses at the table where we showed the speciality bake goods and fruit preserves, daring us to come a riding. He could have took up any girl he fancied, for there were comely maids from all over the County that day but he ended up picking on me. He said the others dulled to ditch water once he seen me and my faery queen locks, said he fancied how the gold and coppery streaks made it like the Sun shone right at me and he said he liked me smiling at him like that. But I think what really got his attentions was my horsemanship. He was giving the Womenfolk each a ride and they were all trying to show themselves off sitting in the English way, as to be seen ladylike I suppose. When my turn come, I was in such high temper I took up my petticoats and held them right between my teeth, swinging my leg on over that Mare's broad brown back just like that. Jonathan turned red as beet-root and stared in wonder with his mouth wide open to the flies. All the lasses who had seen it were laughing till their eyes ran a tearing and holding tight to their sides but it was me he walked home with later on, come evening. And it was me he come for almost every evening after that.

We just went walking together at the first and we talked about the people we knew round the place, the goings on he had seen over by Town, the tales he had heard of things and creatures that could not possibly be but that he wanted to give some credence. Then he told me about his sister Miss Polly, how she had kept their Pappy from marrying her off to the Sheriff's idiot son Hiram by acting all over rashy whenever poor Hiram would come calling. Scratched herself raw just to give old Hiram pause. He told me about his Uncle Rainer who fell in love with a painted picture of a Lady he saw once through the window of the Widow Battle's parlor. Seems he fell so hard and fast there was nothing for it but to go to the Widow and ask could the painting be had for a sum. Missus Battle took pity on poor love struck Rainer and give him the painting to keep and they been living together in Blissful Happiness ever since, the Uncle and his own Sweet 'Art. He told me a lot of things those first weeks and I got to trusting him pretty well. So I told him some things all about where I come from.

He had only heard rumor of the great Atlantic Ocean and could not credit the idea of all that water far as the eye could see, deeper than a man could ever reach and taking some months to float across. So I told him about my Daddy coming from just so far off, about his stern voice and deep laugh and about the order and the cultivation to our lives up until he went off on his Prayer Meeting that Saturday and never come home. How that sent Momma drifting among fits of delirium with much speaking of the old language to people long dead. She never really come out of it and pretty soon she was gone too.

Doctor said it was the Vial Laudanum finally took her. As I told it to Jon, the next thing to happen was I went round all the family looking for someone that would take in a 13 year girl and that was how, after a time, I found myself wedged up between Uncle Ruben and the stone sink back of your old wash house. He did not really hurt me Dearest Aunt, except as he made it I had to leave you once you began to sense the turn of his attentions. It was a lucky thing for me you knew Missus Adams out here in Randolph and paid my fare for travelling the two hundred miles westerly. Sending me off like you did, with a small purse of cash money and a letter recommending my housekeeping skills but failing to mention my condition, was more than I could have rightfully asked you for and I remain eternally grateful for it.

Jonathan knew I had the young ones though he may not have been entirely clear how I come by them. I do not think he had ever really been with a woman himself, at least not entirely, so it was a true Revelation once we got to studying about that part of life. We come to it gradual as I was telling him about some little things a girl likes and once we got there we moved straight on to the confessing of his own welled up desires. We took our time but the feelings only come on stronger and soon enough they got hold of us and carried us away, like feelings always do. Of course I knew what this meant.

No Ma'am it was no surprise, just come a little sooner than I ever would have feared. With the endless trouble my Nancy and Henry were conjuring up, the steady approach of another baby was cause for nothing but worry and alarm. It would not be long before Old Master Adams had me removed from off the property. That would send my children straight to the apprenticeship Authority and slap me away in the Poorhouse for good and ever, free and white though I may be. A woman, I have learned, has no right to anything on this earth but a wealth of soul withering shame.

There were not any choices left to me, though I had heard talk of a Cherokee woman that claimed an ability to heal wrongs and commune over the deceased. She was known to possess a potion that could free a girl from an unwanted child. It seemed soundly peculiar as the potion must be drunk at dusk and would fail if any sunlight touched the skin within the next full day, also the woman was said to live in a big, dead, hollowed out Gum-Tree trunk lying no one knew quite where. I looked but I did not find a trace of her in that short time I had.

The truth of it is I still wanted my Jon Lewis in the worst possible way and he kept coming on by to see me. Then there were some nights he did not come at all and I heard from Polly, the sister, that he had been out with that Dilcey gal. I did not credit her any at first. Then he goes missing for a whole week and I knew it. So right here is where I made up my mind. I was going to lose my living and my children if he did not marry me or at the very, very least give me the money to pay the coming Bastardy Bond. If he refused me I would just have to name him as the Father and he would be bound to pay for the child's living. I reasoned I had nothing to lose as it was all to go straight to Hell otherwise. His Bible quoting family would have an ordeal in accepting me with my two other fatherless babies. I knew that but I hoped and I prayed for Divine Intervention on my three little infants behalf. Then, on an evening when the spring peepers come out from their wintering and the mockingbird began his nighttime singing, I broke the matter to him.

Jonathan was a looking into my eyes with that half dreamy look reserved for those about to be overcome by those intending to come on over, all puckered up for a kiss. He believed till that very moment that he was Master of his fates and a near Heroic specimen of manhood destined for glory and acclaim. Then I spoke my mind and watched his whole face collapse into parts. His eyes got big and watery in his head and his mouth went straight and pale and he did not say a Blessed word. So I went on with spelling it out, putting it all in the best available light with every advantage prominently displayed. I am not without an imagination myself, as you know and this was the greatest effort my mind and heart had ever made. Soon I had a sizably convictive story built up round how I had imagined it could happen. Seeing as we both really loved and needed each other, everyone would soon forgive us and come to Bless our Union and we could have a big Churchy Wedding, soon as next week, in Town.

Jon took a long time coming to my terms but I had a New Faith and was not to be deterred. When I finally broke off, this sweet boy was so stirred by his emotions that he did not dare face me and stood blinking, every direction but mine. Rubbing his hands round like they chafed him he sort of stumbled back up and took hold of his horse while mumbling that he would send me a word, he had some thinking and a planning to do and he would send along a word.

Two weeks and three days and I have his word! Polly come round this noon to tell me that Jon will meet me tonight at the Spring and that he will be bringing something important for me. Important news or anyway something I cannot do without. She was most insistent. I do not doubt him nor that I have the strength to put it all to rights with him on my side! After Polly went off I run back to see to the children who had been locked in again all day and were fit to bust through the walls of that mean little room. They were making an Infernal racket but I just floated over the mess and the noise and the fury. By later on tonight I will have an answer for everyone! I went down to Old Missus Adams to tell her we will be on our way before the baby starts to show. She was in no small way relieved and I believe it is the first and only time I seen that woman smile and soon enough we fell to crying in each others arms. Back in my room I got cleaned up and put on the best thing I have, with the periwinkle blue stripe, combed out my hair and pinned it up nice and run some rosewater over me for the added effect. Both Nancy and Henry were quiet throughout these preparations for the first time in all living memory. My ears fairly rang with the silence as the children went through my ribbons, trying this one and that on me till they thought I looked all right. Then I dug up some clean writing paper and started this letter to you, which I will finish quick as I can and take along to Post at the Guilford Courthouse after we have been pledged. I have kissed the children and tucked them in their little bed and told them I will have Good News come morning. Soon I will lock them up and leave them to their dreams.

From my window I can see a cloudless sky with a quarter moon and the path to Adams' Spring is well marked out, so I might be allowed to avoid the puddles. Fireflies are arising in the fields either side of the trace and that mockingbird is calling out again, clear and close. I can just see the grove of trees round the Spring from this room and beyond that I know the trace goes straight through till it falters at the Deep River crossing. But that will be no trouble for my Jonathan's proud filly!

Dear Aunt, when I think back on all this now I see ill winds a flying at me from every corner, scattering my finer designs and sending fortune spinning ever away. That is, till today. Now with it all settling down I can see clearly how it will come out, how it will have to be and there are strong signs to back me. There is that bird calling that been following me, Polly's blushing and her urging and the silence of my children on this night of all others speaks plainly.

So I will bid you Good-Bye for the time being my only Aunt Esther and let us hope this long delayed letter does not come out runny and stain streaked crossing the River. I beg that you might be happy for me now that I have found my peace and may someday forgive all the trouble I caused as the misfortunes of a thoughtless child. As for me, my heart is fairly singing with hope and with a new love of the bounty and goodness of life and every living thing in God's Creation!

My sincere affections,
Your Niece,
Naomi

⚜

. . . "Go off with me Little Omie and away we will go
Off to get married and no one will know"
She climbed up behind him and away they did go
Off toward the River where deep waters flow
"Jon Lewis, Jon Lewis will you tell me your mind
Do you intend to marry me or leave me behind?"

"Little Omie, Little Omie I'll tell you my mind
My mind is to kill you and leave you behind"
"Have mercy on my baby and spare me my life
I'll go home a beggar and never be your wife"
He kissed her and he hugged her and he turned her around
And pushed her in deep water where he knew she
    would drown . . .

⚜

American folk ballads bear testimony to our hopes and fears. They are composed of human experience and the peculiar perceptions of right and wrong through which we view and interpret the battle raging between good and evil. With these songs, we conjure up forgiveness, consolation, and the power to face and defy the implacable forces that would destroy us: poverty, the wrath of God, and the temptation to stray outside the social contract. Tales of strength and achievement have their place, but the stories that really take hold of us and make the myth personal are those of loss, regret, and the terrible distance of home. A distance each of us walks alone, through a vast and unforgiving landscape, eyed by a harsh and implacable God.

Omie Wise is but one of many murders to be enshrined in the American folk tradition. The number and variety of ballads in which a young woman meets an untimely end at the hands of her lover are so many and so constant a subject as to make you wonder why we honor such excess. What is it about this particular crime that compels us not only to write the songs in the first place but to sing them to each other for the next two hundred years? The girl's undoing is a cautionary tale, but it is her suffering that moves us to listen. The train that runs from righteousness to ruin and on to remorse and redemption is as American as apple pie. Courting disaster, we run away to join the outlaws, the circus, or a rock band till the shock of our fragility forces a return to the confines of the tribe, heads bowed, seeking salvation by Sunday.

"John Brown's Body"
and
"The Battle Hymn of the Republic"

Charlestown, Va, 2d December, 1859.
I John Brown am now quite certain that the crimes of this guilty, land: will never be purged away; but with Blood: I had as I now think: vainly flattered myself that without very much bloodshed; it might be done.

John Brown's final testament, dated on the day he was executed, December 2, 1859. Courtesy the Chicago Historical Society.

SARAH VOWELL

John Brown's Body

During the memorial service at the National Cathedral on September 14, 2001, those gathered in the pews to mourn the more than 2,800 people who were murdered by terrorists three days before sang "The Battle Hymn of the Republic." President Bush sang it. Ex-Presidents Clinton, Carter, and Bush sang it. Watching it on television in New York City, I sang it. And across the sea, at another service in another church, Queen Elizabeth II sang it with tears in her English eyes, having sung the song thirty-six years earlier at the funeral of Winston Churchill. As Churchill himself had sung it along with FDR on the White House lawn in 1943. Because that's when we sing "The Battle Hymn of the Republic"—at wars and funerals. So "The Battle Hymn" was doubly appropriate on September 14. It was a funeral. We were at war.

And yet: there we were, we gathered Americans, Her Majesty the Queen, chanting this beloved battle cry at the terrorists of the world, yet buried inside the melody of the song was the rotting corpse of an American terrorist. Here are the lyrics that used to go to that tune back in 1860, lyrics that honor the terrorist as a hero: "John Brown's body lies a-mouldering in the grave. His soul goes marching on."

I don't throw around the word *terrorist* lightly, but it fits John Brown. Brown, a white man who hated slavery so much that even his friend Frederick Douglass, the famed abolitionist and former slave, wished Brown would shut up about it every now and then. Back in 1856, Brown and his men massacred five pro-slavery settlers from the

South near Pottawatomie Creek, Kansas, dragging them from their homes as their wives and children looked on, screaming. They hacked them up with knives, though Brown shot one man's mangled body in the head just to make certain he was dead for sure.

Then, hoping to incite a slave uprising, Brown led a guerrilla attack on the federal arsenal at Harper's Ferry, Virginia, on October 16, 1859. By the time United States marines under the command of Colonel Robert E. Lee put an end to Brown's mayhem, seventeen people had lost their lives, including ten of Brown's men, two of whom were his sons.

Brown was executed for this crime on December 2, 1859. Riding atop his own coffin to the gallows, Brown looked at the Blue Ridge Mountains and remarked, "This *is* a beautiful country." But before he died, he issued what has come to be called his prophecy. He scrawled, emphasizing words in a way that recalls the italicized warnings against the devils among us in the Puritan sermons he held so dear: "I John Brown am now quite *certain* that the crimes of this *guilty, land: will* never be purged *away*; but with Blood. I had *as I now think: vainly* flattered myself that without *very much* bloodshed; it might be done."

❧

Across the guilty land, Brown's execution was either celebrated or mourned with ringing church bells, depending on which side of the Mason-Dixon Line one hung one's heart. In Concord, Massachusetts, Brown's friends, including Ralph Waldo Emerson, held a service in which Henry David Thoreau called Brown a "crucified hero." Thoreau was so excited about Brown's martyrdom to the abolitionist cause that he cheered that Brown's death gave people who were "contemplating suicide . . . something to live for!" In Philadelphia, 257 medical students of Southern birth—including the future amputator of Stonewall Jackson's arm—stormed an antislavery prayer meeting for Brown's soul in disgust and marched straight to a depot to board a train for Richmond, where they were met by a band playing "Carry Me Back to Old Virginny."

❧

"And," as Lincoln put it in his Second Inaugural Address, "the war came." Then John Brown got a song of his own—sort of. Like every turn in this story, the song "John Brown's Body" is an accident of history.

What happened was that Union soldiers, the 12th Massachusetts Regiment, were stationed at Fort Warren in Boston Harbor. As they went about their duties, the soldiers sang. One of their favorites was "Say, Brothers, Will You Meet Us?"—a Methodist hymn with a "glory, glory hallelujah" chorus.

There was a singing quartet in residence at the fort: Sgt. Charles Edgerly, Sgt. Newton J. Purnette, Sgt. James Jenkins, and Sgt. John Brown.

One day, in December of 1859, news arrived at the fort about the famous abolitionist: "John Brown's dead." Some smart-aleck, thinking of his singing comrade, Sgt. John Brown, is said to have replied, "But he still goes marching around." A soldier named Henry Halgreen reportedly turned this wisecrack into the first verse of the song about his comrade: "John Brown's body lies a-mouldering in the grave/His soul goes marching on." A soldier who played the organ set it to the music of "Say, Brothers, Will You Meet Us?"

So the song was a joke, joshing among soldiers, the sort of ribbing a sergeant in today's army might receive if he had the misfortune of being named Uday Hussein.

⚔

"John Brown's Body" became the 12th regiment's marching song. They sang it in public for the first time on Boston's State Street on July 18, 1861. After that, they sang it marching down Broadway in New York City. They sang it so often they became known as the "Hallelujah Regiment." On March 1, 1862, they sang it in Virginia on the very spot the abolitionist John Brown was hanged. Three months later, Sgt. John Brown drowned while crossing the Shenandoah River on the way to battle. Heartbroken, the Hallelujah Regiment never sang "John Brown's Body" again. But by that time, they were the only ones in the Union Army not singing it. Northern soldiers would sing it on parade, marching from battle to battle, sitting around campfires at night. And since no one had ever heard of *Sergeant* Brown, every soldier who sang the song thought he was paying tribute to the infamous abolitionist.

Lyrics kept getting added on, including one doozy of a stanza about the president of the Confederacy that went, "We'll hang Jeff Davis to a sour apple tree."

A few weeks before Appomattox, about 1,800 black children in Charleston, South Carolina, where the first shots of the Civil War were fired, celebrated the fact that the Confederate Army had fled the town by participating in a victory parade in which they sang "John Brown's Body," including the Jeff Davis bit. Abolitionist Sojourner Truth had already written her own cover version of the song for Negro regiments of the Union Army to sing. As if listening to little black girls and boys sweetly promising to lynch the Confederate president wasn't nerve-racking enough, who knows what terror was struck in the hearts of slave owners who heard armed black men chanting Truth's boast, "We can shoot a rebel farther than a white man ever saw."

In November 1861, some white abolitionists from Boston, including Mr. and Mrs. Samuel Gridley Howe and their minister, Reverend James F. Clarke, were touring a Union Army base on the outskirts of the nation's capital. They heard soldiers singing about John Brown's body a-mouldering in the grave. As the do-gooders made their way back to their lodgings at the Willard Hotel, Reverend Clarke turned to Mrs. Howe and wondered if she might like to write new, more uplifting lyrics to that fine melody of "John Brown's Body."

Not that Julia Ward Howe had a problem with John Brown. She had even hosted Brown at dinner on one of his trips to Massachusetts to drum up money for smiting the slavemongers. Brown had thought Mrs. Howe was "all flash and fire." Howe believed Brown's execution would "make the gallows glorious like the cross." Plus, her husband had been one of the so-called Secret Six who funded Brown's Harper's Ferry raid. Or rather, Samuel Gridley Howe gave John Brown money for his cause and was subsequently shocked, shocked when Brown used it to buy ammunition to shoot at real live Virginians.

The window of Julia Ward Howe's room at the Willard afforded a view of an ad for a company that embalmed casualties of the war and shipped the bodies home. She would recall: "I searched for an old sheet of paper and an old stub of a pen which I had had the night before, and began to scrawl the lines almost without looking, as I learned to do by often scratching down verses in the darkened room when my little children were sleeping. Having completed this, I lay down again and fell asleep, but not before feeling that something of importance had happened to me."

Back home in Boston, she gave the poem to her neighbor, James T. Fields, editor of the *Atlantic Monthly*. He paid Howe four dollars, gave her poem the title "The Battle Hymn of the Republic," and published it in the February 1862 issue. "The Battle Hymn" became a huge hit. Who knew the *Atlantic Monthly* was the *TRL* of its day? Soldiers and citizens alike couldn't stop singing it. When Abraham Lincoln heard it at a rally, it is said that his eyes filled with tears and he yelled, "Sing it again!"

Harriet Beecher Stowe, author of *Uncle Tom's Cabin*, recited "The Battle Hymn" at Boston's celebration when Lincoln signed the Emancipation Proclamation on January 1, 1863. In what is remembered as his "I Have Been to the Mountaintop" address to the Memphis sanitation strikers on the night before he died in 1968, Martin Luther King Jr.'s very last line of his very last sermon was Howe's first: "Mine eyes have seen the glory of the coming of the Lord." When John Steinbeck's wife, Carol, came up with the title *The Grapes of Wrath* for his novel about destitute Okies, Steinbeck was thrilled—not only because it's a catchy name, but because he thought wrapping himself inside the patriotism of "The Battle Hymn" might keep "the fascist crowd" from accusing him of being a communist. (It didn't.)

In the hymn, a line about Christ asks, "Let the Hero, born of woman, crush the serpent with his heel." This shout-out to the Virgin Mary by way of William Shakespeare takes on an extra meaning in light of Julia Ward Howe's biography. Though she was married for thirty-four years, raised six children, and was, in fact, the creator of Mother's Day, Julia Howe was not without ambivalence about domesticity. For example, she wrote a poem entitled "The Present Is Dead"—on her honeymoon. Writing to her sister about what she called the "stupor" of marriage and motherhood, Howe complained, "It has been like blindness, like death, like exile from all things beautiful and good." So in "The Battle Hymn of the Republic" Howe reminds the nation that the Son of God had a human mom who did all the work. Hence, "let the hero born of *woman* crush the serpent with his heel." Howe is rubbing in the fact that even Jesus had to be potty-trained.

Like a lot of your bigger hit songs, the "Battle Hymn" has been ripped off numerous times. Countless renditions have been set to its tune, which is fair enough considering that Julia Ward Howe ripped off a song that was a rip-off of a previous song. There was an 1899 update protesting the McKinley administration's incursion in the Philippines. There was "Solidarity Forever," a number from *The IWW Songbook*, a hymnal for the union that referred to itself as "the Singingest Union of them all."

There was "Gloryland," the official song for the 1994 World Cup, in which Daryl Hall (of and Oates fame) proclaimed to the soccer fans, "With passion rising high/you know that you can reach your goal." And, of course, there is that playground classic known as "Teacher Hit Me with a Ruler," in which students torment their teachers, mock their principal, and set their school on fire.

In the 1950s, around the time of the Korean War, something else happened to Julia Ward Howe's "Battle Hymn of the Republic." A word changed. The line "let us die to make men free" got changed to "let us live to make men free."

⁂

The new wording acknowledged that sometimes war isn't always the answer—plus it's less of a downer. And through the years, a civil war of sorts has broken out between those who would die and those who would live. The Mormon Tabernacle Choir sings "live" on its 1959 Grammy-winning recording of the song. Joan Baez, leading a sing-along at a black college in Birmingham in 1962, went with the traditional "die." In my opinion, "die" is the way to go. When you get rid of the word "die," you erase the most moving idea in the song: that if Christ died for us, we should be willing to die for each other. Why give that up? This is the one clear-cut case where you can ask yourself, "What would Jesus do?" and you know the answer. What would Jesus do? *Die.*

And of course people disagree about the wording. We disagree about everything else in this country. And when we sing the song today, I think we even disagree about what the serpents are that our heels should crush. Some of us see our enemies abroad. Some see them at home. That's the way it's been with this song, all through its history. It gets adapted for one use, then another. The melody is so powerful, the words so strong, that you feel like you really would lay down your life for a just cause—of your own choosing.

When we sing "The Battle Hymn"—and I say "we" because that is how the song is traditionally performed at public events, as a sing-along in which a group of citizens become a choir—we sing about taking action, about marching on, about doing something. And—this is the best part about singing "The Battle Hymn"—you are not standing there alone doing something. You're part of something. The song starts off with "*mine* eyes" and "*I* have seen," and by the end, it's "you and me" and "let us die," or "let us live"—whatever, "us" being the point. We're all in it together. If only for the length of the song.

II

R. CRUMB

"When You Go A Courtin'"

AUGUST 14, 62

MR. MARCUS &
MR. WILENTZ :

RECEIVED YOUR LETTER WITH PROPOSAL FOR BOOK TENTATIVELY TITLED AMERICAN BALLADS, INVITING ME TO CONTRIBUTE. EVERYTHING LOOKED SORTA INTERESTING AND, Y'KNOW, "RIGHT ON" TO ME UNTIL I GOT TOWARD THE BOTTOM OF YOUR LIST OF "BALLADS" AND SAW THE NIGHT THEY DROVE OLD DIXIE DOWN BY "THE BAND" ONE OF THE MOST IRRITATING POP HITS OF ALL TIME. WORDS CANNOT DO JUSTICE TO HOW MUCH I HATE THAT SONG. I HATED "THE BAND" AND EVERY-THING THEY DID — ONE OF THE MOST PHONY, PRETENTIOUS MUSIC GROUPS IN THE HISTORY OF AMERICAN POP RECORDINGS. I ALSO LOATHE AND DESPISE SPRINGSTEEN AND RANDY NEWMAN. I DON'T EVEN LIKE BOB DYLAN! HE WROTE A COUPLE OF FUNNY SONGS IN THE '60s, BUT MUSICALLY HE'S FERSHTUNKINA AS FAR AS I'M CONCERNED... I NEVER UNDERSTOOD THE APPEAL OF THAT GUY.

CALL ME A PURIST OR A "MOLDY FIG" OR WHATEVER... I THINK IT'S ALL BEEN DOWNHILL IN AMERICAN MUSIC SINCE THE COMMENCEMENT OF ELECTRONIC MEDIA... NO ONE HAS YET WRITTEN A COMPREHENSIVE BOOK ABOUT THE EFFECT OF THIS ON OUR POPULAR MUSIC; THE DRASTIC DISFIGURE-MENT OF MUSIC AS A MEDIUM OF EXPRESSION FOR THE COMMON PEOPLE, OF WHAT IS CALLED, FOR LACK OF A BETTER TERM, THE "FOLK PROCESS," AN EROSION AS CALAMITOUS, IN MY VIEW, AS THE DESTRUCTION OF THE RAIN FORESTS, OR THE DEPLETION OF THE SOIL AND WATER TABLE BY EXPLOITATIVE AGRIBUSINESS...

RANT RAVE... I GOT THIS WAY FROM LISTENING TO TOO MANY OLD 78 RECORDS OF THE 1920s, '30s... IT'S PRETTY MUCH OVER MUSICALLY, FOR ME, BY WORLD WAR TWO... IN AMERICA, ANYWAY... THERE'S STILL SOME GOOD INDIGINOUS MUSIC HERE AND THERE... IT'S ALWAYS A THRILL TO ENCOUNTER SUCH MUSIC LIVE, BEING PLAYED RIGHT THERE IN FRONT OF YOU, BUT THAT'S RARE...

IF YOU WANT TO BE COMMERCIAL, YOU SHOULD INCLUDE "MAN OF CONSTANT SORROW", WHICH WAS RENDERED BY RALPH STANLEY FOR THE MOVIE, "OH BROTHER" THE SOUND-TRACK C.D. WENT PLATINUM FOR THAT, AND STANLEY HAD A WHOLE NEW CAREER. IT'S AN OLD "BALLAD" TYPE SONG, FIRST RECORDED CIRCA 1930 BY EMRY ARTHUR. THAT COULD BE THE TITLE OF THE BOOK: "MAN OF CONSTANT SORROW", SUBTITLE, "AMERICAN BALLADS, OLD & NEW" OR SOME-THING LIKE THAT. ANYWAY, JUST A SUGGESTION. THE HUGE SUCCESS OF THE C.D. OF "OH BROTHER" INDICATES THAT ALOT OF PEOPLE OUT THERE ARE HUNGRY FOR SOME MUSIC THAT HAS SOME TRADITION BEHIND IT, SOMETHING DEEPLY ROOTED... PERSONALLY, THE MUSIC OF "OH BROTHER" SOUNDS TO MY EAR LIKE AN ARTIFICIAL RE-CREATION, BUT IT MAY BE A SAD FACT THAT WE WILL NEVER HAVE AUTHENTIC, INDIGINOUS MUSIC AGAIN... IT MAY BE GONE FOREVER... I MOURN... I GRIEVE...

ANYWAY, I'M NOT SURE I CAN STAND TO EVEN BE IN THE SAME BOOK WITH "THE NIGHT THEY DROVE OLD DIXIE DOWN", BUT ONCE IN THE 1980s I ILLUSTRATED AN OLD "BALLAD". I TOOK IT OFF AN OLD RECORD, SEE EN-CLOSED. IF YOU WANT TO USE THIS, I S'POSE YOU CAN. I CAN CHANGE THE TEXT IN THE FIRST PANEL — IT WAS ORIGINALLY PART OF A LONGER PIECE ABOUT SONGS IN GENERAL. SO, LET ME KNOW. IF YOU WANT TO USE IT, I'LL RE-DO THE TEXT IN THE TITLE PANEL.

— R. CRUMB

COPY SENT TO SEAN WILENTZ

...AND NOW, FOLKS, HERE'S AN OLD BALLAD I TOOK OFF AN OLD 78 RPM PHONOGRAPH RECORD CIRCA 1930. IT'S KIND OF A RE-FLECTION ON THE DANGERS INVOLVED IN SEEKING THE COM-PANY OF WILD BACKWOODS GIRLS. THIS IS REAL OLD-TIME RURAL HUMOR. YESSIR, YOU DON'T HARDLY HEAR SONGS LIKE THIS ANYMORE. IT'S AN EXTINCT SPECIES, I GUESS. IT'S CALLED...

"WHEN YOU GO A COURTIN"

THE TWO SINGERS ON THIS RECORD ARE GENIUNE COUNTRY BOYS. IN FACT, THEY'RE A REAL PLEASURE TO LISTEN TO IF YOU HAPPEN TO LIKE THIS SORT OF MUSIC. THEY SING CLOSE HARMONY IN A HIGH, NASAL, UN-EMOTIVE STYLE, AND AC-COMPANY THEMSELVES WITH GUITAR, HARMONICA AND MANDO-LIN. THEIR NAMES ARE GEORGE WADE AND FRANCUM BRASSWELL.

"WHEN YOU GO A COURTIN' LEMME TELL YOU WHERE TO GO — JUST GO DOWN TO THE OLD MAN'S HOUSE, IT'S DOWN BELOW — "

"THE BOYS THEY'RE ALL MARRIED AND THE GIRLS THEY'RE ALL GROWN — THEIR HAIR IS ALL TANGLED AND THEY'VE NEVER SEEN A COMB — "

"THEY CALLED ME IN TO SUPPER AN' I THOUGHT IT WAS TO EAT — "

"I GOT AN OLD DULL KNIFE AN' I CARVED UPON THE MEAT — "

The Rose & the Briar

"When You Go A Courtin'"

SEPT. 16, '02

MARCUS:

YES, YOU CAN PRINT MY LETTER — ANY OR ALL OF IT, WHADDO I CARE, SINCE I'M ALREADY A NOTORIOUS MISANTHROPE AND PARTY-POOPER.

SO, YOU LIKE EMRY ARTHUR'S "MAN OF CONSTANT SORROW" / HE IS A VERY BASIC GUITAR PLAYER, BUT HAVE YOU LISTENED TO "SHE LIED TO ME" ON THE C.D. "THE MUSIC OF KENTUCKY", VOL. 2, YAZOO 2014? THAT IS SOME DEEP, DARK GUITAR PLAYING, VERY INDIVIDUALISTIC... ONE OF MY FAVORITE OLD TIME "BALLADS",,, ALSO ON THAT C.D. IS THE MOST PROFOUND "AUNT JANE BLUES" BY BILL SHEPHERD. UNFORTUNATELY, IT IS REISSUED FROM THE ONLY KNOWN COPY OF THE ORIGINAL 78 RECORD, WHICH IS IN RATHER WORN-OUT CONDITION. IRONIC, WHEN YOU THINK OF ALL THE MADONNA RE-CORDS THERE ARE IN THE WORLD, OR EVEN ALL THE 78s FROM THE 1970s OF, SAY, AL JOLSON, OR RUDY VALLEE, THAT ARE OF NO INTEREST TO ANYONE ANYMORE...

INTERESTING OBITUARY OF ALAN LOMAX ENCLOSED... "THERE WON'T BE ANYWHERE TO GO AND NO PLACE TO COME HOME TO",,,, MOST ELOQUENTLY PUT, MR. LOMAX...

SEE ENCLOSED COPY OF NOTES TO "MUSIC OF KENTUCKY" C.D., IF YOU DON'T AL-READY HAVE IT, FOR GREAT QUOTE FROM ALAN LOMAX'S CORRESPONDENCE TO THE MAN AT THE LIBRARY OF CONGRESS, AND A SHORT BIOGRAPHY OF EMRY ARTHUR TO-GETHER WITH A PHOTO OF HIM.

I'LL TAKE "AUNT JANE BLUES" OR "SHE LIED TO ME" OVER ALL THE POP, FOLK-ROCK, DISCO, HEAVY-METAL, RAP HIP-HOP NEW-WAVE TECHNO CRAP RECORDED IN THE LAST THIRTY-FIVE YEARS! DID YOU SEE "GHOST WORLD" IN WHICH TERRY ZWIGOFF SHOWS AN 18-YEAR-OLD GIRL CONVERTED TO A LOVE OF OLD MUSIC ON HER FIRST HEARING OF "DEVIL GOT MY WOMAN" BY SKIP JAMES? A BIG FANTASY FOR TERRY; THE 18-YEAR-OLD THEN THINKS THE CRANKY, ALIENATED OLD RECORD-COLLECTOR NERD IS A COOL GUY AND THEY END UP HAVING SEX! THAT'S HOLLYWOOD FOR YOU... QUITE A FANTASY /

GOOD MUSIC LIVES ON, THOUGH, IN ODD NOOKS AND CRANNIES. ON THE METRO (SUBWAY) IN PARIS, FOR INSTANCE. COUPLE OF MONTHS AGO, AN OLD WOMAN CAME ON THE METRO, BEG-GING AND SINGING. SHE MIGHT'VE BEEN A GYPSY... "SI VOUS PLAIT, MONSIEUR, MADAME", SHE SANG, OVER AND OVER, IN A VOICE SO PLAINTIVE, IT FELT LIKE IT WAS PULLING YOUR HEART OUT OF YOUR CHEST! IT WAS IRRESISTABLE... HAD TO GIVE HER MONEY... AND ABOUT A YEAR AGO I SAW A TALL, THIN, BLACK, BLACK YOUNG AFRICAN MAN IN A CORNER OF A METRO STATION PLAYING ON A CRUDE, HOME-MADE WOODEN XYLOPHONE OF ABOUT SIX KEYS, BUT THE MUSIC WAS FABULOUS. I HAD TO STOP AND WATCH VERY CLOSELY, STILL I COULDN'T SEE HOW HE WAS ABLE TO GET SO MUCH MUSIC OUT OF THAT LITTLE TWO-BIT INSTRUMENT, I THOUGHT, IS HE HIDING A TAPE RECORDER SOMEWHERE THAT'S PLAYING A BACK-UP TRACK?? BUT NO, HE WAS DOING IT ALL HIMSELF. HIS HANDS WERE A BLUR, HOLDING THE LITTLE HAM-MERS, AND ON HIS FACE WAS A BEATIFIC EXPRESSION AS HIS EYES STARED BLANKLY UP OVER THE HEADS OF THE PEOPLE WALKING BY. AGAIN, THE MUSIC WAS HYPNOTIC — TRANCE INDUCING. HE HAD NO TAPES OR C.D.s FOR SALE,

— R. CRUMB

"Little Maggie"

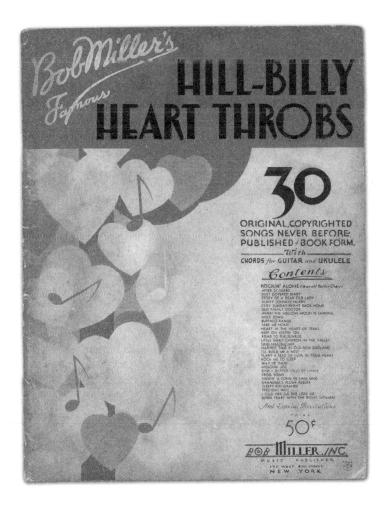

Cover to Bob Miller's Famous Hill-Billy Heart Throbs *(New York: Bob Miller, Inc., 1934). Courtesy of Sean Wilentz.*

JOYCE CAROL OATES

Little Maggie—A Mystery

This was a long-ago time when we were all so young. When Little Maggie first came into our lives. You wanted to think Little Maggie was not a real woman, to cause real hurt and regret. You wanted to think, *It's just a song, it's music fading in the air.*

Some of you have journeyed here to "interview" me. Only surviving child of Blue-Eyed Bill Brandy. Asking do I know the identity of Little Maggie? Did I know Little Maggie? *Was I the model for Little Maggie?*

My age, you have to laugh at such questions. You have to laugh, people are so gullible. My Daddy Bill Brandy used to say *Folks will believe any old bullshit, you say it with a smile. Politicians, they need to add praise God.*

First time I was taken to see my Daddy perform he was all ablaze in light. He was the handsomest man you would ever set eyes on. He had the blackest hair sprouting thick from his forehead and curling down past his collar, he wore a dark blue work shirt like he wore at the lumber mill except it was fresh-laundered and ironed, and he wore a deerskin vest like a mountain man, and a belt with a brass buckle lined up neat with the buttons of his shirt, military style; and clean work trousers and work-boots. He was shy-seeming at first in the bright lights then warming to the crowd, and the crowd warming to him, like a sleepy beast come alive. He was Blue-Eyed Bill Brandy at the start of his career. Played that guitar of his he'd inherited from his granddaddy like his fingers was just alive strumming and picking out notes faster than the eye can follow and the ear can hear. It was nighttime but brighter than the sun on that stage. Blue-Eyed Bill Brandy had eyes like a blue-liquid flame. He was a home-town Vergennes County boy, the crowd went wild for him. His voice was raw like yearning. His voice was their own voice pitched higher. Oh it's something to cleave to your heart through the years, your own handsome young Daddy ablaze in light and this happy cheer come up from the crowd! Something you don't forget, your Daddy enshrined in the wonderment of strangers.

I was three years old. My brother Wes Hardy was five. Our Momma was a young Momma then, happy and proud to be Blue-Eyed Bill Brandy's wife and the trouble not yet come to her marriage. There was our actual name MacGowan, and there was Daddy's music-name Brandy. Why it was chosen over MacGowan was never clear to us. Momma said it was somebody's decision, not Daddy's own. Yet it had to be Daddy's own, we knew. For Daddy was a strong-willed proud man who made his own decisions saying it's like pulling a trigger of a gun: only one shooter, and when you pull that trigger it *pulled*.

Daddy was six feet three inches tall, weighed over two hundred pounds tight-packed with muscle. He'd gone into the lumber mill at Crown Point aged fourteen which was meant to be his life except this miracle had come to him, one day he's Blue-Eyed Bill Brandy at the Vergennes County fairgrounds being cheered by the biggest crowd of people he has ever seen. And Momma staring, wiping tears from her eyes. Clutching Wes Hardy's hand on her left and my hand on her right like she had to grip us tight, to keep a grip on herself. For there was Daddy like a stranger, almost you wouldn't recognize him. So roused, and his face heated. Blue-Eyed Bill Brandy stamping his feet in those boots so hard the stage was shaking! Feet big as horse-hooves, wouldn't want them kicking you! Only thing was, clouds of gnats and moths were attracted to the hot lights you had to be seated close up like Momma and Wes Hardy and me to observe. How Daddy swiped at these damn insects sticking to his eyelashes and lips but never let on to the crowd any least discomfort for that was not Bill Brandy's way with any crowd. This Vergennes County boy the crowd adored. Singing his special song "Little Maggie" in a way like a growl deep in his throat, raw and hurtful and angry and yearning. You could not tell if Bill Brandy loved his Little Maggie or if he hated her. If he was crazy for his Little Maggie or wished to be rid of her. Little Maggie has a drink in her hand she's drinking away her troubles, Little Maggie has a suitcase in her hand she's running away from her troubles, Little Maggie has a .44 pistol in her hand she's gonna shoot away her troubles. Little Maggie is a female not to be trusted, fooling another man. Little Maggie, Little Maggie!—there was not a girl or a woman of any age in that Vergennes County audience didn't want to be Little Maggie sung of by Blue-Eyed Bill Brandy for you could see, whoever Little Maggie was, she'd got inside that man's head.

Little Maggie had a song sung of her which would come to be a famous song, which will not be true of the remainder of us.

⚮

Was Momma jealous that night? Maybe. Did Momma have a suspicion who Little Maggie was? Maybe so. But Momma was mostly overwhelmed by the reception Daddy was getting. Like she had some thought this is the beginning of something you could have no idea where it was headed like the first foothills of a mountain range stretching on hundreds of miles to the horizon.

It was a roused-up audience that night! True, there was drinking, some fooling-around and rowdy behavior at the edges where bleacher-seats gave way to people standing or sprawled in the grass. There was a wanting-to-laugh feeling. For as Blue-Eyed Bill Brandy warmed up, he'd more and more bare his big horsey teeth, had a way of laughing Hey! Whooeee! like playing that six-string guitar and singing in his raw country-boy voice was what he was born to. Through his career it would be said Bill Brandy is a joy to behold, that handsome face ablaze with happiness. Bill Brandy is one to sing his heart out, a performer who holds nothing back. If there are individuals ordained by God to be adored, Blue-Eyed Bill Brandy is surely one of them.

Like rambunctious Little Maggie, he was. In the blazing light, to be envied by those in the shadows.

That night the audience clapped and whistled and kept calling our Daddy back for one more song, though the hour was getting late, and you'd expect folks to be ready to depart. But Daddy seemed to shine all the more. "Little Maggie" was but one of Blue-Eyed Bill Brandy's songs but it was the one folks seemed to favor, so he sung it again, then had a special surprise for the audience: my brother Wes Hardy and me.

(We had been warned this might be. If Daddy felt the crowd wished it. If Daddy felt the crowd merited it. He was so proud of his family he said, he would wish to introduce them at the end of the evening. Momma had said worriedly, she did not think this was a good idea, it would excite us too much especially the little one Lucinda who was me, who had a hard time sleeping many nights as it was, any night of the full bright moon and any night when rain hammered on the roof, but of course Momma would not prevent it, for a wish of Daddy's was to be obeyed. For herself, Momma shuddered at the thought of appearing on any stage, she was a tall awkward shining-haired girl so shy she'd stammer asking a bus driver the fare or making a telephone call to Wes Hardy's grammar school. Momma did not oppose Daddy, however, and dressed Wes Hardy and me for the occasion, and wetted and combed our hair, and tied back mine with a pink velvet ribbon.)

So strange to be brought on that lighted stage where you could not see the audience beyond the first two or three rows, but knew it stretched back into the tramped-down field beyond. So strange, hundreds of eyes staring at you, like through the scope of a rifle. And those damn old gnats and moths darting at us, like Wes Hardy and me were fresh prey. Daddy seized us up in his arms, his face gleaming like a new-minted coin. His eyes had never been so blue-flashing as now. Here is my boy Wes Hardy and my li'l gal Lucinda, Daddy called to the audience, lifting us in his arms, Daddy's hard-muscled arms, Wes Hardy in the crook of one and Lucinda trembling in the crook of the other, both blinking half-blind in the hot lights and so scared we near-to wet ourselves and oh! that Vergennes audience went wild cheering and whistling. Folks love to see a man so manly hoisting his children aloft in pride. Saying in his raw happy voice, God has sent these little ones to me in all their beauty praise God, ain't they beautiful?—giving Wes Hardy a wet smooch, and Lucinda a wet smooch, and the two of us giggling and thrilled to the depths of our child-souls that must be shallow you are thinking, for a child has so little memory, yet that memory is a radiance that will endure until all else has faded and vanished. Wes Hardy was a staring-eyed little boy with his Daddy's black curls, Momma had dressed him like his Daddy in miniature in dark-blue denim, little fringe vest, and brass belt buckle lined up with his shirt buttons military style, and there was Lucinda looking like a chubby little doll, pink ruffled dress, white anklet socks and black patent-leather Mary Janes and her strawberry-blonde hair the color of Momma's hair in curly ringlets pulled back and fastened with a pink velvet ribbon. Praise God, Blue-Eyed Bill Brandy cried, tears spilling down his cheeks, ain't they beautiful like angels come to earth?—and the crowd yelled back, cheered and applauded so Wes Hardy and me understood the answer was *yes*.

This was a long-ago time in Vergennes County, Kentucky, when we were young. Strange to realize that Daddy and Momma were young, too. Great Depression this time would come to be called in the history books. Folks would speak with bitterness and hurt. Folks would say *betrayed*. Place your trust in something big—God, government—and it lets you down and you are changed forever afterward.

Like Momma would come to say of Blue-Eyed Bill Brandy who'd been Billy MacGowan when she married him in the Crown Point Baptist Church. She was Noreen Stuckhart aged nineteen, and Billy only twenty-two himself. A worker alongside Momma's brothers at the Crown Point lumber mill on the Threeforks River, he'd started there right out of eighth grade. It was half the men in Crown Point and vicinity worked in that mill. It was the most-paying of the mill jobs a young man might do with his hands. You could hope to be a foreman one day, but there would not be any union. The change that came over Billy MacGowan in a few years, Momma could not have predicted. This thing with his granddaddy's old six-string guitar! Soon as the old man died and Billy inherited it, there was like a new presence in the house. Like a new spirit restless and excitable. Come home from the damn mill wrung out Billy said, so tired but he'd have a drink and a smoke and take up that instrument and it was like his fingers would come alive and his blue-flamey eyes and he'd get back his strength, amazing to behold. Momma spoke in wonder of this transformation, and sometimes in dread. Momma was hopeful for our Daddy to find employment when the mill was laying workers off. It was steady employment Daddy wished for to support his young family, never would Momma have believed that that guitar would be his salvation no more could Momma have believed that that guitar would be her damnation. Seeing the end of it in the beginning, you are the more lost in wonderment: *why*?

Little Maggie was the source of the trouble Momma wished to blame but who was Little Maggie? Wes Hardy and me believed that Momma never set eyes on this girl. Or even if Momma had good evidence to believe that Little Maggie was an actual girl. Yet Momma was stuck on that. Momma could not see, maybe it was that old six-string guitar that was to blame, bending Billy MacGowan's destiny like it did.

There are some betrayals you can't forgive. Hurts like a spike in the heart.

My memory of our Momma who'd been that shining-haired shy girl now straggle-haired and her eyes red-rimmed like she's been clawing at them, hitting her fist against her heart.

Like every able-bodied man in Vergennes County our Daddy joined up with the U.S. Army to fight the Axis enemy that wished to invade and destroy us. It was a time of excitement like witnessing a barn ablaze. It was a time of fear and dread, that a summons would come that Daddy was hurt, Momma prayed *God protect these children's father, one day at a time.* And so it was, and Daddy returned home unhurt and joyous unlike many soldiers who returned wounded or did not return at all. And when Daddy returned it was not the Great Depression but Post-War. The Post-War Boom, it came to be called. And Blue-Eyed Bill Brandy was of that era for Bill Brandy had the look of a soldier-hero you could trust, a man so tall, broad-shouldered and handsome and his hair so black and eyes a fierce blue, it was a time for Bill Brandy's guitar, and that raw yearning Kentucky-boy voice. Except now Bill Brandy had hired on a manager, a U.S. Army major he'd met over in France now retired to civilian life. Major Brownlee was never a friend of our Momma's, she would claim she had seen into the man's mercenary heart the first sight she had of him. The Major's way of laying his meaty hand on Daddy's shoulder crowing *Blue-Eyed Bill, sky's the limit.*

Little Maggie was waiting back home, just like Momma.

Little Maggie was biding her time.

Now it wasn't the Vergennes County fairgrounds on the crude outdoor stage aswarm with insects, now it was bookings in Lexington, Louisville, Evansville. It was two-day bookings, three-day bookings in Nashville, Knoxville, Chattanooga, Memphis. It would come to be tours not just bookings. It would come to be Indianapolis, Cincinnati, Akron, and Pittsburgh. It would come to be recording sessions in Nashville. Early on, Momma would travel with Daddy for a day or two. But there was no place for Momma and no need for her, she came to see. Still she was proud of Daddy, still she adored Daddy. On the radio you could hear Bill Brandy's voice, so strange! Wes Hardy and me, we'd turn the dial in search of our Daddy's voice which sometimes we would find. The first of Bill Brandy's string of hit singles was "Little Maggie" but in a faster rhythm than we recalled, jivved up some. Since the Army, his far-away time he would not speak of to any of us except to say *I left all that over there,* Bill Brandy had a new kind of speech, only raw-seeming now when he wished. Other times, his voice was smooth and caressing like a cat's fur being stroked.

More and more Daddy was away. More and more Momma waited for him to telephone. Waited for him to send money.

Which he did. For a time.

Momma started to drinking, you'd never expect it of her. It was the Stuckhart family curse she'd said, she would never succumb. But in time she did.

Momma, Wes Hardy, and me weren't living in Crown Point any longer but upriver at Bowling Green. We'd moved from that old asphalt-sided tin-roof shanty on the Threeforks River to a four-bedroom "Georgian"-type house Blue-Eyed Bill Brandy had purchased for his family, red brick and white columns and a three-car sliding-door garage and a grassy front lawn that blossomed bright yellow dandelions in the spring. Post-War the U.S. was everywhere leveling land outside towns, building tracts of cheap housing for veterans to live in with their families but the "Georgian" Daddy purchased for us was no cheap tract house and Daddy would not live in it with us.

It was a shameful thing, our Momma and Daddy "separated." Not divorced (not yet) but "separated." Almost it's a worse time, you have some hope and hope is hurtful. There's songs Bill Brandy sung at this time, that speak to *hope that hurts*. There's songs that made Bill Brandy famous that speak to how Wes Hardy and me felt, left-behind by our Daddy we adored and made to feel scorned, except in the songs Bill Brandy is the left-behind one singing how broke his heart is! Wes Hardy laughed hearing this the first time. Marveling, our Blue-Eyed Daddy is some shrewd old buzzard ain't he, scavengering hurts that ain't even his.

Wes Hardy, I said, that's a mean interpretation! Our Daddy is not any nasty old buzzard. An artist takes from where he can and who, I told Wes Hardy. It's like a strong feeling is in the air, Bill Brandy sets it to song.

Bill Brandy shoves it in his pocket, Wes Hardy laughed.

⁂

I never hated Daddy like Wes Hardy did. Why I have outlived my brother by thirty-two years, eight months, and eleven days.

⁂

Those songs of *hope that hurts* were named by the President of the United States as some of his favorites. But this was later, when Momma and Daddy were divorced.

Poor Momma! When she wasn't drinking she was praying. Which is harder on the nerves to live with, I would not wish to say. You feel sorry for a left-behind woman, then you cease to feel sorry and begin to feel other things.

Momma's face that used to be a plain-pretty girl's face smooth as soap turned into this peevish put-upon face like something left to dry out in the sun. Her hair that was shining turned dry as broom sage. Scaly rashes on her eyelids she'd scratch with her fingernails and make worse like there was a pleasure in it. Drawing the parlor blinds on hot summer days of no more air than the inside of a skillet and setting the record player on *repeat*, hearing again and again Blue-Eyed Bill Brandy singing of his lost love Little Maggie in that raw yearning voice any woman would die for, and Momma is asprawl in her nightgown she hasn't troubled to change out of, barefoot and her hair in a tangle, Noreen Stuckhart drinking her troubles away with gin like Little Maggie herself and wishing she had a .44 to clutch in her hand, and Blue-Eyed Bill stepping through the door unawares. Momma knew each syllable of each of Bill Brandy's six recordings of "Little Maggie" each of them differing considerably from the others except the opening words *Yonder stands Little Maggie*. These, Momma thrilled to for they were always the same.

Wes Hardy cried Momma shame! Look at you.

Momma says Pluck out your eyes, then. Nobody askin' you to look.

Momma's words were slurred like dripping grease. She'd lost all pride. Wes Hardy and me despaired of her. We'd telephone Daddy at whatever number he'd given us "for emergency" and try to speak with him, so he might speak with Momma saying he loved her, just he was so damn busy right now he couldn't talk long.

Momma says Billy, are you with her?

Daddy says This line is bad, Noreen.

Momma says Are you? With her?

Daddy says This line is no good, better say goodnight darlin'.

Yet several times in those years of his fame rising like a helium balloon Daddy returned to Bowling Green with a hope of "reconciliation." In printed interviews we would eagerly read, cut out, and place in albums Bill Brandy gave himself humbly to be a family man. He was a Christian husband and father. He had accepted Jesus Christ into his heart. He meant to do right when and where he could. A few days in Bowling Green where life was slow as a meandering creek in August and Daddy was on the phone making and receiving calls all day long and drinking and in the night we'd hear him and Momma quarreling like radio voices getting louder. Wes Hardy was still living at home, he had not gone away to school as Daddy had wished for him. And Lucinda was still living at home for who would take care of Momma, and Momma begged me. In the night we would be wakened hearing these quarrels and lie listening in dread. A sound of glass and Momma's shriek, *Go to her, then! Go to your whore, adulterer!*

(I have to say, I could not comprehend how if a man and a woman is joined by God, and exchanged holy vows, they could see their way to parting. I shared the fervent beliefs of Momma and her family in this. Male and female they are joined together, husband and wife they will cleave together in sickness as in health till death do they part. I believe this. And if babies come of their love, how can they bear to part? Knowing how the child's heart is rended in the devouring teeth of the elders. I prayed to Jesus Christ asking of Him how can what is uttered out of the heart with eternal love become ash in the light of a later day? Jesus, *how*?)

(You have gathered, I became an outspoken female at a young age. Even to Jesus Christ I did not stint my voice. Little Maggie was my older sister in this: for what choice was there, I came to see by the tender age of twelve, between Little Maggie lifting her shot glass to her lips, leveling her .44 pistol to blast out a man's heart, walking away suitcase in her hand, and poor miserable left-behind Noreen Stuckhart?)

Go to your whore, adulterer! Momma's very words. You are smiling to hear such words, decades later in this new century. Yet for me, Momma's daughter, the shame of those words prevails. Like the memory of the Vergennes County fairgrounds when Daddy lifted me in his hard-muscled arm aloft in the adulation of the crowd, this is a memory that will not ever fade.

And Daddy says to Momma whose heart he has broken not once but many times, *All right then, with your blessing, Noreen, I will.*

Like a minor chord. Slipping-down-sad, with a mean little twist.

Packed his things in a fury and called his driver and was borne back to Nashville that very night with no goodbyes to Wes Hardy and me, that would be proof to us how to Blue-Eyed Bill Brandy his very children *did not exist.*

⁂

In the mail in those terrible years there would come on the average of two or three times a week addressed to "MRS. BILL BRANDY" the cruelest most disgusting pulp-magazine clippings: Blue-Eyed Bill Brandy looking more handsome than ever in the company of glamour women, sometimes their names provided ("Sultry Hollywood Starlet Yvonne DeCarlo") but more often no name ("Bill Brandy's Little Maggie?"). Wes Hardy and me tried to waylay this mail before Momma could lay hands on it.

The only good thing was, Wes Hardy and me realized, the glamour women were always changing. We figured none of them could be Little Maggie, there was so many of 'em.

The cruelest was, in the late 1950s, a two-page feature in *National Enquirer* depicting Bill Brandy and a busty blonde Jayne Mansfield type tenderly cradling in her arms *twin babies*! These were exclusive intimate photos taken with a night-scope lens, Brandy and the shameless blonde basking on some Caribbean hotel balcony oblivious of being seen. Smiling at each other like Daddy and Momma used to smile at each other, and those little angel-twins (a boy, a girl) spittle-smiling up at them. It was so unfair!

This shocking evidence, Wes Hardy threw down in front of me. I was so stunned I near-about fainted.

Oh Wes. It's like Daddy has replaced us. We're too old to be his babies now.

Wes says, No. These are bastards, Lucinda. *We are the legitimate heirs.*

⁂

That was so. Bill Brandy never married any of his whores.

❧

It was a new era. It was a new decade. Songs of *love-in-ashes* would make Blue-Eyed Bill Brandy known to the new generation who scorned country/folk music as old-timey. What came to be called "acoustic guitar" was scorned. It was electric guitar, music so amplified it was more electricity than music ramming and rushing along your veins like you had a seat strapped in the electric chair and electrodes on your skull. Blue-Eyed Bill Brandy was a pioneer in this new sound, which you wouldn't expect of a Kentucky boy born so early in the century. He had a Little Maggie for the new music, too. This Little Maggie was some kind of "revolutionary"—"Free Female." It wasn't a whiskey Little Maggie slugged back it was LSD, it wasn't a .44 pistol Little Maggie clutched but a submachine gun aimed at your heart, America! Blue-Eyed Bill was cruel laughing of them hurt, haggard, hanging-on females that were Little Maggie's left-behind kin, as he laughed of the maudlin old-timey country tunes that enshrined them.

Bill Brandy traveled now in private planes. Bill Brandy traveled now with his band and a crew of technicians. There was the Major and the Major's assistants. There were PR people, hair stylists, makeup girls, and costumers. Bill Brandy's worn-out old granddaddy guitar that had brought him his early fame he brought with him to concerts for some time, brandishing it in the hot strobe lights like a chalice of another era but gradually leaving it behind in safekeeping in his Nashville mansion. It was a custom-made glaring-blue electric guitar Bill Brandy now played. Bill Brandy's new sound was raw and yearning in a new way like a Harley-Davidson revving up. Oh you can't bear such hard-drilling noise penetrating your heart muscles, your belly, and your groin but when it stops you crave it to begin again, more penetrating than before.

❧

Again and again, again hearing our Daddy's new recording of Little Maggie turned up deafening-loud. Wes Hardy had set the mechanism to *repeat* and the volume on high. Wes Hardy was not a seasoned drunk so he'd had only to drink a pint of whiskey washing down a fistful of barbiturates to stop his heart in rumpled bed linen on the top floor rear of the lonesome house in Bowling Green, Kentucky. A note addressed to *My sister Lucinda* saying only *Pray for me*.

Coroner ruled accidental death. Some thought it was the hand of Bill Brandy paying out bribes, to keep the ugly scandal out of the tabloids.

Blue-Eyed Bill Brandy on Johnny Carson who's saying he has been a fan for all his life. Blue-Eyed Bill Brandy displaying the original guitar that's clumsy-clunky to the contemporary eye like somebody shuffling in shoes three sizes too large for his feet. Blue-Eyed Bill Brandy saying you have to have the gift, Johnny. I guess. It's a God-given gift. It ain't anything to do with a man's will, or wish to be rich or famous. It ain't even got anything to do with a man's humility. You have to be born to it. There is nothing to be done if you ain't born to it.

Johnny asks Blue-Eyed Bill to play Little Maggie.

Blue-Eyed Bill rolls his eyes but sure, he's a good sport. This is the song the TV people want from him so OK. Beginning to play the familiar chords *Yonder stands*, Bill Brandy's fingers agile and powerful as they'd been at the Vergennes County fairgrounds many years before, and the damn G-string snaps!

Go on, Johnny says. A snapped string won't stop you will it, Bill?

Johnny looking at Blue-Eyed Bill sort of surprised, frowning.

Bill Brandy? Go on, play for us. "Little Maggie."

The look on Blue-Eyed Bill's face. It's a solemn struck-to-the-heart look. A handsome ravaged face like clay beginning to crack, maybe it's his TV makeup melting, mascara like a sooty tear streak running down his face.

Dead air time, a fraction of a second and it's like an abyss has opened. Blue-Eyed Bill Brandy blinking at the guitar in his hands like he's never seen such an instrument before or (maybe, his fans will agonize through the night) the man has had a stroke, and Johnny Carson hastily winds up the segment in a swirl of music like clockwork.

Momma and me, we stayed up to watch Johnny Carson that night. We were witnesses to Bill Brandy's snapped string. Momma dismayed me making a laughing-crackling noise like a demented hen. I was one of those who agonized through the night.

Every reporter, journalist, TV interviewer has asked Blue-Eyed Bill Brandy the same question: Who is Little Maggie?

Bill Brandy has his quick sly answer: Think I'm gonna tell *you*?

Except today, this reporter persists asking Blue-Eyed Bill if Little Maggie is still alive, after so many years?—and Bill Brandy blinks like he's been prodded in the ribs.

As if, maybe, Bill Brandy had not thought that Little Maggie might be dead. As if he had not given Little Maggie a serious thought in a long time.

Saying, in a weak-smiling way, *Sure. She is.*

Damn reporter persists, Where's she live, Bill? You keep in contact, huh? and Bill Brandy shrugs, and reporter asks, You share your royalties with her, Bill? All the years you been exploiting that gal?

Or, reporter leans closer, pushing the tape recorder a just-perceptible fraction of an inch toward Bill Brandy, is Little Maggie, like, a figment?

Bill Brandy laughs, he is so incensed.

Bill Brandy doesn't dignify these questions with an answer.

Pointing out to this asshole that he has composed and sung many songs in the course of his career: songs of mill workers, miners, truckers, and farmers; songs of being left-behind, and songs of walkin-out-the-door; jailhouse and penitentiary blues; lost-love blues; bankruptcy blues; tryin-to-kick-the-habit blues (drink, nicotine, methamphetamine); an early hit single was "Smotherin Love" (a woman condemned to death for infanticide), a more recent is "Patriot Blues" (post-9/11). So why's it always Little Maggie folks are curious about?

Reporter says Why d'you think, Bill? Little Maggie made you

famous way back in the 1930s. And here you are, country-music legend Blue-Eyed Bill, still going strong. There's some of us wondering about *her.*

Wonder, says Bill Brandy gravely. Wonder is good for the soul.

It's true, Blue-Eyed Bill Brandy is a legend. There's generations of Americans who are his fans. His early records are collector's items. He jokes he couldn't afford to collect himself! Those fierce blue eyes are somewhat faded but still blue. The hair so thick, glossy and coal-black is thinner, threaded with silver his female fans adore. And his torso and upper arms once so hard-muscled are now fleshy. And his way of carrying himself onto a stage calculated like here's a skilled drunk walking a tightrope knowing just how to walk it. Bill Brandy plays mostly in Vegas now, those days of twenty-city tours are ended. The Major says let the mountain come to Moses. (What that means, nobody knows for sure. The Major says it's a saying.) For his Vegas act, Bill Brandy wears a royal blue satin jumpsuit that's a mix of his old mill worker's clothes, including the fringed deerskin vest, and a paratrooper uniform. If he walks kind of stiff on his tightrope it might be because he's tight-laced into a corset. (Just a rumor!) He wears his signature kidskin belt with a big platinum BBB buckle in a design copyrighted and manufactured and sold in the hundreds of thousands annually to his fans. His hand-tooled kidskin boots have a two-inch heel (to compensate for Bill Brandy getting shorter?). Possibly, Bill Brandy has had face-lifts, cosmetic surgery, liposuction. Possibly, some days he squints into the mirror seeing this embalmed face, best strategy is to give the poor bastard a wink *Good mornin', legend*!

Smiling at the reporter now. Trying to think what the question is: something about that bitch Maggie?

Bill Brandy says, fumbling his charm, like it's car keys you can misplace, Friend, I made Little Maggie famous too. Dint I?

Reporter says meanly, Bill, you sure did. Why you're pursued like you are. If you weren't famous, nobody'd give a fuck who you exploited, or how many.

Friend, that sounds hostile!

Blue-Eyed Bill has been known to flare up in a demon temper, punch out reporters who say the wrong thing. He's been known to smash photographers' damn cameras. Wrestle in a rage with a TV camera. But this morning it's strange, Bill Brandy sighs wistful and hurt. One of his faded-blue eyes is leaking moisture. His human-hair hairpiece mixed in with his own coarser hair is slightly askew. Wiry hairs needing badly to be trimmed by a barber are sprouting in his ears, nostrils.

Reporter says Bill, nobody is hostile but your fans worldwide just want to know. Who is, or who was, Little Maggie? There are websites devoted to Blue-Eyed Bill Brandy, ever check 'em out?

Never.

Little Maggie is there, too. There's a tribe of females, some of 'em pretty old, claiming to be your Little Maggie, you check 'em out?

Bill Brandy says No. Don't need to.

How come?

'Cause I know just where Little Maggie is. And it ain't on any damn old website inside any computer, friend.

Bill Brandy snatches up the reporter's tape recorder, tosses it overhand across half the hotel terrace to sink into the chlorine-aqua swimming pool. Interview's *over*.

⁂

This is a hard thing to say. I have tried to overcome the shame.

Fact is, that first time our Daddy brought Wes Hardy and me up on stage with him, that radiant happy time lifted aloft in Daddy's arms that has stayed with me through my life, was near-about the last time, too. Soon as Daddy got called to perform his songs outside Vergennes County he never introduced Wes Hardy and me to any audience ever again and we would come to wonder why, why! Why'd Blue-Eyed Bill Brandy seem to lose his pride in us as his beautiful little angels come to earth. . . .

Wes Hardy used to say with his harsh laugh Lucinda you know why.

Daddy is ashamed of us, I guess?

Got to be. Look at us.

I wouldn't, though. If Wes Hardy dragged me to a mirror to stand beside him exposed, I shoved at him and ran away.

Fact is, that night I was three years old, already I was looking like five. A chubby girl with red-brown ringlets, smooth skin like a rubber doll. I was pretty, I guess!—for a while. But not delicate-like, not that fragile-angel look men prefer. By age five I was looking like eight, by age eight I was looking like ten or eleven, by what's called puberty I was five foot tall and chunky-bodied like a female wrestler weighing upward of one hundred twenty pounds. And growing. And my smooth-doll skin broke out in rashes, pimples, actual warts. And I'd dig at 'em with my fingernails, out of spite. By which time Daddy was mostly gone. Daddy was a voice on a record, or on the radio. *Yonder stands* was my way of thinking about Daddy off standing somewhere yonder with this female none of us had met, Little Maggie who had some power to draw him from us and win over his soul.

Wes Hardy had a bad skin, too. And Wes Hardy walked thumping his heels with spite. But Wes Hardy's main feature was his eyes that were these beautiful fierce-blue eyes like our Daddy's except crossed just so you'd notice it without knowing what you saw, exactly. You'd be looking at one of Wes Hardy's eyes but could sort of sense that the other eye wasn't looking at you, or maybe the first eye wasn't looking at you, so you looked quick at the other eye, and that eye wasn't looking at you, either. And so Wes Hardy was one to make folks uneasy and by age thirteen Wes Hardy liked it that he made folks uneasy like teachers or relatives or Blue-Eyed Bill Brandy himself.

If Daddy can't abide his freaky son, so be it. Wes Hardy laughed his laugh like sandpaper.

Wes Hardy and me were the closest human beings in each other's life and yet, if you asked me were we close I'd have to think. Maybe yes. But maybe no. For I had secrets from Wes Hardy he'd have like to be told, but never was.

Like, what Little Maggie looked like.

While Daddy was still living with us in Crown Point I'd rummage through his things sometimes. Like a little mole burrowing. Early on I seemed to know that Blue-Eyed Bill Brandy was not to be trusted, the more he claimed he loved his family and missed us so, when he was away. And also, I was one to crave any knowledge of my daddy there might be, even forbidden. So in his bureau hidden amidst a tumble of socks I found a little rolled-up packet tied with a red ribbon and inside the packet were six snapshots of a dark-haired girl each inscribed *To Bill Love & Kisses XXXX Your Maggie*. She looked to be about twenty but might've been older, there was a hard glint to her eyes staring right into the camera as into my Daddy's heart. Every family snapshot I've ever seen people are smiling like fools but this Maggie had only the merest trace of a smile in two or three of the snapshots, like she had better things on her mind than smiling. The bones of her face were sharp and her hair was scissor-cut in bangs straight across the forehead so she seemed to be peering out at you bemused. It was a sexual look I did not recognize at the time. In the most shocking snapshots this Maggie was naked carelessly holding a towel against her front with a mock-laughing look like she was about to toss it down or at the man holding the camera. In other snapshots Maggie was holding a glass part-filled with some dark liquid and a cigarette between her fingers trailing smoke. She wore a tight-fitting sweater showing she had compact little arm and shoulder muscles and her breasts were high and firm like muscles, too. Her hips in a pair of men's trousers were narrow as a boy's. I was eager to see if there was any picture of Maggie with her .44 pistol but there was not.

Pretty girls are made for men to love was running through my mind all this while and for weeks, months, and years to come. The riddle was, this Maggie wasn't what you'd call *pretty*. Nor did she look like a woman who would wish to be called *pretty*.

I was sickened to discover my Daddy's secret friend but fascinated, too. Told myself it was Daddy's secret shared with me, I would keep his secret forever. For you could see why Daddy preferred this Maggie to poor Momma who lacked all certainty of herself. Noreen who'd made herself into a *nice woman* and what's that?

Nobody you'd sing about in any ballad. Nobody you'd give five cents to hear sung about.

Quickly I put away Daddy's snapshots I knew to be prized by him. He'd only just returned from a trip, dumped his socks into that drawer and would afterward take away the packet. I would never find it again in that bureau drawer or anywhere else. Yet the memory of Little Maggie would abide with me for all of my life and to this day many decades later it is that dark-haired girl I can shut my eyes to see more vividly than my own face.

It was at Momma's funeral in May 1978 I finally set eyes on that woman. First time, and last.

Never told nobody this fact not even Wes Hardy. By this time poor Wes Hardy was gone.

I was not a young woman any longer. My youth had departed like a wisp of a mare's-tail cloud. You spend your hours waiting for something nice to happen to you like being called upon a stage to bask in the adulation of strangers and when it doesn't happen you just keep on waiting. And finally you are old.

Blue-Eyed Bill Brandy never sang any ballad about that.

Momma's funeral was held back in Crown Point where she had kin. No one in Bowling Green gave a damn about her except to drive past our house (we'd had a twelve-foot brick wall built facing the road to discourage this) taking photos of Blue-Eyed Bill Brandy's cast-off family home. By the time she breathed her last, poor Momma was hollowed-out with the effort of being a *nice woman* that folks might observe (at church, mostly) and her true bitter hating self she kept indoors, the last decade of her life. Eat-away by what you'd swear to be cancer but no doctor could detect and weighed sixty-five pounds when she died, a husk of that tall shining-haired girl Billy MacGowan had married when she'd been nineteen.

Out in the world, in photos and TV footage, you marveled to see Blue-Eyed Bill Brandy handsome and fit, looking young enough to be the son of a woman aged as poor Momma!

Out front of the Crown Point Baptist Church there was quite a crowd gathered on that morning of Momma's funeral. First, I'd thought they was for Momma who'd been Noreen Stuckhart in these parts then it turned out many of 'em was what's called media people. TV camera crews, photographers. The expectation was that Blue-Eyed Bill Brandy would be attending the funeral of his left-behind old wife he'd sung of in certain ballads with such winning ways.

I knew better, though. Had to laugh to see 'em. The great man would never return to Crown Point, why should he? He'd bought all his family big houses in Nashville near his own.

Except for the Crown Point Nuclear Power Plant on the Threeforks

River where the lumber mill used to be, there was nothing new in this place. Young people drifted away if they had the capability and never returned except for weddings and funerals like this.

Momma's relatives, mostly female, mostly old and ailing, made a fuss of me which vexed me as I am an independent woman. At the funeral service I took a dislike to the minister who was a stranger to Momma yet spoke of her as Noreen. There was a woman standing at the rear of the church my eye fastened upon, a stout oldish female with gunmetal-gray hair, bangs straight-cut across her forehead. That hatchet-face, and unsmiling mouth. In a rush I'm thinking *It's her: Maggie.* My heart beat so hard! You'd think that I was angry and protective of Momma, whose life that woman had ruint, but that was not so.

Except she was not called Maggie, she was Midge Kilfeather. A cousin-twice-removed of Momma's who was younger than Momma by only a few months. Kilfeather was the name of her (dead) husband said to be one-quarter Indian. Midge Kilfeather was not liked by her relatives for her rude ways, she'd been wild-behaving as a girl and gotten into trouble with the law, accused of smothering her own baby-born-out-of-wedlock and sent to prison for life except they let her out after nineteen years which was a shock to everybody and a deep embarrassment when she returned to Crown Point and took up serious drinking and married this Kilfeather and the two of them lived in a tin-roof tarpaper shanty in the hills where they spent their time drinking till Kilfeather died and Midge tried to move in with her sisters but they refused to have her. . . . All this I heard so dazed and my mouth so dry I could not speak. Little Maggie! My Daddy had made so much of her!

Maggie was so changed from those sassy snapshots, you would not know the woman except like me you'd prized her in secret so long.

The funeral service passed in a blur for me. I was dry-eyed, so stunned hearing the minister's pious droning voice through a roaring in my head like Niagra Falls.

Midge Kilfeather was not invited to the funeral luncheon at the house of one of Momma's sisters but showed up mostly to stand at the buffet and eat. I perceived she was of my height, a tall woman, and as stout as me, but much older. Like poor Momma, Midge Kilfeather could be mistaken for Blue-Eyed Bill Brandy's mother. Shyly I came to speak with her, as she lifted thick-cut slices of honey-cured Virginia ham in her bare fingers to devour greedily. Midge Kilfeather wore a man's soiled jacket and work pants. Her gunmetal hair was stiff with grease. She smelled of her body and of whiskey. Close up, I saw that her skin was raddled as an old gardening glove. My voice was thin saying Excuse me Mrs. Kilfeather we have not met, I am the daughter of— The woman squinted at me with such a hostile look, I thought she must be drunk even now, unless brain-damaged in some way. Yet I could see the girl-Maggie inside the ravaged face. I could see the dark Maggie-eyes. Only wish I'd seen some kinship in them. Some flash of recognition.

Midge Kilfeather mumbled some words at me. I would interpret them as *Get away! I ain't the one!* in a choked voice might've been sudden anger, or fear. Midge Kilfeather snatched up another slice of ham, pushed her way roughly past me to exit the house.

It was then I burst into tears.

Hadn't been able to cry in the church, or at the grave site. Only now bawling like my heart was broken. The Stuckhart females closed about me quick like a big moist fist. There is such a satisfaction in the faces of such females when at last you cry. Hugging me saying Your Momma is with Jesus, Lucinda. Your Momma is in a better world now, she won't be hurt now. Never again!

There was a triumph in this. I tried to feel it.

But still I was crying, helpless and sick-to-heart, it wasn't like me, nor letting these females I scarcely knew fussing over me like I was one of their own. Oh it was the great shock of my life, this sudden weakness.

I'm shamed to say, in my heart I am crying still.

∝⫯⟆

Yonder stands is a joke to me now. The kind you try to laugh at but can't.

∝⫯⟆

In his Nashville mansion Blue-Eyed Bill Brandy is given out to be still alive, tended to by round-the-clock nurses sworn to secrecy. Long ago Blue-Eyed Bill promised his fans he would live to be one hundred at least. At age one hundred he would give his farewell concert. There is no communication between us of course, I would not expect any word from Daddy after sixty years. Yet I remain confident, I am Daddy's sole surviving heir (legitimate). I am confident that in Daddy's heart he loves his angel-girl Lucinda. There is a triumph in that.

Other day I read in the *Bowling Green Standard* that Daddy's old guitar that had been his granddaddy Alistair MacGowan's guitar was auctioned off for some charity, went to a private collector for $1.8 million and I felt a thrill of pride.

"Frankie and Albert"
or
"Frankie and Johnny"

Frankie Baker in the flesh. St. Louis Post-Dispatch, *February 13, 1942. Reprinted with the permission of the* St. Louis Post-Dispatch, © *1942. Image* © *The St. Louis Mercantile Library at the University of Missouri St. Louis.*

CECIL BROWN

We Did Them Wrong: The Ballad of Frankie and Albert

It is only in his music, which Americans can admire because a protective sentimentality prevents their understanding of it, that the Negro in America can tell his story. It is a story that has yet to be told and no American wants to hear.

—JAMES BALDWIN,
"MANY THOUSANDS GONE"

What Baldwin said about black music is particularly true about the song "Frankie and Albert." Americans can appreciate different versions of the song, like the one by Mississippi John Hurt, because they are simply beautiful. But who wants to know the story of the real people who suffered to bring the song about? Who wants to hear about the life of Frankie Baker? It is a commonly held belief that the great folk ballads arose from the anonymous folk, and that individual creators, or authors, are a misnomer. I believe that the folk song we know as "Frankie and Albert" had a single author, and that this authorship does not take away from the rich contributions that the folk—the people—have made to it.

One Monday morning, October 16, 1899, the readers of the *St. Louis Republic* saw the following item:

"NEGRO SHOT BY WOMAN"

After midnight, Sunday, Allen [Albert] Britt, Colored, was shot and badly wounded by Frankie Baker, also Colored. The shooting occurred at the woman's home at 317 Targee Street, after a quarrel over another woman named Nellie Bly. Britt had been to a Cakewalk at Stolle's Dance Halls, where he and Nellie Bly had won a prize. His condition at City Hospital is serious. . . . The Police pending investigation made no arrest.[1]

The City Hospital record notes that Albert Britt died three days later, on October 19, at 2:15 A.M. By the evening after the shooting, a "barroom bard" named Bill Dooley had already composed a ballad that came to be called "Frankie Killed Allen." As the events unfolded, the ballad grew in the slum area into performances. That the incident contained the ingredients of a good story can be seen from the following article, which appeared in the *Republic* on the day Albert Britt died:

"AMID THE SUFFERING"

Allen Britt's brief experience in the art of love cost him his life. He died at the City Hospital, Wednesday night, from knife wounds inflicted by Frankie Baker, an ebony-hued cakewalker. Britt was also colored and he was seventeen years old. He met Frankie at the Orange Blossom's ball and was smitten with her. Thereafter they were lovers.

In the rear of 212 Targee Street lived Britt. There his sweetheart wended her way a few nights ago and lectured Allen for his alleged duplicity. Allen's reply was not intended to cheer the dusky damsel and a glint

---

[1] Britt's given name was Albert, but he was also known as "Allen." For citations of the primary and secondary sources used in this essay see Notes, Books and Recordings.

of steel gleamed in the darkness. An instant later the boy fell to the floor mortally wounded. Frankie is locked up in the Four Courts.

The writer was so inspired by the imagery of violence and overblown clichés that he got the facts wrong. Britt died from gunshot wounds. In spite of the inaccuracies, the article showed the public interest in the story. The romantic imagery of "dusky damsel" and "ebony-hued cakewalker" obscures the reality of prostitution and pimping.

Meanwhile, like an oyster in a shell, time and tradition produced the pearl of a folk ballad called "Frankie and Albert."

The ballad caught the eye of folklorists very early on. John Lomax included a 1909 "A" version of "Frankie and Albert," "from Texas sources," in his 1934 *American Ballads and Folk Songs*, and he also included a "B version . . . a composite of stanzas obtained from Connecticut, North Carolina, Mississippi, Illinois, Tennessee, and Texas." There were so many different variants—including the three hundred in the collection of the folklorist Robert Winslow Gordon— that Lomax called for "a doctor's thesis" to study them. "No one has ever heard precisely the same song sung by two individuals, unless they happen to be roommates."[2]

In 1962, Bruce Redfern Buckley answered Lomax's call and produced what remains the most comprehensive study of the ballad. In his dissertation, "Frankie and Her Men: A Study of the Interrelationships of Popular and Folk Traditions," Buckley examined 291 versions, of which 186 are complete, thirty-one are fragments, and eight are parodies. The song takes different names; it is called "Frankie and Albert" when it is associated with the incident in St. Louis where a certain Frankie Baker shot her lover, a certain Albert Britt. Buckley calls this the "Folk" type, and he dates it around 1899. The first publication of the song as sheet music was in 1904, under the title "He Done Me Wrong," with the subtitle "Death of Bill Bailey."

---

[2] John A. Lomax and Alan Lomax, *American Ballads and Folk Songs* (New York: Macmillan, 1934), p. 103.

What Buckley calls the "Popular" type was published under the title "Frankie and Johnny" on April 10, 1912, by Tell Taylor, with music and words by the Leighton Brothers. In 1942, Guy Lombardo used the famous lead line "Frankie and Johnny were sweethearts" in a version written by Boyd Bouch and Bert Leighton.

> Frankie and Johnny were sweethearts,
> Oh! What a couple in love;
> Frankie was loyal to Johnny
> Just as true as stars above
> He was her man,
> But he done her wrong.

Frankie goes down to the drugstore to get some ice cream, in this—the Popular type—and the soda jerk tells her that Johnny has been making love to "Nellie Bly." Frankie steals her Dad's gun (he's a policeman), goes back to the drugstore, peeks in on the party, surprises Nellie and Johnny, whips out her .44, and shoots her man. The singer ends with, "This is the end of my story, and this is the end of my song."

> Frankie is down in the jailhouse,
> And she cries the whole night long:
> "He was my man,
> But he done me wrong."

This is a clean version of the Folk type—of "Frankie and Albert," as taken up over the years by Mississippi John Hurt, Leadbelly, Taj Mahal, and hundreds of others. In Hurt's version:

> Frankie was a good woman,
> Everybody knows,
> She spent one hundred dollars
> For to buy her man some clothes,
> Oh, he was her man,
> But he done her wrong.

Here you are in a different world—a different a part of town, as it were. The relationship between the lovers is different. If Frankie is spending a hundred dollars on his clothes, she is expecting more than any sweetheart is:

> She had Albert's .44
> He was her man,
> But she shot him down.

In the Popular type, Frankie goes to a drugstore. In this version, she goes to "de whore-house":

> Rang de whore-house bell,
> Says, "Tell me, is my lovin' Albert here?
> 'Cause Frankie's gwine to raise some hell
> Oh, he's my man,
> But he's a-doin' me wrong."

The artistic way that the story is told sets it off as different from the unimaginative rendering in the Popular type. In the Folk type, on the other hand, Frankie is shown in cinematic terms; each stanza is a minute film scene.

> Well, when Frankie shot Albert,
> He fell down on his knees,
> Looked up at her and said
> "Oh, Frankie, please
> Don't shoot me no mo', babe,
> Don't shoot me no mo'."

Just as minimal art can evoke a larger scene, so these stanzas can evoke entire tableaux with only a minimum of words:

> "Oh, tu'n me over, doctor,
> Tu'n me over on my right-hand side
> 'Cause de bullet is a-hurtin' me so."

He was her man,
But he's dead an' gone.

With a kind of genius particular to this type of ballad, the scene we see—the hospital, the doctor, the dying patient, the corpse—goes far beyond the few words that are used.

In the end of the ballad, Frankie is not hanged or otherwise executed, as she is in the Popular type. Instead, the focus is on her pain—the pain of killing the very person she loved:

> Now Frankie's layin' on old Albert's grave,
> Tears rollin' down her face,
> Says, "I've loved many a nigger son of a bitch,
> But there's no one can take Albert's place
> He was my man,
> But he done me wrong."

Here we have tragedy. In the Popular type, the story simply ends; here, in the last lines, the poet presents his view of the world:

> There is no point to my story
> It has only to show that
> There is no good in men.

Buckley found that the Folk type resisted the Popular type in the early part of the twentieth century, but that as time went on, it began to yield.

⁂

What is the connection between the real life of Frankie Baker and the origin of the ballad in St. Louis? How much of the social drama that surrounded the murder is supported by the ballads?

Richard Clay, a neighbor of Frankie Baker, lived at 34 Targee Street, and he knew both Frankie Baker and Albert (Allen) Britt well. A film projectionist, Clay later met the director John Huston, to whom he told the details of the story. In 1930, Huston published

Frankie and Johnny, an illustrated book on the ballad; two years later, he wrote and directed his first play: *Frankie and Johnny*. According to Clay, he was with Albert on the night Albert first met Frankie, and he was with Albert as he was slowly dying in the City Hospital on October 16, 1899. Frankie was probably in her early to mid-twenties—the sources conflict about her exact age—when she met Albert, a fifteen-year-old boy already well known as a gifted ragtime pianist.[3] Soon after, they moved in together at 212 Targee Street; Albert's parents lived at 32 Targee Street.

Clay described the neighborhood where Frankie Baker lived with Britt as a sporting area. "This society was built around the woman and her mack," his friend John Huston later wrote. "New Orleans had already had her *maquereau*, a colored exquisite, who made their percentage out of the sporting white's weakness for black girls." Now it was St. Louis's turn with the macks. "St. Louis became known as the toughest town in the West. Boogie-joints and bucket shops opened up on Twelfth, Carr, Targee, and Pine Streets. The fast colored men and women lived up to their necks. Stagolee stepped out and made a legend of his Stetson hat. The girls wore red for Billy Lyons. Duncan killed Brady. The ten pimps that bore the dead were kept on parade between the infirmary and the graveyard."

Frankie Baker was born in St. Louis during Reconstruction. When she became a prostitute, she followed in the footsteps of many young black women. Yet according to Clay, by October 1899, she had already "gained notoriety by her open handedness, good looks, and her proud and racy bearings." She was "a queen sport in a society which for flamboyant elegance and fast living ranks alone in the sporting west."

---

[3] In a later interview, Baker claimed she was born in May 1876, which would have made her twenty-three when she shot Albert. Dr. E. I. Silk of the East Oregon Hospital, where she eventually died, affirmed that his records showed that she was born on May 30 but did not specify the year. A subsequent search for her birth certificate was fruitless. Albert's father testified under oath that, at the time of the shooting, she was thirty or thirty-five. John Huston later wrote that she killed Albert while she was in her twenty-seventh year. She appears to have acted older than her age, so it seems reasonable to conjecture that she was in her early to mid-twenties. All that is certain is that she was older—and looked as if she was considerably older—than her lover and eventual victim.

W. C. Handy wrote "St. Louis Woman," a ballad inspired by beautiful women he saw walking down Targee Street near where Frankie lived. "I wouldn't want to forget Targee Street as it was then," Handy wrote in *Father of the Blues*. "I don't think I'd want to forget the high roller Stetson hats of the men or the diamonds the girls wore in their ears."

Richard Clay described Frankie Baker as "a beautiful, light-brown girl, who liked to make money and spend it. She dressed very richly, sat for company in magenta lady's cloth, diamonds as big as a hen's eggs in her ears." Clay remembered that Frankie had "a long razor scar down the side of her face she got in her teens from a girl who was jealous of her. She only weighed about 115 lbs., but she had the eye of one you couldn't monkey with. She was queen sport."

Do the ballads support such a view of Frankie?

On the night of his murder, Albert had played a cakewalk concert. According to the ballad, Frankie shot Albert because of another woman:

> Frankie was a sporting lady
> A red-light hung over her door
> She always paid fifty or sixty dollars
> For every suit that Johnny wore.

According to Buckley, in the general description of the woman in the ballads Frankie is referred to as "a generous good prostitute whose love blinds her and makes her foolish." She is also described as "a good girl" (fifty-five times) or a "good woman" (forty-nine)—but "good" means that she was expected to take care of her pimp.

Clay's account of what happened that night is as follows: "On the Sunday night of the shooting, Frankie went out to look for Albert. . . . She surprised him in the hallway of the old Phoenix Hotel making up to a girl named Alice Pryar [an eighteen-year-old prostitute]."

> Frankie went to the hotel
> Looked in the window so high
> There on the chair sat Johnny
> Makin' love to Alice Pryor.

According to Buckley, about thirty-six ballads have this report; others have Frankie finding Albert in a poolroom, ballroom, depot; in the alley, cell house, whorehouse, etc. As we can see from the report on the social drama, Frankie Baker did, in real life, go looking for her lover, her pimp, Albert. She may have had a reputation of doing this many times.

This episode is an important one in the structure of the ballad. Buckley calls it the "Search" trait; he devotes a lot of time to it, and rightly so. Of more than 200 variants of the ballad he examined, more than 150 have the following stanza:

> She went to the barroom
> Bought a bottle of beer
> "Good morning, bartender
> Has my lovin' man been here?"

She looks for him in a bar, the barroom, the city bar, the saloon, the first saloon, the next saloon, the town saloon, the gin well, the beer shop, the station, on Broadway, at "Sweeny's," at "the Thalia." "She called Albert outside and began quarreling with him," Clay observed. "A crowd gathered and listened to the row. Albert would not go home with her."

The ballad tradition reports this as:

> Frankie called to Al,
> "If you don't come to the woman you love,
> I'll haul you out of here.
> If I'm your woman,
> You're doing me wrong."

In real life, Frankie begged Albert to follow her home; in the ballad, she threatens to kill him if he doesn't.

> "Come to me little Albert,
> I'm callin' through no fun;
> If you don't come to the one love you,
> I'll shoot you with my old gun."

According to Clay, "Finally she went on alone. . . . It was nearly daylight when Albert followed. He found Frankie waiting up for him. There was more quarreling as he got ready for bed. He admitted to Frankie that he had been with Alice in her room at the hotel, and he warned her that he was ready to throw her over for good."

This is exactly what the ballads reported:

> Frankie and Johnny [Albert] were sweethearts
> They had a quarrel one day
> Johnny vowed he would leave her
> Said he was going away.
>
> Frankie she begged and she pleaded
> Cried, "Oh, Johnny, please stay"
> She said, "My honey, I've done you wrong
> But please don't go away."

"She began to cry and said she was going to find Alice Pryar [Pryor]," Clay reported. "Albert said he would kill her if she tried to go. She started for the door and Albert threw the lamp at her. In the darkness, Frankie shot him as he came after her with a knife."

> But Albert said, "Frankie, now listen
> I'm going away from here."
> Frankie said to Albert, "If you leave me
> I'll starve to death I fear."
> Albert went down to the corner
> To get a cool glass of beer
> And here he met Miss Nellie Bly
> Who said, "Let us wander from here."

After he was shot, according to Clay, Albert "made his way out of the house and down the street to the home of his parents. His mother heard him calling. She ran out and found him lying on the front steps in his pajamas. He told her what had happened, and she began to scream, 'Frankie's shot Allen!'" How accurately did the ballad report this incident? A son dying on his mother's front steps is too vivid for a ballad-maker to ignore:

> Albert ran to the doorway
> To make a get-away
> But he slipped and fell,
> And [Frankie] shot him where he lay.

In another ballad, he is "crawling" to his mama's door:

> Well, Albert went to his mama's
> And he crawled up to the door
> "Please come here mama
> I'm shot with a .44."

It was well known that Albert's elderly parents doted on their only son. The only-son trait is a consistent part of the Folk version. In 1934, Alan and John Lomax visited Angola State Penitentiary in Louisiana, where they discovered Leadbelly, the self-styled "King of the 12-String Guitar." One of the songs he played for the folklorists was "Frankie and Albert." The interpretation is stunning, mainly because Leadbelly emphasizes the mourning of the mother for her "only son, the only one." In fact, he makes this refrain more powerful than the powerful "He done her wrong."

"Inside a few minutes," Clay went on, "the word was all over [the neighborhood] that Frankie had gotten her man."

> "Albert was a yeller man
> Coal-black curly hair.
> Everybody in St. Louis
> Thought he was a millionaire
> He was my son, and the only one."

In a 1935 interview about the incident, in Portland, Oregon, after a long reflection, Frankie claimed she knew that Albert was seeing another girl named Alice Pryor. He failed to call her one evening. "I went straight to our home at 212 Targee Street," she told a reporter, Dudley L. McClure, "and went to bed. . . . I wasn't going to let his philandering worry me. I had had experience. Albert wasn't even at Alice's house. They were together all right, but were at a party at a friend's house. Albert was drinking and, as always, was entertaining at the piano. That boy could play!" One must note how Frankie admired his gift for music.

"About three o'clock Sunday morning," she said, "Allen came in. Pansy Marvin [her roommate and friend] opened the door and let him in. I was in the front room, in bed asleep, and he walked in and grabbed the lamp and started to throw it at me. . . . I jumped up out of the bed and says, 'What's the matter with you Al?' and he says, 'What the hell are you doing in this bed?' I say, 'I've been sick and come in where I can get some air,' and he walked around the bed and started to cut me, like this, twice. I asked him, 'Say, are you trying to get me hurt,' and he stood there and cursed and I says, 'I am boss here, I pay rent and I have to protect myself.' He run his hand in his pocket opened his knife and started around this side to cut me. I was staying here, pillow lays this way, just run my hand under the pillow and shot him. Didn't shoot but once, standing by the bed." But in none of the ballads does Frankie ever shoot Albert in her bedroom. Conspicuous in its absence, that is one curious trait that is passed into the song.

Clay believed that Albert threw the lamp at Frankie and they were in the dark when she shot him. Some versions of the ballad use that motif:

> Frankie went down a dark alley
> Heard a bulldog bark
> And there lay her Albert
> Shot right through the heart.

Although the place of the murder, in an apartment at 212 Targee, was widely reported, why does this setting never appear in any of the ballads? Why did the ballad-maker choose a bar or saloon for the scene?

Buckley found that the killing was the most diversified of all the traits in the ballad, but in no version of the song does Frankie reach under her pillow for a gun. In Buckley's collection of the ballads, she gets the gun from beneath her dress thirty-four times:

> Frankie threw back her kimono
> She took out her bright .44
> Root-a-toot-too, three times she shot
> Right through that hardwood door.

In the ballad tradition, Frankie repented the murder:

> Frankie went to the coffin
> She looked down on Albert's face
> She said, "Oh Lord, have mercy on me,
> Wish I could take his place."

In some versions, she goes to Albert's mother and asks for forgiveness:

> Frankie went to Mrs. Johnson
> Fell down on her knees
> Cryin', "Oh Mrs. Johnson
> Will you forgive me please?"
> Said, "I'm sorry I killed your son,
> Won't you excuse me please?"

How does this square with reality? After the shooting, Frankie was taken by the police to the hospital to have Albert identify her. She said that they worked on him a long time before he would do it. He knew he was wrong, she said. "I felt sorry for him. Sometimes they sing that I sobbed and cried, but that's wrong too. I felt terrible of course, but I simply had to protect myself."

The next four traits—Arrest, In Jail, Trial, Judgments—show that there was dynamic activity between the social drama surrounding Frankie's murder of Albert Britt and the rich production of motifs in the ballad.

In real life, Frankie was arrested, and the coroner's jury said that the killing was justifiable homicide in self-defense. Although she was still required to stand trial before a judge, one Willis B. Clark, he acquitted her. "I ain't superstitious no more, because I went to trial on November, Friday, 13, 1899," Frankie recalled, "and the bad luck omens didn't go against me."

In one version of the ballad, Frankie is casual:

> Well when they arrested Frankie,
> Wasn't she dressed up fine?
> Had a bottle of Holland gin
> And a bottle of Newport wine.

In another, she is nervous:

> Frankie said to the sheriff,
> "Oh, what do you think it's be?"
> The sheriff said, "It looks like a case
> Of murder in the first degree."

Verses describe her stay in jail:

> Frankie said to the warden
> "What are they goin' to do?"
> The warden said to Frankie,
> "It's a pardon, my girl, for you."

"Why, the judge even gave me back my gun," Frankie remembered. "Don't know what I did with it. Guess I pawned it or gave it away. Everybody carried a gun in those days. Guess I wasn't so very guilty if the judge gave me back that gun, was I? You know, I was afraid of Albert. He beat me unmercifully a few nights before the big blow-off. My eye was festered and sore from that lacin' when I went before Judge Clark. He noticed it too."

People were upset with the verdict, and the ballads reflected this. Some of them are bitter:

> Judge tried lil' Frankie
> Under an electric fan

Judge says, "Yo' free woman
Now, go kill yourself another man."

Mississippi John Hurt sings about the relationship between
Frankie and the judge as if they were conniving backstage:

> Frankie and the judge walked out on the stand
> Walked out side by side
> The judge says to Frankie
> "You're goin' to be justified."

In at least four versions, Frankie makes a comical quip:

> Frankie said to the Judge
> "Well, let all such things pass,
> "If I didn't shot him in the third degree
> I shot him in his big brown ass."

Buckley cites many stanzas that have Frankie crying over Albert's
grave and asking for forgiveness:

> Frankie was a standin' on the corner
> Watchin' the hearse go by;
> Throwed her arms into the air
> "Oh let me die (by the side of my man)."

Did Frankie go to Albert's funeral and cry? "I had nothing to cry
about," she told McClure. "I didn't feel smart about it, either. I didn't
go to his funeral because I couldn't. I was in jail."

In some versions—the Popular type—Frankie is executed. In
reality, Frankie Baker stayed in St. Louis for a year after the incident.
Two months after Albert died, Frankie heard the ballad for the first
time. And as she walked down the street, people "began singing it so
she ran to Omaha in humiliation."[4]

---

4 *St. Louis Post-Dispatch*, February 13, 1942.

But she couldn't settle in Omaha, Nebraska, because the song had already arrived, and she was haunted by it. She was attracted to Portland, Oregon, because she read about the Rose Festival. She always had had a love for beautiful flowers. So she moved to Portland, but the ballad had arrived there, too.

After some activity in prostitution in the north end of Portland, and after having gone to jail several times, Frankie put away her diamonds, fancy lace, and plumes for good. Around 1925, she began to lead a life of respectability. She opened her own shoeshine parlor and later worked as a chambermaid at the Royal Palm Hotel. In the 1930s, after an illness that prevented her from working, and almost penniless, she spent most of her time sitting alone in her white frame house at 22 North Clackamas Street.

In 1935, when Republic Pictures released the film *She Done Him Wrong*, starring Mae West and Cary Grant, it disseminated Frankie's story to an even wider public than the ballad had done. "When the Mae West picture was in town," Frankie told a journalist, "men and women would gather in front of my place and point. Some of them would come in and get a shoeshine, and probably ask me if I was a St. Louis woman. They even called my home and asked me silly questions. I'm so tired of it all; I don't even answer anymore. Autograph seekers pester me too, mostly by letters. Some of them enclose money, and those, of course, aren't so bad. What I want though is peace—an opportunity to live like a normal human being. I know that I'm black, but even so, I have my rights. If people had left me alone, I'd have forgotten this thing a long time ago. Now they can start paying me."

In April 1938, Frankie filed suit against Republic Pictures for damages of $200,000. She lost the case. But Republic had released a film called *Frankie and Johnny*, starring Helen Morgan, in 1936, so in 1942 Frankie sued once more.

She lost again—but what came out of the various depositions was a treasure for folklore scholars. It was during this trial that the most revealing aspect of ballad history and ballad-making became apparent. The trial was held in St. Louis; when Frankie returned to press her case, she was nearly sixty-six, and as witty as Mae West. When asked who Albert was, she replied, "He was a conceited piano player," adding that "he had been staying at my house off and on for a couple of years, although I knew he went out once in a while with Alice Pryor." She was asked if she wore diamonds as big as goose eggs. "Only an average size one," she said. Did she buy Albert hundred-dollar suits? "Not necessarily." What ever happened to Alice Pryor? "I heard she passed out."

Representing Republic, Meyer H. Lavenstein of New York and Hugo Monnig of St. Louis wanted to show that the song could not have been based on the Frankie Baker incident, and to prove that the song existed prior to 1899. They called Sigmund Spaeth, an authority on popular songs and ballads. Fifteen years before, in 1927, Spaeth had written a book in which he stated that the ballad "Frankie and Johnny" was based on the Frankie Baker incident. He said that "St. Louis was the home of not only 'Frankie and Johnny,'" but also of "Stagolee" and "King Brady." Now, after receiving an expert witness fee of $2,000, Spaeth took the opposite position, claiming that the song had not originated in St. Louis and that Frankie Baker had not inspired its creation. On Frankie's side were Joseph L. McLemore and Robert L. Witherspoon, and witnesses Charles Marshall, Mariah Jones, and Richard Clay. The lawyers and witnesses for Republic were all white, and the lawyers and witnesses for Frankie Baker were all black. The jury was composed of white men. The outcome of the trial was hardly surprising.

The film was screened for the jury, but since all the characters were cast as whites, the white jurors had a hard time seeing how they could have been drawn from Frankie's life. "Frankie Baker wants to appropriate for her own use one of the finest ballads of American folklore," Monnig said in his closing argument. "If you give her a verdict, she will have a claim against anybody who ever sang the song. Send her back to Portland, Oregon, and her shoeshine business; for an honest shine, let her have an honest dime. Don't make her a rich woman, because forty years ago, she shot a little boy here in St. Louis." Frankie had her day in court, and according to one reporter, "brightened the lives of all St. Louisians in a dreary winter filled with bad news from the Pacific theater."

Back in Portland, Baker became a lifetime member of the Urban League. In the 1950s, she was admitted to a mental hospital; at her hearing, she told Judge Ashby C. Dickson that she had killed her sweetheart back in St. Louis in 1899. She also told him that she came to Portland a hundred years ago. It was obvious that she had completely lost her mind, except she had not forgotten the incident that changed everything in her life.

Frankie Baker's tale illustrates how the mass popular hunger for lurid stories destroyed her privacy and ruined her life. As John David wrote in 1978 in an unpublished dissertation, "Surely Frankie Baker must have felt the inherent contradiction between the aim of democracy—to enrich the citizens' everyday life—and its modern means of achieving that goal. Frankie's claims against Republic Pictures were a product of the ballad's popularity, made possible by America's perfection of techniques for widening experience. 'Frankie and Johnny' was a melody hummed by young and old alike, yet Frankie felt strangely forgotten. Haunted by melody, she fled across the United States, but she could not escape." She would say that people she encountered were surprised to find that she was still alive; they always thought she had died many years earlier. Now that she really is dead, she has been completely forgotten.

⁂

The Targee Street area was so notorious that it supported three ballad-makers, Tom Turpin, W. C. Handy, and Bill Dooley. Tom Turpin, owner of the Rose Bud Saloon, wrote popular ballads, which he played and copyrighted. One of the best known was "The Bowery Buck," a satiric ballad about a young black man taking his girlfriend to a show, only to be told by the white ticket salesman that Colored people are not allowed.

W. C. Handy overheard two women talking about their lovers. One of them used an expression so striking that he kept it in the back of his mind for two years until he found the right place to put it: "My man's gotta heart like a rock thrown in the sea."

Both Handy and Turpin were refined, educated musicians who expected that their ballads would be played in the parlors of middle-class Americans and the concert halls of class-conscious music lovers.

Bill Dooley was different. He worked on the street corners. He was not trained in music. But if Turpin and Handy are the Christopher Marlowe and John Marston of the late-1890s St. Louis slum, then Bill Dooley is its Shakespeare. In his "Frankie Killed Allen," Bill Dooley's use of imagery is bold and his characterizations of Frankie and Albert are tragic and unforgettable.

Turpin's ballads are so specifically about his particular place and time that they have become lost to history. Handy's ballads are so musically brilliant that they are remembered as a universal expression of the blues. Dooley's talent, on the other hand, was to create unforgettable people in emotional situations that could be found anywhere in both folk and popular cultures. It is difficult to do better than Frankie, her lover, and the refrain "He did her wrong."

What distinguishes Dooley's use of the refrain is his subtlety. Writing the night after the shooting, then adding details in the days that followed, he placed the words in the mouths of the different characters in the ballad: Frankie, "Mr. Bartender," Albert, friends, and the judge. When Frankie comes into the bar, she says to the bartender, "He was my man, but he done me wrong." The bartender replies, "Yes, he was your man, and he did you wrong." When Albert is confronted by Frankie, he concedes: "I am your man, but I did you wrong." Even the judge, when he acquits Frankie of the murder, tells her, "He was your man, but he did you wrong." Each character delivers the line to reflect his or her limited understanding of the total situation. The different ways in which the line is delivered have the effect of creating both the characters and the mood of their milieu at the same time. The scene is not complete: the reason why there are few interior scenes in "Frankie"—and why the actual crime scene, a bedroom, is missing—is that Dooley, writing from the perspective of a street person, didn't know that world. The closest he comes is the kimono: somehow, he found that striking detail.

One of the first to name Dooley the author of the "Frankie and Albert" ballad was Ira Cooper, a reporter for *The Palladium* in St. Louis. Writing in 1899, Cooper claimed that the composer of the ballad was an "itinerant" black man. "On the night following the shooting," Cooper wrote, "Bill Dooley, a Negro pianist and song writer, composed a sorrowful dirge which was played thereafter in many Negro saloons and resorts."

In 1942, in Frankie Baker's second suit against Republic Pictures, her attorney, Joseph L. McLemore, claimed that the ballad was written by Bill Dooley. "Dooley," McLemore said, "along with W. C. Handy, composer of 'St. Louis Blues,' and Tom Turpin, were the most prolific writers of ballads in the Gay Nineties."[5] McLemore emphasized the point that all three men "improvised ballads on news events," and that Dooley "was the most prolific of them all." McLemore went on to give a detailed appreciation of Dooley's genius. "Dooley had a flair for writing catchy tunes. And 'Frankie and Johnny [Albert]' was the catchiest of them all." Then McLemore described Dooley's distribution practice: he would "sell his compositions on the streets of St. Louis at 10 cents a copy." The night after the murder, Dooley had already had a version of the ballad performed, another observer reported; he was playing it himself on street corners.

Dooley moved to Detroit, where he became a street-corner preacher; he was killed there in 1932.

On the second day of the 1942 trial, Nathan B. Young, a St. Louis lawyer and amateur researcher of Negro folklore, took the stand. He said that in the 1890s, when Dooley wrote "Frankie and Albert," it was the practice of "Tin Pan Alley" songwriters to "come here to St. Louis Negro clubs, listen to the improvised songs, then go back East and write their own versions." While Turpin and Handy would be able to protect their ballads by copyright law, Dooley had no such protection. He knew, as Shakespeare knew, that others would steal and manipulate his work, so he had to compose his ballads in such a way that they would survive the more pernicious appropriations. In spite of a hundred years of exploitation by hundreds of songwriters, the originality of Dooley's composition remains intact.

At the conclusion of his study of the "Frankie" ballads, Bruce Buckley wondered why there were so many similarities between the "Stagolee" ballads—about the Christmas night 1895 shooting in St. Louis, of Billy Lyons by "Stag" Lee Shelton—and "Frankie and Albert."

---

[5] *St. Louis Post-Dispatch*, February 17, 1942.

There were countless similarities. In "Frankie":

> People all said to Frankie,
> "Little girl why don't you run?
> Don't you see that police chief?
> With a .44 smokeless gun?"

In "Stagolee":

> Stagolee, Stagolee
> Why don't you cut and run
> For there comes the policeman
> And I think he's got a gun.

"A study of Stagolee and its relationship to Frankie would make clearer which tradition came first in the verses found in Frankie," Buckley wrote. But the question is misleading—that is, it takes us away from the most likely answer. Yes, there are many floating passages in both ballads, but such fragmentary stanzas alone cannot explain why these two ballads are so alike in both structure and imagery. What can explain it is that both can probably be traced to Bill Dooley.

We often think that folk songs spring from the anonymous public, or the folk. But in time, place, and style, the "Frankie" ballads, like the "Stagolee" songs, point to a single author. This doesn't mean that the people didn't help produce the ballads; on the contrary, the people *did* help produce them, by contributing to their transmission. It may be that, yes, to create a great folk ballad, you need a village—but you may also need an untaught genius.

"Delia"

Blind Willie McTell recording in an Atlanta hotel room for John and Ruby Lomax on behalf of the Folksong Archive of the Library of Congress, November 5, 1940. The story goes that Ruby Lomax, on a field recording trip with her husband, found McTell completely by chance while he was entertaining at a pig 'n' whistle stand. The next morning, in the Lomaxes' hotel room, McTell played his 12-string guitar, sang, and told stories for two hours, of which forty minutes was committed to tape. The Lomaxes came away with more than a dozen previously unknown McTell compositions, including the first recording of his version of "Delia." Courtesy of the Library of Congress

SEAN WILENTZ

The Sad Song of Delia Green and Cooney Houston

Delia, oh Delia,
Where you been so long?
Everybody's talking bout ya',
Now you're dead and gone.
One more round, Delia's gone,
One more round, Delia's gone.

—ERIC BIBB, "DELIA'S GONE,"
ON *PAINTING SIGNS* (2001)

Son of a bitch.

The curse is ubiquitous and supple, mild enough today for prime time. It can connote a hard turn of luck. It gets said in commiseration or as a shout of glee. In the white South, slurred—*sum*-bitch—it passes as a semi-obscenity, more emphatic and vulgar than "jerk" and less offensive than the usual four-letter words. But in the poor, rough, and black Yamacraw district in the western end of Savannah, Georgia, on Christmas Eve night in 1900, it was a curse so "wicked"—according to one version of "Delia," aka "Delia's Gone"—that when fourteen-year-old Delia Green called her fourteen-year-old lover, Moses "Cooney" Houston, a son of a bitch, he shot her dead.

That version of the song does not reveal why Delia cursed Cooney, what the curse actually was, why Cooney's outrage turned lethal, and why anybody should care, let alone sing about it. Most of the other versions are equally elliptical, including the one Bob Dylan sings on *World Gone Wrong*, recorded in 1993. In the album's liner notes, Dylan does offer a vivid interpretation of the mystery that turns out to be mostly on the mark: "the song has no middle range, comes whipping around the corner, seems to be about counterfeit loyalty."

Dylan's accounting, even with its tentative note, is truer by far to what happened than the most widely listened-to "Delia" to date, by the late Johnny Cash. "Delia's Gone" is the overpowering first track on Cash's album *American Recordings*, which, when released in 1994, won Cash a new following among music fans of the rap-and-grunge generation. Cash sings in the first person as an unnamed, calculating killer who, dealt some unmentioned hurt that is almost certainly infidelity, has tracked the "low-down, triflin'" Delia to Memphis, tied her to a chair, and blasted her to death with a submachine gun. The killer's conscience bothers him after he lands in prison, but the song ends remorselessly, with a passive-voice line that shifts the blame back from the murderer to his victim:

> So if your woman's devilish
> You can let her run,
> Or you can bring her down and
> Do her like Delia got done.

It's all very different from what Dylan sings and writes—and from the version of "Delia" that Cash recorded in 1962. Although also sung in the first person, Cash's earlier rendition leaves the killer's motive unclear and ends with his being shackled to a ball and chain, dogged by guilt and Delia's ghost. According to Cash, he found the new "Delia's Gone" in the same part of his imagination where he found "Folsom Prison Blues"—a revision by an artist "older and wiser to human depravity" than he once was. Whether out of wisdom or vicarious, play-acting evil, a young 1990s public, on the verge of the gangsta boom, loved it.

Or perhaps the young public loved another even more fanciful version of the story, as presented on the video that accompanied Cash's song and that got heavy airplay on MTV and CMTV. There, the supposedly anorexic, heroin-chic Calvin Klein model Kate Moss played Delia, the perfect white pop woman-child victim for a certain kind of modern American ballad psychosis. Delia Green was also a woman-child, but if we don't know much at all about what she looked like, it's obvious that she was no Kate Moss. And Cooney Houston, the truly disturbing character in the actual story, was nothing like the persona that Johnny Cash inhabited—except that he, too, seemed to overcome whatever guilt he felt about his crime.

⚜

Thanks to the research of John Garst, we know more about the facts behind "Delia" than we do for most American ballads. At around 3 A.M. on Christmas Day, Delia Green, "a colored girl," one newspaper reported, died of a gunshot wound to the groin at her home at 113 Ann Street, where she resided with her mother. The police arrested a light-skinned Negro, Cooney Houston (sometimes referred to as Mose), and booked him for murder. There was never any question about who pulled the trigger, only about why.

The shooting occurred at the home of Willie West and his wife, Emma, one block from Delia's home. There is conflicting testimony about what was happening at the Wests'. Some witnesses said that the place was filled with drunken carousers, most of them women. Others said the group was small, everyone was sober (or that everyone was sober except Houston), and that the assembled were standing around the Wests' organ in the parlor singing "Rock of Ages." As it was Christmas Eve, a time of special celebration and feasting for Southern blacks since slavery times, perhaps there was some truth to both accounts—in which case, the singing of "Rock of Ages" may have been more profane than pious. In any event, Cooney Houston appears to have been what one witness at the trial called "full," which today would be "loaded."

After the shot rang out, Willie West chased Houston, caught him, and handed him over to patrolman J. T. Williams. Williams later testified that Cooney immediately confessed to shooting his girlfriend, saying that they had argued and that she had called him a son of a bitch and so he shot her, and he would gladly do it again.

At his trial, Houston and a supporting witness named Willie Mills told a different story. In the midst of a drunken party, supposedly, West bid Cooney to retrieve his pistol from a repair shop, which Cooney did. The boy placed the gun under a napkin. After Cooney returned from a second errand to get more beer and whiskey, he and a friend named Eddie Cohen got in a friendly tussle over the gun, which went off; the bullet accidentally hit Delia.

Houston's second story convinced nobody. Another witness testified that Willie Mills, Houston's corroborating witness, was not even on the scene at the time of the shooting. Eddie Cohen, identified as Emma West's second cousin, swore that he had already left the house when the killing occurred and that he had not struggled with "this boy" over a pistol. The jury found Houston guilty but recommended mercy. The judge, Paul F. Seabrook, sentenced him to life in prison instead of death.

Reports of the murder made it into the leading local newspapers, the Savannah *Morning News* and the Savannah *Evening Press*. Even when the victim as well as the perpetrator was black, murder was news enough for white editors and reporters. Alleged black-on-white attacks, and the lynchings that sometimes followed, were bigger news, of course.* Still, Delia Green's murder at least rated a couple of stories,

---

* Four years after Cooney shot Delia, two black men, Will Cato and Paul Reed, were convicted of murdering a white family in Statesboro in nearby Bulloch County. A mob summarily removed Cato and Reed from jail, doused them with oil, and burned them at the stake. The Savannah *Morning News* abetted both the prosecution against the two and their lynching with numerous sensational stories. "WILL LYNCH PRISONERS AS SOON AS CONVICTED," one headline ran during Cato and Reed's trial. The hysteria lasted long after Cato's and Reed's deaths, leading to a rash of assaults by whites on blacks that caused a full-scale black exodus from Statesboro. Years later, Blind Willie McTell would sing (and, in 1927, record) his now-famous "Statesboro Blues." "Reach over in the corner, hand me my travelin' shoes," McTell sang, "you know by that, I got them Statesboro blues"—but he was describing visiting the town, not leaving it. Born outside Augusta, McTell had settled with his family in Statesboro around 1907, when he was about eight—after the antiblack hysteria had died down. Thanks to McTell's powerful song, Statesboro is remembered for being a

if only to affirm to white readers that drunkenness and violence were endemic to the bars and bawdy houses of Yamacraw.

In contrast to the newspaper accounts, the ballads ignore that both Delia and her killer were scarcely in their teens. It is a crucial ellipsis, which changes everything about the song. At the time, the press emphasized how young the two were. (The first dispatch, in the *Morning News*, noted that Delia was a mere girl, "but 14 years old," yet said nothing about Cooney's age. The *Evening Press*, published hours later, got the full story: "Boy Killed Girl," it reported on page 5.) Some versions of the ballad lightly imply that Delia lived with her parents, but it is only an implication; and plenty of poor young adults live with their parents. By saying nothing more, the songs mislead about what happened. Cooney's murder of Delia was not simply a crime of passion arising from a lovers' quarrel; it was a crime of passion involving two lovers barely out of puberty. It was a childish murder. It was precisely the opposite of Johnny Cash's deliberate mayhem, engineered by a cold-blooded killer.

According to the differing accounts in the trial transcript, this is roughly what transpired between Delia and Cooney:

Cooney:	"My little wife is mad with me tonight. She does not hear me. She is not saying anything to me." (To Delia): "You don't know how I love you."

Mutual cursing followed.

Delia:	"You son of a bitch. You have been going with me for four months. You know I am a lady."
Cooney:	"That is a damn lie. You know I have had you as many times as I have fingers and toes. You have been calling me 'husband.'"
Delia:	"You lie!"

About fifteen minutes after the argument ended, Cooney started for the door, turned, pulled out a pistol, and fired. He had boasted of a grown-up fantasy about himself and about Delia. (It sounds as if the

---

pleasant place, "up the country" from Savannah, rather than for the long-since-forgotten events of 1904. In 1940, and again in 1949, McTell, having traveled widely and made Atlanta his base of operations, would record his own version of "Delia."

sex was real, although boys in their early teens are known, historically, to lie extravagantly about far more equivocal sexual encounters. But the common-law marriage was not real, or so Delia insisted.) Delia broke up whatever was between them and verbally cut him dead. She was not his "little wife." She was a lady and thus not guilty, by definition, of serious improprieties. He was low, a son of a bitch. Cooney, the boy, turned hot, saying in so many words that he had fucked her twenty times, and that that made her his. But Delia's curse still burned in Cooney's brain, almost certainly fueled by alcohol; and when he tried to one-up her, Delia hit right back, treating him (as one account put it) with "supreme contempt." Minutes later, she was bleeding to death and Cooney was out the door.

It is a commonplace that, in passionate conflicts, women are agile with words whereas men get frustrated and violent. Something like that seems to have happened here. Add the strong possibility that Willie and Emma West's place, later described by Houston's lawyer as a "rough house," was actually a bordello, and that Delia Green may have been one of the Wests' younger prostitutes, and the scene looks familiar enough. ("Some gave Delia a nickel/Some gave her a dime," runs one version of "Delia.") Yet Delia's words painted a different picture: she was neither a common whore nor Cooney's "wife," she said; she was proper. Saying so with a curse got her killed by her disgruntled boyfriend, who may have been angry that she had turned to prostitution and was jealous of her johns.

Whatever the case, these two were children. Even by the hard standards of the Jim Crow South of 1900, most people saw Delia Green and Cooney Houston that way. The fictionalized characters Frankie and Johnny, in the classic American ballad of jealousy and murder, worked by mature if maddened design. (Although the actual "Johnny," Albert Britt, was barely older than Cooney, Frankie Baker appears to have been in her twenties.) With the real-life adolescents Delia and Cooney, the words cut deeper and the killing came quicker.

❧

"Boy Charged With Murder," blared a front-page headline in the Savannah *Evening Press* on the eve of Houston's trial, three months after the shooting. At the trial itself, age—and, more subtly, race—made all the difference. And in the ever-elliptical ballad renditions, the courtroom drama is almost always the soul of the song.

Houston stood accused as an adult. (There was then no juvenile justice system in Georgia.) The defense made a great deal of Houston's youth. Cooney, now fifteen, showed up for his arraignment the day before the trial dressed in short pants. The *Morning News* reported that he had "the round cheerful countenance of many mulattoes" and that he "seemed to be rather above the average of negro intelligence." He "gave no outward indication of being possessed of the 'abandoned and malignant heart,' which the law says shall be inferred to exist" in cases of murder.

In a later petition for clemency, Houston's white attorney, Raiford Falligant, an eminent young member of the Georgia bar, laid out the case for the defense. Houston, Falligant said, was "a mere child" at the time of the killing. He had "got into bad company and so unfortunately committed the act that he now suffers for." It was all a tragic accident. Cooney "was crazed by drink in boisterous company for the first time in his life and . . . the crowd he was with and in got him drunk."

The truly shocking part of the proceedings came immediately after the jury delivered its verdict of guilty. Houston's mother, described by the *Morning News* as "an old black woman of respectable appearance," broke down and sobbed. Cooney stood up, emotionless, at Judge Seabrook's command.

"Houston," said the judge, "you have been indicted and tried for the crime of murder. The jury has seen fit to accompany its verdict with a recommendation to mercy, and it now becomes my duty to impose the sentence directed by the law. I perform this duty with some pain and some reluctance; I dislike to condemn one of your youth and apparent intelligence to life imprisonment. In so doing I exhort you to be a man, even in confinement, to repent of your past evil deeds and strive to earn the confidence and respect of those placed in authority over you."

But Cooney did not cooperate. Gaily, he thanked the judge and pranced out of the courtroom in a bailiff's custody, "calm and as debonair," the *News* dispatch said, "as if the experience through which he had just passed was a matter of every day occurrence and of no particular importance."

"Delia"

As the convict waited to be taken to prison, a sheriff's deputy asked him how he liked the verdict and sentence. "I don't like it at all," he answered, "but I guess I'll have to stand it." The next day, the *News* reported that Houston's age had "saved his neck" and that he had endured the ordeal "without turning a hair."

What actually happened may have been more pathetic. Cooney, scared out of his wits, could easily have been mustering some teenage bravado. Or maybe, dazed and confused, he simply tried, too late, to show a last bit of respect to the judge, as he'd been instructed to do by his lawyer. ("Thank you, sir," is what Cooney said.) But that is not how it came across in the papers. Instead, it seemed as if a young black— literally a boy—made light of the grimmest of occasions, sassed a white judge, and showed not regret but a twinkle of triumph. He was a killer, no matter his age—and he had beaten the system by cheating the gallows. He was not ashamed. He was not pitiable. And he'd fooled everybody.

Outrage at this travesty—or, perhaps, a knowing cynicism about such outrage and the white newspaper stories that provoked it— pervades the many versions of "Delia." Just as there is nothing about the killer's age, there is nothing about the racial tingling caused by Cooney's reported light-hearted words and demeanor. (Like other ballads, "Delia" has evolved as a universal tale by not citing either Cooney's or Delia's skin color. Most versions seem actively to avoid doing so by giving Cooney another name—"Cutty" or "Curtis" or "Tony," or something else—thereby eliminating any allusion to "coon.") But there is almost always something about a courtroom exchange between the judge and the killer. It might be as simple as Bob Dylan's lines, swiped from Blind Willie McTell, in which "Curtis" asks the judge about what would be his fine—as if he'd get off that lightly—and the judge replies, "Poor boy, you got ninety-nine." It might be closer to the reported facts, as in the version that Arthur Bayas and Nemser Lipton include in their 1978 compilation, *The Best Bluegrass Songbook—Yet!* (In this "Delia," the judge sentences "Tony" to ninety-nine years, and the prisoner says, "Thank you, your honor treated me fine," knowing that the judge could easily have said, "Nine hundred ninety-nine.") It might, as in McTell's almost jaunty version, have the judge ask "Cutty" what the fuss was about, with the accused replying that a bunch of gamblers (McTell also calls them "rounders") had come between him and Delia. Or it might be more involved, as in the "Delia" performed by Koerner, Ray, and Glover:

> Monday he was arrested, on Tuesday he was tried
> The jury found him guilty and the judge said "Ninety-nine"
> Delia's gone, one more round and Delia's gone.
>
> "Ninety-nine years in the prison, hey, judge that ain't no time,
> I got a brother in New Orleans doin' nine hundred ninety-nine"
> Now Delia's gone, one more round and Delia's gone.

Of the best-known modern versions, only Cash's psychotic murderer from 1994 escapes a showdown with the judge.

The songs also usually speculate about the killer's sorrow or lack of it—and the uselessness of that sorrow as far as poor Delia was concerned. Commonly, there is a description of the convict in his cell drinking from a silver cup (sometimes it's a humbler, prison-issue tin cup), while Delia's in the graveyard and she won't ever get up. (McTell, in a 1940 recording, has "Cutty" drinking in a barroom, scot-free. McTell also sings that Delia "may not never wake up," which in its uncertainty could connote the Resurrection or could be something more ghoulish.) Sometimes Cooney, or Cutty, or Tony, or whatever his name happens to be, is tortured by his deed. Sometimes he tells the jailer he cannot sleep, since all around his bed at night he can hear little Delia's feet. But the bottom line is always harsher. Delia is dead, Cooney is alive, and all the penitence in the world cannot change that cruel fact.

Thus, in their elusive way, the songs about Delia and Cooney actually get to the emotional heart of the matter as it happened—or as it appeared to happen—more than a century ago. They are not simply murder ballads, they are trial ballads—and ballads of irredeemable injustice, even though justice was done and hard punishment meted out. Bob Dylan guessed, incorrectly, that Cooney was "a pimp in primary colors"; but he also got him right: "he's not interested in mosques on the temple mount, Armageddon or world war III, doesn't put his face in his knees & weep & wears no dunce hat, makes no apology & is doomed to obscurity." The truth about Cooney Houston and about Delia Green just turns out to be less clear-cut and even sadder than Dylan suspected.

⚶

Moses "Cooney" Houston served just over twelve years of his life sentence. On October 15, 1913, Georgia Governor John M. Slaton signed an order approving his parole. Subsequent unconfirmed reports say that Houston got in trouble with the law again after his release, that he moved to New York City, and that he died around 1927, which would have made him a little over forty.

The merciful Governor Slaton soon found himself in trouble of a different kind. Five months before Houston's release, the dead body of a fifteen-year-old white girl, Mary Phagan, was found in a pencil factory in Atlanta. In a controversial and still notorious trial, Leo Frank, the factory supervisor and a New York–raised Jew, was convicted for the crime on the basis of tainted evidence, and sentenced to death. The verdict caused massive civil-rights protests, which led to an unsuccessful appeal to the United States Supreme Court. In Georgia, public opinion was equally inflamed against Frank, whom the local district attorney called "a wealthy yankee Jew." In June 1915, Governor Slaton, who believed that Frank had been unfairly convicted, commuted his sentence to life in prison. Hounded by an irate public, his effigy burned and cursed, Slaton was soon voted out of office and forced to leave the state. On August 16, 1915, an armed mob lynched Leo Frank, which sparked new protests, and which today remains a subject of outrage and shame. The authorities filed no charges in connection with the crime.

No one has discovered who Houston's friend Eddie Cohen was and why someone with that name was Emma West's second cousin. Nor is it clear how Raiford Falligant came to be Houston's lawyer.

Delia Green is buried at Laurel Grave Cemetery South, in Savannah, amid trees covered with Spanish moss. The exact location of her unmarked grave was forgotten long ago.

"The Wreck of Old 97"
and
"Dead Man's Curve"

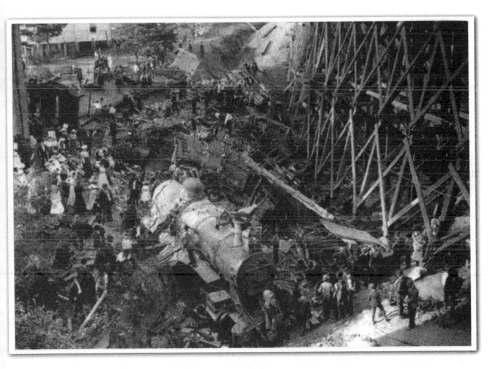

Wreck of Fast Mail No. 97 Sept 27, 1903
Danville Va. *The accident occurred on September
27; this image, taken from a glass negative, was
made several days into the cleanup. Eleven men
died: five railroad workers (including the
engineer Joseph Andrew "Steve" Broady) and six
postal workers. By the time this picture was
taken, much of the debris had been cleared away
and the engine had been set upright, but the
remnants of the smashed Post Office railroad cars
are visible to the right, aside the Stillhouse Trestle.
Editors' thanks to G. Howard Gregory.*

DAVID THOMAS

Destiny in My Right Hand:
"The Wreck of Old 97" and
"Dead Man's Curve"

Here's a quick and easy way to parse the American Character out of the high-fat-content homogenized beverage that is Western multicultural society. Find The Neptune Pub in Brighton, England. It's along the seafront west of the Lawns. Ask the barmaid to play the song "Wheels" (from the album *The Gilded Palace of Sin* by The Flying Burrito Brothers). My drinking buddies know all the words. They'll sing along . . . up to a point. That lyric, the line that goes, "And destiny is in my right hand"—that's where they stumble. They mumble across it, or take a swallow of beer, or, most likely, come over all ironic. There's a reason. They're foreigners.

Consider two American ballads. One, "The Wreck of Old 97," appears at the beginning of that Magnetic Age of Sound inaugurated by Thomas Edison's invention of the phonograph/microphone. Another, "Dead Man's Curve," appears at the dawn of that age's "golden" era. Across that timeline, the narrative voice evolves out of sight of its starting point and the expectations of its audience expand, enlarge, and engorge exponentially. Yet these two songs, for all of that, are remarkably similar.

These are popular songs, written to be sold in the marketplace. But whereas "Dead Man's Curve" is identified with one musical group, Jan and Dean, "The Wreck of Old 97" is not linked to anyone and has been recorded by many different singers and many different groups over the years. Such anonymous popularity speaks of a universality more often associated with an "amateur" folk culture than a media-driven pop industry, and "The Wreck of Old 97" is considered by many to be a typical folk song. Except that after Edison, the culture of folk music seems to go into free fall. Shorn first of its religious basis, then of a political vitality, and finally of its brooding and dangerous soul, it washes up in 2004 as self-obsessed, dithering, fearful and cowardly. It's more useful to propose that, after Edison, folk music in American culture enters a state of metamorphosis brought on by the forces that shape the Magnetic Age. At the other end of that process, folk culture emerges reborn in the person of Elvis and all that flows from him. A moribund stump of Nostalgia Folk lingers on. Consider that both ballads are the products of the pop industry of their time. Both are also the products of the folk culture of their time.

Both these ballads are rooted in a specific American geography. Sites of the major train wrecks that occurred on either side of the end of the nineteenth century are dotted across America, but the ones that became the subject of popular ballads are predominantly Southern and, more specifically, Appalachian. (Pennsylvania and New York railroads "produced" far more train wrecks yet yielded far fewer ballads about them.) Did the citizens of the heartland of a New South find something especially moving and poignant and gripping in the wrecks of such magnificent engines and the deaths of the crews that mastered them? And, assuming that not every balladeer would have been Appalachian, why did balladeers gravitate more often to an Appalachian setting for these tragedies than, say, a Pennsylvanian one?

An imperative that derives from a gestalt of geography, sound, and culture fixes and vitalizes and drives certain musics. Consider the Delta regions of Arkansas and Mississippi, the Flats of Cleveland, the Los Angeles River Basin, the South Side of Chicago, and the way in which, in the late 1980s, Yakutsk musicians in the Arctic regions of Siberia became obsessed with the music of Pink Floyd. All the best young bands sounded like Pink Floyd except somehow more immediate and more authentic. It was a cargo-culture phenomenon.

Asked to explain how a renegade copy of *Dark Side of the Moon* could galvanize an entire subculture, one musician said, "The sound reminded us of the snow."

Sensation is the base language of human consciousness—what we know we know because we have successfully encoded experience as a complex of sensation, a hieroglyph. Sound as a description of the architecture of space can be a startlingly efficient hieroglyph incorporating symbolic, metaphorical, geometrical, sensual, and historical perspectives. As the Magnetic Age matures, the ability to manipulate the scale of sound adds a significant narrative component to musical activity. It follows that the soundscape of physical geography would become an acoustical frame shaping musical activity not only in regard to a locally recognizable palette of ideas and sounds, but also in regard to a parochial set of musician intentions and audience expectations. It is not remarkable that the car-and-surf culture of the Los Angeles River Basin would produce a song like "Dead Man's Curve." What is remarkable is how a simple throwaway ballad could identify and then imbue with romance various locations in the virtual landscapes of countless midwestern towns, lending significance and perspective to nasty little bends in the road everywhere, propagating dead men's curves in locations far removed—like Johnny Appleseed, planting seeds wherever fertile soil could be found.

As we consider the similarities of these two ballads, it is notable that each is a morality tale of untimely death in which the protagonists, the locomotive engineer and the teen racer, are cast as sympathetic figures and accorded heroic status as they die while in personal control (or not!) of powerful technology. And, it is the willful and even foolhardy determination of the two protagonists to achieve personal glory that calls down such calamity. Steve Broady drove his train too fast (and the actual facts of the wreck indict him for foolhardy recklessness). The teen racer threw his XKE into a man-killer bend. Still, there is not a hint of reproach found in the songs. The writer of "The Wreck of Old 97" even goes so far as to ignore the bald, incriminating facts of the story. Why? The ballad form itself dictates certain shapes—formulaic, sentimental, voyeuristic, and epic. Also, powerfully evident here is the courageous and unflinching

American notion of manifest destiny—personal, geographic, and philosophical all jumbled up together and urging characters as diverse as Thomas Edison and Elvis Presley, Robert Johnson and Henry Ford, Dwight Eisenhower and Jack Kerouac on, ever on, into the technological frontier of the soul.

What the Ballad Wants, the Ballad Gets

A ballad needs a hero, not complication. The untimely death of a young man doing his duty is tragic and poignant, engaging and full of poetic possibility. The death of many in a senseless or random event is not. The balladeer gets paid for heroes, not victims. The popular train-wreck songs almost exclusively documented those wrecks involving the loss of just the engineer and a few brave crew who, according to the lyric writers, died doing their duty to the last possible moment. Few train-wreck ballads recounted the loss of passengers. There is no heroism (and therefore no meal ticket) in riding into eternity tourist class, punched ticket in hand. Note as well the singular absence of ballads about plane crashes where loss of passengers is great and, therefore, one would think, greatly "tragic." The notable exception is Woody Guthrie's "Deportee (Plane Wreck at Los Gatos)," where the motivation is not public sales but the advancement of a political agenda.

The ballad, as a form, is fueled by the kind of moralizing that lives next door to Schadenfreude. Doubts and complex dilemmas are not helpful. Bathetic redemption or melodramatic fall is better currency. Note how the chorus to "Dead Man's Curve" works. Designed to suggest a Greek chorus/inner voice, the backing vocals warn of impending disaster with the enthusiasm of a Parisian knitting circle gathered round a guillotining, while at the denouement, after the surviving teen racer confesses contritely, "I guess I found out for myself that everyone was right," he is embraced prodigal-son–like as the chorus glories in a self-satisfied, nearly triumphant(!), "Won't come back from Dead Man's Curve!"

There is as well the voyeuristic component that is injected into "The Wreck of Old 97." Most versions of the song conclude with a verse warning women everywhere not to speak harshly to their husbands lest said husbands be overtaken by fate and never return home . . . from the bank or convenience store or office-supply superstore, presumably, as well as from a mail run on the Southern Railway. The not-so-subtle underlying suggestion is that a no-doubt-juicy marital problem played some role in the doomed mindset of the engineer. But Steve Broady was a bachelor. What the ballad wants, the ballad gets.

Significantly, the protagonists are *not* the subject of any moralizing concerning addiction to speed or reckless behavior. Quite the opposite. And the writer of "The Wreck of Old 97" goes to some trouble to concoct a poignant fiction disguising the conduct of the engineer. It's a fiction reinforced by any number of singers who emphasize by repetition the verses that speak of the failure of the air brakes (or loss of "average"). The suggestion is that the wreck was an unavoidable, fated event. But Southern Railway's accident investigation, which led to the company's paying compensation to the families of the wreck's *other* victims, concluded that engineer Broady bore sole responsibility. He may have been "whittling"—a dangerous practice that involved speeding into curves and braking going around them—a practice known to lead to a potentially fatal loss of air pressure. Yes, the air brakes failed, but only because Steve Broady recklessly emptied them.

But is it not in the American character to forgive, to edit away, or to overlook the tragic flaw that might be found in a hero, in the good man who finds himself in a bad situation and yet who behaves boldly, impetuously, even recklessly, in order to stamp the moment with the seal of his own personality . . . to Live Free or Die? What American balladeer would fail in his social duty to rejig events appropriately? So Steve Broady drove fast, too fast . . . but Old 97 was turned over to him at Washington Station already running late and what was a man, a Sanctified Possessor of the Right Stuff, what was such a man, engineer of the fastest train running, what was he to do but make up the time or bury himself and his train and his comrades in hell making the attempt? Criminal irresponsibility can be massaged gently into Flawed (and Epic) Heroism with surprisingly little effort. And is it not the presence of such a flaw that makes a hero recognizable to an American as a version of himself, of his own flawed and cruelly

"The Wreck of Old 97" and "Dead Man's Curve"

average state, of what he can aspire to, or take warning from, as a template of how he himself might survive such a journey with his own frail flesh and fragile bones, baptized into an impersonal, unpredictable world of hurt? And how much more will be forgiven the protagonist engaged in a symbolic or iconic role, the man who stands in for all of us, the man who races inside the now moment with his hand firmly gripping the lever of destiny?

Elvis was there . . . first . . . again. Check into the Days Inn Graceland/Airport at the Brooks Road exit of I-55 at the edge of Memphis in August going somewhere else and you'll find yourself dropped into the middle of Elvis Death Week and a motel full of Elvis People gathered in welcoming boom-box circles around the pool. Sure, Elvis had a drug problem, the conversation may go, but he was only a man, an innocent hounded by Dark Forces as he tried to walk the narrow road of being The One True King of Rock 'n' Roll—a backbreaking undertaking by any reckoning. He made mistakes, Elvis did, but he had a good heart and a generous nature, the Elvis People will say. And even the man's last headlong, self-destructive lunge is not only understood, not only forgiven, but it is recognized as an unavoidable consequence of the man's pursuit of destiny. He is recognizable. As an American hero. As a man. Not perfect.

Is the teen racer of "Dead Man's Curve" a hero, an American hero? Does he fit the suit prepared for him by the balladic formula? Certainly not as a hero in a societal context, and any bravery—to which the teen racer doesn't even seem to aspire—is not in pursuit of a benefit to others. A cheap and easy out would be to categorize the teen racer as a kind of Hollywood antihero of an emerging subculture—which, of course, is social-worker baloney and serves to undercut and denigrate the principle of Heroism. The heroism of the teen racer must be considered in the context of the evolution of sound and narrative voice across that Magnetic Age that separates the two ballads. More of this later.

Finally, the ballad aspires to the epic, and the American ballad will often locate that quality at the technological frontier. Note that "Old 97" was not "old" at all. It was one of the fastest, most modern, sophisticated machines of its day, and the specific engine that was wrecked was, at the time, only nine months old. (Similarly, the Jaguar

XKE and the Corvette that figure in "Dead Man's Curve" were the fastest and sexiest machines available to the average citizen.)

The locomotive engineer was a man for the epochal. He was the astronaut of his day. He drove the machines that defined the moment. He drove them at speed. And in his hand he gripped the buzzing key to the future. The rails he traveled were the veins through which Progress itself flowed. He pulled in the far ends of the world, and through him mysteries were revealed, closed frontiers opened, and the dark places illuminated. He was master of time and space, and the engine he had mastered was imbued with great and enduring symbolism, the quality of its very being capable of illustrating deep and abiding truths, as is evidenced by countless folk and pop songs ever since. Even now, with the railroad long relegated to graffiti-sprayed container haulage, the train holds a powerful place in the poetry and imagination of the American people. American writers who have little experience of it intuitively understand its iconic content/hieroglyphic significance to American culture and have been hard-pressed to find an adequate metaphorical substitute. Robert Johnson ("Love in Vain"), A. P. Carter ("Worried Man Blues"), and Lawrence Ferlinghetti ("Starting in San Francisco") all testify to that.

But the train is John the Baptist to the automobile. Everything that can be said of the train as an icon, as a metaphor, as an emblem, as a philosophical tool, is merely by way of an introduction to the automobile.

An Outline of the Significance of the Magnetic Age

Thomas Alva Edison is the father of Elvis. The moment the phonograph/microphone is conceived, the delivery of Elvis becomes simply a matter of allowing for the passage of sufficient time. Like a pregnancy. Year Zero of the Magnetic Age is 1877. The vast complex of magnetic and then digital technology that follows from a stylus scratching the vibrations of the human voice onto a cylinder will produce a foundational reordering of all that can be expected of human expression. The fracturing of scale and its purposeful manipulation characterize the age, and the most important consequence of that fracturing is the investiture of the single human voice as the mediator of experience, arbiter of meaning, and, eventually, in the pop celebrity hysteria of the twenty-first century, guarantor of being. (I am known, therefore I am.)

Consider Edison's epochal reading of "Mary Had a Little Lamb." The sound of the spoken word up to that moment has been largely incidental to the business of broadcasting words. The human voice reverberates briefly, loses amplitude rapidly, and almost instantaneously is inaudible. But now, come Edison's invention, the spoken word can be preserved, transformed into an object, and thereby invested with meaning, portent, and significance beyond the basic understanding of the words voiced. Scale is fractured at the most fundamental level. The consequences are staggering. The technological frame of the microphone makes redundant massed choral voices and the restrictive vocal techniques required by purely acoustical venues, the volume of accompanying musical instruments, and the formalities of hierarchical production methods. Instead, highly individualized and intimate forms of singing become possible. New characters previously excluded from the marketplace of mainstream culture—crooners and bluesmen, cowboys and hillbillies—find a voice. A heightened sense of theatricality expands the range of available narrative techniques. The single human voice acquires an immediacy and palpable humanity. The singer is no longer a faceless musical functionary but a man of hopes and fears who exists in a moment and in a place and in a time and then is gone. Musical activity is invested with a sense of mortality, and the singer is established as mediator between musicians and their intentions, and the audience and its expectations.

What is meant by scale?

Hearing is bilateral. Sound arrives first at the ear closest to the source. An instantaneous and involuntary process of triangulation identifies that source and locates the hearer relative to it. If the scale is "real" and a function of the known world—in other words, if there is a 1:1 correspondence—then the hearer can locate himself accurately within a knowable geography. At work is that sixth sense, which is the body's awareness of itself as a location in space. On an internalized map, this is the weight that consciousness perceives itself as possessing. But what happens if technology is applied that allows scale to be artificially fractured? And then what happens if an entirely rewritten and reconceived sonic lexicon is introduced?

Musical activity and the sound of it can be very distant cousins. The act of plucking a string and the thing that happens inside the head of a listener as a consequence of that plucking must be considered as distinct and sometimes barely related events. Even the simplest vibration pattern encounters a profusion of reflective surfaces and, conforming to the geometry of a specific space, ceases to be simple. Every surface absorbs and reflects frequencies differently. Delays and echoes are introduced. Space conforms the sound of any musical activity to its own shape and character. What is heard is a representation of that space and everything that happened in it. Even humidity and temperature will print. The sound of the musical activity is also a distinctly colored voicing of the intention and method of the musical activity. Framing is introduced. In the Magnetic Age, the musician/composer must choose not *whether* but *how* to engage this framing as a "partner" in the musical process. Meanwhile, technology and technique have evolved so that musicians can completely rewrite the sonic lexicon with tools that are essentially designed to manipulate attributes of space. Sound engineers are not electricians but architects of real, as well as virtual, spaces. Scales are fractured and reassembled in quite startling ways, and if what is heard cannot be imaged on a 1:1 basis, then the sense of body awareness must still locate itself on a map that must be internalized and within geographies that must be invented in order to accommodate the space that is perceived.

The listening experience in the Magnetic Age can be likened to unpacking Russian matryoshka dolls. Frames are framed within frames. Consider how the intentions of a band of musicians are passed through the spatial characteristics of a variety of microphones, reshaped by the virtual soundscapes generated in the recording studio, injected with all manner of often-unintended sonic flotsam and post-production jetsam, finally to be broadcast imprinted with the virtual space and scale of a set of biased loudspeakers. Extruded into the no-doubt-eccentric spatial characteristics of the listener's living room, the matryoshka doll is unpacked and revealed. It's been a hellish journey.

But now, at an involuntary and synthaesthetic level, this complex of frames within frames and modulated scales provokes a negotiation in that gestalt of all the senses we recognize as consciousness—causing it to resonate, to triangulate, to establish perspective so as to generate the final Grand Context in which Meaning can happen. It's Pavlovian. The bell rings and the listener salivates Meaning. Posed an audio-geometric question, the listener answers by reflex. And even if the scale of what is heard is nonsensical and cannot be readily imaged, at an involuntary level gears will grind away until something—anything—shows up as an explanation or a context. For human beings, there is no acceptable alternative to Meaning. It's the great craft secret of the Brotherhood of Musicians and the mechanism on which all of music hangs as an art and as a language.

It is the ungraspable, uncontrollable, unexpected, unintentional, unprocessed nature of sound itself, distinct from the musical activity that generates it, that as a frame becomes such a powerful narrative voice. Sound forces questions and confusions, doubts and mysteries, accidents and the unexpected. It throws up ambiguities and undermines contrivance and artifice. It poses questions with no set answers: "What does this mean?" "Why is that there?" It forces contexts then suggests explanations not in a logical sequence of linear thoughts but in a jumbled collage of hieroglyphic sensations. It provokes the imagination and, most importantly, most critically, it personalizes the listening experience.

Destiny in My Right Hand

Now consider these two ballads in the context of the timeline of this Magnetic Age.

The narrative voice is transformed.

"The Wreck of Old 97" purports to be a third-person accounting of the "facts" of an actual event, the telling of which will serve to edify and instruct. And though the engineer protagonist may have been a headstrong individualist, he is framed within a social order, and the tragedy that overtakes him is shaped in such a way as to reinforce that order, not challenge it. The scope of the narrative is broad, invoking details of the geography of a significant stretch of the eastern seaboard. The time, weather, and setting of the accident are noted in the first verses in the same way that a newspaper journalist establishes the Who, What, Where, and When in the first paragraphs of a story. Next, the How and Why are revealed, albeit with imagined dialogue and some extravagantly fabricated personal detail injected to channel the drama properly. The story unfolds inexorably along a strictly linear path and is neatly wrapped up with a moralizing homily in the last verse. It is a recognizable artefact of its time and in keeping with the expectations of its audience. A tone of understatement and flatness belies the high melodrama and nearly bathetic emotional manipulation being perpetrated. And a flatness of vocal delivery characterizes recorded versions of the song—that same phlegmatic, long-suffering delivery common to the sort of folk music this ballad seeks to invoke.

A half-century later, the narrative point of view in "Dead Man's Curve" is shifted 180 degrees. The singer is fully invested as mediator, and through his office the audience navigates a dramatic musical soundscape of incident, surprise, and ambiguity.

The mediation of the singer (actually singers, in this case) transforms the ballad from the relatively simple social exchange that is the intent of "The Wreck of Old 97" into an object, a work of art that presumes its own significance. Instead of the God's-eye, arm's-length perspective of "The Wreck of Old 97," the audience is presented with a concoction of first-person narrative, attitude, theatricality, oddly mocking personal angst, and some hard-to-define self-observational ambiguity, i.e., punk snottiness. And though the use of "pure" sound as a distinct poetic voice will continue to evolve, and techniques for its usage become far more sophisticated, the use of the musique concrète of the car tires squealing and engines crashing is still a significant step toward the eventual realization of the data-overload school of found sound and analog synthesization that in the 1970s will seek the final liberation of sound from the hegemony of musical activity. And though this use of sound effects may be dismissed by sophisticates as hard-core cornball, it speaks of an urgency and a youthful, enthusiastic yearning to expand the palette of expression. Note as well that, though the musique concrète may occur first as simply a melodramatic flourish, it is then repeated as a compositional element.

As the Venerable Bede is to William Faulkner, so is the use of musique concrète in "Dead Man's Curve" to the shape of things to come.

Note, as well, how the ballad's shifting points of view employ the First Person Detached to great effect as the singer/protagonist observes himself and his actions from various angles and with various shades of self-awareness and various degrees of detachment. This perspective is characteristic of the best of rock music and marks the golden era of the Magnetic Age. It is the true legacy of Elvis Presley, the incorruptible Homer of the Inarticulate Voice, the man who took the moribund folk forms of hillbilly country-western and rural blues and brought to them the power and universality of Abstraction. (Elvis's rendition of "Heartbreak Hotel" is one of the more sophisticated early expositions of the First Person Detached—note how it is through the bellhop, ostensibly a peripheral character, that Elvis the singer establishes the perspective that most brutally examines his own actions.)

Because of the First Person Detached voice, the audience for "Dead Man's Curve" has a blinkered, slightly claustrophobic view of the ballad's geography, which is found to consist of little more than a couple of street names, a nameless hospital, and an oblique reference to the actual location of the man-killer bend. But in the Magnetic Age, the transaction between singer and audience is based on trust, intimacy, identification, and subjective experience. A cooperative spirit is implicit and, consequently, a minimum of journalistic detail concerning Who, What, Where, and When needs to be on offer. The diminished size of the external geography, in any case, is necessary to allow time for the mapping of the internal geography that is the psychology of the teen racer . . . the inner space that is as dynamic with its attitudes, perspectives, and ambiguities as the Big Out There with its racing engines, screeching tires, and hospital emergency room. Surfing the moment of the eternal now, the narrative voice is positioned as the interface between these inner and outer spaces that mirrors the role of the singer himself in the Magnetic Age; the mediator, the doorkeeper, who alone grants access to all the observation decks of this two-minute, sixty-four-bar wonder, and who positions himself between the intent of the musical activity and the listener.

It is this geometry that at least partially accounts for the emergence of the automobile as the preeminent icon for the later part of the Magnetic Age.

Ike Turner's "Rocket 88," recorded in 1951, is often cited as the first rock 'n' roll record. Appropriately, it's about a car. Of its age, the automobile is as compelling a philosophical model as Plato's Cave. The automobile is about space, scale, and perspective. Old thinking confuses it with materialism or, absurdly, male sexuality. There's a poster at the airport quoting Maya Angelou about the roads being full of big cars going nowhere fast. This image may be popular, but it is evidence of confused thinking, equivalent to describing a room full of meditating monks as a pajama party.

Consider how the geography of the automobile mirrors that of the First Person Detached. A windshield frames the Big Out There in wide-screen, cinemascope-like proportions, the interface between inner and outer space. Think "I Am a Camera." Except this Camera can be directed freely through any landscape framing moments and ideas, stories and peoples, fictions and eternities . . . at speed . . . at the streamlined chromium edge of the eternal now moment . . . whilst inside, in inner space, a radio frames a broadcast signal which in turn frames a recording which is in itself a complex of frames within frames, wheels within wheels, and all the while the individual in question operating in either of the heavily symbolic roles of Driver or Passenger is navigating across a no-doubt-whacked landscape from within this resonating soundscape frame-container and all the scales are fracturing very artistically and the gyroscope of the sixth sense of body awareness is flipping around, getting pleasantly enervated or irrepressibly enthused about what exactly is the distinction between internal and external geographies . . . and that's what's called "cruising" . . . and in America the real artists do not work with marble or paint or ink or sound or cine film only, the artist can also be a slob with a quart of oil and a set of spark-plug wrenches who understands that the automobile is a way of examining and testing, and of being examined and being tested—by the world, the flesh, and the devil— because if the truth is like a mirror in which a man can see who and what he really is, then geography is also like a mirror, not as clear and sharp but still useful because the space we inhabit speaks to us not only of our own hopes and fears but also of those of our fathers and forefathers and represents continuity which cannot lie . . . look or look away . . . look or look away . . . look or look away . . . SEARCH! . . . geography is the teacher (the driver is the preacher) . . . so musicians engage in a dialogue inside that blurred zone between soundscape and landscape perfectly in tune with the Magnetic Age, which is another way of saying the American Age That Redeems Civilization and as Edison is to Elvis so Eisenhower is to Kerouac, the symbiosis, the ying and the yang, demonstrating how, again, technology and vision, the engine and the art, are inseparable in that it is Eisenhower who conceives of an interstate network of Big Roads/Big Sky but it is a Kerouac who must arrive to describe how to use it . . . at velocities . . . a skill to be mastered by a new kind of engineer, the driver, who, like the locomotive engineer before him, has access to new people and new places, fueling the imagination, exciting the senses, elevating the spirit, and who, like the locomotive engineer before him, travels the roads over which Progress itself flows, and who, like the locomotive engineer before him, is an individual, a man alone, destiny gripped firmly in his right hand.

Unlike the locomotive engineer, though, he is Everyman.

Finally.

Emerson and Thoreau smile. Whitman laughs aloud.

"Buddy Bolden's Blues"

Photo mural of the Buddy Bolden Band, with the only known portrait of Buddy Bolden, New Orleans, circa 1905, in Herbsaint Bar and Restaurant, New Orleans, 2004. Pictured from left to right, back row: William Warner, C clarinet; Willie Cornish, valve trombone; Bolden, cornet; Jimmy Johnson, bass. Front row: Frank Lewis, B flat clarinet, and Jefferson Mumford, guitar. (Missing: Cornelius Tillman, drums.) Photo by Ken Jackson, Herbsaint © 2004 by Ken Jackson.

LUC SANTE

I Thought I Heard Buddy Bolden Say

The Union Sons Hall stood at 1319 Perdido Street, between Liberty and Franklin, in the area of New Orleans known in the late nineteenth and early twentieth centuries as Back o' Town, which was among other things the unofficial black prostitution district, as distinct from the official white one, Storyville, a few blocks away. The hall was built sometime after 1866, when several "free persons of color" formed the Union Sons Relief Organization of Louisiana and bought a double-lot parcel for its headquarters. The only known photograph of the place was taken in the 1930s, a decade or so after it had become the Greater St. Matthew Baptist Church, and by then it certainly looked like a church—although this being New Orleans it is not impossible that it always had a steeple and Gothic arched windows. Anyway, it was a church on Sunday mornings for much of its existence, originally leased to the First Lincoln Baptist Church for that purpose. On Saturday nights, meanwhile, it was rented for dances which lasted until early light, so that the deacons must have put in a hard few hours every week washing up spilled beer and airing out the joint before the pious came flocking. At night it was known as one of the rougher spots in a rough area. It was razed in the late 1950s, along with most of the immediate neighborhood, its site now lost somewhere under the vastness of the Louisiana State Office Building.[1]

It is remembered solely because of those dances, and primarily because some of them featured Buddy Bolden and his band. Jazz is too large and fluid a category of music to have had a single "eureka" moment of origin, let alone a sole inventor, but just about everybody agrees that no nameable person was more important to its creation than Buddy Bolden. He was a cornet player, born in 1877, and he got his first band together sometime around 1895. He was known for playing loud—stories of how far his horn could be heard sound like tall tales, but they are so numerous there must be something to them—and for playing loose and rowdy. He was by all accounts the first major New Orleans musician to make a virtue of not being able to read a score. You can begin to get an idea of how distinctive his band was from looking at photographs. The traditional-style brass bands of the era wore military-style uniforms, complete with peaked caps, as their parade-band successors do to this day; the getups proclaim unison and discipline, even if the New Orleans version allowed for more latitude than was the rule among the oompah outfits active in every American village of the time. The orchestras—the term was then applied to non-marching musical agglomerations of virtually any size or composition—dressed in mufti, but their sedate poses attest to rigor and sobriety. The John Robichaux Orchestra may have had a big drum, as shown in an 1896 portrait, but its legendarily virtuosic members look as serious as divinity students, and by all accounts they played as sweetly.

Buddy Bolden's band, on the other hand, is clearly a *band*, in the sense in which we use the word today. In the only extant photograph, circa 1905, each member has chosen his own stance, with no attempt at homogenization. They all rode in on different trolleys, the picture

---

[1] This piece draws heavily on Donald M. Marquis's *In Search of Buddy Bolden, First Man of Jazz* (Baton Rouge: Louisiana State University Press, 1978; New York: Da Capo, 1980), a heroic piece of historical detective work that represents pretty nearly the last word on Bolden, who nevertheless remains a specter about whom more stories can be refuted than proven. Mention should also be made of the Web site maintained by Carlos "Froggy" May—www.geocities.com/BourbonStreet/5135/Bolden .html—which has stayed abreast of more recent scholarship, faint trickle though it is.

says, but up on the stage they talk to each other as much as to the audience. Drummer Cornelius Tillman is unaccountably absent. Shy Jimmy Johnson disappears into his bull fiddle. B-flat clarinetist Frank Lewis sits gaunt and upright as a picket. Willie Warner holds his C-clarinet with the kind of delicacy you sometimes see in men with massive hands. Jefferson "Brock" Mumford, the guitarist, looks a bit like circa-1960 Muddy Waters and a bit like he just woke up fully dressed and out of sorts. Willie Cornish shows you his valve trombone as if you had challenged his possession of it. Buddy Bolden rests his weight on his left leg, holds his little horn balanced on one palm, shoulder slumping a bit, and allows a faint smile to take hold of his face. You could cut him out of the frame and set him down on the sidewalk outside the Three Deuces in 1944, alongside Bird and Diz, and then the smile and the posture would plainly say "reefer." You could cut him out of the frame and set him down on the sidewalk outside right now, and passing him you would think, "significant character, and he knows it, too," and spend the rest of the day trying to attach a name to the face.

You can't hear the Bolden band, of course. They may actually have cut a cylinder recording around 1898, but the beeswax surfaces of the time were good for maybe a dozen plays, so it's hardly surprising that no copy has ever been found. And then Bolden suddenly and dramatically left the picture. In March 1906, he began complaining of severe headaches, and one day, persuaded that his mother-in-law was trying to poison him, he hit her on the head with a water pitcher. It was the only time in his life that he made the newspapers. His behavior became more erratic, he lost control of his band, and then he dropped out of that year's Labor Day parade in midroute—no small matter, since the parade was an occasion for strutting that involved nearly every musician in the city.

Not long thereafter, his family had him committed for dementia. His induction papers cite alcohol poisoning as the cause, but modern scholars suggest it might have been meningitis. In any case, he remained incarcerated and incommunicado in the state Insane Asylum at Jackson until his death in 1931, age fifty-four. He missed the leap of the New Orleans sound to Chicago and beyond, the rise of Louis Armstrong (who, born in 1901, may have remembered hearing

Bolden play when he was five), the massive popularity of hot jazz that finally allowed acquaintances and quasi-contemporaries such as Freddie Keppard and Bunk Johnson to record, however fleetingly or belatedly. His name became known outside Louisiana only when white researchers from the North began knocking on doors in the late 1930s. He achieved worldwide fame as a ghost.

But let's get back to the Union Sons Hall. It's a Saturday night in July 1902, and the temperature outside is in the lower nineties, with eighty-three-percent humidity. The hall is typical for its place and function, an open room maybe twenty by fifty feet, made of white pine that hasn't seen a new coat of paint in a few decades, with no furniture besides a table for the ticket-taker and a series of long benches lining the walls, and no decor other than some old bits of half-shredded bunting tacked to the molding about ten feet up. There's a small raised stage at one end, with nothing on it but a few chairs and maybe Tillman's drums. People start trickling in around nine. They are local people, mostly single and mostly young, teamsters and plasterers and laundresses and stevedores and domestic servants and barbers and sailors and cooks. A few pimps and prostitutes are in the company as well, and a number of persons of no account, bearing names that may right then mean plenty in the neighborhood but will be preserved only as marginalia in the police records: Grand Jury, Cinderella, Pudding Man, Hit 'Em Quick, Ratty Kate, Lead Pencil, Two Rooms and a Kitchen. Someone may be selling glasses of beer from a keg in the corner, but many in attendance will have brought stronger sustenance in pint bottles. Within half an hour the room is already fetid with cigar smoke. As more and more people crowd in, the heat rises, and the air circulation slows to an ooze, and the air gradually becomes a solid—a wall composed of smoke and sweat and beer and rice powder and Florida water and bay rum and musk and farts.

By this time the band has been playing for a while. They have walked in through the crowd, carrying their instruments, jumped onstage and fallen to without fuss or fanfare. All of them are seated except Johnson behind his bass, but they stand to take solos, and then the footlights reflected by tin disks make them look distended and not quite real. They have begun, per tradition, with the sugary stuff,

"Sweet Adeline" and "A Bird in a Gilded Cage," maybe even given the nod to the sacred up front: "Go Down Moses," "Flee as a Bird." Maybe they've allowed some blues to trickle in, or proto-blues from the age-old fakebook: "Careless Love." To our ears they're playing these chestnuts pretty straight, with none of your cubist reconfiguration of the standards—that will come a couple of decades later, with Satchmo—but on the other hand the tunes are densely filigreed with embellishments and arabesques, and when Bolden plays you hear not so much the perfection of technique as the full range of the human voice. After a while they start to want to rag it, though, and Bolden calls out his transition number, "Don't Go Way Nobody," and then they throw down with "My Bucket's Got a Hole in It," which maybe Buddy wrote. By now they are as loud as if they stood in front of Marshall stacks, and the inside temperature is the kind to make cartoon thermometers balloon dangerously at the top, and the people on the floor are crazy, doing the Shimmy and the Ping Pong and the Grizzly Bear, shouting and stomping, losing sundry articles of clothing, in some cases dropping down cold along the wall.

But the band needs air. They need to fill their lungs to blow, remember? And the air is this yellow soup with filaments of monkey shit running around in it. So Bolden stands up, slices laterally with his hand, and the music stops, abruptly, right in the middle of the third chorus of "All the Whores Like the Way I Ride." Then he stomps hard once, twice, three times to get the crowd's attention. "For God's sake open up a window!" he bellows. "And take that funky butt away!" The crowd laughs. People look around to see who the goat is or to shift blame away from themselves, while a man wielding a pole topped with a brass hook finally pivots open the tall windows. Everybody knows that this will mean noise complaints and then probably a police raid, but nobody leaves. Finally Bolden blows his signature call, and the machine starts up again. Afterward, people straggling home keep hooting, "Take that funky butt away!" For days they shout it in the streets when they're drunk, or they approach their friends very seriously, as if to convey something of grave significance, then let loose: "Take that funky butt away!" Various Chesters and Lesters in the area become "Funky Butt" for a week or a month, or for the rest of their natural lives. And then the hall, which everybody calls Kinney's, after the head of the Union Sons, starts being referred to as Funky Butt Hall, and the name sticks.

A week later the Bolden band is playing a dance at the Odd Fellows and Masonic Hall, a couple of blocks down on Perdido and South Rampart. In the second part of the set, right after "Mama's Got a Baby Called Tee-Na-Na," when everything is getting loose, Willie Cornish stands up and starts singing: "I thought I heard Buddy Bolden say/Funky butt, funky butt, take it away. . . ." There is a silence from the crowd, and then pandemonium. People can't believe what they're hearing. It's as if the band had looked into their minds. And the song is more than a joke. It's a fully worked-out rag, immediately memorable on its own merits, while the words are irresistibly singable, a banner headline set to music. If there were records available, and people owned record players, storekeepers would not be able to keep copies on their shelves. Within a week or two, dockworkers are singing it, and well-dressed young people are whistling it, and barbers are humming it, and drunks are caterwauling it. New verses proliferate. The tune, which instantly calls up the memory of the original words, is annexed by comedians and political campaigners and every sort of cabaret singer. Most of the versions are filthy, some are idle, some topical. For a long time the song goes unrecorded on paper, since even its title is unprintable, until an enterprising—not to say larcenous—ragtime publisher finally copyrights a wordless piano arrangement entitled, for some reason, "St. Louis Tickle."

༄

For anyone who spent time at the dances and parades of black New Orleans at the very beginning of the century, though, the song will remain Buddy Bolden's monument, his living memory for decades after he is first locked up and then stone-cold dead, as the long line of graybeard interviewees of the earnest young Northern jazz fans knocking on doors from the 1930s to the 1960s will attest. Buddy Bolden wrote other songs, some of them—although attribution is always uncertain—more famous than he ever was, but "Funky Butt" is not merely his song; in alchemical fashion it has replaced the man himself. But no version of the lyrics was set down until an entire generation and then some had gone by.

Jelly Roll Morton, the Ancient Mariner of New Orleans jazz, finally recorded it three times in 1938 and 1939, once with the all-star New Orleans Jazzmen (including Sidney Bechet, Sidney de Paris, Albert Nicholas, Wellman Braud, and Zutty Singleton) and twice solo, accompanying himself on piano. The first of the solo recordings was made at the Library of Congress, where Morton spent three weeks reminiscing, orating, quoting, and singing for Alan Lomax's disc recorder, laying down songs and versions of songs so lavishly obscene they were not issued commercially until 1993. Morton copyrighted the song in his own name the next year, but for Lomax's recorder he paid tribute to Bolden—"the most powerful trumpet player I've ever heard, or ever was known."[2] This was around the same time that Bunk Johnson was alleging to William Russell and Stephen Smith that he had played with Bolden (he had to fiddle with the dates a bit to make his case), and five years after E. Belfield Spriggins published, in the *Louisiana Weekly*, the very first serious article on jazz ever printed in the state, in the course of which he gave Willie Cornish's version of the origin of "Funky Butt":

"It seems that one night while playing at Odd Fellows Hall, Perdido near Rampart, it became very hot and stuffy and a discussion among members of Bolden's band arose about the foul air. The next day William Cornish, the trombonist with the band, composed a 'tune' to be played by the band. The real words are unprintable but these will answer: 'I thought I heard Old Bolden say/Rotten gut, rotten gut/Take it away.'"[3]

Very little else has ever surfaced about the song or its origin. Russell

---

[2] *Anamule Dance*, volume two of *Jelly Roll Morton: The Library of Congress Recordings*. Rounder Records 1092. Also see Alan Lomax, *Mister Jelly Roll* (New York: Grove Press, 1950).

[3] E. Belfield Spriggins, "Excavating Local Jazz," *Louisiana Weekly*, April 22, 1933, p. 5. Quoted by Marquis (p. 109), who sadly notes that "in 1965 Hurricane Betsy struck [Spriggins's] house and totally destroyed all the notes and records of his very early jazz research. His wife reports that he has been in such a serious state of depression since that he will not or cannot speak to anyone including herself."

and Smith's assertion that the number was "inspired by some 'low-life' women who had worked on a boat with the band"[4] sounds bizarre, and it was possibly concocted by Bunk Johnson. Morton remains the only person to have recorded the song who heard it played by Bolden's band. All three of his versions are consistent in lyrics and tempo—most contemporaries agreed that they are far too slow. There are reminiscences galore of the song's scatological variant lyrics, but none ever seem to have been published, and Morton's version, in a series of recordings notable for probably containing the most uses of the word *fuck* prior to 1987 or so, is remarkably chaste. Besides the main verse, which is all most people know—funky butt, take it away, open up the window, let the bad air out—there is a second one in Morton's published version and on his second solo recording, about Judge Fogarty sentencing somebody to thirty days' sweeping out the market (a frequent punishment for minor infractions then), and something about Frankie Dusen (a trombone player who took over Bolden's band when he became incapacitated) demanding his money. Edmond "Doc" Souchon, a local musician, recalled a version from his childhood: "Ain't that man got a funny walk/Doin' the Ping Pong round Southern Park/Black man, white man, take him away/I thought I heard them say."[5] Bolden's biographer, Donald Marquis, suggests that the tune predated Bolden, that it was carried down the river, and he cites as corroboration words that do sound older than 1902:

> I thought I heer'd Abe Lincoln shout,
> Rebels close down them plantations and let the niggers out.
> I'm positively sure I heer'd Mr. Lincoln shout.
> I thought I heer'd Mr. Lincoln say,
> Rebels close down them plantations and let all them niggers out.
> You gonna lose this war, git on your knees and pray,
> That's the words I heer'd Mr. Lincoln say.[6]

---

[4] In *Jazzmen*, edited by Frederick Ramsay, Jr., and Charles Edward Smith (New York: Harcourt Brace, 1939; New York: Limelight Editions, 1985), p. 13.

[5] *Jazz Review*, May 1960.

[6] Marquis, pp. 109–10, quoting Danny Barker, "Memory of King Bolden," *Evergreen Review*, March 1965, pp. 67–74.

Jelly Roll Morton's recordings, for all their testamentary aspect and intent, can actually be seen as marking the start of a second life for at least one aspect of the song. Although *funk* is a versatile word, with secondary denotations of fear and depression and second-order thievery, the phrase *funky butt* would have clearly signified an odoriferous posterior for at least a century before Bolden famously used the phrase, and in context it can still be so interpreted. In the glossary of hepcat jive that Mezz Mezzrow inserted at the end of his memoir, *Really the Blues* (1946), *funk* is defined as "stench," and *funky* as "smelly, obnoxious." In less than a decade, however, the meaning of the word had begun to turn, at least in jazz circles, particularly on the West Coast. The scat singer King Pleasure, backed by Quincy Jones, put out a record called *Funk Junction* in 1954, and 1957 saw the issue of *Creme de Funk* by Phil Woods and Gene Quill, and of *Funky* by Gene Ammons's All-Stars. In 1958 beatnik fellow-traveler John Clellon Holmes employed *funk* in a strictly musical sense in his novel *The Horn*, and not much later the word was being applied favorably to a performance by Miles Davis. By 1964 even the *New York Times* was throwing it around.

The word was in general currency from the early 1960s on as a musical term signifying some combination of authenticity, earthiness, greasiness, muscularity, perspiration, and the presence of one or more of the following: fuzz-tone bass, hoarse cries produced on the bottom register of the tenor sax, a bottom-heavy and high-hat-intensive drum style, and a particularly dirty sound obtainable on the Hammond organ. The turning point came in 1966, when Arlester Christian wrote, and recorded with his band Dyke and the Blazers, the epochal "Funky Broadway," which was covered and made into a huge hit by Wilson Pickett the following year. The way *funky* was employed in the lyrics did not refer to music, although it retained many of the cluster of meanings associated with musical use: authenticity, earthiness, greasiness, etc. All of these dovetailed with and enlarged usefully upon the word's original olfactory denotation, welcoming the noxious odor and giving it a room and a new suit without actually rehabilitating it. From there it was a short step to Arthur Conley's

"Funky Street" (1968), Rufus Thomas's "Funky Chicken" (1970), Toots and the Maytals' "Funky Kingston" (1973), and "Funky Nassau" by The Beginning of the End (1973), among many. James Brown virtually bought the franchise, from "Funk Bomb" (1967) through "Ain't It Funky," "Make It Funky," "Funky Side of Town," "Funky President," "Funky Drummer," and scads more from all quadrants of meaning by a man who spent a year or two calling himself Minister of the New New Super Heavy Funk. He had no peers atop the funk pyramid, or at least that was the case until George Clinton (of Funkadelic) concocted something like a theology of funk. (One of my proudest possessions is a T-shirt I can't fit into anymore that is emblazoned with the legend "Take Funk to Heaven in 77"). Clinton, in full evangelical feather, instituted a principle of spiritual surrender he termed "Giving up the Funk." This was *mana*, total communion with the life force manifested as a fried fish.

Funk has climbed down from those heights. It has been devalued by George Michael's "Too Funky," and the Eagles' "Funky New Year," and "Funky Funky Xmas" by the New Kids on the Block, not to speak of the lingering memory of Grand Funk Railroad. But the word has not been shucked. It is still too valuable. It appears in hip-hop strictly as a place-marker (the Notorious B.I.G.'s "Machine Gun Funk," Too Short's "Short but Funky," OutKast's "Funky Ride," etc.), but it is a place-marker that will not go away anytime soon. Payments are kept up on the word. Its license is renewed. It is periodically removed from the shelf and dusted off and cradled, occasionally taken for a spin to shake out the knots. The day will come before very long when it is immediately necessary once again, when all of its putative substitutes have been tarnished and made risible, when "ghetto" has been redeveloped and "real" has become irredeemably fake—when it will have acquired a previously undreamed-of nuance temporarily undetectable by the white middle-class ear. It awaits a further development of the process set in motion on the rickety stage of some fraternal hall in uptown New Orleans in the year 1902 or thereabouts. It permanently embodies the voice of Buddy Bolden, speaking through a cloud.

13

JON LANGFORD

"See Willy Fly By"
and
"The Cuckoo"

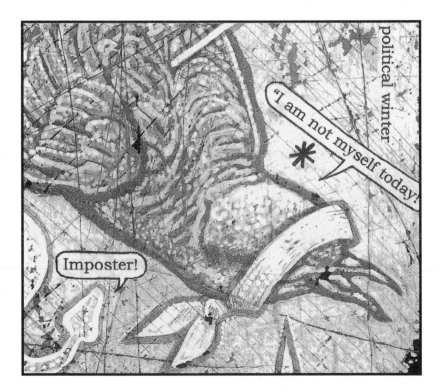

In this suburb of Babylon
They don't like to wait
They kill the messenger
'Cos the message was late
Kill the child starving at the gate
predicting the ruin of the state
See Willy fly by
in the by & by, in the never you mind, in the Dollar store light, in the there you go, in the wait & see, in the them & us the us & them, the them & me
He's the exception that proves the rule
ALL YOUR DREAMS are a lie!
How much will you swallow?
CUCKOO
when Willy flies by

"The Coo Coo Bird"

as recorded by Clarence Ashley, 1929

Gonna build me

Log cabin

On a mountain

So high

So I can

See Willie

As he goes

On by

Hmm-mm

Hmm-mm-mm

Hmm-mm

Hmm-mm

COO COO

There's something ROTTEN round here nobody forgot all the rest on the bottom WHITE MEN still on the top

fantasticis aparicionibus

Walk and talk with Suzie
Shoot to cripple and maim
Shoot to kill again and again and again and again

bird is the sign

VOTE OFTEN

political winter

"I am not myself today!"

Half heard
half remembered
half understood

Imposter!

like Rock'n'roll's strange journey from a slang term for sex, thru a teen dance craze to savage Big Business — the Cuckoo's playful song of rebirth & fertility has become propaganda & marketing for the Big Lie and finally a harbinger of Doom...

This verse written by Bob Wills and Mayor Daley

The Rose & the Briar

190

Hmm-mm-mm

Hmm-mm

Hmm-mm

Hmm-mm

Oh the coo coo

She's a pretty bird

She wobbles

As she flies

She never

Hollers coo-coo

Til the fourth day

July

END OF WINTER
SEX
NO!
NO LIES
THE VOYAGE
DISEASE
EXILE
PERSECUTION
CARNAGE
COO!
COO!
Gonna build me a house on a mountain so high I'll sit in my car and stare up at the sky
WOBBLE
A PRETTY BIRD
THE DREAM
MORE SEX
THE AMERICAN DREAM
JULY 4
$
THE DREAM & LIE OF THE
CUCKOO
HERE BE MILLIONAIRES

I've played cards
In England
I've played cards
In Spain
I'll bet you
Ten dollars
I beat you
Next game

Jack a Diamonds
Jack a Diamonds
I've known you
From old
Now you've robbed my
Poor pocket
Of my silver
And my gold

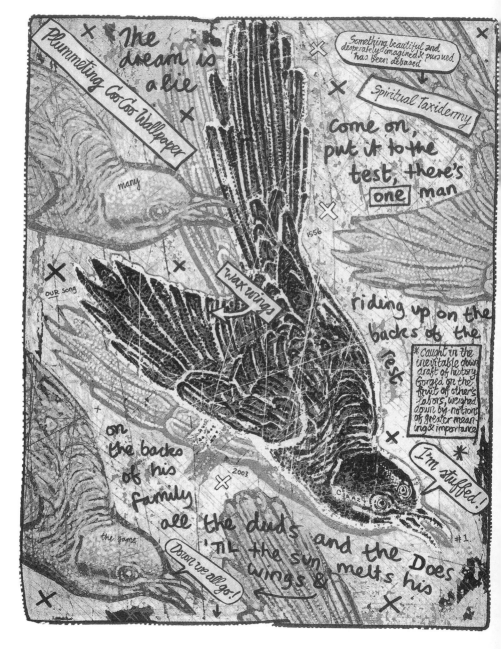

Hmm-mm-mm

Hmm mm mm

Hmm-mm

Hmm-mmm

Hmm-mm-mm

Hmm-mm-mm

Hmm-mm

Hmm-mmm

I've played cards

In England

I've played cards

In Spain

I'll bet you

Ten dollars

I beat you

This game

The Rose & the Briar

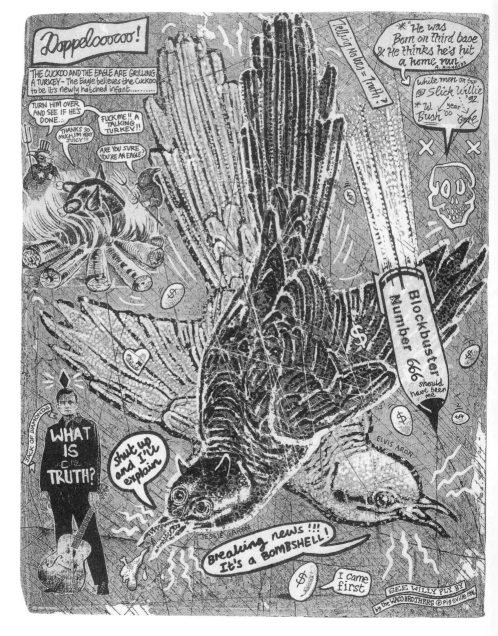

Oh the coo coo

Is a pretty bird

She wobbles

As she flies

She never

Hollers coo coo

Til the fourth day

July

III

"Volver, Volver"

,

Fast & Fresh Deli, 84 Hoyt Street, Brooklyn,
New York. *Drawing by Paul Berman, 2004.
Courtesy of the artist.*

PAUL BERMAN

Mariachi Reverie

I.

Up the street from Macy's in downtown Brooklyn is a modest little shop called Fast & Fresh Deli, which, at a glance, appears to be a down-at-the-heels grocery-and-sandwich shop like thousands of others in New York, but turns out to be, at second glance, a bit of Mexico City transplanted into the distant north. I stop at that place a few times a month and order beef tacos, and I sit on a stool at the counter and listen to the boom box above the stove. And, like everyone else at Fast & Fresh, sometimes I find that one song or another has thrown me into unexpected moods and reveries, and little stabs of savory emotion compete for my attention with the equally savory stabs of cilantro and raw onion in my mouth. More than once the boom box has played a mariachi classic called "Volver, Volver"—"To Return, To Return"—in the version belted out by Vicente Fernández, the Mexican mariachi king. A reedy organ proclaims a few opening notes, two trumpets blare a melodious fanfare, the greasy beef dissolves into the grainy corn tortilla, and— surely I'm not the only one to have had this experience, seated on a stool at Fast & Fresh—my heart swells.

How many times I have heard "Volver, Volver"! I walk through the New York streets, and phrases from that song seep from the back doors of restaurants, where the dishwashers are toiling. I hear the song in the Mexican groceries that have popped up everywhere in

New York during these last few years. I hear it on the sidewalks of an East Harlem that long ago ceased to be Italian (except for a few lingerers), and is scarcely even Puerto Rican anymore, though it pretends to be, but has managed to become, in its tastes and storefronts and in the look of the passing crowds, an outpost of Puebla, Mexico. Or I listen as one of New York's innumerable mariachi bands strikes up the song in a restaurant. Or someone drives past in a beat-up old car, and the song comes vibrating out the windows—"Vol-vair, volll . . . VAIR!" And each new time the song recurs, I am somehow reminded of the previous times, until the merest phrase from that song sends me hurtling downward into caverns of fathomless nostalgia.

The most sensational rendition I have ever heard was in San José, Costa Rica, many years ago. It was Christmas Eve. Costa Rica is an agrarian place, and every year horsemen come into the capital from the farms and go cantering past the cathedral and the main plaza and through the streets in an equestrian parade called "el Tope," showing off their most spectacular horses and waving at cheerful crowds. I was late in getting to the parade and had to make my way into one of what are called the "popular" barrios—which is to say, the poor people's districts—to catch the tail end. The parade had gotten a little bedraggled by then. Even so, horsemen came trotting by dressed in the finery that you see in the old-fashioned Westerns, the ancient Spanish costumes from centuries ago—the embroidered short jackets and bolero hats and the magnificent tooled boots. Sometimes, as the horsemen cantered by, they pulled on the reins and their horses reared and pranced—"el Tope," the prance—and girls in the crowd laughed and waved and ran into the street, and now and then a horseman scooped up a girl with one arm and with a single swoop seated her on the back of his saddle and trotted off, the horse swaggering its silky flanks and the crowd cheering at the merry scenes of rapture.

The crowd had grown a little beery by the time I arrived, and the aluminum cans spilled across the sidewalk and onto the street. And yet, just as the beer seemed to have won a final victory over the tropical afternoon, the most magnificent horseman of all came lazying along on a stolid white horse. This grandest of horsemen was a mariachi singer, dressed in a short, white embroidered jacket and studded tight pants, with a gun holstered to his thigh. The horseman held the reins with one hand and a microphone with the other, and behind him rolled a big sound truck with the horseman's broad white charro hat atop the cabin, next to the loudspeaker. The horseman braced himself on his stirrups to firm up his diaphragm, and, with the loudspeaker blaring the background music, he held up his mike and belted out his own version of "Volver, Volver":

> Este amor apasionado
> Anda todo alborotado
> Por volver!
> Voy camino a la locura
> Y aunque todo me tortura,
> Sé querer!

> This impassioned love
> Keeps me all stirred up
> To return!
> I'm going straight into madness
> And though everything tortures me,
> I know how to love!

That singer was magnificent. His voice was as big as his horse.

> Nos dejamos hace tiempo
> Pero me llegó el momento
> De perder.
> Tu tenías mucha razón.
> Le hago caso al corazón
> Y me muero por volver.

> We left each other long ago,
> But the moment of heartbreak
> Has come.
> You were very right.
> I listen to my heart.
> And I'm dying to return.

He rose still higher on the stirrups and gestured to the crowd. And everywhere along the sidewalks, the tipsy and uproarious people took up where he had left off, bellowing out the chorus in a burst of beer fumes—a raucous crowd, thousands of people, bawling the words in unison, every single person at the top of his lungs, in a roar:

> Y volver, volver, volll-VERRR!
>
> And to return, return, ree-TURRRN!

The horseman answered:

> A tus brazos otra vez!
> Llegaré donde estés.
> Yo sé perder, yo sé perder.
> Quiero volver, volver, volver.
>
> To your arms once again!
> I will come where you are.
> I know how to lose, how to lose,
> I want to return, return, return!

And he went once more through the song, until the crowd, swaying to the music and waving their cans, roared once again, "Volver, volver, volll-VERRR!"

II.

I worry that, describing the song in this way, and in recalling the mariachi horseman of Costa Rica and the tipsy crowd, I am giving the wrong impression of this song. Or I may be feeding an ignorant prejudice—a notion of mariachi as music for drunkards and louts, something crude, artless, a music for roughnecks and the uneducated, and not for anyone more refined. But no, no—there are jewels in this music. Besides, I don't want to sneer at the crowd. Even feelings that are roared in the street may have their justification. And there are traditions to consider, which suggest refinements and emotions of their own, unto the most fantastic complications.

Those costumes, to begin with, the studded pants and the beholstered uniform—there is something to say about that. I have a CD of what is supposed to be the earliest and most classic of the mariachi orchestras, the Mariachi Vargas de Tecalitlán, which was founded in 1897 in Jalisco, Mexico, on the West Coast. A photo in the album brochure shows the Mariachi Vargas in its early days, when the instrumentation consisted of two violins, a wooden-box harp, and a more-or-less standard guitar called a *guitarra mariachera*. Everyone dressed in white linens, short neckties, and straw sombreros—the traditional *campesino* clothes of long ago. But that was then.

By the 1930s, mariachi orchestras had come to include several violins, the wooden-box folk harp (sometimes replaced by an accordion or even an electric organ), a couple of trumpets, and three kinds of guitars—a standard guitar; a tiny round-backed *vihuela,* which I suppose might be considered a lute; and an acoustic bass guitar called a *guitarrón,* as big as a cello. The costumes likewise evolved, until they had arrived at what is standard today—the tight, studded pants opening onto cowboy boots, the broad silk neckties or scarves, the short brocaded jackets, and, for the singer and sometimes for the entire orchestra, an enormous, broad-brimmed charro hat of the sort that Mexican restaurants hang on the wall. Plus the singer's gun and holster, strapped to his hip. These costumes have something in common with a matador's uniform—flamboyant costumes of an armed aristocracy. Here is homage to the Spanish Empire and its medieval virtues, and yet homage as well to the rustic spirit of Western Mexico—a mix of European martial arrogance and humble farm life. You don't see anything like this in the conventional folk culture of the United States, except maybe in a few corners of the magnolia-and-moonlight Confederacy, where people have gone on dreaming of Sir Walter Scott, or in the Western rodeos, where the gringo cowboys were always doing their best to imitate the Mexicans, anyway.

From a strictly musical standpoint, mariachi has a few idiosyncrasies that someone accustomed to the conventions of American pop and folk music might fail to notice, and the first of those peculiar musical traits is surely this same mixture of the elegant and the rustic. Violins in a mariachi orchestra are not country fiddles. They are classical instruments, and vibrato is everything. Mariachi violins do tend to get a little wavery and screechy now and then, even on some of the best recordings (which adds a touching note of frailty to the music—the pathos of the out-of-tune). But the violins are not supposed to be frail and feeble, and in better orchestras the violins do produce, at least sometimes, a pure and rich sound, tasty and sweet— the delicacy of a zarzuela orchestra from the musical theatre of Madrid, or a light opera from the Paris music halls. (According to one of the theories about mariachi and its origins, the music owes something to the occupying French Army of the Emperor Maximilian, during France's 1860s adventure in Mexico.)

But there are trumpets, too, and the trumpets tend to be played with the ferocity of a bullfight band—sometimes bleating noisily, often a little sharp (though some of the trumpeters do know what they're doing, needless to say, and are perfectly capable of performing with the greatest delicacy, sometimes with a sweetening mute, like the trumpets that accompany Caribbean trios). And so, in a mariachi orchestra, the violins rustle like flowers and the trumpets roar like farm animals. The orchestra might end up sounding in one passage like a slightly peculiar opera orchestra, and, a moment later, like a jaunty country band, inebriated and aggressive. And, in that fashion, mariachi orchestras go teetering forward—refined and rustic, sweet and braying, orchestras of the high and the low—like nothing else I have ever heard.

The rhythms, too, play with ideas and customs that depart pretty radically from the customary rhythms of American folk music and pop music. A traditional mariachi song might lurch from one pattern to another within a song—sometimes varying the tempo, sometimes the syncopation, tripping from one Mexican hat-dance complexity to the next, or settling for a moment into a rhumba or a two-beat gait. Variation is the thing, not monotony and groove—a variation that descends from Spain and not from Africa (except when the orchestra strikes up a rhumba). The rhythms are meant for dancing, but, at least in some of the more traditional mariachi songs, the dancing is supposed to be elaborate and formal, a "shoeing" or *zapateando* that requires certain specific steps and a lot of well-defined heel-tapping and skirt-swishing. And yet the most striking aspect of all has got to be the singing, and this, once again, because of the range of variation.

A first-rate mariachi singer commands several vocal techniques and might very well put every one of those techniques to use in a single song—a syrupy crooning, an open-throated singing in the broad style of Italian opera, an occasional sob, and a series of yelps, which come in regional variations. A yelp from Jalisco, where mariachi got its start (and all mariachi seems to have remained, in some respect, Jalisciense, no matter where the orchestra makes its home), is a high-pitched, extended *ay-ay-yi-iiii* that can sound genuinely weird. This is not the cheerful *yippee-yi-yo* of a singing cowboy—this is a cry of anguish, unto insanity, something hair-raising, a wild tone. And, having done all that, a singer might conclude his phrase by sliding down a fourth, as if slipping alcoholically from his chair to the floor, from F to C. And these vocal maneuvers and techniques, in their marvelous variety, their idiosyncrasy, humor, intensity, and virtuosity, make for a lyrical exposition that is, in the end, theatrical in the extreme—passionate, tender, raucous, violent, operatic, lunatic, demagogic, and hammy beyond all hamminess. All of which is performed above the courtly-and-rustic instruments and the varying syncopations—a music that has very little in common with the main impulses of American folk and pop, and everything to do with the folk and theatre traditions of Spain and probably France, too, long ago.

But now I worry that, having pointed out a few mariachi oddities, I may have made the music seem excessively exotic or foreign from American life, as if this kind of music were nothing but an immigrant import. That would be a big mistake—even if, nowadays, there do seem to be a lot of immigrants, and some of them have formed orchestras, and entire neighborhoods seem to feel a civic obligation to turn up their boom boxes in order to augment the public joy. No, mariachi ought to count as, in its fashion, an authentically American music. Or so I want to argue, and I will cite highest authority.

For what does it mean, really, to be American—what are the distinctly American qualities? The qualities of the United States, I mean, and not of the Americas as a whole. An unanswerable question, you may say. But there is a way to answer, and that is to glance at the first group of people to pose this question in a recognizably modern version.

Those people were the poets and intellectuals of the generation that came of age forty or fifty years after the American Revolution—writers like Longfellow in Massachusetts and Whitman in New York, who wanted to know what it meant to be American, and what America's purpose ought to be. The Revolutionary generation, the Founding Fathers, had answered those questions with legal and political principles. The writers who came along a few decades later wanted to speak, instead, about culture and history. They wanted to dig up folk traditions from the past, the unique qualities of American life, and to discover in those qualities a sap and vigor capable of shooting upward and blossoming in the future. They knew very well that American culture was rooted in the English past, but they also wanted to show that American culture drew on other roots, far, far from the British Isles—and the farther, the better.

Longfellow mooned over the shores of Gitchie Gumee precisely because the Indians offered an indigenous tradition that was not England's—because the Indians helped define what was distinctively American, just as the last of the great Eastern Woodlands tribes were being pushed across the Mississippi. That was a big theme for the writers of Longfellow's time—for Thoreau, Parkman, Cooper, and so many others, each one of them fascinated by the Indian past. And, on that same logic, Longfellow and William H. Prescott and Washington Irving and more than a few other writers insisted on taking seriously the Spanish origins of the United States—the origins that could be found in the Southwest mostly, though also in Florida, New Orleans, the Northwest, and other places from the days of Spanish greatness: "When the flag of Spain unfurled/Its folds o'er this western world," in Longfellow's phrase.

Spain had spent several hundred years as England's hated enemy, on grounds of imperial rivalry as well as religion, and the American writers knew they were being slightly insolent in claiming a Spanish heritage for themselves. But insolence was itself an American trait. Whitman loved the Spanish on that count. He pointed to what he called, in the title of one of his essays, "The Spanish Element in Our Nationality," and he even set about incorporating a bit of fake Spanish into *Leaves of Grass*—"As I lay with my head in your lap camerado," and that sort of thing (though the correct Spanish word would be *camarada*). "Comrade Americanos!" Whitman cried out. His was the original Spanglish in literature. He loved the word *libertad*. Saying "liberty" in Spanish gave those syllables an extra dignity. Or maybe the Spanish word signified a bit of American solidarity with the freedom fighters of monarchical Spain and Latin America. *Libertad* was the key to Whitman's "A Broadway Pageant"—which is to say, he plunked down his Spanish word in the center of Manhattan.

But the "Spanish element" attracted these writers for another reason, too. These people, every one of them, were Romantics, and the Romantic writers in every country went looking for medieval roots and eternal national characteristics and historical destinies, and they tended to find these many things in a dream landscape that everyone described as Spain. The Romantics were a little nauseated by the ravages of liberal civilization and by the bleached-out Protestantism and rationalism of the Northern countries, and Spain was, for them, the great alternative. It was a pure land of medieval tradition and high passion, a land of the pre-bourgeois and of Catholic nostalgias, of impetuous emotion, a land of the gut and the heart and not the brain. Even the cruelty of the Spanish Inquisition had its perverse allure. The French Romantics were especially excited by these Iberian qualities, and they threw themselves into composing even more fake Spanish than Whitman ever did. Victor Hugo was always salting his plays, poems, and novels with passages of fake-Spanish dialogue, and sometimes even a bit of correct Spanish. It made him feel he was saying something rougher and more violent than could possibly be said in French.

These writers wanted to resurrect the literary and song traditions of the Middle Ages, if only they could figure out where to find those lost traditions; and here Spain was truly useful, not just in the zones of fantasy. People in Spain were already nostalgic for the distant past—more keenly nostalgic, I think, than anyone else in Western Europe. The Spanish enthusiasm had long ago turned into a tradition of its own. In whole regions of the Spanish countryside, people did remember the medieval lyrics. The Spanish were in this respect Romantics before Romanticism. They had long ago set the old lyrics into print in the *Romancero*, the medieval songbook. And these authentic traits of Spanish life drove the poets in other countries into ecstasies of artistic inspiration.

Hugo found in the *Romancero* a way of writing immense stories in a fragmentary lyric fashion, as if composing ballads to be sung to guitar accompaniment, in the Spanish fashion. Whitman never even tried to do anything similar. Yet he, too, went out of his way to sing the virtues of Spanish tradition. He did this in an essay called "British Literature," where he recommended Cervantes and the tales of *el Cid*, meaning the *Romancero*, in preference even to Shakespeare. This was carrying the anti-British insolence a little far. Whitman couldn't help himself. The multicultural was one of his tropes, and the more multiculti he was, the more democratic and even nationalist he felt. But I can imagine that, in nodding to Spain, Whitman meant to express something more than openness to a polyglot world. He felt the same inspiration that Hugo felt. It was a feeling for the grand sweep of human affairs—a feeling for whatever is overarching in world history—the universal and not the parochial or the particular.

In its many ballads, the *Romancero* told stories of kings and knights and lovers, but the nineteenth-century writers glimpsed in those separate tales a larger, vaguer story. This was the immense epic of the *Reconquista*—the Christian crusade to retake Spain from the Moors, a seven-hundred-year affair. This was not a narrow theme—this was the very struggle that, at its end, sent the conquistadors, as if propelled by giant catapults, across the Atlantic to continue the same crusade against ever-new populations of Moors, and to convert the Western Hemisphere to the Christian cross. This was the story of all mankind (if you could get yourself for a moment to picture Catholicism's progress, and mankind's, as the same). Something in the notion of composing a fragmentary verse epic of universal history did seem to appeal to the author of *Leaves of Grass*. You can see another version of the same influence still more clearly in Longfellow and his "Tales of the Wayside Inn" and other ballads. Longfellow wanted to compose a national epic in lyric fragments—the national epic that, for him, too, was going to speak of universal progress, from servitude to freedom. Longfellow's ear was tuned to English tradition. Yet, he, too, went out of his way to acknowledge the Spanish heritage, and not just in his translations of Lope de Vega and other writers. He wrote "The Bells of San Blas" on a

Mexican theme—which is to say, Longfellow made a point of acknowledging the Spanish heritage not just in faraway Spain, but in places where the Spanish flag unfurled across the Western world.

The heritage of the Spanish *Romancero* was, in any case, a living thing in the United States of Longfellow's day. In New England, Spanish legacies (yes, even in New England) had mostly died out by the nineteenth century, but maybe not entirely. Longfellow remembered them in his poem about the Newport Jews—legacies courtesy of the Sephardic. But in other places, farther south, the Spanish heritage had never ceased to flourish. The conquistadors brought the *Romancero* to the Western world just as much as they brought the cross and the sword. And the *Romancero* and the culture that surrounded it—the nostalgia for the Middle Ages, the tradition of heroic ballads—took root. New variations of the old "romances" or ballads sprang up in all of the Spanish regions of the New World, and those regions included the zones eventually incorporated into the United States.

The Mexican scholar Mercedes Díaz Roig compiled a fascinating volume a few years ago called the *Romancero tradicional de América,* and, in her catalogue of the Romances of the Western Hemisphere and its several regions, she included a section on the Latin American zone known as Estados Unidos, which had generated some highly traditional "Romances," unknown in other places. None of this ever withered away. For what are the *corridos* of the American Southwest today, and of northern Mexico—what are those two-beat and three-beat polka-rhythm ballads about wetbacks, bandits, and the like, the "narco-*corridos*" with their drug-smuggler heroes? Those are living fruits of a very old tree. The "Spanish element" that Whitman and Longfellow wanted to claim for the American nationality, the *Romancero* and its New World legacies, the Catholic memories, the peculiar Spanish nostalgias—these are things of the present, not just of the forgotten and exotic past.

IV.

In drawing a few connections between the mariachi orchestras and these older Spanish traditions, I don't want to turn the mariachis into conquistadors, and I don't want to attribute the typical lyrics of mariachi repertory to the old *Romancero* and its heritage. The *corridos* tell elaborate stories and are visibly in the grand tradition, and this is not true of the more typical mariachi lyrics (though mariachi orchestras do perform *corridos*, sometimes). Still, there are many ways to tell a story, and the mariachi orchestras do tell a story. The costumes by themselves conjure the past. And that gun on the singer's hip, the mandatory gun—what is that, if not a sign that the singer is a warrior, and these are warrior songs, ballads that a wandering knight might pluck on his guitar? The *Romancero* expresses one kind of medieval nostalgia, and here is another. Jorge Negrete, the mariachi film star of some sixty years ago, sang a hit called "El Charro Mexicano" on this theme—on the glories of his own brocaded sombrero, silk tie, pistol, guitar, and spurs. And Negrete concluded, like a knight warbling his creed:

> Soy la noble tradición!
> Soy el charro mexicano,
> Noble, valiente, y leal!

> I am the noble tradition!
> I am the flashy Mexican dude,
> Noble, valiant, and loyal!

Then again, the mariachi orchestras have a history of their own, something modern, and I think that, at least in Mexico, audiences understand this, too, if only by intuition. The Mexican Revolution broke out in 1910 and proved to be vast and traumatic—the largest and most violent single event to occur anywhere in the Western Hemisphere in the twentieth century. The revolutionary generals warred with one another, which was a disaster that lasted twenty years. Eventually, though, the generals had the good sense to join together in the massive national organization that became known, in time, as the Party of the Institutional Revolution, the PRI. And the PRI turned out to be wonderfully successful at creating a sense of order and unity in Mexico, in the name of nationalism and revolutionary ideals.

The greatest of those early PRI leaders was Lázaro Cárdenas, who became president in 1934—a kind of Franklin Roosevelt, except more radical. And Cárdenas, with his cunning and his vision of a Mexican future, set out to construct not just order and peace but something more, a national culture. Mariachi music had gotten started, as I say, in Jalisco in the late nineteenth century. Cárdenas came up with the inspired idea of bringing the best of the Jalisciense orchestras, the Mariachi Vargas de Tecalitlán, to Mexico City to play at his inauguration. Then he put the orchestra on the payroll of the Mexico City police department and took the musicians on tour with him around the country, and in this way set about creating a revolutionary popular culture for Mexico as a whole. Mexican radio and film arose in those same years, and the people who built these new industries likewise turned to mariachi in search of a national culture, something with commercial appeal, which they increased by adding trumpets to the original set of instruments (or, at least, that is one version of how trumpets came to play a part in the mariachi orchestras) and by making the uniforms standard for everyone. Mariachi orchestras appear in some 200 movies from the Golden Age of Mexican filmmaking, which is pretty astounding, if you try to picture the experience of sitting in a Mexican movie theatre during these last many decades.

Mariachi offered a revolutionary answer to a fearfully difficult question for Mexicans—namely, how to compete with the commercial music and film products from the United States, and how to do so without turning to Spain, the oppressor from the past. The PRI's achievement was to bring together impossible contradictions into a single, disciplined, national organization. Mariachi did something similar in the alternative universe of music. Mariachi gathered together medieval memories, revolutionary populism, knightly arrogance, rustic humility, *campesino* rebelliousness, and the modernizing drive of the national state and the radio and film industries, not to mention a cult of Mexican regionalism—and somehow, by pickling these things in a spirit of tragedy and pathos and nationalism, ended up with a marvelous and moving mythology, musical and theatrical at the same time.

Does that seem impossible? You must see the movies of Pedro Infante. There is a scene in *Las Mujeres de mi general* (Ismael Rodríguez, 1950) where the great star leads an army in the revolution, scandalizes high society by proposing to marry his low-class camp-follower, and serenades the young lady by organizing what appears to be the entire revolutionary armed forces in the middle of the night to put down their rifles and pick up guitars and sing to her in the stony streets, with the radiant young lady replying with lyrics of her own from her balcony—a glorious noir-filmed scene that expresses the eternal values of ardent love, military valor, Mexican nationalism, revolutionary commitment, disdain for the prejudices of the past, and reverence for the virtues of the past, not excluding the crucifix on the wall. Now, that's movie-making!—Not to mention choral harmonizing! Not to mention guitar-playing! Not to mention those fabulous hats!— the hats that grandly perpetuate the image of the gigantic sombreros worn by Emiliano Zapata, the most radical of the rural leaders from the most radical period of the revolution, when the *campesino* millennium seemed plausibly at hand and the age of oppression and injustice seemed to have disappeared into the past. (Not to mention, in addition, that Manuel M. Ponce, one of Latin America's finest classical-music composers, arranged the serenade.)

And so, in those years of the mariachi boom, from the 1930s to the 1950s, a story hovered behind the mariachi orchestras that audiences could instinctively recognize. It was the story of the Mexican Revolution in its many impossible complexities—the revolution that was forward-looking and backward-looking at the same time, feudal and populist and sometimes even socialist. This story underwent a few twists and turns of its own in the next few years, and the new twists added still more echoes and themes to the music. The 1930s to 1950s were glory years for the PRI. But the whole structure of Mexican life began to sag after a while, and, by 1968, a new generation of sophisticated young people had come of age, filled with impatience at the Institutional Revolution and its byzantine and heavy-handed customs, and fed up with the commercial arts of the official culture. The new cultural radicals saw in the old mariachi orchestras the music of an authoritarian culture of the older times—the culture of the one-party state and the feudal past. Mariachi began to appear, in the eyes of the cultural radicals, as a music of a slightly loony male domination, in an antique style that no one in his right mind could tolerate anymore. Now, this last complaint was not always fair. Lola Beltrán was one of the greatest of the mariachi singers, and her throaty and fiery singing expressed the same kind of hot-blooded ferocity as that of her male colleagues, or maybe even hotter, if that were possible, which it is.

But the hot-blooded style, whether male or female, was itself a sign of a macho universe—a lover's universe in which the amorous and the murderous were erotically entwined, and the holster on the singer's hip symbolized a lover's tyranny, and violent jealousy seemed the highest expression of ardor. The radical sophisticates of 1968 couldn't abide that stuff any longer. Plus there was the rigidity of the music itself. The 1968 student uprisings were genuinely massive in Mexico, especially in Mexico City; and, as everywhere that year, those uprisings were about music as much as anything else. They were uprisings against the old state-sanctioned music, in favor of different kinds of music, which seemed liberating and exciting to the students. And what kinds of music were those? Cuban-influenced protest music—but also a few styles and performers from the English-speaking world. The radical students took to listening to the Beatles and Joan Baez—the anti-machistas, singers of the gentle instead of the violent (except sometimes), singers who were positively cute and wistful, singers who did not wear guns on their hips. The older, revolutionary generation in Mexico found this hard to take. The revolutionary elders accused the young people of being Soviet agents, and this accusation tended to mean, in regard to music, that young people had forsaken the national patrimony not just for Fidel Castro's cultural productions but for crappy music from the historic enemy across the border, and from the historic enemy's linguistic forebears and allies—musical treason, in a word. But then, for the younger people, English-language music was not really the point.

Up-to-dateness was the point. The same kind of people in Mexico who grooved to gringo musicians in 1968 went on, in later years, to become the fans of the new Cuban dance bands, not because of any association with Fidel but simply on grounds of musical hipness and love of artistry—this, together with a continued revulsion for the patriarchal and feudal memories that seemed to cry out from the old mariachi orchestras. I have watched people respond in very similar ways to mariachi in Nicaragua, where the music established itself long ago, thanks to the influence of Mexican recordings and movies. During the violent struggles between the left and right in Nicaragua in the 1980s and 1990s, the sophisticated leftists of Managua and the universities tended to be fans of American folk and pop music in the 1980s (as well as of the Cuban-influenced protest music) and then went on, in later years, to become the lovers of Afro-Caribbean dance music. But the rural enemies of the Managua leftists were solidly the fans of mariachi. The Sandinistas answered to one set of musical tastes, the contras to another. Wall posters in the Sandinista towns might feature José José or some other Mexican or Spanish pop star, but wall posters in the contra zones of the faraway rural districts were likely to feature Vicente Fernández, grinning from under his charro hat.

Or maybe the controversies over mariachi in the last few decades have had to do with a relatively simple sense of past and present—a feeling that mariachi comes out of a long-ago time that, in some people's eyes, seems, in its antiquity, a little repulsive. There is in Mexico a genuinely large class of people who are mendicant musicians, people who roam the streets begging for coins or hoping for a commission to go perform at someone's party or to go stand under some woman's window and serenade her. It's hard to believe, but these people, some of them, have been organized into the PRI, where they make up the rank-and-file of the street-accordionists' union and other sturdy structures of what used to be the giant party-state. But the street musicians express nothing of what once used to be the PRI's commitment to the modern and the efficient. Those musicians are the failed, the ancient, the impoverished. There is something appalling about them, in their studded, tight-fitting uniforms that long ago decayed into rags, carrying their dented instruments and radiating an air of hopeless poverty and even of crime.

Mariachi orchestras wander around Plaza Garibaldi in Mexico City looking for work, and those musicians can be a pretty fearful sight, as if at any moment they might turn into Pedro Infante's guitar-playing serenaders in reverse, and might put down their guitars and violins, and pull out guns, and finish you off, quick. There's a bit of a homosexual desperado underground in some of this, too, at Plaza Garibaldi (a natural component of a music that so insistently exaggerates the masculine), which makes, all in all, a frightening scene: run-down, pathetic, ragged, and impoverished, a vista of every wretchedness of ages past. Yet those same musicians, for the equivalent of five or ten dollars, can still break your heart with a well-performed rendition of this or that classic of the repertory, depending on your command. And everyone knows it. In Mexico and in Central America, too, people on the left as well as on the right, the sophisticates and the anti-sophisticates, the sexual Neanderthals and the sexual progressives, all of them, so far as I can judge, with a few curmudgeonly exceptions, do seem to have a soft spot for mariachi. And who could not?

V.

"Volver, Volver," then. On second thought, I once heard a rendition that was even more astonishing than the horseback performance at the Tope parade in San José. This was at Radio City Music Hall, in New York, in the mid-1990s. Vicente Fernández was performing. Radio City is an enormous auditorium with seats for several thousand people, and tickets for that performance cost sixty dollars, which was expensive; even so, those thousands of seats were sold out, and crowds were clamoring at the entrance. And who were those fans, demanding their seats? Mexicans and Central Americans almost entirely, most of them young, and more men than women.

This was not the new, young, prosperous Mexican-American middle class, except for some. This was an audience of immigrant proletarians who had spent a huge portion of their week's pay to get into that concert hall. A sizable percentage of New York's restaurant dishwashers must have been in attendance, together with any number of construction laborers and random workers, throwing away their money in an extravagant gesture. And why were they doing so? It was easy to imagine. The Mexican Revolution was the single largest social or political event of the twentieth century in the Western Hemisphere, and the Mexican emigration to the United States may well end up as the single largest such event in our new century.

Already there are said to be twenty million Mexicans in the United States, an astounding figure. These people have been wrenched out of traditional settings and thrown into modern American life, at its bottommost rung, without families or wives or girlfriends, living a kind of half-existence in which they toil in the United States, send most of their earnings back home to Mexico, and dream of their own return, someday—immigrant existences in which their wallets are in the United States and their hearts are in Mexico. And so, those young men may have lost their women and their hometowns and everything they used to know and love, but for sixty dollars, they could have Vicente Fernández and his Aztec mariachis—"Chente" Fernández, the mariachi king. They could count on Chente to re-create for them, on the Radio City Music Hall stage, everything they did not have. And Chente proved reliable.

His orchestra was in full uniform, with short jackets and studded pants, deployed across the enormous stage—guitar, *vihuela, guitarrón*, several violins, two trumpets, folk harp, and electric organ. The great man himself bounded onto the stage with his charro hat in his hand, which he immediately set down. He launched into one beloved hit after another. There have been a lot of these hits, for thirty years now. He began with current songs, in the knowledge that present-day music always carries less emotional weight. This was a man who knew how to send his concerts aloft on a proper orbit, starting at a level of mere excitement and then arching slowly upward into the heavens of sheerest hysteria, where the oldest hits, like shiny stars, are forever twinkling. The audience enjoyed those current hits, the ones he played at the start. The cheers were already loud and boisterous.

Chente's performing style was peculiar. The music required vast extremes of emotion and hammy theatricality, and not least a genuinely athletic vocal skill, opera-style in full vibrato. All the while he strutted dramatically up and down the stage, sometimes leaning on one of the stage wings, then racing to the other side, the image of energy and stamina, in his brocaded jacket. Yet, as he sang, a constant stream of audience members, one or two at a time, made their way up the auditorium aisle, past the bodyguards, to the foot of the stage, where they held up concert programs for Chente to autograph. He idled to the front of the stage, knelt on one knee to reach down, and regally affixed his signature, even as he went on singing. It was pretty strange to see him do this, given the exuberant nature of his songs and his own singing—an odd kind of distancing, to use the theatre term. The singer on his knee signing concert programs made you reflect that his many outlandish emotions and his thrilling vibrato and his athletic strutting were merely an act that he had repeated ten thousand times, and he could perfectly well sign autographs while he sang, and maybe he was contemplating his post-concert dinner, too, and perhaps he was reminding himself to hire an auditor to keep an eye on his accountant. And he never missed a beat or dropped a lyric.

A woman came to the foot of the stage and handed up a little girl of about four or five for Chente to kiss. He did kiss her, then stood her upright on the stage while he knelt at her side. I wondered if this wasn't a setup—if the little girl wasn't actually the guitarist's daughter, who had spent her entire life being dandled on don Vicente's knee and standing next to him on the stage to be cheered by enthusiastic crowds. Every single person at Radio City must have expected the girl to burst into tears or to leap from the stage into her mother's arms. The little tyke did nothing of the sort. Chente wooed her tenderly with his giant tenor voice, the violins and guitars serenaded from the rear of the stage, and the girl suddenly smiled and accepted her homage and even kissed his cheek—a coup de théatre (which, by the way, reprised a scene from Pedro Infante's *Las Mujeres de mi general*). Then another few people straggled to the foot of the stage to have their concert programs signed, and Chente went back on his knee, autographing still more programs. And still the hits came, one after another, sung at full throttle, and the guitars plucked and strummed, and the violinists sawed away, and the trumpets played fanfares and countermelodies.

I was never bored—that would have been impossible at such a performance. But I did wonder, after a while, at what moment the intermission was going to arrive. Chente's performance was a high-energy extravaganza, and I noticed that the sturdy *guitarronista* at the rear supported his heavy instrument from a cord around his neck without any sort of stand or prop to share the weight, which must have put quite a strain on the man's back. The other musicians, too, must have been pretty tired, standing upright in their natty uniforms without a single chance to sit or even stretch their legs. The concert had begun at 8, and by 10:30 it was reasonable to wonder how much longer these guys could go on.

But there was no question of an intermission. Nor did anyone ever leave the stage, except Chente himself for a moment, only to return at full volume. The audience had been enjoying their beers, and, after a couple of hours, people were fairly drunk, streaming up and down the aisles on their way to the bathrooms. Someone dropped a paper cup of beer on me from an upstairs balcony. After a while, a straggle of people began to make their way to the foot of the stage to pass along to Chente flasks containing something or other, and the great man took swigs from the flasks and smiled and passed the flasks back down, and went on singing. I did think he had begun to stagger a little, and after a while I concluded that Vicente Fernández had become drunk on stage. At least, he seemed to be.

A good many mariachi songs are about liquor and drunkenness— songs of alcoholism, really, though the alcohol mostly figures in a larger theme, which is the topic of masculinity and its tragedies. This is, finally, the single most insistent theme in the mariachi songbook, at least on its *ranchera* side—songs of one hero after another who has had to embrace failure, the tragedy of the defeated, the rage and self-pity and the alcoholic hiccups of heroes who have struggled in life and in love and have gotten knocked down at every turn, and who hold their heads high even so, and have learned how to lose, and how to maintain their masculine dignity by singing at top volume with a bravura rebellious spirit, no matter what. Some of these songs tell the story of farm laborers who never make any money and never get their girl and live a migrant life, and keep going, nonetheless—songs of labor and suffering.

Chente launched into "De un rancho a otro"—"From One Ranch to Another"—one of his greatest hits. The crowd roared. The size and depth of that roar made me realize that, at Radio City, the audience consisted very largely of people like the wandering farmworker in that song—people who had made their way through God-knows-what miseries from Mexico to New York, and had taken jobs at the lowest of low pays, and had shown an insuperably tough spirit, and had kept at their labors, and damn well deserved the recognition they were getting from a song like that. On the other hand, I found myself reflecting that Vicente Fernández himself was hardly such a person. His listeners were the oppressed and the exploited of New York, and he himself was a wealthy pop star who was probably staying at the fanciest of hotels, swathed in satin. Such were my thoughts as I sat in the center of the orchestra section, wiping the beer suds off my shoulder.

But then Chente himself must have worried, from his place on the stage, that somewhere in the gigantic hall an audience-member like me might be harboring just such thoughts, perhaps even questioning his bona fides in regard to toughness and grit—the principal topic of his own songs. Or, who's to say what he was thinking? He did seem to notice, after a while, that he was singing into a microphone, which was not an unusual thing to do, especially in a hall as cavernous as Radio City. And yet, he seemed to ask himself, does a man, a real and authentic man, a man with indomitable spirit—a *man*, in short—need the aid of something as petty and artificial as a mike? He stared at his mike, astonished. In a disdainful gesture, he put it down—the ugly, electronic thing. And, as if naked, he went on singing, unamplified, unprotected, unaided, his voice suddenly reduced to mere human scale—a shocking change, the real voice suddenly audible, the kind of voice that you never get to hear in pop concerts, the actual vibrations. Yet he sang with genuine technique, up from the belly and chest, his voice warbling with a giant vibrato, and, by God, those powerful throbs filled the hall—the voice of a slightly dented and battle-hardened opera singer who knows how to make enormous buildings resonate to his own implacable will. The audience could barely believe its eyes and ears.

It was not just that Chente was visibly drunk and that it was 11 P.M. and there had not been an intermission, and the man had been singing for three hours at the top of his lungs. By throwing away his mike, that man had just managed to drink his audience under the table. The mere mortals in the audience went on dragging themselves up and down the aisles to the bathrooms, reeling in their drunkenness and exhaustion. Chente was reeling a bit himself, from one side of the gigantic stage to the other. Yet he was visibly stronger than before, stronger than the microphone, stronger than the giant auditorium. He was Samson. He was saying, in effect, to hell with technology. To hell with the modern age and its electric cords and props! To hell with anything but the lonely hero! And behind him, imperturbable, inexhaustible, the guitarists went on plucking and strumming, the violinists bowed, the trumpeters blared, the harpist plucked—one rhythm piling onto the next, from one ranch to another, hit after hit. And, as the evening wore on, the hits wended ever farther into the past.

VI.

"Volver, Volver" is one of the songs that made Vicente Fernández's career—one of his oldest hits. It is a song with the simplicity of a folk tune, but it is, in fact, carefully confected, the composition of one of Chente's earliest arrangers and conductors, Fernando Z. Maldonado, a mainstay of mariachi sophistication. Maldonado arranged and did some of the conducting for the album *¡Arriba Huentitán!* from the early 1970s. The mere sound of the opening notes—a throb from an organ—is bound to drive fans into frenzies of recognition and expectation. I once heard Chente perform this song years ago at Madison Square Garden, where he sang with his son, Alejandro Fernández. Alejandro dresses in mariachi costume, but he is really an ordinary pop singer—a good enough singer, with a respectable ear and a syrupy voice that is pleasant to listen to, within its limited range. Alejandro has become a big star in Latin America in the last few years, thanks to his pretty face and tousled hair—or rather, thanks to his very skillful arrangers and composers. The tours Alejandro used to make with his dad back in the 1990s must have done him a world of good, introducing him to a popular audience. The comparison with Chente was never in Alejandro's favor, except from the point of view of youth. Still, father and son made a moving duo, when I saw them. The two of them brought mom on stage to take a bow, which sent the audience into ecstasies of family values.

And then father and son, on the stage of the Garden, lit into "Volver, Volver," with gusto, and hammed it up, too, stretching out the syllables, "VOL-VAIR, VOLLLLLL-VAIRRRRRR!" in a contest to see which set of Fernández lungs could hold out longest. It was a tie. The audience was thrilled. Hamming it up killed the song, to be sure. Alejandro was a little too young and sweet for the grainy edge the song requires, and he seemed to drain all the scariness out of his dad. All in all, the old man was better off performing this song by himself at Radio City, even if he was drunk and his audience was drunker.

So, then, back to Radio City. The reedy electric organ began to throb. The audience erupted in excited recognition that Chente was about to sing his greatest hit from *¡Arriba Huentitán!* The trumpets announced their opening fanfare, and, holding the mike once again, Chente broke into the wildest yelp I have ever heard, a painful *ay-yi-iiiiiii-yi!* at an impossibly high pitch—a yelp of sheer anguish, of tragedy, of rebellion, the yelp of a man who cannot be held down, a hyena's gulping laughter.

Fernando Maldonado's composition and arrangement are deceptively simple, such that, in the opening trumpet fanfare, you are already getting a melody, which you don't yet recognize as melody but which turns out to be the countermelody to the one that Chente will soon enough begin to sing:

> This passionate love
> Keeps me all stirred up
> To return!

The trumpets answered with a commentary of their own, and the *guitarrón* went loping forward at a packhorse gait, as if there was all the time in the world. This is a true *ranchera* song, reeking of farm life, a song where you can almost smell the horse and the saddle. But the key to the song rests on a single point, which is the range of Chente's vocal technique. You hear it on the album. He sings at first with a soft crooning—the sweet, echo-chamber sound of a pop star cradling the mike. It is strange to hear this saccharine singing so immediately after the hair-raising hyena scream. The crooning almost makes you put the yelp out of your mind, in the expectation that "Volver, Volver" will be a sentimental song of yearning and the bittersweet.

But when he turns to the chorus, "Volver, volver, volll-verrr!" a couple of the guitarists join him in singing, and they belt out the words in vibrato harmony, with Chente barking his words with operatic violence. Then he sobs, and he yelps again like a laughing hyena, and he's back to crooning, and again to belting out "volll-verrr!" operatically with his guitarists. Nearly every line is sung with a vocal technique different from the last, as if he were conducting a conversation among four different voices, every one of them his own: the sweet crooning, the operatic lyrical, the operatic violent, and the hysterical yelping. This is Chente's gift, his ability to raise his voice a notch in intensity, and then up a thousand notches, the ability to erupt, to go from soothing to sulfurous in no time at all, as if, all along, the man had been set to explode. And then, seething lava, he lapses back again. He is not everyone's favorite mariachi singer, and I think this is because some of the other all-time greats can outdo the sweetness of his voice. Pedro Infante, to return to him, commanded a singularly tender voice. Javier Solís, to cite another of the classic stars of the past (whose great hit "Payaso" was likewise composed by Fernando Z. Maldonado), always seems more touching than Chente Fernández—Solís, with his air of pugilistic toughness that manages to be ostentatiously vulnerable, too.

But I have never heard anyone outdo the violence of Vicente Fernández's eruptions. He sings correctly, without any sort of idiosyncratic warp, but when he goes rocketing upward from his crooning to his big-throated opera acrobatics, the abrasive edge in his voice is undeniable, and you get the feeling that Chente possesses in his own throat and chest the full range of tonality that is commanded by his warbling violins on one hand and his fanfare trumpets on the other, and maybe even a wider range, and he could out-sing them all, if he chose to do so. It is thrilling to watch him shift from one of those registers to the other. You catch your breath at the impetuosity of it all. And the hyena laughter puts an exclamation mark on his range—the animal cry of a man whose emotions seem to be veering unsteadily from one phrase to the next, as if he were tottering between the merely emotional and the utterly distraught.

There are wilder songs than "Volver, Volver." He sings "Amor de la Calle," which is still another of Fernando Z. Maldonado's compositions—a song that carries Chente deep into the realms of the heartbreaking, the hysterical, the ridiculous, the histrionic, and beyond. Nothing so extreme crops up in his rendition of "Volver, Volver," though you do feel the potential for it. But "Volver, Volver" has the surpassing virtue of offering, in its chorus, a chance for audiences to sing along. And so, at Radio City, the great Chente, staggering from those many swigs from flasks passed up to him on the stage, having already proved his ability to fill the hall with his own, unamplified operatic voice, joined with his singing guitarists to belt out the chorus, "Vol-ver! vol ver! VOLLL VERRR!" And thousands, literally thousands, of voices joined in. The massed dishwashers of New York, the construction laborers, the people who had made their way northward through routes unknown to anyone but God, the people who must have been living in terror of the immigration authorities, the young men who had left wives and children and parents at home, far away in Mexico—these people, who had splurged extravagantly on their concert tickets, roared out the words unprompted. And with the exquisite poignancy of the heartfelt and the true, they sang, en masse, "To return! return! REEE-TURRRRN!"

They were singing to the accompaniment of an orchestra that, by its uniforms alone, evoked feudal memories of the Spanish Empire and the nostalgia of a perfect village life that had never existed. There was a touch of the Mexican Revolution in their singing—the Revolution that Lázaro Cárdenas had set to music more than half a century earlier by instituting the Mariachi Vargas as the orchestra of the Institutional Revolution. But that audience was singing, finally, an anthem of their own experience—an anthem of the immigrant tidal wave, of the people who had fled the beaten-down villages and the tired old city of Puebla or the provinces of El Salvador or some other place for a worse life, but a better paycheck, in the faraway United States. These were the people who had made their way from one ranch to another until they had arrived at whatever toilsome lot may have been theirs in New York. And they were singing their plain desire—"To return, return, return!"

You may ask, was this really a ballad? This was a ballad. These lyrics expressed something more than a sentiment or an affirmation. The lyrics and the loping rhythms and even the costumes told a story, which was the story of many millions of people undergoing the hugest of historical experiences, the uprooting of the Mexican rural world that had already made a revolution early in the twentieth century and was now making another revolution, if only by fleeing to other climes.

"To return!" To return to what? you might ask. To Mexico, or maybe to the distant tropics of Central America. To the feudal world of the Catholic Middle Ages, maybe. To the Mexican Revolution and its grand promise. To the lovely celluloid plaza where Pedro Infante led his soldiers in song and wooed his girl. But, most of all:

> To your arms once again!
> I will come where you are.
> I know how to lose, how to lose,
> I want to return, return, return!

—a few thousand balladeers, drunk on their own emotions, heartbroken and inconsolable, except by song.

But I don't mean to reduce "Volver, Volver" to a sociological phenomenon. For who am I, plunked down on my stool at Fast & Fresh, with nary a worry about the Federal immigration laws, and no far-away rural village where I imagine someday returning? Mine is a non-*campesino* heart. And yet it swells. Vicente Fernández's rendition comes to an end on the boom box, some other song starts to play, I pay six bucks for my tacos to the dueño behind the counter, and he and I exchange a few wisecracks in Spanglish, our common language. And then, having passed all of fifteen minutes at his excellent deli, I am out on the street again in this modern day of ours, where some people, less astute than Longfellow and Whitman, may think the Spanish Middle Ages have nothing to do with us, and the Mexican Revolution was not our revolution, and we have no reason to pore over the intricate pleats and folds of the American nationality—this modern street where, in spite of the Brooklyn appearance of things, my ears go on ringing with Spanish fanfares and Mexican rhythms and vibrato choruses and lunatic Jalisciense shrieks.

"The Foggy, Foggy Dew"

Burl Ives, before the country knew him. Cover of
The Wayfaring Stranger, *Stinson SLP 1, 1949.*
Courtesy of John Rockwell.

JOHN ROCKWELL

"The Foggy, Foggy Dew"

I was born in 1940, which means that my life knits into this story. When I was still young, my parents got a long-playing record machine when they first came out in 1948. We had several prized discs, all of which helped shape my musical tastes. The ones that come to mind were the Beethoven and Brahms violin concertos with Jascha Heifetz (my father had played violin as a boy), Broadway musicals such as *Oklahoma!* and *South Pacific*, and albums by Paul Robeson, Mahalia Jackson, and Burl Ives. In retrospect, my love for black music came from Robeson and, even more, Jackson, and my love for operatic singing came from Robeson and Ives.

The Ives record we had was a 10-inch Stinson LP (SLP 1) called *The Wayfaring Stranger*, released in 1949. It was Ives's first long-playing record, although it contained 78-rpm takes from as far back as 1940. Now my parents are dead, but I still have their LPs; I'm looking at the Ives right now. The songs, all Anglo-Scottish-Irish as filtered through Appalachia and the Midwest and latter-day compilers like Cecil Sharp and Carl Sandburg, were edited by Alan Lomax.

They include atmospheric mood pieces like the title song and the haunting "Black Is the Color"; narrative ballads like "Henry Martin," "Brennan on the Moor," and "The Bold Soldier"; gentle, humorous, and children's ditties like "The Sow Took the Measles," "Buckeye Jim," "Jimmy Crack Corn," and "The Fox"; and an eerie, distinctly erotic ballad called "The Foggy, Foggy Dew." These are all charming or better. But "Black Is the Color" and, most important for the purposes at hand, "The Foggy, Foggy Dew," did much to define my notions of music and of romantic love, and I hold those notions especially dear.

I want to write here about that ballad and its variant versions, about Burl Ives's performance of it, and about the social and musical context that made it beloved—by me and by millions. That context is sometimes described as genteel, as opposed to vulgar (the musicologist H. Wiley Hitchcock uses the more genteel terms *cultivated* and *vernacular*). More often than not in these rock 'n' roll days, the genteel is excoriated as everything stultifying that the ruder energies of Appalachian folk music, Delta and Chicago blues and rock 'n' roll blew away. I love the manly rough stuff but want to defend our softer feminine side. Or white. Or old. All of these being the softer halves of dualities the critic Robert Christgau, who writes of "the great war between the genteel and the vulgar" and who sides passionately with the vulgar, has deployed to describe this schism.

The folk tradition led by Ives and Lomax—and also including, in the middle of the twentieth century, John Jacob Niles and Richard Dyer-Bennett—was a cultivated effort to reclaim and preserve the folk past. This was not true folk music, unmediated from oral tradition. These were educated men who researched their sources. Their predecessors dated back to early-nineteenth-century German efforts to reclaim folk traditions for nationalistic ends, an effort replicated all over Europe and one that similarly gentrified peasant roughness into bourgeois respectability.

The American movement was born of assiduous study of printed editions, field and commercial recordings, and sought-after encounters with real folk singers in the back country. "I'm not a folk singer," Ives once said. "I am a singer who just happens to like to sing folk songs." Dyer-Bennett made a similar distinction between true folk music and what he did, which he called minstrelsy, in a sense that would not earn much currency today. What followed in the folk-music movement of the 1960s wasn't any more authentic, not that folk authenticity is an absolute virtue; the best of it was an authentic expression of self. Either in their popsier folk-rock manifestations or in the tougher kind, replete with newly composed songs in a folkish idiom, the folkies had created their own idiom, had become their own folk.

Burl Icle Ivanhoe Ives did have rural roots. He was born in 1909 into a tenant-farming family in the Bible Belt of southern Illinois, and learned his first songs from his family, which had been in the United States for nearly three centuries, and especially from his tobacco-chewing grandmother, Katie White. He rode the rails in the 1930s, picking up songs where he could. All that could count as authenticist credentials. But later, drawn to the American cultural capital to better himself both vocally and professionally, he trained his tenor classically at New York University.

What emerged, with genteel tenors like Ives and Dyer-Bennett (who was so genteel he was actually born English, and who sang in white tie and tails), was a kind of folkish music that harked back to the parlor of late-nineteenth-century America. I can still remember my beloved grandfather, who was born in 1879, singing Charles K. Harris's weeper, "After the Ball." This was the first great Tin Pan Alley hit, from 1892, and it launched the commercial pop-music bandwagon of the century to come. The way Ives and Dyer-Bennett sang folk ballads came as close to my grandfather's parlor sentimentality as to Appalachian keening.

The motivations for these early folk revivalists were both non-commercial, reflecting the leftist idealism of the 1930s, and commercial. Ives sang in New York clubs and on Broadway, had his own radio show, and eventually sold records and made films. Of his later career—he died in 1995—I have little to say here, liberated as I am from suffering under direct correlations between artistic worth and political correctness.

Ives became fat and at least outwardly jolly, although his imposing Big Daddy in *Cat on a Hot Tin Roof*, on Broadway and in the film, hinted at a darker side. Some of his early fans shunned him after he named names before the House Committee on Un-American Activities. The chief name he named was that of Pete Seeger, with whom he had once appeared as part of a group called the Union Boys '44. For thirty years after that, he hardly performed in New York. But a concert in 1993 at the 92nd Street Y in Manhattan reunited Seeger and the by-then-wheelchair-bound Ives, presumably signaling a healing of long-past rifts in the folk community.

The young Ives was thin and muscular (he played football professionally) and had a wonderfully pretty voice. It was highly, even painfully sensitive, yet never effete, and it was masterfully deployed, with expressive shadings of pitch, lively rhythm, and a magical ability to shade the modern tenorial chest voice into various gradations of so-called head tone and falsetto. It was singing that gave immense pleasure in itself, but also made an expressive point. It sounded mid-American, full of the sturdy optimism and poetic undercurrents that defined the heartland.

And it was still close enough to operatic style to allow people to make a smooth transition from Enrico Caruso's Neapolitan folk songs and John McCormack's Irish ballads to a more direct, more American voice. In the course of the nineteenth century, operatic singing in general and tenor singing in particular had grown louder and more assertive, better to make a proper sonic impact in ever-larger halls with ever-larger orchestras. Those changes in turn reflected a shift of patronage from the aristocracy in palaces to the newly ascendant bourgeoisie in concert halls.

Before, despite the pyrotechnics of the castrati and star sopranos, much operatic singing, with its soft high notes and almost conversational declamation, was closer to Ives's cultivated folk singing than to Caruso. "Head tone" defines a light, gently nasal tone that can easily shift upward into falsetto. Tenors started taking their high notes "from the chest"—belting them out athletically—by the middle of the nineteenth century. Late-century verismo opera in Italy and Wagnerian opera in Germany placed a new premium on manly vocal strength and ringing high notes.

Henry Pleasants, the late vocal critic and Foreign Service agent, argued that modern electronics permitted a restoration of the conversational ease of seventeenth-century bel canto singing, and he used Frank Sinatra as his poster boy for that theory. Light tenor singing of the Ives sort could only enjoy a comeback with the advent of recordings and concert amplification. As halls grew ever larger, no natural voice, however pumped up (Rudy Vallee used a megaphone), could hope to fill them. But three scrawny kids with guitars and a big amplifier and monster loudspeakers could eventually do so with ease.

During the twentieth century, however, people grew tired of operatic belting; they didn't need it anymore. They turned instead to the renewed conversational naturalness that the microphone permitted. Operatic outbursts began to sound mannered and strange, a homegrown version of what we hear as the swooping screeches of Chinese opera. Ives's voice was in that sense transitional: it had the sheen and finesse of opera without its latter-day Puccinian vulgarities and without the pretensions of operatic ritual. It was genteel in expressive impact without being genteel in social conformity. And it moved people. As Ives's youthful singing shaped my images of romance, millions of others felt a similar longing for an emotion that conformed to gentility but subverted it at the same time. But amplification and recording also made untutored folk singing commercially viable, and hence led directly to our era of putatively vulgar popular entertainment.

It was not just crooners and arena-rock musicians who benefited from the electronic revolution. The enormous impact of radio in the 1930s and '40s—Ives had a popular radio show early on—helped to build individual careers but also to disseminate entire genres, like folk music. People like my grandfather sang "After the Ball," which as a mega-hit had quickly become a part of folk music, from sheet music and from memory. Radio and recordings, offering the option of hearing performances and unfamiliar music passively, may have blunted personal music-making. But they led to a huge expansion of available repertory, and hence helped transform our musical experience.

⁂

John McCormack recorded "The Foggy Dew" in 1913, but here's where the story of this song, or these songs, gets complicated—as it does with so many folk songs whose attribution is undocumented in oral tradition. Originally there were two "Foggy Dews," both love songs but with different words and melodies, one from Suffolk in England and the other from Ireland (McCormack's version, of course). During the struggle for Irish independence, new, political words were overlaid onto the McCormack song, recalling the 1916 Easter Rebellion, and that version is still often heard (Sinéad O'Connor recorded it with the Chieftains on their *Long Black Veil* album). There is even a time-honored pub in Dublin called The Foggy Dew. It has a Web site.

Ives sang the English song, called "The Foggy, Foggy Dew," and it too exists in many versions, although always recognizably with the same roots. Originally it was pretty racy—so much so that Ives spent a night in jail in Mona, Utah, in the '30s for singing a song so unsuitable for Mormon ears. But the version Ives sang by the time he made recordings is less sexually explicit and more elusively poetic.

Ives's recorded version—as collected by Sandburg and included by Lomax in his *Folksongs of North America* (with only one "Foggy" in the title) and by Ives himself in his *Burl Ives Song Book*—is in three verses, each ending with the refrain "Was/Just to keep her from the foggy, foggy dew." It tells the tale of a young weaver who woos a "fair young maid" but makes the mistake of keeping her from the aforementioned dew. One night, she comes to his "bedside," weeps, cries, and is held by the weaver "just to keep her from the foggy, foggy dew." In the third verse, he is again alone, but now with his son (presumably from the fair young maid), and every time he looks into his son's eyes, they remind him of her—and of winter, and part of the summer, "And of the many, many times I held her in my arms/Just to keep her from the foggy, foggy dew."

Aside from its evocation of a common English climatic occurrence, the foggy dew is a metaphor for whatever you want it to be. For me, it clearly implies mystery of the sort beloved of Romantic painters, with their ghostly churchyards and ruined buildings. Dew means ghosts and spirits, the romantic Wilis of the ballet *Giselle*, will-o'-the-wisps, trolls, and faeries. For humans, it means unfulfillable romance but also death, an English version of Wagner's love-death, a state attained in his opera *Tristan und Isolde*. Isolde's love-death takes place in Tristan's home in Cornwall, just across England from the birthplace of "The Foggy, Foggy Dew."

The music, especially in Ives's singing, is particularly haunting, because while it is firmly in a major key (G major, in his recordings and his songbook), his bard-like tone and phrasing and the tune itself evoke the modal plaintiveness of an older time, before the codification of modern Western harmonic practice. The tune achieves this illusion in part through the suggestions inherent in its foggy romantic aura and lamenting lyrics ("ah me! what could I do?"). In more specific musical terms, there are its chantlike eighth-note reiterations of the same pitch ("only, only thing that I did," on four rapid Gs and four Bs in the same bar) and quasi-modal emphasis on the subdominant, a third above the tonic of G, rather than the more comfortably common dominant, up a fifth. Ives's singing on the Stinson LP—oddly, *Poor Wayfaring Stranger*, an otherwise wonderful CD on the British Flapper label, which collects a great amount of early Ives material, including my Stinson LP, includes a faster, feebler take of this one song—is controlled yet vulnerable, with a superb use of *voix mixte*, the typically French eighteenth- and early-nineteenth-century blend of head tone and falsetto. It breaks your heart, even in a supposedly cheerful major key.

The reason Ives was arrested in Utah was that two earlier, longer versions of this same song are more explicit. Here, with only slight variants in the first three verses: "Many's the night she rolled in my arms/All over the foggy dew." After she weeps and cries, she announces, "Tonight I'm determined to sleep with you/For fear of the foggy dew." The next verse goes on: "All through the first part of that night/How we did sport and play."

In one version, included in Lomax's *Folksongs*, the final verse pictures the happy couple later in life. "I never told her of her faults"—presumably meaning her unashamed expression of sexuality—"and never intend to do/Yet many a time as she winks and smiles/I think of the foggy dew." The other version, sadder and closer to the Ives, finds them after their passion is spent regretting the prospect of children. She marries another. The last verse is the same one Ives sings, full of regret.

⁂

Around the time of Ives's first recordings in the early 1940s, Carl Sandburg called Ives "the mightiest ballad singer born in any century." But does that make "The Foggy, Foggy Dew" a ballad and, more precisely, an American ballad? The music dictionaries disagree as to how recently the term *ballad* in folk music came to imply narration. Some suggest that until the late seventeenth century, the difference between ballad and song was slight to non-existent. The German *Musik in Geschichte und Gegenwart* identifies the first reference to ballad as a narrative song from 1761. The English *Grove Dictionary of*

Music and Musicians argues that "ballad tunes are a part of the general body of folk music, only hypothetically separable from the mass of lyric folksong."

Still, however far back into the Middle Ages its roots may lie, "The Foggy, Foggy Dew" does indeed tell a story, however short—and many ballads dealing with love are indeed short, as opposed to long historical narratives or Bob Dylan's tale-telling. And I would argue that the song's very Americanization, which could be interpreted as a blunting of the song's initial suggestiveness, is actually poetically superior. I like the supposedly bowdlerized version; the romanticism, the fear and excitement aroused by that mysterious foggy dew is purer. But then, I'm genteel.

The "genteel tradition" as defined by George Santayana represented a secularization of Puritan rigor into middle-class propriety. Its polite presumptions—its "cool abstract piety," as Santayana called it—became every American's "tyrant from the cradle to the grave." There was, to be sure, more to this denaturing of Calvinism than mere philosophical entropy. As Charles Hamm argues in *Yesterdays: Popular Song in America,* the Civil War had exhausted America, and the troubles of the conquered South were best kept far away.

"Nostalgia had run its course elsewhere in the Western world by 1865," Hamm writes. But in America popular song was turned into escapism. The parlor was the domain of women, who have retained a disproportionate power on cultural boards of trustees to this day. Scorn for gentility can easily slip into scorn for women. Men deal with war and money and politics; women deal with children, the kitchen, and culture. Soft-grained tenors have had a long appeal in the parlor; they're the olden-day equivalent of the romance novel. Leslie Howard, not Clark Gable.

The latter part of the nineteenth century was the lull before the twentieth-century storm, musical and otherwise. Eventually, even the parlor grew weary of such sentimentality, the popular mood having shifted to ragtime and vaudeville, and the piano to the player piano to the phonograph and radio. After the Golden Age of Tin Pan Alley songwriting and the treacle of Hit Parade pop, the folkies—or at least some folkies, those who weren't determined to become one with the working man—appropriated the genteel tradition. But gentility had mutated by then. With two wars and the Holocaust, it became ever harder to cling to the old pieties, however secularized. In that sense, the late '40s and early '50s—Pleasantville—were the last ebb of gentility before the hellhounds of rock 'n' roll were unleashed.

Lomax collected a lot of rougher music, and so did Harry Smith. I love that music. But there seems no reason, insisting upon your love, to scorn everything else. If the purist folkies booed Dylan at Newport in 1965, rock critics repaid the favor by mercilessly attacking such genteel latter-day folkies as Joan Baez and James Taylor, not to speak of our sappier country-pop balladeers (Ives made a couple of country albums himself late in life). Softness, and hence gentility, has never died. Most obviously, in Britain, are the post-operatic soprano warblers like Sarah Brightman, Charlotte Church, and now Hayley Westenra. Add to them an ongoing undercurrent of female confessional rock—recently, Tori Amos, Sarah McLachlan, Liz Phair before she went pop, Jewel, Dido—and you have a persistent gentility, bubbling under in the age-old war with ruddy vulgarity. Female politesse versus crude, manly vigor.

Thus, Taylor and a few other confessional males aside, it is no accident that gentility has survived in the persons of women singer-songwriters. Christgau's "dustbin of gentility" is a lovely phrase, but it lines him up all unconsciously with men and manly women. Rock, the true successor to folk, was always a boy's game, with "chick singers" looked at askance. The prejudices of capitalists and soldiers and other regular guys have been absorbed by rock 'n' roll. The only real folk music is the kind that slides into punk rock. The only good chick singers are the tough ones, preferably lesbian.

The manly bias of rock 'n' roll intellectuals masks their indebtedness to the long philosophical tradition, extending back to Plato, of rationalist moralism. The beautiful is wantonly open to unregulated feeling; the good and the true must claim precedence over roiling passion and mere surface allure. But in the nineteenth century, American gentility was infected by German Romantic Idealism, through the agency of Emersonian Transcendentalism. Feminine equality became less a weak reduction of art to manners than a threatening challenge to rational righteousness: a conduit for feeling, suppressed by extramusical ideology, as a virtue in itself.

These are of course sweeping generalizations, just like Christgau's notion of a Manichaean struggle between the genteel and the vulgar. Real life is more complex than that: things overlap; tendrils entwine. Burl Ives appealed to the genteel but thought of himself as a friend of the working man. He was a manly football player with a sweet, some might say effeminate voice. His music drew from many sources and appealed to many audiences.

His "Foggy, Foggy Dew" started out as an English folk ballad, became American in words and music and cultural ownership, attained gentility in versions by Ives and Dyer-Bennett, and even—rather unsuccessfully—in an artsy folk arrangement by the higher-than-highbrow English composer Benjamin Britten. It is as much a part of our folk culture, our genteel culture, our culture, as any ballad ever born.

For me, as a boy with my beloved 10-inch LP, this ballad in this performance helped define vocal beauty, shaping my taste forever. And it embedded deep within me an ideal of romantic beauty and romantic love that has colored my entire life. Not determined it, but colored it. It may be a genteel song, but genteel people suffer passions and pain, too. Who knows what tensions and longings seethed in the parlor? In our age, which prizes the authenticity of roughness, gentility reinforces my lifelong conviction that beauty, even when seemingly contained within the strictures of form and tradition and gentility itself, can have haunting power. Beauty can be strength; the genteel can be real.

"Come Sunday"

Duke Ellington and Mahalia Jackson on the cover of Black, Brown and Beige, *originally released by Columbia Records in 1958. Courtesy of Columbia Records.*

STANLEY CROUCH

"Come Sunday"

How big does a person have to grow, down in this part of the country, before he's going to stand up and say, "Let us stop treating men, women, and children with such cruelty just because they're colored?"

— MAHALIA JACKSON

In the second week of February, 1958, Duke Ellington brought the great gospel singer Mahalia Jackson into a Hollywood studio and recorded one of the masterpieces of the twentieth century, a somber yet elevating religious ballad called "Come Sunday." No doubt about that. The way Ellington and Jackson sounded together has yet to be equaled in the world of jazz, because we have not since had such a great jazz orchestra and we have not heard again a voice of such spiritual breadth and depth. Their meeting was a pinnacle for the music of New Orleans. The Crescent City is where Jackson was born, having left at sixteen for Chicago, where she would soon be noticed for singing with stirringly individuated passion, volume, and rhythm. We can always hear what was made of that New Orleans music at the hands of the peerless Ellington, whose art was so thoroughly shaped by the influences of Sidney Bechet, Louis Armstrong, King Oliver, and Jelly Roll Morton. But the music that Mahalia Jackson made with Duke Ellington was, above all else, created in recognition of a reckoning. It was created during a tumultuous moment in the history of this nation, at a time when a social wrong that should have been taken care of about eighty years earlier was no longer going to be accepted by those upon whom it had been imposed. It is in this distinct context that what those two superior artists brought off together should be understood. Such awareness neither increases nor decreases their artistry, but it surely deepens our understanding.

In 1958, America had not yet descended to the low place where it now resides, caught in commercialized sexual desperation and hungering for something of spiritual value that cannot be reduced to a spotted trend or packaged like dead sardines in oil. There was still serious religious music in that year, and Mahalia Jackson was its most shining symbol. Within her marvelous brown being, the entire heritage of the religious music from slavery and the spiritual music that came after bondage was given communicative residence of a special kind. She was a woman of large beauty and regal presence. Her voice was humbling because it was absolutely pure in its impersonality, which meant that it sounded unlike personal expression or autobiography or belief. She possessed the quality that all great religious singers must have—the ability to give the impression that they are not telling you what they believe or what happened to them somewhere in the world at some time, no, but what was always true in every time and in every place.

That was the source of the purity in her sound, and that purity was also an instrument of innovation because she and the composer Thomas A. Dorsey took the traditional spiritual—or plantation song of worship—and created an extension called gospel. With her huge and compelling voice, so accurate in pitch and so perfectly developed for the expression of nuance, the singer from New Orleans had, with a succession of recordings and public performances, made a world for her art and had remained beyond reproach. To hear her was to have a transcendent spiritual experience that was not beyond criticism but was surely beyond bloodless commentary because, in the world of God, people need to sing something or play something or just listen.

Jackson had built up quite a career by the time she met Ellington in the studio after arriving by train in Los Angeles at Union Station, which has a floor plan in the shape of a cross and an exterior that is a hybrid of Spanish Mission, Moorish, and art deco styles. She had appeared on concert stages across the nation and in Europe, had been heard and seen on radio and television, and had proven in person to be one of the most impressive performing artists on the face of the earth. Jackson had neither dreamed of nor expected any of that. Her wishes were spiritual, but the mechanics of her time had made it possible for her to sell millions of records and for her voice to be in far more homes and ears than she could ever have imagined. It had all been an unprecedented surprise.

By 1958, she was revered by her listeners for making unspoken conditions of feeling audible and exalting. The brown diva from New Orleans, who had done scullery work, picked plantation cotton, and studied how to "do" Negro hair in Chicago, certainly was treated by the Negro Red Caps who carried her luggage and then the waiters and porters on the train from Chicago to Los Angeles with the special respect reserved for Negro nobility. She was one of those who had earned aristocratic status through their deeds and, therefore, had proven the truth of the democratic ideal. Her meals had to be given that special touch and her quarters made especially comfortable and each of her wishes attended to with the eloquent passion of *service,* as opposed to servitude. She may well have been asked for autographs and, however used to it, might have almost felt overwhelmed by the fuss they made of satisfying her every desire. But that was how people of her level of achievement were handled, and they, far more often than not, proved themselves true aristocrats by the grace with which they received the very best that someone could offer them.

But at that time, there was trouble in the land. It had been building in the four years since Senator Joseph McCarthy had been brought down through the instrument of television by Edward R. Murrow and censured by the Senate. The abuse of power and the danger of lies in high places were made clear, and the sting of that public recognition of such abuse was national. McCarthy had been proven to be a demagogue. The senator from Wisconsin had sensed that the country was in the mood for demagoguery and he had made the most of it. McCarthy had lied, he had exaggerated, he had created the kind of public paranoia that almost always grants more power to those who say they are protecting society, and he did his best to make the committee gavel sound like the crack of doom. We can say from this distance that Senator McCarthy, in the wake of a world war against the very obvious evils of European totalitarianism, was in the process of bringing American democracy as close to that very evil as he possibly could—though we can never be sure whether or not McCarthy was fully aware of everything that he was doing when he claimed to know the location of Communist spies here, there, and everywhere. But the most important fact of the matter is that unchallenged lying in high places is antithetical to democracy and its effects are nothing less than evil. In the wake of the McCarthy years, and the understandable obsession with freedom of speech and censorship, something that was to reshape the entire United States had already jumped off.

That something had been renewing itself since the end of the Civil War and had most recently drawn an enormous amount of fresh wind from the 1954 Supreme Court decision *Brown v. the Board of Education*. Led by the remarkable Thurgood Marshall, an NAACP legal team had argued against school segregation before the nation's highest court and had won. So in that same year that McCarthy fell, the unchallenged consistency of the lying at the center of segregation and racism took a serious hit. Goliath was down on one knee. The destruction of segregation at large was the next job. Both those genteel whites and redneck crackers residing below the Mason–Dixon Line were about to learn that there were native-born citizens who had an interest in living in the United States and, thank you very much, having their constitutional rights as well. A new storm in the sky that would later be called the Civil Rights Movement was in motion.

By 1958, young men and women were shattering and battering and challenging Southern racist conventions at every opportunity. It was not so much that Negroes had *finally* had enough; they had *always* had enough. The bigoted white man had always been a serious pain. The only difference at that point was that communities that had been largely independent—usually with some version of their own schools, churches, and businesses—were making use of their secular and religious resources for organization, for support, and for the numbers necessary to have their way and tear the house of segregation down.

Duke Ellington, who was ever-attentive to the troubles and triumphs of his people, had in mind what seems to have been a complexly supportive message to those who were in the midst of that Southern battle. It was a message in music that spoke with an understanding of slavery, of tenant farming, of exclusion, of segregation, and of the heroic gratitude for merely living that is at the center of the bittersweet joy of jazz and of Negro culture at large. Ellington had no doubt about whom he needed to project that spiritual missive, to nail its notes upon the air of the world. There was just the one. He and she had been talking about doing some music together for years, and now, when he reached her by phone, the answer was an unqualified yes (though she actually hoped her deeply admired Ellington would not try to take her out of her spiritual world). He gave her the dates and sent her some music with no words, just notes.

Ellington had decided to reach back to January of 1943 for the music that he would adapt for the recording. It was from his single piece of symphonic jazz, *Black, Brown and Beige*, which had premiered in New York at Carnegie Hall. Ellington called the piece "a tone parallel to the history of the American Negro." It was nearly an hour in length and traced the Negro from slavery through the end of the Civil War and then into the North. The long work contained extraordinary invention in melodic, harmonic, and rhythmic terms. There was protean, uplifting zest, as well as sumptuous, romantic, and prayerful lyricism—every aspect counterpointed by the ambivalence that went with living in America and the unfinished business that was still at hand. Part of its singular charisma came from the way in which Ellington made use of all kinds of black American music, from field chants and marches to very urbane and seductive melodies. It was all personal, and every bar drew upon Ellington's massive compendium of remembered experience—his many gigs in small clubs where pistols might be drawn and fired; the greasy, after-hours piano battles where he learned his trade; the Harlem clubs owned by murderous gangsters; the uptown Negro days and nights of great parades, style, dancing, inimitable food, and brave, wistful dreams; the Savoy Ballroom, where his band took on the best of the day as they played for couples in love or looking for love or for some hot and sensuous affirmation hiding behind a silent mating call; and every college he worked in, black or white, from coast to coast, not to mention all of the private, the very private, and the very, very private parties. The music told a story that began in the plantation fields of the South and ended in a penthouse on Sugar Hill in Harlem, with plenty of Negro life between those extremes. It was the most ambitious jazz piece of its time and remains a formidable achievement. Yet, as he was to learn over and over, Ellington's work was beyond the ears of the critical establishment, which largely hated it and said, essentially, that the boy needed to stay in his own backyard and not attempt to go beyond his own talents or the depths of his idiom.

Ellington was deeply hurt by the rejection of his work and chose never to pursue the symphonic form again, even so imaginatively remade for his own purposes. *Black, Brown and Beige* was never performed in its entirety after that, though he presented excerpts from it in his concerts. Along with his shorter pieces, he continued to write long works—which he usually called "suites," whether they were or not—but none of *Black, Brown and Beige*'s length or of its expanded ambition. Though Ellington's hero-worshipping supporters deny that his musical horizons were so stunted by his detractors, I don't think there can be any other explanation for his artistic behavior after that fateful night in January 1943.

Nearly four years after the Supreme Court's monumental decision of May 17, 1954, Ellington had conceived of something that was, as he knew, unexpected. Why not redo his extended work and focus its development on "Come Sunday," with Mahalia Jackson delivering what would amount to a prayer in support of the movement that Ellington and Jackson and every member of his band had been a part of since their first day on earth? It could work. The band was in *very* good shape since it had fired up the Newport Jazz Festival in 1956 and shot Ellington back up to the top of his profession after a low time in the valley of the business. They had been strutting, usually without barbeque, roaring with fury when it was necessary, and laying it on with finesse when there was just no other way to do it. It wouldn't bother them—as if anything ever did. They had been around the world, had traveled by every possible means, had blown all kinds of stuff in everybody's faces—gangsters one night, society types the next, high school boys and girls falling in love the night after that. They had been to the mountain top and they had been treated like slop. You couldn't tell them anything.

You couldn't tell Duke Ellington anything, either. He had been through it all, experiencing elevation and humiliation, something that was hard to avoid if one traveled the entire United States, East to West, North to South. During the era of segregation, an entirely different pattern of travel arrangements had to be made, one in which people learned that separate but equal was surely separate but very rarely—if ever—equal. In Ellington's case, it was much the same as it was for all bands once they traveled by bus behind the Cotton Curtain and knew themselves to be where the enemy regime was in full power. When they could find no lodgings, they had to stay at the homes of local Negroes, who might well supply them with meals much better than one could get any place other than the finest hotels. Or they might find themselves in the local whorehouse, sleeping downstairs while Ellington spent the night upstairs, with the girls. The Negroes who attended their dances Down South were separated by ropes or, as was often the case, waited until the white folks were done and then hit the floor. If there were no Southern dance halls, Ellington and his band would play tobacco barns, where country Negroes and their girls showed up, some nearly reverent, others stooped or made gangly by too much of that moonshine. Everything could be all right or it could be far from all right. Even in the 1950s, long after Ellington had been an internationally respected artist, trumpeter Clark Terry was told a harrowing story by other band members after he joined the organization. When the band was in Carbondale, Illinois, a gangster shot into the floor during a tirade that ended with his cutting Ellington's tie off just below the knot and demanding that he dance for him. The road could be wonderful, it could be awful. That was how it was and anybody who says anything different is lying.

So by the time Ellington got Mahalia Jackson in his musical circle, he had many things on his mind and there had been some horrific things happening Down South of late; they lay in the air like the sweet stench that follows battle and had to be in both Ellington's and Jackson's thoughts. For one, in the summer of 1955, Emmett Till, while visiting from Chicago, had been murdered in Mississippi for getting fresh with a white woman (what would that constitute now?). The casket at his funeral in Chicago was open, and his hideously unrecognizable corpse was viewed by thousands because Till's mother wanted the world to know what those rednecks had done to her boy. As for those gallant men who considered murder not too much but just enough to protect the soft pink purity of Southern womanhood, they sold the details of how they killed the boy to a magazine after their acquittal on September 23, 1955. That murder roared through black America, waking those who had slept through the malignant evils of racist violence and the toy courts of the South. Till's mother said of the tragedy, "Two months ago I had a nice apartment in Chicago. I had a good job. I had a son. When something happened to the Negroes in the South, I said, 'That's their business, not mine.' Now I know how wrong I was. The murder of my son has shown me that what happens to any of us, anywhere in the world, had better be the business of us all."

It was the business of the music that Duke Ellington intended to make with Mahalia Jackson but he had to figure out a way to elegantly walk over the eggshells of her extreme religious beliefs and her refusal to ever sing any blues. She was adamant about that. That is where Ellington's genius for adjustment came in. He was still smarting from the critics' rejection of *Black, Brown and Beige* when he premiered it fifteen years earlier, but he had figured out a way to ram at least some of it down their throats and make them like it. Most importantly, he had figured out how to create a piece of music focused on the American Negro that would culminate in the appearance of Mahalia Jackson. It would be his statement on racial matters and on the inevitability of victory over segregation.

What he had in mind was not propaganda but a fully artistic statement about things as they actually were at the time. But in order to make the music work for Mahalia Jackson, and to keep her from feeling aesthetically abused, he had to streamline his marvelous composition so that it did not take in that much of the city or tell too much of the tale of the people on Sugar Hill—not everything, anyway. In the original concluding section, a waltz eventually gave way to a slow, symbolic coupling that would not do at this time. Ellington would keep only the heraldic opening movement, with slight adjustments, and shape it into three parts, or tracks, that formed an overall ABA structure, the first introducing or alluding to all of the themes but focusing on the South; the second introducing the contrast between religious gravity and blues; the third introducing a picture of the Negro in the world of Harlem, where such an astonishing culture of limitless style and groove had been created. What Ellington now conceived of as the first part was perfect, because it told the story of slavery and was also possessed of a feeling of determination and of struggle, both emotions undergirded by a melancholic longing and a high-mindedness. In the second track, we hear the first of the two themes that Jackson will sing, "Come Sunday," contrasted with some rowdy blues. With track three, an extraordinary variation on the first track, Ellington set up the New Orleans priestess with a big, proud, mocking fanfare of roaring, stomping city music, which was also vitally urbane, meditative, even lonely, yet maintained awareness of its spiritual roots (represented, again, by the trombone statement of "Come Sunday" near the end of the track). It was symbolic of how much things had changed as Southern Negroes, formerly sure-enough hicks, became city dwellers well adjusted to the pace of their environment and ready for more opportunities to present themselves. The work song, the spiritual, and the blues—separately, in counterpoint, or intertwined—went the furthest and the deepest. They were all there. That was side one.

In the days of the long-playing record, with about twenty minutes on each side, Ellington decided to make the first side instrumental and the second side, opening with "Come Sunday," two vocals separated by a violin feature for Ray Nance. It was a shrewd decision, because those who had no use for jazz or who had no use for such sophisticated jazz composition could just turn the record over, looking for their Mahalia, and be knocked to their knees. Now the original fifty-seven-minute work had been trimmed to thirty-six minutes and was, for all practical purposes, a different piece of music with vastly different ends in mind. With no pronouncements, Ellington wanted the world to hear how deep his commitment was to Negro history and culture. He also wanted everyone to know how strongly he felt about racial justice and how deeply he believed in the necessary support of God.

Writer Patricia Willard, who was then doing public relations for Ellington and had been given the assignment of making sure that everything was all right with his guest singer, recalls that Ellington and Jackson had suites across the hall from each other at the Watkins Hotel near Adams and Western Avenue. Some of the band may have been at the Watkins Hotel and others might have been scattered around Los Angeles because, as Willard remembers, "They may not have been welcome in Hollywood just yet. They soon would be but, at that time, they may not have been." Willard also recalls that Jackson did not take her assignment lightly. "Mahalia was in such awe of Duke Ellington. She was nervous because this man was one of her idols and she wanted to be good enough. She was very humble."

The session took place at Radio Recording Studios in Hollywood. Mahalia Jackson knew her music when she arrived in Los Angeles and was to learn the lyrics either before going to the studio or at the session itself. Ellington made her the star of the sessions that she attended so that she would focus only on what she was going to do and he would use his musicians solely in an accompanying or obbligato role. He would record the other material after she was done. She didn't need to hear the other music; all she needed was to give her soul over to the notes that were there for her to fill up with the light that was in her voice.

"The thing about 'Come Sunday,'" says Wynton Marsalis, "is that it brings together a lot of different American music. It alludes to many different forms, first the pentatonic sound of the Spiritual and the fiddle ballad, then the I–IV progression that is central to the blues, then the movement to the relative minor, which was done a lot in fiddle tunes as well as American popular songs. The use of the augmented V chord, which is always evocative of the blues, and when it precedes a dominant II chord, connects us to the sound of 'Mood Indigo.' It also has, in the final turnaround, the type of triadic inversions that we find in almost all Afro-American church music. And the AABA form is the classic form of the American popular song. So what it all adds up to is a summary of a number of American things, including that allusion to Ellington himself, to 'Mood Indigo.' But then, why should he leave himself out? There's nothing more American than Duke Ellington."

Though the words have been dismissed as banal, even by so great a writer as Ralph Ellison, I have to disagree with all detractors because, from the very opening, it all becomes clear what Ellington had in his thoughts and there is hardly a more straightforward way to say what he wanted to say. This deeply private man enjoyed the freedom of being absolutely explicit. He also knew that if there was anyone on the earth who could give the meaning the majesty with which he felt it, he now had that person in the studio, standing there in all her heavy brown beauty. The melancholic gentility on her face was characteristic of those who knew both the universal weights of life and the specific burdens of color, but that knowledge had been given an added strength by the blessing that is the capacity for the expression of unlimited purity. It was the disarming authority that Mahalia Jackson gave him in spades as she made even clearer the obvious emotion Ellington had put in his lyrics.

> Lord, dear Lord of love
> God almighty
> God above
> Please look down
> And see my people through
>
> Lord, dear Lord of love
> God almighty
> God above
> Please look down
> And see my people through

Knowing the troubles and the dangers facing the Negro people, whether in political situations or not, Ellington was offering a prayer that these people, who had been so abused on every level, who had been disappointed so often, be looked out for, taken care of, and gotten through what was surely the bloody and sacrificial road that lay ahead.

Next there was a cosmic sense of order and recognition of the fact that always stood up above all others: no matter how much darkness there was, no matter how black and unlit the night might be, all of it would pass, and light, of every sort, was a forthcoming fact. The great Jackson, as much aware of that fact as Ellington himself, let those words and notes loose with so much confidence that they needed no overstatement to achieve a convincing state. The idea is a simple one, but the way she sings the words that are the nouns and what she does with the adjectives and the verbs creates the wonder and the inevitability that only our most special singers have within their power.

> I believe the sun and moon
> Will shine up in the sky
> When the day is gray I know it's clouds passing by

Out there in the struggle that is not about color but is about the nature of living, discord and turmoil arrive and lie like rings of thorns inside the mind that needs those thorns removed and their wounds, if not healed, at least attended to with what results in the experience of that stranger called comfort. The Negro, even when it was illegal, learned that there was a God who lived somewhere above all that the world had to offer or used to oppress, above bondage or sheer bad luck, and that He could be met on Sunday, with nothing more than belief, which was the ticket that allowed entrance into something called peace. If no other day, Sunday was there, waiting. With her expansive and intimate lyricism, Jackson again makes each word, each image, and each state that is referred to, both earthly and unbound, some mixture of opposites made true by the clarity of her emotion.

> He'll give peace and comfort
> To every troubled mind
> Come Sunday, O come Sunday
> That's the day

The fatigue that arrives with abuse is always the servant of defeatist feeling. The tiredness that is experienced as the weight of all wrong seems never to lighten, the blows that strike the soul arrive as if from a tireless machine, and the universe appears, for all purpose, to have become an infinite and deaf ear, capable of hearing nothing—not whining or wishing or praying. A man as private as Ellington, who said his prayers every night and who must have often felt nearly overwhelmed by the complex of artistic personalities, deadlines, and the treacherous dictates of show business, had learned to lean up against something that was as invincible as it was invisible, as quirky as all get-out but, finally, right there when it was needed. At Newport, just eighteen months earlier, the great spirit of God, appearing in the flesh as a blonde overtaken by the swing of his band and the searing blues tenor saxophone of Paul Gonsalves, had pulled Ellington up from the dregs into which his career had fallen. Incapable of sitting still, this all-American sandy-haired heifer jumped up and started dancing with so much liberated soul that she sparked the crowd to near-hysteria and gave Ellington's career another wind strong enough for the bandleader to capture the cover of *Time* magazine. So Ellington knew—yes, he did—that there was always that resource out there, effortless and infinite, capable of reversing fortune or defining it. That was as true to him as the facts of spring and should be understood together. Jackson, who had lived for so many years in the world of prayer, which could take place anywhere and at any time, and who also looked upon life as a great gift beyond all suffering and all want, again connects two things that seem outside of logic with the lyric power of her diction, her time, and the control of her voice's timbre.

> Often we'll feel weary but He knows our every care
> Go to Him in secret He will hear your every prayer
> Lilies of the valley they neither toil nor spin
> And flowers bloom and spring time birdies sing

The importance of *knowing* that one can be heard by the highest of high authorities has to be repeated, because that is a central message of the song. If all else has been exhausted and has exhausted you in the process, you may have to get down on your knees in private, or in the secrecy of your mind, and ask for what you truly need. Jackson reiterates that with an empathetic sincerity, the sound of having been there, too, giving the words *secret* and *prayer* a feeling of safety as well as a lilting tenderness in the way she lifts up off the note and pushes in more depth at the same time.

Often we'll feel weary but He knows our every care
Go to Him in secret He will hear your every prayer

Finally, Ellington is talking about the South, where the Negro worked from "can't see in the morning to can't see at night." Those sore muscles, those calluses, that aching back, those tired feet meant almost nothing when Sunday arrived and it was possible to dream into the face of God, to think about a future different from the hard present. Something like transcendence could happen then and give the kind of strength not only to get through a difficult life but to support those who would risk their lives trying to change things from the way they were to another way altogether. Jackson, having known what it felt like to pick plantation cotton during the week and to feel free on Sunday, sings the final words with the illuminated recognition that is not a flight from the world, as so many would have it, but a stepping into a deeper understanding of the meaning of freedom.

Up from dawn 'til sunset
Man work hard all day
Come Sunday, O come Sunday
That's the day

She then hums a chorus, the language gone and the music delivered with a voice that is beyond words but that amplifies all of the feelings that they were written to express. At this point, Jackson becomes the mother of us all, those hums arriving on Sunday morning accompanying the smells of breakfast in preparation; she becomes the mother at the bedside of the sick; she reminds us, through her ascendant tenderness, of the reverential empathy that underlies all of the dreams and the facts of civilization. There it was. Ellington had had his way and had made a masterpiece with the aid of an artist of unparalleled quality, one of the geniuses of feeling that America has been so lucky to produce. Her second song, "The Twenty-third Psalm," is also a masterpiece, and it perfectly concludes the recording with a foreboding solemnity that constitutes tragic recognition of great danger yet assumes ultimate salvation. But we will not discuss that right now. We will end by letting Jimmy Woode, who played bass on the date, tell us about the effect Jackson had. "At one point, Duke decided to turn out the lights and have Mahalia sing 'Come Sunday' a cappella. Now, as you know, the band at the time was full of alcoholics, knuckleheads, dope shooters, kleptomaniacs, gamblers, and just about any kind of person you would meet in a band. They were all there. These men had been through it and they had been around. They were, you might say, rough customers. So we're all standing or sitting in the dark listening to that wonderful and incomparable sound of Mahalia Jackson, who was just singing her heart out. Beautiful beyond belief. And don't you know that when those lights came back on, there was not a man among that wild bunch who did not have a very, very obvious tear in his eye."

"El Paso"

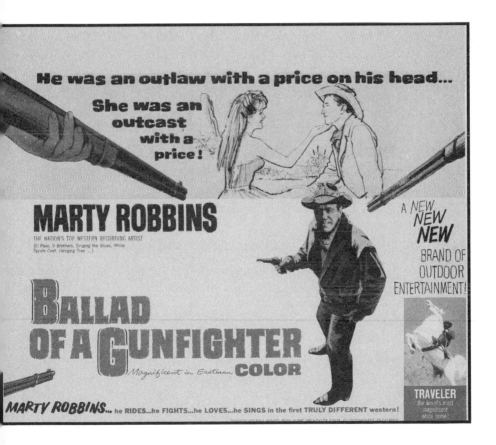

The singer as gunslinger. Poster for the original release of Ballad of a Gunfighter, *starring Marty Robbins, directed by Bill Ward, Parade Pictures, 1964. Courtesy of Sean Wilentz.*

JAMES MILLER

"El Paso"

I don't consider "El Paso" a country-and-western song. It's a cowboy song, early American folk music from the western United States. It's not an old song—I wrote the song—but it's the type of song that you would have heard eighty years ago. That's not country-and-western.[1]

—MARTY ROBBINS (1925-82)

As a multimedia child of the early fifties, weaned on the cross-merchandising of six-shooters and lunch pails blazoned with pictures of Hopalong Cassidy and Davy Crockett, I naturally assumed that cowboys and the songs of the West were a key part of my patrimony. I was encouraged in this assumption by my parents, who had a copy of the famous John and Alan Lomax anthology, *Best Loved American Folk Songs.* My mother would sometimes play songs from the book—"Home on the Range," "The Old Chisholm Trail"—on our upright piano.

For John Lomax, this music shed light on "that unique and romantic figure in modern civilization, the American cowboy"—a figure that Lomax dramatically placed "on the skirmish line of

---

[1] Quoted in Alanna Nash, *Behind Closed Doors*, p. 446. For full citations, see Notes, Books and Recordings.

civilization. Restless, fearless, chivalric, elemental, he lived hard, shot quick and true, and died with his face to his foe."[2]

For my mother, cowboy songs had no special significance; they were simply part of an American boy's common culture, like baseball and apple pie. But for my father, the ballads cut closer to the bone in ways that I didn't understand until I was much older.

He was born in 1920, on Cactus Hill outside Bartlesville, Oklahoma, where cowboys still tended cattle. The son of an oil worker active in the local union, he had grown up watching the films of Gene Autry, listening to the Western swing of Bob Wills and his Texas Playboys—and helping his dad recruit new members for the union. The first in his family to receive a Ph.D., he had a scholarly interest in Western music as well. Besides the Lomax book, he had acquired a number of the albums of union songs and folk music, including cowboy ballads, recorded by Woody Guthrie, Burl Ives, and Pete Seeger for Moses Asch and his Asch label in the 1940s.

As I grew older, I put away my toy spurs and coonskin cap. But I never quite outgrew the Western music I was raised on—which helps explain my continuing affection for one of the greatest cowboy ballads of the twentieth century, Marty Robbins's "El Paso."

༺ঙ༒ঙ༻

Marty Robbins was of my father's generation and came of age at the height of the Great Depression. But whereas my father grew up in the Dust Bowl, Robbins was from the outback of Arizona.

Born in 1925 in a high-desert homestead outside of Glendale, northwest of Phoenix, Robbins was one of nine children. His father, an immigrant from Poland, was only intermittently employed—the family was sometimes forced to live in a tent.[3]

One of his earliest memories was of listening to the tales of the Wild West told by his maternal grandfather, Bob Heckle, a former cowpuncher and Texas Ranger who had also traveled with medicine

---

[2] John A. Lomax, *Cowboy Songs* (1925), "collectors note."

[3] Colin Escott, notes to *Marty Robbins at Town Hall Party*. Bear Family DVD 20007 AT (2003).

shows, hawking books of his own cowboy poetry. "The stories that he would tell me were cowboy stories that he heard around the campfire," Robbins later recalled. "My grandfather inspired me to be a cowboy, I guess. That's what I wanted to be. Because I thought a lot of him, and he was a cowboy, you know."

Grandpa Heckle died when Robbins was six, but the boy was hooked: he became an avid reader of Western fiction (and would later in life publish a Western novel of his own). He picked cotton so that he could see the latest Westerns at the local picture show.

"I first started praying to be a cowboy singer," Robbins once explained. "I wanted to be Gene Autry. I wanted to ride off into the sunset."[4]

And so the young Robbins became a singer of cowboy songs, coming to master the "western" part of country-western—a mishmash of tall tales, old Irish music, and minstrel hokum. He doubtless knew the first popular recording of a cowboy ballad, "When the Work's All Done This Fall," a song based on a poem written by Montana cowboy D. J. O'Malley in 1895, reprinted in John Lomax's first book, *Cowboy Songs and Other Frontier Ballads*, in 1910, and sung by Carl T. Sprague, once a real cowboy too, in the 1925 recording that turned it into a Western standard. (It would be recorded by Robbins himself thirty-six years later.)

In 1929, the Arizona Wranglers, from Phoenix, recorded "Strawberry Roan," the saga of a bucking bronco that couldn't be broken; it became the basis of a 1933 movie, *The Strawberry Roan*, featuring Ken Maynard, Hollywood's first "Singing Cowboy," who delivered the song in an abrasive nasal monotone. (Robbins would record "The Strawberry Roan," too, in 1959.)

As a result of the growing popularity of musical Western films, demand started to outstrip the supply of more or less genuine cowboy songs. This created an opportunity for new singers and new songwriters, like the Sons of the Pioneers, a Hollywood-based harmony group with no firsthand experience of the frontier but a knack for imagining what it was like and writing tunes that evoked its

[4] Quoted in Nash, *Behind Closed Doors*, p. 442.

wild beauty. Their 1934 recording of "Tumbling Tumbleweeds" was a national hit, and a year later the song became the centerpiece of the film that turned Gene Autry into a Hollywood star—*Tumbling Tumbleweeds*.

A veteran of medicine shows, Gene Autry had first achieved fame as "Oklahoma's Yodelin' Cowboy," performing on radio station KVOO in Tulsa, Oklahoma, before moving on to WLS and joining the cast of its *National Barn Dance* in Chicago. Autry had style; he sang with a bluesy twang, like the Singing Brakeman, Jimmie Rodgers, but his delivery was relaxed and his diction clear, like Bing Crosby, the Old Groaner.

In *Tumbling Tumbleweeds*, as in the many films that followed, Autry wasn't only a cowboy who happened to sing; he was *Gene Autry*, frontier good guy. Invariably playing himself, he was miraculously able to defeat crooks and killers with a song and a sunny disposition—or, if that failed, some sharp shooting. Even in the depths of the Great Depression, a Gene Autry film seemed to promise, there was one place in America where justice would prevail. That was back home on the range—"where you sleep out every night, and the only law is right," as Autry sang in "Back in the Saddle Again," his radio theme song.

⚜

In December of 1959, my radio theme song became "El Paso."

At a time when the radio was full of watered-down rock 'n' roll sung by pretty boys bereft of talent, Marty Robbins and "El Paso" had the narrative arc of an epic film. The music was lilting, the singing gorgeous. The recording lasted for nearly five minutes, an eternity by the standards of the time. The lyrics told the story of a cowboy who kills, and in turn is killed, all for love of Felina, a Mexican girl. Even more memorably, the outlaw narrates his own death. He sings of the bullet going deep in his chest, the girl kissing his cheek, and his very last words: "Felina, goodbye!"

At the time, I was twelve years old. Though the killing spree of Charles Starkweather and Caril Fugate had terrorized my hometown of Lincoln, Nebraska, the year before—and though my grade-school teachers had taught me to duck and cover in the event of nuclear war—I knew little about life and less about death. An introvert by temperament, I spent much of my youth daydreaming. Thanks to *Gunsmoke* and *Have Gun Will Travel,* two favorite TV shows, the image of a lawless frontier was vivid in my mind. But most of the time, it bore no resemblance to the world I thought I knew.

That winter, my family drove across Iowa to Moline, Illinois, to celebrate Christmas with my mother's extended family, the Anderson clan. There were six brothers and sisters still living on the banks of the Mississippi in 1959, all of them descended from Swedish stock, all of them still churchgoing Lutherans like my mother, and they were one image of a good community—loving, cozy, civilized.

Grandpa Anderson worked at the local Chevrolet dealership, which one of his older brothers owned. On this visit, I was to earn some money and learn some discipline by helping him take inventory in the parts department. It was a dirty job. The weather was bleak. Driving to the dealership every morning under sleet-gray skies, I would warm up by listening to the radio—and what warmed me the most was hearing "El Paso."

I tried to interest my grandfather in the saga of the amorous outlaw and his inevitable death. But "El Paso" left him cold. Like most of the other members of his clan, grandpa Anderson was a loyal company man and a lifelong Republican, with little interest in the wilder side of life. He didn't much like Westerns, he explained, and he would rather listen to Dinah Shore—Chevrolet sponsored her TV show, after all.

∽∐∾

Marty Robbins recorded "El Paso" in the course of an all-day session held in Nashville, Tennessee, on April 7, 1959. The session produced twelve songs that would appear later that year as a long-playing album entitled *Gunfighter Ballads and Trail Songs.*

A cast member of Nashville's "Grand Ole Opry" since the early 1950s, Robbins first achieved fame in the country field by writing and singing love songs in a smooth, sweet tenor, like Eddy Arnold in the 1940s. When sales of his love songs began to sag, Robbins tried his hand at rock 'n' roll. In 1954, he cut a version of Elvis Presley's first record, "That's All Right," and had a country hit with it, unlike Presley. He cut a version of Chuck Berry's "Maybellene" and had a modest hit with that, too. Then, in 1956, his version of "Singing the Blues" became a number-one country hit, edging out Elvis Presley's "Hound Dog."

The following year, Robbins traveled to New York to work with veteran pop producers Mitch Miller and Ray Conniff. Targeting Presley's teen audience, Robbins recorded a new composition of his own, and in the spring of 1957 "A White Sport Coat and a Pink Carnation" rivaled the mainstream popularity of Presley's "All Shook Up." More pop hits followed—"The Story of My Life" in 1957, and "Just Married" in 1958—all of them featuring the kind of close-blended vocal accompaniment that Presley had made a fixture of his hit recordings with the Jordanaires.

To reproduce the sound of his pop records on the road, Robbins hired a group of vocalists, the Glaser Brothers, a trio of Jewish farm boys from Nebraska. "We grew up in Spaulding," recalled Jim Glaser many years later, "and the nearest town was sixty miles away. The town wasn't on our side. A lot of people thought you had to be illiterate to like country music." Ironically rescued from a life of rural idiocy by their mastery of song forms symbolically associated with rural idiocy, the brothers joined Robbins and his touring show.

"In those days, Marty traveled in two cars, or sometimes station wagons," Jim Glaser says. "Marty carried a little ukulele, made by the Martin Guitar company, and would often pass the hours and miles by singing every song he could think of, with Bobby and me adding harmony. Many of the songs were Western songs, and it was during this time that Marty decided to do an album of these songs."

Robbins also began to make up new Western songs of his own. One of the first was "El Paso"—inspired, he would later say, by driving through the West Texas town on a family car trip from Tennessee to Arizona.

"The song took him several months to write," recalls Jim Glaser: "Each time we went out on tour, Marty would sing the latest verses. . . . By the time we accompanied Marty into the studio to record the song, we had it down so well that it only took four takes to get the final version, and two of those were false starts."[5]

"El Paso" shares some of its ingredients with the Western music that enchanted Marty Robbins as a boy. The song as a whole projects an aura of authenticity, like the ballads of Carl T. Sprague; it is sung with the sort of open-hearted sincerity that Gene Autry made a trademark; and the vocal blend of Robbins with Jim Glaser and Bobby Sykes evokes the freedom of the open range as surely as do the soaring harmonies of "Tumbling Tumbleweeds."

But the *music* itself bears no resemblance at all to the sorts of songs sung by Sprague, Autry, and the Sons of the Pioneers—and neither do the lyrics, which invert the exaggerated optimism of the singing cowboys of the 1930s.

Robbins's West is a dangerous place of large passions and empty violence, where death and eros are intertwined. Though *Gunfighter Ballads and Trail Songs* included such traditional numbers as "Billy the Kid" and "Utah Carol," its keynote songs were "El Paso" and "Big Iron." Here he evokes a specifically American fear of falling on the wrong side of the skirmish line of civilization, a fear that also informs the noir Westerns that Hollywood had begun to make after World War II: from *Red River* and *Winchester '73* to *High Noon* and the TV series *Have Gun Will Travel*.

There are decent men in this West—but they are loners and outriders, and there is always a chance that a good man's blood brother will turn out to be evil incarnate (as happens in *Winchester '73*). The Paladin character in *Have Gun Will Travel* is a bounty hunter with a brain and what seems like a good heart—though where he found his moral compass is obscure, not least to some of the outlaws he brings to heel. (For the album cover of *Gunfighter Ballads*, Robbins wore *vaquero* black, just like Paladin.)

---

5 Memo from Jim Glaser to Norma J. posted on her Web site devoted to Jim Glaser: http://norma100.com/glsrobbns1.html.

The unrequited lover who narrates "El Paso" is not quite beyond good and evil. He expresses shock at his ability to kill a stranger in a jealous rage. But he is irresistibly drawn by his love for Felina, who is "wicked" and "evil" and "casting a spell." His violent end is as sublimely preordained as that suffered by any hero in Greek tragedy.

The song is cast in the form of a *ranchera,* the Mexican brand of "ranch" music associated in the 1940s with Jorge Negrete and Pedro Infante, impassioned singers who were also Mexican movie stars, personifying on screen "El Charro Cantor," Mexico's version of the Singing Cowboy. The outlaw who sings "El Paso" tells his story in an operatic idiom that his Mexican maiden will surely understand. The song is taken at a brisk waltz tempo characteristic of *ranchera*— mariachi horns would be a natural addition. (In 1960, when Robbins tried to recapture the epic spirit of "El Paso" by recording a new gunfighter *ranchera,* "San Angelo," he in fact added mariachi trumpets.)

The music itself proves how porous cultural borders can be. Robbins's cowboy is trapped by a passion that bursts forth in a song-form that belongs to another world. Virtue and vice blur along this borderline. In the badlands the song evokes, power grows out of the barrel of a gun—and death seems almost a form of deliverance.

<hr/>

A similarly ambiguous moral universe was dramatized in the most popular Hollywood Western of 1959, *Rio Bravo,* a movie set in an anarchic border town much like the "El Paso" of Robbins's song. As in "El Paso," much of the action takes place in a cantina. "Every man should have a little taste of power before he's through," declares an outlaw who has just been forced to lay down his guns by the town's often unreliable deputy sheriff, an alcoholic gunslinger played by Dean Martin. As the film's director, Howard Hawks, famously quipped, he had made the movie, in part, as a rejoinder to *High Noon* with its picture of a high-minded lawman who must beg for help. "I didn't think a good sheriff was going to be running around town like a chicken with his head off asking for help."

The taciturn sheriff in *Rio Bravo,* played by John Wayne, gets help without asking for it. The sharp-shooting rifleman takes his name from the hostile power that he has mastered: "Chance" is fearless, independent, and a natural-born Stoic whose virtue is tested not just by killers but by a lady of low repute, like Felina from "El Paso."

When outlaws roll into the border town to spring a comrade from jail, the gang's leader tells the cantina's band to play "The Cutthroat Song"—a sinister mariachi that the Mexican Army used to break the will of the men defending the Alamo. Waxing philosophical, Chance explains the meaning of the music: "No mercy for the losers."

The *ranchera* in "El Paso" is similarly evocative. From the moment the music starts, it rushes forward to embrace death—like the cowboy who sings the song.

⚜

The Nashville recording session for "El Paso" involved four musicians in addition to Robbins and the Glaser Brothers. The players—Louis Dunn on drums, Bob Moore on bass, Jack H. Pruett on rhythm guitar, and Grady Martin on lead guitar—included several members of Nashville's A-Team, as the city's best pickers were called. The most important of these was Grady Martin, whose calling card was an uncanny ability to alter his sound to fit the needs of virtually any song— from the fleet boogie-woogie he plays on Red Foley's 1949 recording of "Chattanooga Shoe Shine Boy," to the thundering 12-string guitar riff that he uses to open Roy Orbison's 1964 recording of "Oh, Pretty Woman."

But all of Martin's other achievements pale beside the gut-string solo he improvised for the recording of "El Paso." For chorus after chorus, the guitarist accompanies Robbins's narrative with a nonstop sequence of runs, flourishes, and fills that are more redolent of Gypsy flamenco, or of Les Paul's playing on "Vaya con Dios," than of anything commonly heard in a *ranchera* or an ordinary Nashville session.

Martin's guitar becomes a second solo voice. It dances and gallops, and it makes the song seem to lift off the ground.

⚜

As a result of the popularity of "El Paso," Marty Robbins was able to fulfill a childhood dream. He starred in a Hollywood Western, *Ballad of a Gunfighter* (1964).

Like Gene Autry in all of his films, Marty Robbins appears as himself in *Ballad of a Gunfighter*. He is a frontier Robin Hood who steals gold that he gives to the local padre and the poor of San Angelo, a Texas border town. The town's cantina is home to a bordello full of Mexican maidens, including Felina from "El Paso" and Secora, the heroine of that song's sequel, "San Angelo."

In the film, "Señor Marty" falls in love with Secora. With the help of the padre, he tries to convince Secora that there is good in everyone, even a whore like her and a thief like himself—to become good, all you need is love.

The soundtrack opens with symphonic variations on "El Paso" and climaxes with Robbins's recording of "San Angelo." A corrupt sheriff traps Robin Hood by kidnapping Secora and forcing her lover to ride into an ambush. As in the song, Secora dies—and so does Marty Robbins.

The religious imagery could not be more explicit. In the film, the padre smiles beatifically as Secora and Robbins die. The cowboy is a kind of saint—a martyr, redeemed by his transcendent love, a love stronger than death.

⁂

Years after "El Paso" first captured my fancy, I asked my paternal grandfather to tell me about his life. We talked in the living room of a refrigerated bungalow in suburban Houston, where grandpa Miller had moved after he retired from the Phillips 66 petroleum company. He had worked as a roustabout for Phillips for almost his entire adult life.

Since I had developed an interest in the history of the American left, I pressed him about his political beliefs as a young man. Almost offhandedly, he revealed a fact that even my father didn't know: Phillips had banished him from Tulsa to remote Shidler, Oklahoma, to punish him for his union activism. A onetime socialist, he became a lifelong Democrat with a sharp sense that there is no justice in this world.

The ice broken, we kept talking—he was normally a man of few words. Before settling down to raise his family in Oklahoma, he explained, he had gone north to find work in the coal mines of Kansas. His earliest memories were of Texas at the turn of the twentieth century. As a teenager, he had hawked newspapers on the streets of Fort Worth. He recalled traveling in a covered wagon, and he recounted how, as a child, he and his parents had had a frightening encounter with Indians on the open range (nobody got hurt).

The West that Marty Robbins conjured up in "El Paso" never existed, of course, any more than the West depicted in "Home on the Range" or in John Wayne's *Rio Bravo* did.

But as I came to understand while talking to my grandpa Miller shortly before his death, the West was a bigger part of my real patrimony than I had previously understood. Though not a cowboy, my grandfather had certainly lived on the skirmish line of civilization—and he had certainly fought the good fight in a morally uncertain universe.

And that is another reason why I still warm to hearing Marty Robbins exalt a lost world of rough passion and stoic courage—in what may be the last great cowboy ballad.

"Trial of Mary Maguire"

One of the Texas courthouses where the trial of Mary Maguire did not take place. County Courthouse, Zapata County, Texas, *photograph copyright 1997–2004 by Brett Cameron and Ted Lerich, reprinted by permission. This picture, and those of the 253 other Texas county courthouses, can be viewed at www.texascourthouses.com.*

ED WARD

"Trial of Mary Maguire"

No, you probably haven't heard it.

There's no reason you should have. It wasn't a hit, even a regional one, and it came and went like many another pop record. It's a record that tells a story that never happened, sung by a guy nobody's heard of, a record that never sold. It's not the kind of hyperkinetic faux-Motown the Northern Soul brigades in England love, nor is it the gospel-drenched drama of what the Brits call Deep Soul, so it's never shown up on any of the compilation or single-artist soul albums that come out in England each year. So why bring it up? Because it keeps running around in my head.

⚜

I'm embarrassed to say that I managed to live for thirteen years in Austin, Texas, five of those years as the music columnist/critic/reporter for its daily paper, constantly looking for stories, yet I never ran into or heard of Bobby Patterson. He might even have played in Austin while I was living there, but since I'd never heard of him, it's unlikely I would have gone even if I'd known.

According to Bill Dahl's liner notes for *Soul Is My Music: The Best of Bobby Patterson* (on Sundazed Records, a reissue label in Coxsackie, New York, that is better known for surf and psychedelic obscurities), Bobby Patterson was born on March 13, 1944, although Dahl neglects to say where. Unlike the vast majority of soul artists, he didn't grow up singing in church. His father was a big blues fan who played harmonica, albeit not professionally, and Bobby grew up going to shows with him, hanging out in bars and playing the jukebox, and, after getting a guitar at the age of thirteen, playing live. He must have been good: at sixteen, he won a talent contest that earned him a contract to record a single for Liberty Records and a plane ticket to L.A. so he could do it. The record, though, never came out.

By the time he entered the University of Texas at Arlington, he was recording for small local labels and playing around the Dallas–Fort Worth area with his band, the Royal Rockers. At school, he met John Howard Abdnor, Jr., who constantly mentioned that he was going to get his father to start a record label. Bobby remained skeptical: Abdnor Sr. was in the insurance business, not the record business. But sure enough, one day John Jr. showed up with a record on the Abnak label, and Bobby began to get ideas.

In fact, he got to record before the boss's son did (John Jr. showed up as half of Jon and Robin & the In Crowd, who in 1967 had a Top 20 hit, produced by Dale "Susie Q" Hawkins, with "Do It Again a Little Bit Slower"), cutting his first single for Abnak in January 1966 with his new band, the Mustangs. Like Bobby, the Mustangs were all young—as young as sixteen—and yet all were veterans of the local club scene.

Although Abnak is remembered today (to the extent that it's remembered at all) as the home of the Five Americans of "Western Union" fame, pretty standard white-bread pop music, it's clear that Bobby Patterson and the Mustangs represented something special to Abdnor Sr. and his crew. Once the label began to have regional hits, it spun off the Jetstar label for Patterson and any other soul acts it might acquire (none, as it turned out). Bobby and the band had their own rehearsal studio in the basement of the insurance company, and enjoyed hanging out there, shooting pool and playing ping-pong and working on their act. When they weren't there, they were probably touring, playing fraternity dances, doing the club circuit, traveling around Texas and Oklahoma, and trying to get their records played on the local radio stations. Or else they'd be at Summit Studios in Dallas, recording one.

It would be tedious to go over the many records Bobby Patterson and the Mustangs recorded, showing how each one tried and failed to make it onto even the local charts, and Dahl does an excellent job in the liner notes to *Soul Is My Music* (from which I've culled the facts here). The album contains forty of their best songs, which are well worth hearing. Well, thirty-nine songs; "Trial of Mary Maguire" is on there twice.

It came after Patterson had, at long last, a hit. "T.C.B. or T.Y.A." was a funky, Joe Tex-ish workout (Tex is a big influence on Patterson) that got as high as 36 on the national soul charts in April 1969. It never went near the pop charts, but even what seems on paper to be a very mild triumph was a big deal for such a tiny label toward the end of the era of tiny labels. It may also have been hindered by its title, which Bobby always explained meant "take care of business or turn yourself around," but which most people knew as "tear your ass." I guess it's equally possible that it was *helped* by the title.

Having tasted success, Abdnor knew it was time to storm the pop charts. He'd hired a house songwriter, Ray Winkler, best remembered these days for Jim Reeves's "Welcome to My World," a huge crossover country-pop smash from 1964, and Winkler and one J. Jones and one J. Carroll came up with "Mary Maguire." Here's Bobby from Dahl's notes: "Ray must have been around sixty-something then. 'Trial of Mary Maguire' was something that he had wrote a long time ago that John took a liking to and wanted me to record. He sent me to Memphis to record that thing. I cut it here ⌈in Dallas⌉. I went to Memphis, I came back here and cut it again. He just kept having me trying to cut that thing, trying to get it in a pop vein. It just wouldn't lend itself to R&B or pop." The hot producer/engineer Chips Moman produced the Memphis session. "Chips said 'Man, I can't do no better than you done on this thing. What more can you do with it?' So when I got back to Dallas, we wound up using my track. We cut it up there, but John didn't like it, so we didn't use it. He said 'I like yours better.' I said 'I thought you said mine was too funky!' So he said 'Well, we're gonna go with yours.' "

Studio costs weren't what they are today, but even so, sending Bobby to Memphis and working with Chips Moman couldn't have been cheap. Abnak had quite an investment in "Mary Maguire." It did them no good: the record disappeared as quickly as Bobby's other ones. This was worse news for Abnak than for the Mustangs, who, after all, worked live dates all the time and made money from them. And although there were a few more Bobby Patterson records on Jetstar, Abnak folded in 1970, and Bobby went to Jewel Records in Shreveport—probably the hottest place at the time for the sort of soul-blues mix Patterson did—where he wound up doing some producing. He got further into the business end by becoming a promotion man for Malaco Records, which remains America's top soul-blues label, and finally he returned to Texas, got back into performing, and as I write holds down a morning radio shift on KKDA, an AM station in Prairie View.

🐾

They were so sure of themselves. "Mary Maguire" was a natural. And Bobby sang the hell out of it, too. Why didn't it work?

Playing the two versions back to back is revelatory. The first, the Memphis/Chips Moman version, starts with an organ, suggesting the solemnity of the courtroom, perhaps, for a good twenty seconds, and it's easy to imagine Bobby, standing alone under a spotlight, as he begins to tell the story. His voice is solid and sincere, which it has to be: the story itself is not going to be particularly believable, so the teller has to make us believe it. Moman's production here is a textbook Southern soul template: the organ, subtly joined by an electric bass, then strings gently insinuating their way in as the bass marks out the rhythm, joined by rolling martial drums. But there are already problems, and they don't lie with the production. Patterson has trouble rendering the lyrics, fluffing the last word of the second line, which then has to be followed by some amazingly clumsy songwriting: "In form, too small for a woman" reads okay on the page but utterly confuses the ear, something you'd think a professional songwriter would have learned to avoid. There's no blaming Bobby for this, either. It's just flat-out a bad line, and it comes way too early in the song for the ear to forgive.

The instrumental track builds and builds for two verses as the details of the story pile up. Orphaned, and in charge of her two younger siblings (the youngest of whom is two), Mary Maguire, this child-woman, has stolen some bread and is on trial for the theft. The details laid out, the backing reaches a climax, and the first chorus comes in, with the judge reminding her that if she's guilty, she'll have to pay. The chorus is backed by rather subdued female vocals, which serve to punch out the "if you're guilty" hook. After the judge speaks, things settle way down, with a plaintive tone from the strings and a couple of rolls on the drums, after which the bass comes back, the organ leaks into the strings, and Mary offers her defense: she couldn't get a job, the weather was bad, and the children were hungry. It wasn't, she says, really stealing. Up pops the judge (it's chorus time again) and reminds her again that if she's guilty, she'll have to pay, and now, two minutes and twenty-three seconds in, it's time for the payoff. A modulation changes the song to a slightly higher key. Nobody in the courtroom thinks she's lying (well, she's not; she admits she stole the bread), but there's another blown line thanks to poorly managed backup vocals (which sound like an overdubbed Bobby and a woman) on some crucial words that sound like "as they gazed into her eyes." Then the judge makes his last appearance—to let Mary off, of course—and then comes the song's last, but fatal, songwriting mistake: rhyming, within two short lines, "self" and "myself." Even with Moman's classically churchy Memphis arrangement and production, even with the second rhyme occurring on a note sung with more passion than Bobby has yet put into the song, energy that he obviously has been saving for just this moment, there's a feeling of deflation. Nor does it help that the chorus, which takes the song out into a fade, repeats yet another rhyme, "himself," twice.

Though Moman and Patterson both did exemplary work on the Memphis version of the record, there are good reasons for Abdnor's ambiguous feelings about it. At the time "Mary Maguire" was recorded, radio programming was evolving into today's pseudoscience. Compared to contemporary microniched programming, it was primitive, but programmers were beginning to analyze aspects of records that had almost nothing to do with their content but everything to do with the way listeners were supposed to attend to them. The goal was to keep listeners at the same station, to avoid a "dialout" to another one or, worse, turning the radio off. The listener would have to endure the song before getting to those all-important commercials that brought the station's income. Of course, commercials, too, were sources of dialout, but they were short and rarely produced the reaction—"Yuck! I *hate* that song!"—that resulted in the immediate dialout. A commercial tends to be thirty seconds or less; a song could be up to three minutes.

And there was one of the problems with "Mary Maguire": the Memphis version, as smooth and beautiful as it was, came in at 3:43. This was a record that was going to the pop stations, the same ones that had played the Five Americans and put them into the Top 10. Pop stations had played long songs before: Bob Dylan's "Like a Rolling Stone," which had been played at its whole six-minute length, and then the Doors' "Light My Fire," which had received far more airplay with an edited version. In the time it took to play "Like a Rolling Stone," you could play two songs and a commercial and have time for the deejay. But let's face it: Bob Dylan was Bob Dylan. People already knew who he was before "Like a Rolling Stone," and he'd even charted earlier that year with "Subterranean Homesick Blues," so even pop radio knew what he was up to. Bobby Patterson was not Bob Dylan. No way could Jetstar force its way onto commercial pop radio with a song—even a masterpiece, which they had to have been convinced this was—almost four minutes long.

There were a couple of other technical problems, one being that intro. If you had a long intro, the deejay tended to talk over it, or fade it down, and that disrupted the flow of the song. The faster you could get into the song, and the faster you could get to the chorus or the first hook, the better off you were. The Memphis "Mary Maguire" takes almost a minute to get to that first chorus, and that's risky. But there was no way to shave the intro. The bigger problems were the two verbal miscues and the badly punched-in harmony vocals. Given what was at risk, there was ample reason to hesitate to release the record.

It's kind of hard to tell from the quote from Bobby cited above, but it would appear that he'd started on the Dallas version before he went to Memphis, then came back and finished the Dallas recording. It wouldn't cost too much to come up with a finished second version, even if it had to be done from scratch, because there was no way a Dallas studio would cost as much as a Memphis one with a big, hit-making track record.

The Dallas "Mary" is as completely different a record as you could make and still be faithful to the song. The intro is a split second: a quick slap of the snare, and then a quick descending line played by guitar and bass, and there's Bobby with the first line. Replacing the organ and strings is a gospelly group of female backup singers. As the first verse builds, some strings—a small section this time—add color and drop out, and then we hear the bass again, with the treble setting much higher than in the Memphis session, and bumping around while a small horn section—almost certainly the Mustangs themselves—does a staccato "diddle-iddle-it" riff.

But it's the chorus where Bobby's arrangement really kills Moman's: instead of having the chorus girls sing along with Bobby, they echo his words—"GIL-lay!"—to drive the point home. And this is well before we're a minute into the song. And instead of what we now realize was a dead space after the end of the chorus in the previous recording, Bobby interjects a guitar sting into the silence and then the bass joins him for that same descending figure with which the record started. Brilliant—it's a second hook!

The second verse, then, puts all the elements behind Bobby—strings, girls, horn riff—and he's got the backing to really take off on his vocal. We now sense Mary Maguire pleading because, as a good soul man, Bobby's learned how to plead for his life, and he makes it seem that's what's at stake here. The second chorus swells up, and then Bobby uses the sting and descending line to do the upward modulation, making it look easy, and we're into the final verse just like that, with the bass still jumping and strings putting down a pad, and the girls doing a wonderful arpeggio—"bummm . . . bummm . . . bummm . . . !" apropos of nothing, but giving some charming variety to the proceedings. And after repeating it, they re-sing it as "aaaahhhh," to blend with the strings. Corny? Hell yes! You pull out *all* the stops on something like this. Then, in this version's only misstep, at the end of the last chorus, the chorus isn't so much sung again as it's repeated, as in *mechanically* repeated. This sounds to me like they copied the last chorus and edited it on—and, in fact, I think I can hear the edit. The fade is quick and dirty; it's a real shame that a better way couldn't have been found to end the record. It does, however, get out in just under three minutes, so in those terms, Bobby had made a record radio could play. Radio, of course, didn't agree.

For days after I first heard *Soul Is My Music*, having ordered it on a whim from the Sundazed publicity guy, thinking it might make a nice piece for my "rock history" slot on NPR's *Fresh Air* program, I couldn't get "Mary" out of my head. I kept hearing girls going "GIL-tay" in the back of my mind. These are things you look for in a pop record when you're trying to make a hit single. So it's worth considering for a minute why the record didn't make it.

First, there was the record company. It was small, based in Texas, and best known for its other label, which put out tame white pop-rock. Still, they'd had a hit with this same artist with "T.C.B. or T.Y.A." and presumably knew a little about getting heard on the national scene. Now, of course, I have no idea what Abdnor's strategy was, but I do know what I would have done in his place: get the momentum going on the black stations and then cross it over to pop. Hell, that's not even thinking—that's what everyone did in those days, that's how it worked.

Imagine a deejay at a soul station who remembered the long scream Bobby opened "T.C.B" with, the James-Brown-by-way-of-Joe-Tex rhythm groove that vamped underneath it, the Stax-like horns under the chorus—all clichés, but imaginatively regrouped. Now the guy working the Jetstar account has shown up with . . . this? Who's Mary Maguire, anyway? I've never heard of her. And what's this storytelling shit? A quick look at the number-one soul records for 1969 and 1970 shows only one song that could be conceived of as a narrative, Brook Benton's "Rainy Night in Georgia," and that was by an established star on a major label. It, too, had been written by a professional songwriter with Nashville connections, Tony Joe White, and it was probably in play at the same time as "Mary" was. It also did exactly what "Mary" was supposed to do: went number one on the soul charts and number four on the pop charts, peaking in March 1970.

Of course, there was no way to start this record on the pop stations. They were deluged with their own hopefuls, thanks to the aftershocks of the post-Woodstock explosion in rock bands. The bigger stations were going through the nightmare of trying to balance this onslaught with enough "good" music so they didn't lose the older consumers who were the targets of most of their advertising; the number-one pop singles in

1970 alternated between things like "Raindrops Keep Fallin' on My Head" and various Motown records ("I Want You Back" and "ABC" by the Jackson 5, "War" by Edwin Starr) and, incongruously, "Thank You (Fallettinme Be Mice Elf Agin)" by Sly and the Family Stone. This was mostly soft, reassuring music; the only veteran rock band represented is the Beatles, and they're only there with "Let It Be" and "The Long and Winding Road," both from a final album so overproduced that it was reissued in a "corrected" version in late 2003. "Mary," though, would have fitted in there nicely. Its message of justice tempered by humanity was as uplifting as that of "Bridge Over Troubled Water," another number one that year. But again, it would have had to have started moving on black radio, and that was not about to happen.

I think it's down to the song. What, other than the prestige of hiring a guy who'd had a massive hit, inspired Abdnor to hire Ray Winkler, is beyond me. It's not like Bobby couldn't handle a country tune: one of his earliest recordings as a teenager was of the Ernest Tubb classic "Walking the Floor Over You," and the porous membrane between country and soul is well documented. Bobby's idol, Joe Tex, was the most country of all soul singers, using Nashville songwriters and musicians, and his label, Dial, was based there. Brook Benton was about to have a hit with a Tony Joe White song. But the difference between Ray Winkler and Tony Joe White is telling. Winkler's is an old-fashioned narrative, with a beginning (verse one), a middle (verse two), and an end (verse three and its chorus). Tony Joe's is far more impressionistic: we spend the whole song trying to figure out what the narrator is doing besides missing his girlfriend, why he's out in the Georgia rain, and, at the end, why he's holed up in a boxcar. You could actually have a conversation about this song, about what's happening to this guy. Mary's story is cut and dried. There's absolutely no room for interpretation here: you're being told what happened, and that's it, no ambiguities, no boxcars, and, to cite an earlier model that people were still chasing at the time, no whatever it was that Billie Joe McAllister and his girlfriend threw off the Tallahatchie Bridge.

But it's not as if bad songs didn't make it, either, especially if they referred to real events: "Abraham, Martin, and John," anyone? Here was another problem. Nobody had ever heard of Mary Maguire or her trial, for the excellent reason that it had never happened. There was a lot of injustice going around in those times, especially in the black community, and a record that could capitalize on it and grab the public imagination would have been controversial, but welcome in some circles. A young black woman standing trial and facing serious jail time for stealing some bread for her two orphaned younger siblings? You *bet* you could get that record played. When's the trial? Where?

Oh.

In the end, though, the reality was probably much more mundane. Dahl's liner notes make veiled references to John Abdnor, Jr.'s personal problems, quoting Bobby as saying, "John Sr. really got tired of messing with it because he was such a problem," and notes that about six months after "Mary Maguire" came out, Bobby and the band were let go and the label ceased to exist. With the Dallas "Mary" having been finished after Bobby got back from Memphis in early December 1969, there probably wasn't much time or energy after the first of the year to get a head of steam going behind what wasn't fated to be a hit in the first place. Sometimes things like that just happen.

⚜

A few years ago, I read a pop-psych article that suggested you should pay attention if a song won't stop playing in your head, that you should listen to the song and see what it is your subconscious is trying to say to you. Having once spent the better part of a year with a melody I couldn't place cropping up over and over, and having finally and accidentally discovered that it was the first movement of Schubert's String Quintet in C Major (D. 956, op. posth. 163), I'm not sure this is a great diagnostic tool. (It's too late for me to die of syphilis at thirty-one, after all.) But I tried it with "Mary Maguire" and saw, in my mind's eye, my local supermarket.

The story of Mary Maguire, fictional though it is, is a real one. Especially under California's "three strikes" law, but also in other states, notably Florida, we have, over the past couple of decades, seen this story—or at least the first two verses—acted out on a disconcertingly regular basis. I saw the story reported locally several times when I worked at the daily paper in Austin. In most of the cases that I remember, though, it was a father who did the stealing in a last-ditch attempt to keep his family fed while he looked for work, which, for one reason or another, he could never find. In more than one case, the men were given long prison sentences because the law's the law and we can't make an exception in your case and there's one more damn Mexican/black/Cuban guy off the streets. Certainly people have been stealing food as long as there's been hunger, and the only difference between these cases and others stretching into the past is, usually, the severity of the sentence (in some cases mandatory) and some reporter who decides it's news and manages to get it into print.

And it's not like I don't know something about hunger. I'm a freelance writer, and I've gone through several periods of near-starvation due to money not showing up when it should, or lack of any work at all. When I first moved to Berlin ten years ago, I was shocked (although in retrospect, I don't know why) to discover that the American media didn't want any stories from Germany that didn't reinforce their prejudices. Unfortunately, I didn't know any neo-Nazis, and it was seven years before I saw my first one, getting off a train from the countryside. I wound up selling magazines in the subway, eating every other day, drinking a lot of water to fool my stomach into thinking it was full. It took me a year of this before I found my footing again, and I had a good stretch. Then, a year ago, change of management at both of the publications for which I wrote the majority of my stuff saw me totally on the outs. It's the kind of thing you can't ever predict—it's not about how good you are, it's about who you've been associated with, and I was associated with two people who were gone. By association, I wasn't welcome.

So I sat down to write this in another of these periods. By the grace of German laws, which make evictions very difficult, and the forbearance of a generous landlord, I've still got a roof over my head, but the food's all but run out and there's no money due for a couple of weeks. I've seen this before, and I'll probably make it through to the other side again. But since you've asked, no, it doesn't get easier each time.

Still, I realized as I saw that picture of the supermarket when I played "Mary Maguire" to myself mentally, I've never stolen food. I'm the guy who gets caught, and I always have been. It's not worth the risk. I'm a pretty inventive cook: ask me sometime about the week I lived on five eggs and thirty-five cents.

"Trial of Mary Maguire"

Then it came to me. I hate my local supermarket, and I've even written a longish essay about why that is, and how I found out why it is. Editors don't get it, of course, but ordinary people who've read it like it and think it's a realistic snapshot of the way things are in Germany these days. (Hint: Nazis have nothing to do with it.) But the supermarket is where I have to go to get most of what I want. Once a week, when I have money, I walk a couple of miles to a department store, since they have much better food sections than regular grocery stores do, and I buy things that are too exotic for where I do my daily shopping: Parmesan cheese, beef, shrimp, and fresh pasta. But nearly every day, I'm at the Extra.

You see all kinds of things there; the show is as much a reason to go as the food, and it's of a much higher quality. The first thing you see when you walk in is a huge poster of a lens, informing you that you're being watched "for your protection." The entrance and the checkout lines are both alarmed.

A couple of weeks ago, I saw a young Vietnamese couple there. I'm not sure why I noticed them, except that he bore a slight resemblance to the Vietnamese guy who runs the corner fruit and vegetable stand where I pick up most of my produce, and it was odd that he'd be there instead of at his own shop. But I was wrong; the woman definitely wasn't his wife. They seemed deep in conversation, not really paying attention to what was going on around them. I didn't pay them any more mind and went about my business.

When I was standing in the checkout line, I became aware of a commotion. There was no time to see what it was: as I stood there, the Vietnamese guy streaked past, two full bags of groceries in his hands. He was out of there before anyone could chase him, and I felt myself go through three distinct emotions:

What?

Stop!—*Run!*

He's gone!

৵৴৶

"GIL-tay!"

"Down from Dover"

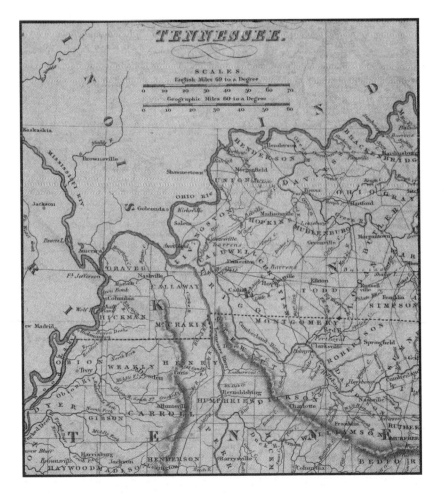

Map of the States of Kentucky and Tennessee,
1831. Courtesy the Map Division, the New York
Public Library, Astor, Lenox and Tilden
Foundations.

ERIC WEISBARD

Love, Lore, Celebrity, and Dead Babies: Dolly Parton's "Down from Dover"

It was 1993 and Whitney Houston's version of "I Will Always Love You," featured in the film *The Bodyguard*, had been crisscrossing the planet for months. A fellow critic, once a punk and now a pro-pop snob with all the same arrogance, learned I had Dolly Parton's 1970s original. He asked to hear it, expecting that the slick remake had it all over the homespun early version. My roommate tagged along. She was an ex-punk too, but of the communal kind: lately, her favorite music fix was singing Mexican story songs with the workers in the restaurant where she cooked.

Parton's "I Will Always Love You" got to both of them, from different directions. Credit it to her homey yet ersatz voice, which evokes Tennessee mountain music here, pop universality there; to her songwriting, as she adopted a slightly archaic form to convey unabashed romanticism in what amounts to an epistolary power ballad. How many roots artists have an understanding of the synthetic tender enough to rival any postmodernist? But with that, in Parton's case, comes a commitment to evoking her origins that outlasts the wigs, plastic surgery, and Hollywood moves. The original "I Will Always Love You" doesn't cross over to you. It asks you to cross over to it.

Part one accomplished, I figured I would cinch the conversion and switched from the 1975 *Best of* to the 1970 one, putting on "Down from Dover." It starts with as dramatic an opening couplet as I know:

> I know this dress I'm wearing doesn't hide the secret I have tried
> concealing
> When he left he promised me that he'd be back by the time it was
> revealing

Each line extends the length of a normal pop verse; the writing is formal-sounding at times and rigorous; the verbal stresses pulse metrically.

> The sun behind the cloud just casts a crawling shadow o'er the
> fields of clover
> And time is running out for me I wish that he would hurry down
> from Dover

Parton, in her early twenties when she recorded the song, seems younger in years and older in time: a child from the land her forebears left, not raised for this kind of fate, clinging to genteel language even as her man's failure to return forces her beyond the social pale.

For three belabored verses, as her parents send her away and her term comes due, the music keeps to a basic figure planted in the modal starkness of Appalachian music. No one and nothing is going anywhere in this song. There isn't a chorus, just the repeated refrain— a musical resolution that is never a narrative resolution. Still, the production has the gloss of turn-of-the-seventies pop: candy melted onto something still crunchy underneath. And in a verse where she looks back and sings that it was love that led her astray, the only love she'd ever known, the mood alters: a diva emerges.

Then the singer goes back into the void, to stay:

> My body aches the time is here it's lonely in this place where
> I'm lyin'
> Our baby has been born but something's wrong it's much too still
> I hear no cryin'

Country songs usually have a twist; that's part of their charm. The twist here is that there is no twist.

> I guess in some strange way she knew she'd never have a father's
> arms to hold her
> And dying was her way of telling me he wasn't coming down from
> Dover

I've never played "Down from Dover" for someone and not seen his or her jaw drop. Can you *believe* this? That was a *Dolly Parton* song? For folks like me—Northern, urban, younger than Parton, raised on the punk/pop divide, working out our notions of "roots" in a confusion of potted histories and indigestible catalogue reissues—the song amounts to an epistemic break. The most successful and enduring a pop icon that country ever produced was also capable of writing and recording music as old as the hills. This was a mainstream country record. And it can rip your heart out. Why, given how famous Dolly is, didn't we know about this?

For decades now, jaded rockers have been doing what I did to my friends: shoving country songs of a certain earthiness in people's faces like smelling salts. Screw your psychedelics; try some moonshine. Gram Parsons taught the Byrds and Keith Richards that lesson in the 1960s. The Mekons brought the message home to me when in 1985 they started investigating honky-tonk existentialism on *Fear and Whiskey*. Soon, Mekon Sally Timms covered "Down from Dover" in the same spirit as the Mekons had Hank Williams's "Alone and Forsaken": as a ditty for floating off the edge of the world.

If you didn't grow up with them, pursuing songs like these almost constitutes a new kind of ballad-hunting. I don't want to overromanticize this: there's a world of "alternative country" listeners who love country's dark stuff. The German performer Rowland S. Howard, for example, of the postpunk goth bands the Birthday Party and These Immortal Souls, covers "Down from Dover" in brooding live sets that span traditional genre categories to include Leonard Cohen, Ricky Nelson's "Lonesome Town," the psychobilly Gun Club, and the traditional "All My Trials." Blue material, one and all.

Even so, "Down from Dover" remains just hidden enough to be shocking when first encountered. It wasn't a hit, or even released as a single, since the assumption made at the time was that country radio stations would never play a song about an unwed mother. Nor did it enhance Parton's heartwarming superstar image, so it was eventually dropped off her résumé. As of this writing, with the 1993 compilation *The RCA Years* out of print, the original version isn't available on a CD you can order from Amazon.com, which is saying something.

Still, Parton and those around her ranked it with her key accomplishments: that's how it got on that early *Best of*. Skeeter Davis included a rather lightweight cover on her *Skeeter Sings Dolly*, calling the tune "my favorite in the album." Alanna Nash placed it in the pantheon in her 1978 biography, *Dolly*. And in 2001, Parton herself revived it, doing a new version of the song for her album *Little Sparrow*. "When I write and sing that stuff, it takes me to this place where I don't go any time with any other music," she told an interviewer.

Parton was in a folk phase at that point, recording overtly traditional music for the independent folk label Sugar Hill. She was, you might say without thinking about it too hard, going back to her roots. Yet she was still mixing in stuff like a cover of the southern grunge crew Collective Soul's "Shine," and even "Stairway to Heaven." Because when you get down to it, what kind of roots does someone like Dolly Parton have?

"I was on TV before we *owned* one," she once said. Yes, she grew up in a Tennessee mountain hollow, the child of a sharecropper dad and a mom who married at fifteen and bore twelve children; she ate stone soup for supper and was ridiculed at school for wearing that famous coat of many colors, stitched together from scraps of fabric, that her mother made for her. However, beginning in elementary school, she appeared regularly on Cas Walker's television and radio programs, recorded in the relatively urbane nearby college town of Knoxville; there's a publicity photo that dates back to 1957, when she was eleven. And her mom made her that coat because young Dolly, of all her children, most loved flashy things. Like Bob Dylan, a few states up and over in Minnesota, with whom she shared an early fixation over *Gunsmoke*, Tennessee's Dolly Parton was a child of postwar America, soaking up a folklore and poplore in unsiftable combinations.

In her memoir *In the Shadow of a Song*, Parton's older sister Willadeene offers a clue: a list of folk songs the siblings absorbed growing up. (This part of Dolly's heritage too has been obscured over time: a later edition of the book, retitled *Smoky Mountain Memories*, omits the passage.) They are: "Barbry Allen," "Eastbound Train," "The Letter Edged in Black," "Two Little Babes," "Little Bessie," "Letter to Heaven," and "Little Son Hugh." "Barbara Allen" is a well-known Child Ballad—a spurned man dies for love, his maiden regrets it and dies too, and from their bodies grow a rose bush and a briar that meet in a lovers' knot. "Little Son Hugh" would seem to be the more obscure (and creepy) ballad "Sir Hugh, or the Jew's Daughter," in which a child is murdered for ritual purposes by a Jewish or gypsy woman, then gives instructions for his burial. "The Letter Edged in Black" was a country hit, a mawkish tale of a man whose mom dies before he can reconcile with her. "Two Little Babes" is probably "Babes in the Wood," about two children who die in the forest and are covered up gently by the animals there. "Little Bessie" is in the voice of a girl being called to heaven. "Eastbound Train" is likely the bluegrass staple "Last Ole Dollar," about a man taken by fate and the railroad far from his loved ones.

As for "Letter to Heaven," if a folk source exists it has been obscured by Dolly's original, recorded first for the 1963 album *Million Seller Hits Made Famous by Country Queens* and then rerecorded for the 1971 *Joshua*. Parton wrote it, or her version, as a teenager, and the early recording is one of her first, released on an LP side of what purported to be Kitty Wells covers; the other side of the truckstop record is by a different performer. The stakes were low, so alongside three actual Wells covers Parton snuck in "Letter" and two old folk songs, the only ones she would record for much time to come. "Two Little Orphans" is not "Two Little Babes," but a different ballad about young children dying of neglect. "Little Blossom" in its original was a temperance tract, about a drunken father who, with demon rum possessing him, murders the little girl who has gone looking for him. (Hank Snow wrote "Answer to Little Blossom" from the perspective of the father, sitting in prison.) Parton's version, though, concentrates on the girl, stopping at the moment when "poor Little Blossom was dead" and not bothering with the father bemoaning his actions.

"Letter to Heaven" is akin to the old ballads, but less elemental—more a domestic tale played for maximum sentiment. A grandfather helps his grandchild write a letter to her dead mother, but as the child is going across the street to mail it she is hit by a speeding vehicle and dies. Now she'll get to deliver her message personally, says the postman passing by. On *Joshua*, where "Letter to Heaven" closes the album, the song is given a professional sheen: Dolly harmonizes with her narrator self and stands partially outside the song. But on the 1963 release, she sings in a much less confident upper register, like a schoolgirl giving a parlor recital. With the metronomic beat of a piano keeping waltz time behind her, you'd be forgiven for imagining that the "big auto" that hits the child is a Model T.

Dolly Parton was born in 1946. In her 1983 concert video, *Dolly in London*, she introduces "Down from Dover" by saying, "That's a song that I wrote when I was about eighteen years old and when I first started recording they wouldn't let me record this on the radio because they said it was too controversial at the time." The words are a bit confusing—record the song at all? or release it to radio as a single? perform it on Cas Walker?—but if the dates are remotely accurate, they suggest she wrote "Down from Dover," first unveiled in 1970 on *The Fairest of Them All*, in about 1964, perhaps not long after "Letter to Heaven." Both are folk songs filtered through the teenage sensibility of a child performer from a rural background. One who, if you can believe what she has said consistently throughout her career, is proudest of her accomplishments as a songwriter. And who returns obsessively, within all the legacies and possibilities she has to choose from, to the creature who gives title to the flip side of her first single: "Girl Left Alone."

As I searched for "Down from Dover" on the Internet, I found this proposed project by the Goblins, a Chicago garage band. If your label will put it out, they'll record it:

> *The Goblins Sing Songs of Child Abuse and Mortality Made Famous by Dolly Parton* (EP). Songs: "Down from Dover," "I Get Lonesome by Myself," "Bloody Bones," "Malena," "Jeannie's Afraid of the Dark," "Me and Little Andy," "The Party," "Letter to Heaven."

These songs and others like them span Parton's career (*Little Sparrow* includes a sequel of sorts to "Down from Dover" called "Mountain Angel"), though it's hard to know whether she wrote most in her younger days, when she was churning out tunes in batches of up to twenty a night. In "Me and Little Andy," a hungry and abandoned little girl shows up with her dog at the singer's door one evening; both are dead by morning. Parton plays the girl in a singsong voice; it's maudlin beyond belief. The song was first released on *Here You Come Again*, the 1977 album that represented Dolly's move from Nashville to Hollywood and Top 40 pop.

But she hardly thinks of "Me and Little Andy" as a pop tune. She performs it on the 1983 concert film, saying, "A lot of folks that follow my career know that I write a lot of sad songs and this one is absolutely pitiful." The camera closes on just her head as she staccatoes the cute baby-in-distress part, face almost buried under makeup and a two-ton wig: "Ain't ya got no gingerbread/Ain't ya got no candy/Ain't ya got an extra bed for me and little Andy." Before moving on to "Down from Dover," she acknowledges the applause this way: "Well, I can see you love them old sad songs, just like I do. I love country music, it's my favorite of all."

From 1967 through the mid-1970s, Parton's boss was Porter Wagoner, twenty years her senior, who had a nationally syndicated TV show. The two released a series of duet albums at the same time that Parton was putting out solo albums, all on RCA. The duets, initially, sold more copies than Parton's solo work. Wagoner had a knack for recitations, in the style of Hank Williams's Luke the Drifter numbers, that convey chilling outcomes with numbed stoicism—most famously, "Green, Green Grass of Home," whose jailed protagonist will only see that grass again when they hang him and put him under it. Porter and Dolly were born to work together. "The Party," with Wagoner narrating Parton's tale, stars a couple who go to a swingers' night one Saturday, leaving behind their children, who had asked to go to church the next day. There's a fire, the kids burn to death, and all end up in church after all. "I Get Lonesome by Myself" has both an abandoned five-year-old, played in that eerie cute voice by Dolly, and laconic narrator Porter, who in telling the woeful story suddenly realizes the girl he's met is the child he once abandoned.

One could go on and on. The girls in desperate straits can also be women in thorny positions. *The Fairest of Them All*, the album on which "Down from Dover" first appeared, begins with "Daddy Come and Get Me," a Parton song about a woman thrown into a mental institution by her cheating lover. "Chas" features a character lusting for the husband of the crippled woman she tends, who in the last line is revealed to be her sister. "Robert" is addressed to a rich boy who doesn't realize that the girl he's crazy over is his half-sister. "I'm Doing This for Your Sake" parallels "Dover," but with the child put up for adoption. "Mammie" finds a woman struggling with the wildness in her blood.

Yet the one song from *Fairest* still readily available is "Just the Way I Am," a bouncy thing defending Dolly's right to cry at night and chase butterflies. Yes, it was a single. But "Daddy Come and Get Me" was a bigger single. Even when Parton's darker material was popular, it has been purged from the catalogue. "Jeannie's Afraid of the Dark"—about a little girl who dies prematurely and has a light left permanently burning over her grave because, well, you guessed it—was said to be Porter and Dolly's most requested duet when their vinyl-era *Best of* was released. It's not on *The Essential Porter Wagoner and Dolly Parton*, the longer 1996 CD-era collection.

Alt-country favorite Robbie Fulks covered "Jeannie" on a 2000 album of such half-erased songs, *13 Hillbilly Giants*. He writes in the liner notes: "These inhabitants of an unkinder, less gentle nation would not have thought to deny that our lives are marked not only by sentimental indulgence but insuperable limits. Their songs don't flinch before despair, self-loathing, God, sex and its discontents, insane happiness, or plain insanity."

But what is "Jeannie's Afraid of the Dark," or "Down from Dover," if not a sentimental indulgence? Consider a different cover version of "Down from Dover." Skeeter Davis didn't exactly wreck the song; she just shlocks it slightly, wailing out at the end for God to take her, too, if he's going to take her baby. But Nancy Sinatra and Lee Hazlewood's rendition—which, like Davis's, came out in 1972—is full-on parody. It's done as a duet. Hazlewood, in his beyond-cynical, enervated way, pops in to leer, "She could not refuse me when I needed her," and the like. Sinatra camps up the ending.

Still, it is imaginable that Dolly and Porter themselves did "Dover" this way at some point; their best duets, like "Fight and Scratch," were often about lovers cackling as they abused each other. Perhaps an archivist will unearth a goofy version of "Dover" done for one of the TV shows. By 1970, when the song came out, Wagoner and Parton were up to seventy-eight half-hour episodes a year. From 1968 to 1975, the two released twelve duet albums and a *Best of*; Dolly on her own released sixteen albums on RCA and four anthologies. They did a couple of hundred live dates a year as well, leading a troupe that included the comedian Speck Rhodes, who blacked out some of his front teeth for down-home charm.

These were revue shows, revue albums: hokum, giddyup, and pathos swirled together in whatever manner worked. "Mule Skinner Blues (Blue Yodel No. 8)," Dolly's first good-size country solo hit, is a Jimmie Rodgers cover, but with whips snapping loudly in the mix it might easily have been a Nancy-and-Lee number. Or a variant on Serge Gainsbourg's "Bonnie and Clyde."

Country, folk-rock, pop with a Vegas tinge—by 1970, a lot of musical genres were blurring. Buck Owens in Bakersfield and Wagoner-Parton producer Bob Ferguson in Nashville were more than capable of giving country a kind of party rhythm not so unlike what dancers in go-go boots might have been dancing to in the urban discotheques. Wagoner's most prominent musician, Buck Trent, was known for playing electric banjo. And plenty of Parton's greatest "folk" songs, like "My Blue Ridge Mountain Boy," have thoroughly pop aspects.

When Parton speaks of "Down from Dover" in interviews, she still sounds frustrated that it didn't get a shot at the charts. "There are songs that you love that you think could be hits, like a favorite song of mine from an album is a song called 'Down from Dover,'" she told Larry King on CNN. "And it's like—it's a song that people have heard if they're big fans. But, you know, I just like some songs, and I think, man, I would have thought [that] would have been a hit, and nobody cares."

"Down from Dover" as thwarted commercial move? It wasn't all that implausible, given the range of downbeat sentiments that country had been airing for Parton's whole life, not to mention Top 40 hits like Bobbie Gentry's "Ode to Billie Joe" and all the teen death sagas, like "Tell Laura I Love Her" and "Last Kiss," which were charting in Parton's developing years as a morbid teen songstress. Parton has often expressed frustration with her career, and especially with Wagoner, wanting more room to be a traditionalist at certain times, to leave country behind altogether at others.

By 2001, in contrast, she sought to have "Down from Dover" be *less* pop. Resurrecting it for *Little Sparrow*, she used the Irish band Altan to give the folk elements of the song more prominence, though so preciously that the results are no less a pop concoction than the original. She also included a verse Wagoner had made her cut, in which the pregnant girl finds shelter on a farm taking care of an old lady who "never asked me nothing." Wagoner was right: the edit shortens the song and a sense of compressed time is part of what gives "Down from Dover" a modern tension different from the old folk ballads, where bad things happen more matter-of-factly, without pop perils of Pauline.

Has Parton fought so hard for "Down from Dover" because there's an autobiographical component to it—or to any of what critic John Morthland once called her "dead baby specials"? Her brother Larry died shortly after birth, not quite stillborn like the girl in "Dover"; he had been "her" baby, the sibling it was her turn, as next oldest in line, to help raise, and a photograph of his dead little body is included in Parton's autobiography. In an earlier family trauma, mom Avie Lee Parton, heavily pregnant with Willadeene, left her husband over his drinking and carousing. A girl alone, Avie Lee walked through the forbidding pines to her parents' house and stayed there the first year of Willadeene's life. There was vicious talk in Dolly's high school that she was a slut, that she had been gang-raped behind a lumberyard, that her youngest sister Rachel was actually her illegitimate child. And Parton tells of finding a small grave with the name Dolly Parton on it and her dad figuring it was the stillborn child of distant relatives.

Parton has never had children herself; whether that was intentional or a physical matter is one of several aspects of her life that have always remained blurry in interviews she has given. Her much-mocked relationship with Carl Dean, her husband since 1966 and a former housing contractor, inverts all the standard folk-song gender stereotypes: she's the one who roams, while he's a determined homebody. There's a female companion, Judy Ogle, Dolly's best friend since high school, who by Dolly's account sleeps in the same bed with her on the road—and Dolly says she likes to sleep naked. What was her relationship with Porter all those years they pretended to be husband and wife on records? And most famously, are those breasts real?

It's easy to ascribe bad intentions and gossipy narratives to Parton A celebrity, by definition, cannot be emblematic of tradition. Dollywood, the theme park Parton planted in her hometown in Tennessee, is both a tribute to her origins and an implicit statement that Dolly, personally, is now bigger than the place where she came from. Laurie Anderson's "Walk the Dog" took potshots at Parton for singing "Tennessee Homesick Blues." Anderson parodied Parton, in a voice pitch-altered to mimic her intonations while still betraying no real sense of human origins whatsoever. "*You* know she's not gonna go back home. And *I* know she's not gonna go back home," Anderson jabbed. The Drive-By Truckers, by contrast, don't attack Parton in "18 Wheels of Love." Singer Patterson Hood simply rasps about how his depressed mom hooked up with a trucker and "they got married in Dollywood by a Porter Wagoner lookalike." The Wagoner part is made up; the Dollywood part isn't. But there's no way to be sure. Parton has gone from songwriter to someone songs are written about: an icon for the conflation of pop and folk, biographical and manufactured, wild and plastic.

This can't help affecting how one hears "Down from Dover," which to a certain extent has to be uncoupled from the woman who wrote it to be experienced as anything like a folk ballad. Sally Timms of the Mekons has repeatedly covered "Down from Dover." I know of three recorded versions. On the first, done for the Sally Timms and the Drifting Cowgirls *Butcher's Boy* EP in 1987, and also included on the LP *Somebody's Rocking My Dreamboat*, it's enough that she's simply reclaiming the song—asserting its power as a punk predecessor. On the Sally Timms and Jon Langford 2000 release, *Songs of False Hope and High Values*, she and her collaborators have become acute preservationists, finding a deeper droning musical undercurrent than Parton's folk version managed. In between, tacked onto the 1995 *It*

Says Here EP, there's a live take, the most evocative, recorded in New York with friends playing guitar behind Timms and the crowd chattering loudly and somewhat indifferently. In this rendition, the song itself feels as weatherbeaten and forlorn as the person it is describing.

I never get that sense with any of Parton's versions. "Down from Dover" may be updating a folk narrative, but the person it is happening to is special, a common sort singled out to represent the multitude under an enormous spotlight. Stardom, melodrama—these are topics venerable enough to parallel the transformation of folk song to pop song. In *The Rise of the Novel*, for example, Ian Watt notes of Samuel Richardson's eighteenth-century novel *Pamela*, with its fifteen-year-old damsel in distress trying to preserve her chastity: "What was new was that Richardson attributed such motives to a servant-girl." Her plight is meant to make the reader churn, and Watt's account of how it works could just as easily apply to Parton's tearjerker:

> This combination of romance and formal realism applied both to external actions and inward feelings is the formula which explains the power of the popular novel: it satisfies the romantic aspirations of its readers in a literary guide which gives so full a background and so complete an account of the minute-by-minute details of thought and sentiment that what is fundamentally an unreal flattery of the reader's dreams appears to be the literal truth . . . it confuses the differences between reality and dream more insidiously than any previous fiction.

Carry this process through the invention of photography and recording, through cinematic close-ups and folksy heroes of consumption. By the time of "Down from Dover," the confusion of reality and dream is even more insidious. For in Parton's music she is both author and, to an indeterminate extent, character.

There is almost no way to talk coherently about the overlap of all these kinds of transformations. So Parton cuts through all the confusion about origins and ambitions, who she was and who she is now, with a simple word: *love*. In her 1994 memoir, *Dolly: My Life and Other Unfinished Business*, she makes a big deal of being the person in her family who forces everyone to say they love each other. She tells of how her father reacted when she tried to exact the word from him:

> "Aww, you know I love you'uns" (a mountain word meaning more than one).
>
> "Not you'uns!" I kept on. . . . I want to know if you"—I emphasized the word by poking my finger into his chest—"love me," I said with an emphatic point toward myself. He tried to look to one side, but I held his face firmly. He blushed and sputtered and finally said haltingly, "I love you."
>
> That must have been the crack in the dam. Once the top man had fallen, it was easier to teach the rest of the Partons to say "I love you." Now it is something we all do freely.

This is the kind of love that the girl in "Down from Dover" thinks she has conceived. The love that the mountain heroine of Lee Smith's epistolary 1988 novel, *Fair and Tender Ladies,* is imagining when she sets down, at age twelve and circa 1912, her semiliterate ambition: "I want to be a famous writter when I grow up, I will write of Love." A love that would both sanctify the folk experience and transcend it, banish it. An "I Will Always Love You" kind of love.

It's telling that Dolly Parton's biggest hit, "I Will Always Love You," is about leaving someone, not staying with them. And that she wrote it about her business partner. She was quitting Porter Wagoner because his understanding of her career stopped at country showmanship and her understanding of her career aspired to pop monumentality. From the Cas Walker show to leaving for Nashville the day after high school graduation, from *Nine to Five* to Dollywood, that elevation of self has been the drama of her life. It makes her no less of a folk artist, because she has never seen the stories she grew up on and learned to rewrite as anything but universal. Still, the difference between a Child Ballad and "Down from Dover" says a good deal about what happened to the folk impulse as pop culture engulfed it—and how much further our understanding of this process has yet to travel.

Parton relishes how hard she is to sort out. Describing her triumphant first appearance in front of Johnny Carson's audience, she said, "If I could get their attention long enough, I felt they would see beneath the boobs and find the heart, and that they would see beneath the wig and find the brains. I think one big part of whatever appeal I possess is the fact that I look totally one way and that I am totally another. I look artificial, but I'm not." Yes, we can play her old songs and marvel. But she's looking at us and marveling too.

Let's return to that 1983 concert in London. Dolly takes note of the punks in her audience, then says, "I don't take no punk off nobody! I was the original punk rocker," telling a story of how she dressed wild at fifteen and her mom thought Satan had got her, then going directly into a tale about the tent revivals her grandpa's church staged. I expect her song "Daddy Was an Old Time Preacher Man"; instead, she does Neil Diamond's "Brother Love's Traveling Salvation Show." Then she starts talking about Elvis, and how after she saw him on *The Ed Sullivan Show* (she'd have been thirteen), she would pretend that she was Elvis—had he been a woman. "They'd have shot me from the neck up, huh?" The concert is starting to make a lot of sense now: were any of the orchestra members recruited from the King's old Vegas crew? Dolly does "All Shook Up," then "Me and Little Andy," then "Down from Dover."

A grand piano launches her into the song. The younger Dolly rushed the lines, keeping the meter rigid. Now she hits heavier stresses, waves her arms around, represents having a child in her arms when she sings "I won't have a name to give it," goes into that long-familiar little-girl voice as she reassures, "Momma everything's gonna be alright"—not "that's all right mama," but close. Then she gets to the dramatic moment, the pop moment, the female Elvis moment, where the full band kicks in and she bellows that there was no way she could have refused her lover. The tragedy of the song plays out and her eyes go a bit dead. The camera is shooting her from below as she pumps her fist to say that baby knew she'd never have a father's arms to hold her. There's a drum roll out of the Elvis-concert *2001* fanfare; the camera pulls all the way back to acknowledge the sweep of what has taken place.

"Well, is that enough sadness?" Dolly laughs. "It is for me." And she goes straight into "Here You Come Again," her first thoroughly noncountry hit. Later, she tells us she learned how to please an audience long ago: "Make 'em laugh, make 'em cry, scare the hell out of them and go home!" And how it was always her desire to travel around and be a star. Then, for her encore, dedicated to the audience, "I Will Always Love You." "I do wish you joy," you hear her pledge on her way out the door, "but above all, I wish you love."

"Sail Away"
and
"Louisiana 1927"

TYPICAL HIGHWAY SCENE

M-39

Typical Highway Scene, *photograph, Louisiana, 1927. Mississippi River Flood of 1927 Album, Mss. #4373, Louisiana and Lower Mississippi Collection, LSU Libraries, Baton Rouge, La.*

STEVE ERICKSON

"Sail Away" and "Louisiana 1927"

andy Newman's "Sail Away" and "Louisiana 1927" are the same song written and sung from opposite sides of America's original sin. Each shares virtually the same melody; each is hymnal, with evocations of the promised land in the first and a terrible flood in the second. The second song's story is a consequence of the first's, in which a New World slave trader of the early eighteenth century, standing on the shores of Africa, makes his pitch to what he supposes to be a continent of suckers. No more worrying about a square meal, he sings, no more scuffing up your feet running through the jungle. "You'll be as happy as a monkey in a monkey tree," he assures them, the seduction ending only moments before the irons are clapped shut: "Y'all gonna be an American." It sounds more like a threat than a bribe, and it is. "Used to fill up the boats," Newman would crack years ago, whenever he sang the song in concert.

Two centuries later, a Louisiana farmer stands on the edge of his crops watching a torrential downpour wipe out his life. "They're trying to wash us away," he concludes; who "they" might be couldn't be more beside the point. The forces of both heavenly and earthly power are aligned against him, and are as huge as the drenched sky that overwhelms him. The farmer is beset by the ramifications of a sin he never had any real part of—he's the "cracker" son of another cracker's son, barely affording his home let alone the ownership of other human beings—but a sin that has stained the soil beneath his feet for hundreds of years anyway. Not incidentally, the song is sung from the vantage point of an America at the peak of prosperity and also on the cusp of oblivion, three years before the Great Depression would descend and with foreign totalitarianism still out of mind if not out of sight. When people talk about American innocence, as they do every time they imagine America has lost such a thing, as though an America that wiped out its original inhabitants and built itself out of slave labor was ever innocent, this is one of the moments they're talking about, deep in the Jazz Age, deep in the twenties that "roared." But deep in the mud of his Louisiana home, the farmer knows a deluge is coming.

It doesn't seem likely Newman thought all this out, let alone positioned "Sail Away"—recorded two years before "Louisiana 1927"—as a prequel. But not even taking into account the titles of later albums like *Land of Dreams* and *Trouble in Paradise*, some intent on Newman's part to engage the conflict between the American gothic and the American banal is incontestable. I first heard "Sail Away" when Randy Newman sang it at a UCLA Royce Hall concert in 1971. Performed without any accompaniment other than his own piano playing, the song was delivered for laughs, amid the mirth of other songs such as his nuclear serenade "Political Science," which somehow seems a little less absurd in the early '00s than it did in the early seventies. So it wasn't apparent how truly insidious "Sail Away" was until the recorded version was released a year later as the title track of his third studio album. Against a swell of strings, the song was as irresistibly gorgeous as it was toxic. Before irony became cheap cynicism calling itself an aesthetic, Newman was an ironist in the classic sense, which is to say nothing was ever played just for laughs, and its very beauty was what was most appalling about "Sail Away," nothing about it more swooning and majestic than the chorus itself that beckoned an entire people into subjugation and death in the name of a dream that betrayed itself before it was ever dreamed. Stephen Foster by way of the Hollywood soundtrack factories that famously employed two of Newman's uncles to the tune of ten Oscars and would later employ the nephew himself to ubiquitous effect, "Sail Away" recalled the opening scroll of the movie *Gone With the Wind*, which sighs wistfully for lost lovely days "of Knights and their Ladies Fair, of Master and of Slave." In the way *Gone With the Wind*—without the compensating advances in film art, an even more odious film than *The Birth of a Nation*—romanticizes racism and renders it benign, "Sail Away" was also fully aware of its own malignancy as the movie never is, in an era that fashioned itself enlightened and constantly congratulated its capacity for indignation. The self-righteousness of his times was what Newman most despised about them.

❦

History is rarely so symmetrical, but exactly midway between the writing of the Declaration of Independence, in 1776, and 1954, when the Supreme Court ruled school segregation unconstitutional and the modern age of American racial consciousness began, Abraham Lincoln addressed the matter of American innocence on the occasion of his second inauguration as president. No man was ever as transformed by the presidency as Lincoln. Seen by some as a folksy if occasionally eloquent political hack upon his compromise selection on the third ballot of the 1860 Republican Convention, in terms of experience and résumé one of the least qualified men ever elected to his office, he barely kept himself together in the first year of his administration as the country came apart. But sometime in the second and third years, fired by not only social catastrophe but also personal misery, haunted by a dead child and an unhinged wife who was, for all intents and purposes, a collaborationist with the very adversary Lincoln was fighting, he changed. The most mystic of presidents, the opportunist in him joined with the prophet; and as the nineteenth century's most compelling American evidence that character is destiny, the Civil War became for Lincoln a moral crusade of a dimension that George W. Bush might appreciate if his moral sense was half as moral. Not a struggle to end slavery in 1861, by 1865 the Civil War had become something for Lincoln that only the end of slavery could justify, so that when he finished the second inaugural address on March 4, 1865, it was foremost the assessment of Frederick Douglass that mattered to him.

In defiance of the conviction long held by the country that God was on its side, Lincoln didn't merely hint but explicitly stated that no such thing was true. He argued that in fact the country had, for all its short history, existed as an affront to God in its embrace of slavery, that the Civil War was in fact God's retribution against America for the sin of slavery, that if the nation was destined to fight another 250 years of civil war—one year for every year slavery existed—in order to redeem itself, if the nation was to shed its blood to the last drop in order to cleanse itself of the sin, then that was what it would do. With the end of the Civil War finally in sight, in essence Lincoln declared that nothing should be so democratic as blame itself for the war, and so he reached out to the other half of the country that cost him so much personally, in order that his countrymen should redeem together not just an American place but an American idea that had no time or place. Having accepted the burden of American sin, he attested to the power of an American dream dreamed by better angels. Shot six weeks later on a Good Friday, Lincoln became the American Jesus, which—as the deification of men will do—more than anything else had the effect of minimizing his human heroism and the revelation that was his mortal life.

By all accounts Lincoln's delivery of the second inaugural was underwhelming. Witnesses reported he looked awful, croaking out the words as though death hovered nearby, which it did. As in a sepia version of the movie *Blow Up*, photos of the event, enlarged and studied closely, unmistakably reveal John Wilkes Booth in the crowd, feet away from the target he was already stalking. Nonetheless, the second inaugural address remains the most radical speech ever given by a president. If a president today said anything remotely like it, there would be a movement to impeach him; he would be considered guilty of the kind of treason that the more exuberant voices of the political right love so much they name their books after it. In the little more than two years between the Emancipation Proclamation on New Year's Day 1863 and the second inaugural, Lincoln subtly recast the meaning of the country, starting the country over without saying so (except for the one muted allusion in his 1863 Gettysburg speech to "a new birth of freedom"), and it's a beginning the country has resisted ever since. In the South 140 years later, perfectly intelligent, progressive, racially tolerant people still refuse to acknowledge that the Civil War was about slavery at all, unless in the way that the northern states were enslaving the southern. So maybe in fact we live now in a third America that struggles to reconcile the first, which existed between 1776 and 1861, with a second that existed only in Lincoln's mind between 1863 and 1865, even as 1862 was a limbo in which no sort of America existed at all because Lincoln hadn't yet become the visionary who could imagine it. In any event, the second inaugural address is the ballad of a thin man, the missing middle of a trilogy that begins with Randy Newman's "Sail Away" and ends with "Louisiana 1927," a ghost song at once there and not there, which the country hears but won't sing.

⌘

Little more than a year before Lincoln's second inaugural, the greatest American songwriter of his time died in Bellevue Hospital in New York City. Stephen Foster wasn't yet forty. By then his fortune had gone the way of his marriage; in fact, it was during his honeymoon that Foster took the one and only trip of his life into the Deep South that his music so yearned for in songs like "My Old Kentucky Home." An embodiment of the deep ambivalence of the American experience, Foster grew up in Pittsburgh and worked for a while as a young bookkeeper in Cincinnati, where he would gaze longingly at Kentucky across the Ohio River. His compositions at once rendered a slave's lot bucolic while, at the same time, in a song like "Nelly Was a Lady," imparted an anguished humanity that would now seem like liberal sentimentality but was scandalous in a day when calling a black woman a "lady" was a scandal. A Northerner who wrote what some now consider racist songs, Foster nonetheless legitimized (in the eyes of white society, anyway) the vernacular of Southern black blues that would also influence such white songwriters of later generations as Jerome Kern and George Gershwin—all while he flitted around the edges of the abolitionist movement socially without ever becoming part of it politically. A letter he began just before his death, that never got beyond the salutation to "Dear friends and gentle hearts," hints at despondency and even suicide, although the coroner concluded to the contrary. In January 1864, with the fate of the union still very much in doubt, never to know what became of his country, he died in its most mysterious hour; one of his final songs was "Beautiful Dreamer." As much the century's quintessential American as anyone, Foster was born not only on the Fourth of July but on the same Fourth of July on which both Thomas Jefferson and John Adams died.

History is rarely so symmetrical, but almost exactly one hundred years later—one hundred years and nine months, to be precise—a quintessential American of the twentieth century, the Civil War more than sixty years behind him, sailed the New World back to the Old and bound it by the silver chain of an air stream, perhaps to mock the Old World, perhaps out of longing for it. Only Charles Lindbergh's flight from New York to Paris could have so captivated the country that it was distracted from a flood for the ages. As Lindbergh flew, Louisiana was in its seventh week of rain, the Mississippi River moving as a wall of water that killed hundreds and left more than half a million homeless and a lake of 30,000 square miles where none had been. The farmer peering up at the sky in Randy Newman's "Louisiana 1927" is searching not for any airplane but celestial doom. The Lindbergh flight was so much the event of its day that it defined the decade until the end of it, when a massive economic collapse on Wall Street made it seem as though the 1920s never happened; eighty years later, Lindbergh's flight has no resonance at all for most people, unless the murderous careen of airplanes into skyscrapers counts. On the other hand, songs and books about the Mississippi flood continue to appear. Ostensibly taking place in the 1930s, Joel and Ethan Coen's 2000 film *O Brother, Where Art Thou?* ends with it.

Foster (caught between an abolitionist conscience and a racist sensibility), Lindbergh (caught between true heroism and, later, a fascism that meant to defile heroism), and the Louisiana farmer (caught between covenant and damnation) are prisoners of the American contradiction, wandering a landscape that both aspires to and loathes Lincoln's vision of redemption. It's a landscape for which Randy Newman composed his greatest soundtrack before he ever composed an actual soundtrack. After a more conventional career of writing good songs for singers such as Gene Pitney, P. J. Proby, and (when he was lucky) Dusty Springfield, Newman—early in his own recording career—rewrote Foster's "My Old Kentucky Home" as a Todd Browning movie by way of a Flannery O'Connor story, an antebellum nightmare where the porticos are parted to reveal a tribe of inbred white freaks squatting in the slave quarters. Almost certainly Newman feels the American contradiction on a personal level rather than a social one, let alone a spiritual one, let alone one of Lincoln's mysticism; but as someone who perhaps has professed his atheism a little too loudly and a little too often, Newman plays the mystic chords of memory anyway, every time he sits down to the piano. As someone raised first in New Orleans and then Los Angeles, his sojourn across the landscape of contradiction ultimately may have taken the form of a search for identity rather than a search for country or God. But that assumes in America there's a difference.

"Sail Away" remains the ultimate Randy Newman song, the song where various strands of his genius definitively merge. It can't be recorded successfully by anyone else; while other singers can't be blamed for having tried, great songs not exactly falling from the sky like Delta rain, its bitter bewitchment and violation go too far beyond satire. As "Sail Away" refracted through Lincoln's second inaugural, "Louisiana 1927" is the song of the more fully dimensional artist, empathetic and novelistic. It also has been recorded by other people; perhaps predictably, the best of these versions is that of Louisiana native Aaron Neville, from 1991. "Sail Away" is great in its singularity, although it has the sense of a fable that presumes to speak universal truths, while "Louisiana 1927" is great in its universality, although it has a sense of specificity that fixes it to an exact geography and page of the calendar, with cameos by President Coolidge surveying the havoc ("Isn't it a shame," he says, "what the river has done to this poor cracker's land?"). Newman easily assumes the voice of both slaver and farmer, the first in its easy bravado and the second in its plainspoken pathos, while both still share a common American naivete. In 2003, the author returned to these songs on *The Randy Newman Songbook, Vol. 1*, only to find America hasn't yet caught up to either the acknowledgment of national abomination in the first or the humiliation of national promise in the second. Once again, as when I originally heard him play "Sail Away" more than thirty years ago, on *Songbook* it's just Newman alone with his piano. But a lot has happened in those years, including most recently, it would seem, the shattered possibility that America yet might come to know itself, that America yet might become the country it doesn't just want to be but believes it already is. Newman couldn't play the songs for laughs even if he wanted to; they're not funny anymore, not even a little. Maybe they never were. Now they're sung from a kind of exile. On *The Randy Newman Songbook*, "Louisiana 1927" comes early on, right after a song about God as the supreme misanthropist, and "Sail Away" comes near the end, before a song about Karl Marx. Listening to the *Songbook*, we travel back through time, and by the time we get to "Sail Away," it's as though the bottom has dropped out of Randy Newman's America and we've tumbled after it, winding up where it began, Paradise and its Fall in one and the same moment, prologue having circled the clock backward to become elegy.

"Lily, Rosomary
and the Jack of Hearts"

Before the gambling wheel got shut down.
Diamond Jim seems to be absent, but the
Hanging Judge may be on the scene. Leadville,
Colorado, *circa 1880–1910. The words "4000*
(Backroom of 4005)" and "not Pioneer Club,
12/20/79, ADM"— are handwritten on back of
photoprint. Courtesy the Denver Public Library,
Western History Collection, Call Number X-296.

21

WENDY LESSER

Dancing with Dylan

When my son was a baby, I would often put him to sleep by dancing around the living room with him in my arms. Various melodies provided the necessary soundtrack, but the one I remember best, eighteen years later, is "Lily, Rosemary and the Jack of Hearts." I used this song so often that friends of mine, watching this bedtime process, worried that the tune would sink too deeply into my son's subconscious: "He won't be able to go to college without bringing along *Blood on the Tracks*" was how they put it.

The effects were not quite that dire, but for a few years there he did develop quite an enthusiasm for Bob Dylan. Until he was about five or six, my son and I would ride around in my car listening to Dylan tapes and chewing gum (both activities that were mildly frowned upon by my husband); we called this our party on wheels. Eventually the charm wore off, or my Dylan tapes wore out, or some other life event interfered with that particular game, and we never went back to it. Even I, alone in my car when my son was at school, stopped listening to Bob Dylan on the cassette player. But his songs, when I hear them now, still have the power to move me irrationally—if being moved by a song can ever be said to be rational.

My own history with Dylan is a straight, narrow path going back to my early adolescent years. Straight, narrow, and unadorned: there is nothing on either side of it, nothing diverting it from its course, because I was the type of kid who rarely listened to pop music. I bought the Beatles albums, of course, because they were socially and culturally necessary. But when I think back to the Beatles, I recall them almost as a single point in time, whereas Bob Dylan is a continuous presence from then to now. As with the Kennedy assassination or one's first kiss or an important childhood taste or smell, I remember exactly what I was doing when I listened obsessively to each album or song.

Bringing It All Back Home: My mother, the only weird and adventurous person in our suburban neighborhood, had checked the album out of the local library and brought it back home, where I listened to it daily until the next-door neighbor (who had liked my mother's earlier selection, Joan Baez) asked to borrow the latest library record. It was duly sent over to her, and I listened out my bedroom window as she put it on, her living room and my bedroom being separated only by a sliding glass door, a small patio, and a solid but thin redwood fence. "I ain't going to work on Maggie's farm no more! No, I ain't"—Screeeech! The needle was ripped from the record and the album returned to us, my mother's stock as local cultural advisor having suffered a precipitate drop.

"Rainy Day Women #12 & 35": I was on a family trip up the California coast, visiting Mendocino for the first (possibly even the last) time. A dance party was advertised on the bulletin board of a local crafts store, implying that everyone was welcome, so we went. I remember the strobe light and the Indian bedspread; it must have been the first time I'd seen either of those artifacts. And I remember the throbbing, pushy, hilariously self-mocking song—"Everybody *must* get stoned"—that twanged on the record player for the duration of our stay at the party. (We didn't stay long.) It was the summer of 1966 and I was fourteen years old.

Blonde on Blonde: I checked the album out of the college library and played it over and over to myself. A man who loved Bob Dylan, and whom I thought I loved, and who might have loved me, had just spent the night in my college room not sleeping with me but debating whether he should. Exhausted, I sent him home at daybreak and then sought out the record—not as reliving nor as relief, but as something in between, a painful pleasure akin to fiddling with a loose tooth.

And, finally, *Blood on the Tracks*. I say "finally" not because it was the last Dylan album I bought—I know I own *Saved* and perhaps one or two from even later—but because it was the last one to have a profound effect on me. I first heard it in the summer of 1975, when I was just back in America after two years in England. It was a very hot summer in Boston, and I was staying with friends who had a nearly unfurnished and definitely un–air-conditioned apartment, but the Spartan accommodations were redeemed by the presence of this one album. I remember listening to it and thinking *This is the best thing Bob Dylan's ever done* and then *So there's something good about America after all*. The two thoughts were intimately linked: Dylan's personal achievement was somehow to America's credit. (1975, as you may recall, was not a good year for feeling patriotic about America.) At the time, the songs I liked best were "Tangled Up in Blue," "You're Going to Make Me Lonesome When You Go," and "If You See Her, Say Hello." That may tell you something about the mood I was in that summer, but it is also a reasonable response. I still think *Blood on the Tracks* is Dylan's best album, and I still think other songs on it are probably better than "Lily, Rosemary and the Jack of Hearts." But when I was asked to think about American ballads, that is the song that instantly leapt to mind.

Partly, this is because it is so obviously true to the ballad form. It tells a story in memorably sequential stanzas, and the story itself has all the requisite elements of a ballad: love, betrayal, death, martyrdom. Even if you don't listen closely (and for many years I did not listen closely at all), you can still glean the fact that there is some kind of love triangle or rectangle involving the three title characters and "Big Jim." If you *do* listen closely, you begin to pick up much more. Lily, a cabaret actress, is the established mistress of Big Jim but has betrayed him with the Jack of Hearts. Rosemary, Jim's long-suffering wife, stabs her husband in the back with a penknife and goes to the gallows for it. There is also a heist subplot, involving the Jack of Hearts' gang tunneling through a wall to get to a safe—probably owned by Big Jim, though this is never made explicit. But it turns out that quite a bit about the story is not made explicit.

When a traditional ballad leaves gaps in the narrative, it is because the audience is presumed to know the story already and can therefore be depended upon to fill the gaps itself. But "Lily, Rosemary and the

Jack of Hearts," though it feels very much like a traditional story, is not one. As far as I can tell, it has no clear antecedent in American literature or history. Someone told me he had heard a rumor that the story might come from Faulkner's novel *The Hamlet*, so I read *The Hamlet*, with much pleasure but with no sense whatsoever that it had anything to do with "Lily, Rosemary and the Jack of Hearts" (except that in both someone gets away with someone else's money—hardly a distinguishing feature in American plots). I also spent some time tracking the Diamond Jim Brady story. We are never given Big Jim's last name, but we *are* told that he "owned the town's only diamond mine," and since American towns patently do not have diamond mines, I figured this was some kind of Dylanesque clue. And for a while I seemed to be onto something: the real Diamond Jim Brady lived from 1856 to 1917, which put him in the right period for the Wild West shenanigans described in the song, and though he collected jewels rather than mining them, he *did* have an affair with an actress named Lillian—or so Preston Sturges asserted in his screenplay for the 1935 movie *Diamond Jim*. But the trail went cold there, in that this real-life "Big Jim" was a highly urban *bon vivant* and philanthropist, much more likely to eat himself to death than to be stabbed in a small-town cabaret by a resentful wife.

So the questions raised by "Lily, Rosemary and the Jack of Hearts" cannot be quelled by a diligent scrutiny of history or legend. There are, however, some distant relatives of these characters in other songs Bob Dylan has sung. Big Jim's diamonds, for instance, connect him up to both Diamond Joe (a much-despised employer of Texas cowboys) and William Zantzinger, who "killed poor Hattie Carroll/With a cane that he twirled 'round his diamond ring finger"—not to mention the Jack o' Diamonds, who appears in the liner notes of *Another Side of Bob Dylan* as well as in a number of folk ballads. And that Jack, of course, gives us a strange link between Big Jim and the Jack of Hearts in this song. The jacks of hearts and diamonds are traditionally a knavish pair, and Dylan may obliquely be suggesting that the charming Jack and the exploitive Jim are flip sides of the same personality.

Lily certainly doesn't view them that way, but then, Lily herself comes from a rather mixed-up background. I don't just mean the "broken home" and "lots of strange affairs" referred to in the song, but also her balladic history as a betraying female. There's a traditional song called "Lily of the West" that Dylan himself recorded early in his career. It appears in other versions, Anglo-Irish as well as American, with the main character's name varying from Flora to Molly, but the gist of the lyrics is that this Lily of the West deceived the singer with another man, whom he was therefore impelled to kill. So much for the purity of lilies—although the balladeers needn't have read Shakespeare's Sonnet 94 to conclude, for similar botanical reasons, that "sweetest things turn sourest by their deeds;/Lilies that fester smell far worse than weeds." (I have verified this truth myself, when I've failed to throw out cut lilies on time.) If "Lily, Rosemary and the Jack of Hearts" is in some ways a rewrite of the "Lily of the West" material, the main curiosity lies in the fact that Dylan has made Big Jim, formerly the sympathetic narrator, into the scary bad guy, and Lily into the captive heroine who is "precious as a child." By asking us to side with the woman instead of the betrayed man, he severely alters the traditional ballad's structure, though some of that earlier woman's haunting duplicitousness manages to seep into Dylan's Lily, as well as into her Jack of Hearts.

Still, knowing about the other Lilies and Jacks does nothing to help us untangle the plot questions raised by "Lily, Rosemary and the Jack of Hearts." Nor can they be answered satisfactorily by a close examination of the song's lyrics. Take, for example, the burning central question about the fate of the Jack of Hearts. Does he survive the story, or does Big Jim kill him? You could read it either way. All we're told, in the penultimate stanza, is that "the only person on the scene missing was the Jack of Hearts." Even the dead and the near-dead are present—Big Jim "covered up," Rosemary "on the gallows"— so the fact that he is missing doesn't say anything, one way or the other, about the continued existence of the Jack of Hearts. It does seem typical, though, that he is simultaneously "missing" and "on the scene," an oxymoronic trick that is characteristic of this elusive figure. It is not even clear, for instance, that he is a real man rather than a playing card. At one point we hear about Lily drawing him up during a game of five-card stud, and at another point he is "face down" in the corner. It's even weirder than that: he's "face down like the Jack of Hearts," and if he's only *like* the Jack of Hearts, then who is he? Big Jim thinks he recognizes him ("I *know* I've seen that face somewhere"), but he might just be recalling the profile he's seen repeatedly in the poker deck.

Lily too seems to recognize the Jack of Hearts, in that she greets him with "I'm glad to see you're still alive, you're looking like a saint." The first half of this line suggests prior acquaintance, but the second half seems wildly inappropriate, as does her warning that he shouldn't touch the wall because "there's a brand-new coat of paint." Later, after Big Jim's death, the cabaret is closed for repairs, and the wall of the room two doors down from Lily's will no doubt have to be patched after being tunneled through; but why would Lily's dressing room have a coat of wet paint *now*, before all that has happened? In general, Lily seems ditzy to the point of craziness—why, for instance, does she bury her dress away after taking it off?—so I'm not sure we can take her word for the fact that the Jack of Hearts is an old flame of hers. (There is a missing stanza, performed at a demo session in New York and still floating around on the Internet, that makes the relationship explicit, but it is a terrible stanza, and it is to Dylan's infinite credit that he excised it from the recorded version. It contains lines like "Lily's arms were locked around the man that she dearly loved to touch/She forgot all about the man she couldn't stand who hounded her so much." I don't even know how that could *scan*, much less be credibly sung.) The printed lyrics tell us that in all Lily's checkered career with men, "she'd never met anyone quite like the Jack of Hearts," which does suggest that she *had* at some point met him; but when our master of ambiguity records the song, he drops the "d" ("she never met . . ."), managing to imply that perhaps she never did, even now.

If we decide that the Jack of Hearts is mortal flesh rather than slick cardboard, it is still not clear whether he survives the encounter with Big Jim. How seriously are we meant to take Lily's first words to him, "Has your luck run out?" Is this just her way of commenting on the bad penny's return, or is the song hinting at his fate? Dylan tells us that when Lily's door burst open, "a cold revolver clicked" (and we are surely meant to hear "Colt revolver" as well); but a revolver can click either *before* it fires, when the trigger is cocked, or *as* it fires, if it misfires or is empty. Because of the jump cut at this point in the song—we go straight down to the scene by the river, where the Jack of Hearts' successful accomplices are waiting for him to show up—we don't actually see what happens after that click. We only gather the circumstances of Big Jim's death later, by deducing from the available facts: Jim, we are told, died of "a penknife in the back," and Rosemary, who was "lookin' to do just one good deed before she died," who had earlier seen her reflection in a knife, and who was standing beside Jim as he threatened (or shot) the Jack, is now on the gallows. The implication is that she stabbed him either to save or to revenge the Jack of Hearts. But if the Jack of Hearts is dead, where's his body? If he's alive, why are his accomplices stuck waiting for him to show up? (Though even this is ambiguous. The published lyrics have them waiting on the ground for "one more member who had business back in town. But they couldn't go no further without the Jack of Hearts." In the recorded version, they "waited on the ground. . . . For they couldn't go no further without the Jack of Hearts," and to my ear the shift from "But" to "For" turns a rather emphatic and seemingly terminal statement about the Jack's nonappearance into a causal explanation for their possibly temporary wait.) And why, if the Jack of Hearts is alive and Jim is dead, hasn't Lily taken off with the Jack? Perhaps he knew better than to saddle himself with a woman who "had to have something flash every time she smiled." This line, by far Dylan's most scathing remark about Lily, occurs only in the recorded version, where it replaces the anodyne "had that certain flash every time she smiled." The "something" that flashes every time she smiles could be either a big shiny jewel or a photographer's flash powder (do I detect the phantom appearance here of yet another Brady, Mathew?), but either way it's a pretty hard requirement to live with.

None of these questions, of course, has a firm answer. The song wants us to hope that the Jack of Hearts made it out alive; whether it wants us to *believe* that is less clear. This, finally, may be what is best about "Lily, Rosemary and the Jack of Hearts," this gap between what we feel we know and what we actually know. The song comes across as a fully told tale of love and loss, a sustained narrative from beginning to end, but it's actually riddled with holes, strange rents in the fabric of rational existence through which the Alice-in-Wonderland-ish Jack of Hearts can make his escape.

⁂

The relationship between the seeming simplicity of the plot and the actual complexity of the narrated events is rather like that between the music of the song as you carry it in your memory and the specific rendition in Bob Dylan's voice. "Lily, Rosemary and the Jack of Hearts" is the kind of tune whose repetitiousness can drive you up the wall, once you've taken the broad outlines of the melody into your mind. The only way to get rid of this idiot-ghost version is to play the recording once more and listen to how Dylan alters each stanza: by modulating his voice from song into speech, by occasionally varying the melodic line, by pausing in unexpected places, or by otherwise changing the standard pattern, which is basically a five-line stanza that shifts between two simple sets of chords. Unfortunately, the cure only works for as long as you are taking it; the minute you stop listening to Dylan, your own simpleminded version will come thrumming back again.

While you have it on, though, try dancing to the music. You may discover, as I did, that the motions which come most naturally to you, when you're listening to this song, are the movements of American square dancing. A forward-and-back four-step, a sideways slide, a pivot turn—you can almost imagine do-si-do–ing with your corner to some of these musical phrases. No wonder the song seems so different from everything else on its album. It has a different ancestry entirely: not the mournful ballad of individual loss, but the relatively cheery recollection of a public disaster. I can recall square dances from my childhood gym classes that were set to the burning of Chicago or the ghoulish deeds of a female axe-murderer, and it is this tradition that "Lily, Rosemary and the Jack of Hearts" harks back to. The rhythm and the orchestration are foot-tappingly enjoyable. They put us in the social world of bluegrass fiddlers and dance-hall accordionists, rather than in the more plaintive realm of barely accompanied solo balladeers. *Don't think twice, don't listen too closely, just dance*, the song insists. Not, perhaps, what we expect of a ballad, which is supposed to tell us a story in stanzas; and not what we expect of Bob Dylan, whose songs are famous for their literary density. But trust Bob Dylan to get to the root of things (the word "ballad" itself comes from *balar* or *ballare*, meaning "to dance"), and trust him to approach that point from at least two contradictory directions at once.

"Nebraska"

*Charles Starkweather as James Dean. The killer
in his jail cell, 1958. © Bettmann/CORBIS.*

22

HOWARD HAMPTON

"Nebraska"

Someday, I'd like to see some of this country we've been travelin'
through. —THEY LIVE BY NIGHT, 1949

> But I ride by night and I travel in fear
> That in this darkness I will disappear.
>
> —BRUCE SPRINGSTEEN,
> "STOLEN CAR," 1980

> Ever'where that you look in the day or night
> That's where I'm a-gonna be
>
> —WOODY GUTHRIE,
> "TOM JOAD," 1940

I want this picture to be a commentary on modern conditions,
stark realism. . . . —SULLIVAN'S TRAVELS, 1941

DOUGLAS, WYO., JAN. 29 [1958] (AP)—
CHARLES STARKWEATHER, 19, RUNTY
NEBRASKA GUNMAN SOUGHT IN NINE SLAYINGS,
WAS CAPTURED TODAY IN THE BADLANDS
NEAR THIS WYOMING COWTOWN.

A TENTH MURDER VICTIM WAS FOUND NOT FAR
FROM WHERE STARKWEATHER WAS CAPTURED. . . .

WITH STARKWEATHER WAS CARIL FUGATE,
THE 14-YEAR-OLD-GIRL WHO FLED WITH HIM
FROM LINCOLN, NEB., WHERE POLICE SAID
HE KILLED NINE PEOPLE. INCLUDED AMONG
THE VICTIMS WERE CARIL'S PARENTS.

THE TWO TEENAGERS WERE RUN TO EARTH IN RUGGED
COUNTRY WHERE OLD WEST GUNMEN OFTEN HOLED UP.

"THEY WOULDN'T HAVE CAUGHT ME
IF I HADN'T STOPPED," STARKWEATHER SAID.
"IF I'D HAD A GUN, I'D HAVE SHOT THEM."

STARKWEATHER SAID HE SHOT
HIS NEBRASKA VICTIMS IN SELF-DEFENSE.

"WHAT WOULD YOU DO," HE SAID,
"IF THEY TRIED TO COME AT YOU?"

The harmonica notes come from a long way off, a cloud of dust
moving deliberately across an empty field until the particles are under
your skin, vague apprehension insinuating its way out of the dim past
smack into the Big Nowhere of the present. The surroundings—
barren plains, dilapidated farms, deserted two-lane highways—feel
claustrophobic, an immense prison without walls. Yet from the midst
of this open-air, foreclosed-soul landscape, a daydreamy vision
appears, rising up couched in the formal, static cadences of Once-
Upon-a-Time: "I saw her standing/On her front lawn/Just
a-twirlin'/Her baton." The pair go "fer a ride, sir," and in the next
breath, ten nameless people have died in their wake. "From the town
of/Lincoln, Nebraska/With a sawed-off .410/On my lap/Through the
badlands/Of Wyoming/I killed every/Thing in my path." Just like
that, not a speck of remorse. No shock, ego, or pride. The singer-
narrator's voice is preternaturally calm and steady—tender you could

almost say—with the barest hint of a broken smile: a dead man looking back on these terrible events as an out-of-body experience, a bad dream come true. He could be sitting on a porch somewhere, carefully picking the simple melody on a secondhand guitar; the instrument's acoustic, but his rocking chair is the standard prison-issue electric model.

In Bruce Springsteen's 1982 song "Nebraska," opening the sparse, quiet album of the same name, circumscribed reality and tenuous existence gradually bleed into the cornered shadows of film noir, the badlands shrouded in outlaw myth, the folklore of the dirt-poor and the dust-bowled-over. It unfolds as a recurring American reverie, a movie you have watched over and over again but have never gotten tired of: boy meets girl (just a couple of star-crossed, gun-crazy kids, one or both from the wrong side of the tracks), something awful's bound to happen, violence follows as night does the day, and the couple has to flee for their lives with nothing but the shirts on their backs. As a young Henry Fonda laments to doe-eyed Sylvia Sydney in 1937 in *You Only Live Once*: "The bottom's dropped out of everything!" Only there's no bottom in "Nebraska" to begin with: "They declared me/Unfit to live/Said into that great void/My soul'd be hurled." Dead or alive, jury or no jury, the singer is already there—he's beaten them to the punch line. "At least for a little while, sir," he and his baby got to play house: "Me and her, we had us some fun."

There aren't telltale signs to pinpoint the time. The song has a measured stillness that's equally modern and ineffably archaic; "Nebraska" would have been no more or less curious and displacing in the '50s or the '30s than it was when it came out of deep in musical left field in the early 1980s. Though the elements are wholly archetypal, the details are mainly drawn straight from the historical record of the most sensational mass-murder case of the 1950s, the happenstance rampage of Charlie Starkweather and Caril Ann Fugate that briefly catapulted the teens to national infamy. ("I always wanted to be a criminal," Starkweather told the Lincoln sheriff, "but not this big a one.") "Nebraska" recites the places, the number of fatalities, the caliber of the shotgun, practically the verbatim plaintive-fool words Starkweather wrote from jail ("But dad i'm not real sorry for what I did cause for the first time me and caril had more fun . . ."), the verdict, all in that patient, true-to-life monotone. Somehow the snippets of wire-service copy and court transcripts only reinforce its fablelike qualities, presented not as dead facts and figures but tattered phantoms floating across a mute landscape. They mingle with the meticulous, nearly covert allusions, echoes, and literary devices Springsteen adds: the way he politely addresses the listener as "Sir," the offhand delivery of the classic pre-execution line, "You make sure my/Pretty baby/Is sitting right there/On my lap" (consciously or not, recalling the condemned Fonda in *You Only Live Once*: "You can sit on my lap when they throw the switch"), and the clipped way his last words neatly paraphrase Flannery O'Connor's story "A Good Man Is Hard to Find."

"Sir, I guess there's just a meanness/In this world," is how the singer reckons his deeds and himself, invoking the self-evident with an honestly puzzled, it's-not-for-me-to-say shrug. The deferential quality Springsteen adopts has a double edge to it: partly Elvis the Good Son who dutifully reported to the Army not long after Starkweather and Fugate were arrested, raised to be respectful of his elders and obey the Authorities. The other part comes from "The Misfit," as O'Connor's mournfully well-mannered escaped killer names himself in "A Good Man Is Hard to Find," who comes upon a stranded, petty, bickering family by the roadside and, together with his accomplices, kills them all. "She would of been a good woman," The Misfit pronounces brusquely over the grandmother's body, "if it had been somebody there to shoot her every minute of her life." That's the generator humming beneath "Nebraska," the live wire under Springsteen's breath: it comes from a place where faith and nihilism are close to indistinguishable, where Elvisoid yes-sir-no-ma'am piety meets the flat, hard midwestern litany of Dylan's "With God on Our Side," where The Misfit's claim, "I was a gospel singer for a while," trips over Luke the Drifter, the persona Hank Williams assumed to sing homilies and parables of the Lord. Elvis the Drifter, Luke the Misfit, Camus's Stranger in the tobacco-spitting image of Hank "I'll Never Get Out of This World Alive" Williams—Starkweather country was a long way from the moral certainty of Woody Guthrie deadpanning "Mean Talking Blues," or going down that road singing

"Tom Joad," though maybe the distance traveled down this no-exit stretch of Interstate was the whole point.

Springsteen was traveling incognito, not singing as a strict version of his subject (no "Ballad of Charlie Starkweather" here) so much as assembling a pointillist-blank composite picture from a thicket of American reference points, some obvious and plenty squirreled away from plain sight. Where Guthrie made Depression-era bank robber "Pretty Boy Floyd" seem like an Oklahoma Robin Hood ("If you'll gather round me children/A story I will tell"), the singer of "Nebraska" presents himself as an anti-Everyman, a fella who'd as soon kill decent folk as look at them. Much as Springsteen must want to understand where Charlie Starkweather came from, it sounds like he wants to escape the shadow of "Bruce Springsteen" even more—desperately looking for a way to slip out from under the burden of being the overly famous all-pro working-class hero, sainted musical vox populist, the full-on secular gospel paragon of rock 'n' roll virtue, which is to say a walking, preaching, boring oxymoron. That accounts for the weird air of liberation inside the serene negativity of "Nebraska": both killer and singer get a reprieve from being themselves, and both kind of sneakily like how being—playing—the Other feels. The real Charlie said he wasn't mad at anybody, he just wanted to "be someone"; here Bruce's name means nothing with capital-punishment N.

Condemned and damned, the drifter miraculously escapes his chains, those of this world and the next. Diving into the void in slow-as-molasses motion, the man with a surfeit of future jumps into the shoes of somebody who has none at all, while the boy nobody becomes a murky tabloid legend. Switching places, bodies, the singer trades in immortality for the murderer's state of nihilistic grace. Why, it could have been a drive-in movie, featuring Jerry Lee Lewis in his first leading role as "The Killer" (AKA "BABY SNATCHER," as contemporaneous headlines referred to him), and in her film debut as his milkshake-mademoiselle accomplice, his thirteen-year-old cousin and child bride Myra Gale. Moral panic! Teen terror! Anarchy in the streets! "Those were the happiest years of our lives," Myra/Caril would muse in the voice-over. But for the prison scenes, a touch of rigor and mortality, à la Bresson directing *Big House, U.S.A.*—a man escaped, clothes exchanged, a body left behind to throw the warders off the scent, with the face and fingerprints blowtorched off.

Minimalist and eerily cinematic, "Nebraska" effectively translates the imagery of a rather more high-toned movie into folk song: *Badlands*, Terrence Malick's 1973 art-hothouse treatment of the Starkweather case, whose beautifully framed views of flat fields, tumbledown farmhouses, narrow doorways, burning dollhouses, and inert pod people turned Western panoramas into a delicately ravishing series of neon Vacancy signs seen through a telephoto microscope. (Springsteen had previously lifted the title for a grandiose song on the 1978 album *Darkness on the Edge of Town*—a show-stopping number packed to the gills with hope-against-hope and defiant whoa-whoa-whoa-whoa optimism.) Like a prematurely postmodernist John Ford film, *Badlands* parades stock characters across frontier-ish vistas doubling as lunar landscaping (mostly Colorado standing in for Nebraska, Montana, and the Dakotas), using the actors as sock-puppet signifiers to mouth ornate, contrived banalities. Springsteen ditches the movie's clinical disregard and downward-looking perspective on "inconsequential people" (as *New Yorker* lit-nitwit Renata Adler once dismissed the socially and intellectually unworthy), while retaining the feel of long-shot tableaux and finely composed interior setups. "Nebraska" internalizes those lulling rhythms the way *Badlands* orchestrates spaciousness (skies, riverbanks, horizons, farmland) as oppressiveness or at least a constant looming absence. (The absence of anything to do, for starters: boredom as nature, and vice versa.) Springsteen's narration is no less artistic than the faux-naïf pronouncements of Sissy Spacek's blank-teller Holly or preening Martin Sheen's overcooked James Dean sausage Kit, but a lot more matter-of-factly believable. Springsteen sticks closer to the facts, where every ironic-poetic embellishment Malick adds only serves to score cheap points off the fatuousness of the young killers and even their victims, whose deaths will seem less like cold-blooded murder than inadvertent euthanasia—putting the poor human cattle out of their misery, that is if they weren't too blind, deaf, and numb to recognize it as misery in the first place.

"Nebraska" deftly lifts the corn-fed picture of Holly and her twirling baton, then lights out for different territories. ("Laughing," the garage-dadaist band Pere Ubu's love-is-strange riff on the movie's Huck Finn/Swiss Family Robinson riverside idyll, sticks closer to the script of *Badlands*, both invoking and subverting its gum-snapping absurdism: "My baby said/If the Devil comes, we'll shoot him with a gun!") The film returns us to an instantly recognizable yesterday, that received version of America in the late 1950s, hemmed in by sterility and affectless kitsch on one side and white-trash clutter on the other, where Springsteen gets at something more inscrutable, a sense of human experience reverberating beneath the mythic and/or banal. He doesn't view "Nebraska" as a world apart, inhabited by little more than stiff-necked marionettes, monstrosities, and crash-test dummies whose heads are stuffed with true-romance and true-crime pulp: he strikes a fine balance between mundane reality and what Pauline Kael called "the glamour of delinquency," the fifties' first inchoate wave of alienation given iconic status by Dean and Marlon Brando. In "Nebraska," those two strands of life (real and dream) intersect, commingle, fuse, as they do in photographer Robert Frank's road-trip classic, *The Americans*.

Much as Flannery O'Connor's hard-nosed allegories did, Frank's storied 1958 book of black-and-white portraits (luncheonette waitresses, urban cowboys, black motorcyclists, transients, society matrons, elevator operators, gamblers, funeral attendees), roadscapes, and self-generating symbols (phantasmic flags, jukeboxes, bumper stickers, gas-station signs, crosses) captured Springsteen's imagination. Whether by way of direct influence or innate affinity, *The Americans* provided a template for *Nebraska* (the album-cover image was chosen for its similarity to Frank's *U.S. 285, New Mexico*). This is especially true in the way Springsteen here speaks to the idea of America as undiscovered country—vast tracts of recondite life tucked away inside of public images, conventional wisdom, official explanations. Jack Kerouac penned a metaphysical carny-barker introduction to *The Americans*, extolling the way Frank "traveled on the road around practically forty-eight states in an old used car (on a Guggenheim Fellowship) and with the agility, mystery, genius, sadness and strange secrecy of a shadow photographed scenes that have never been seen before on film." But Kerouac's hype is on the mark for once. The plain, singular Americans Frank immortalized constituted the real *Subterraneans*, uncanny camera subjects belonging to a stranger and more unimagined nation than was apparent in either the Eisenhower or hipster-beatnik-intellectual visions of America.

The odd stoic/empathic framework for "Nebraska"—its parched landscape and interior boundaries—can be seen in the unadorned details of Frank's photos: the shrouded body and chilly bystanders of *Car accident—U.S. 66 between Winslow and Flagstaff, Arizona* (also calling to mind Springsteen's earlier "Wreck on the Highway"), the holy-ghostly *Crosses on scene of highway accident—U.S. 91, Idaho*, the stark-weathered farmhouses of *U.S. 30 between Ogallala and North Platte, Nebraska*, the dust-blown family in *Butte, Montana*, straight out of Guthrie and *The Grapes of Wrath*, the plastic wreaths and bulky foot-tall white crosses on display in *Department Store—Lincoln, Nebraska*, with a sign reading, "Remember your loved ones—69¢." They're emblems of what endures, or what doesn't, premonitory souvenirs of a Nebraska Death Trip rolling across such plains like a shadow, casting its pall and moving on. After the dead are buried and guilty sentenced, though, that never-before-seen America of itinerant laborers, congenital outsiders, displaced personalities, and invisible lives is left as it was, absorbing those brief events as it would any natural disaster. Thus Springsteen's straightforward, impassive performance holds itself in suspension, defying its own gravity. There's that aw-shucks glint you could take a dozen ways, how he overinflates "ride" so letting the air out of "died" will sound onomatopoetic, the lip-smacking relish invested in "snaps my forehead back," the gallows mouth organ nearer to Morricone than Guthrie, the unforgiving refusal to rush to either judgment or execution. Instead of speed, urgency, a neon moral, he gives us what *The Americans* offered, the tip-of-the-iceberg feel of people and time standing still. Waiting as the American pastime: for a bus or a hearse, for the next man or woman through the door or last call, for the jig to be up or their ship to come in, for their steak sandwich or orange whip, for Christ to rise or the jukebox to bring forth "Smokestack Lightning."

Yet the memory of Charlie and Caril would be cast into the whirlwind, dispersed almost before their separate trials concluded in

1958 (death for him, life for the by-then-fifteen-year-old Fugate, who when the verdict was read sobbed, "No! I'd rather be executed!"). Eclipsed, its place in public semiconsciousness would be taken by fresh crimes, trials, killer serials: bits and pieces of sensational Americana ranging from Perry Smith and Dick Hickok killing the Clutter family in Holcomb, Kansas (later immortalized by Truman Capote's *In Cold Blood* and the film featuring Robert Blake as Smith), Jerry Lee and Myra Gale, Chuck Berry's conviction on white-slavery charges (transporting a fourteen-year-old Indian girl from El Paso, Texas, to St. Louis for what the Mann Act designated "immoral purposes"), the stabbing death of Lana Turner's boyfriend Johnny Stompanato at the hands of her fifteen-year-old daughter Cheryl, Oswald and Ruby, Richard Speck, Texas Tower sniper Charles Whitman, Charlie Manson. By the time Springsteen wrote and recorded "Nebraska," even *Badlands* was a faint memory, a half-forgotten movie that wouldn't really be revived until Quentin Tarantino paid homage to it in the 1990s with his screenplays for *True Romance* and in particular *Natural Born Killers*. So Springsteen stepped into a vacuum, humming his executioner's song, shedding stock-in-trade romanticism and earnest concern like a snake-oil-skin suit. The song drew its power from his refusal to explain himself—that refusal silenced the reservoirs of tabloid noise, as even the token justifications ("we had us some fun," "there's just a meanness in this world") were as hollowed-out as the narrator's conscience.

Nebraska the album was something else again: alternately (sometimes simultaneously) brilliant and bathetic footnotes to the title ballad, a string of morality plays, stern lessons in economic determinism, quavering parables, explanations grounded in the salt of the Guthrie earth. Models of social conscientiousness and good intentions that spelled out everything "Nebraska" left twisting in the wind, the likes of "Mansion on the Hill" posited a vast moat of inequity separating rich from poor (stuck on the outside looking in, like so many winsome Dickensian lawn urchins) as an unreal estate development owned and operated by the nascent Reagan Administration. The whole scenario was a reassuringly morose throwback to the Great Depression, with the unnamed but omnipresent Reagan presiding over wrack and ruin like a Grand Imperial Wizard of Oz, part Hoover sweeper and part anti-FDR. It was a landscape of defeat, gloom, and impending catastrophe—"Them wheat prices kept on droppin'/Till it was like we were gettin' robbed"; "I got debts no honest man can pay;" "Deliver me from nowhere"—but mainly presented as cut-and-dried, symmetrically boxed in. The dead dog along the roadside in "Reason to Believe" had about as much chance of making a run for it as the doleful family locked inside "Used Cars," windows rolled up, their every petty humiliation affixed like a bumper sticker or a "Kick Me" sign.

"Atlantic City" Greyhound-bused you right out of "Nebraska" and back to Springsteen's familiar Jersey stamping ground: night and the city, small-time dreamers, chorus hooks, mandolins under the boardwalk, irresistible Late Show melodrama ("Maybe everything that dies some day comes back"—The Eternal Rerun). There was the tragic "Highway Patrolman," a hushed dance of death between blood ties and doing the right thing, fate made synonymous with social dislocation. "Johnny 99" offered up extenuating circumstances, copping a rollicking folkabilly plea: "Your honor, I do believe I would be better off dead." "Open All Night" pursued Chuck Berry's "You Can't Catch Me," though it couldn't touch his élan or souped-up language. "State Trooper" put the same Berry echoes into Springsteen's earlier "Stolen Car," headed straight into the "wee wee hours" of "Nebraska," voice and solitary electric guitar poised to fall off the edge of the world. ("Mister State Trooper, please don't stop me.") "My Father's House" was decked out in formal folk regalia, pious and biblical as a headstone: "Where our sins lie unatoned."

"You see, you see the symbolism of it. . . . It teaches a lesson, a moral lesson, it has social significance. . . ." That's the Bruce Springsteen of 1941 talking, not Woody Guthrie, not even a singer at all but the fictitious film director John Lloyd Sullivan (played by Joel McCrea as a half-baked exemplar, half naïf-savant and half well-intentioned bonehead) in Preston Sturges's curb-crawling "land yacht" of a motion picture, *Sullivan's Travels*. You know the archetypically all-American story: fresh off a statement picture about "Capital and Labor destroy[ing] each other," hotshot director Sullivan wants to make a Capra-cum-*Grapes of Wrath* magnum opus, "a true canvas of the suffering of humanity" called *O Brother, Where Art Thou?* When the studio bosses impugn the strapping, $4,000-a-week golden boy's experience in the area of misery and deprivation—"What do you know about hard luck?"—he resolves to embark on a sociological research expedition into the lower depths, posing as a derelict. Picking up the most glamorous bum-moll in the history of Western Civilization (Veronica Lake, who makes a swell tough-sweet cynic and in hobo drag suggests a disturbingly fetching fourteen-year-old boy), they ride the rails ("You're like one of those knights of old who used to ride around looking for trouble," she laughs) and rub elbows and other parts with the dispossessed, getting a lice-size dose of the plight of the poor.

Sullivan's Travels takes in screwball and slapstick comedy, mock and poetic realism, freewheeling absurdity, monochrome romanticism, satire of the Chaplinesque, and a coda of gooey rationalization so nightmarishly uplifting it all but obliterates questions of sincerity or self-parody. Like Sturges and his double Sully, Springsteen wrestled with what it meant to be a popular artist in America, with a nagging sense of obligation and unworthiness. *Nebraska* is in parts Springsteen's *O Brother, Where Art Thou?* (most literal-mindedly in the fraternal tragedy of "Highway Patrolman," but also in "Used Cars" and "Mansion on the Hill"); elsewhere, it's *Sullivan's Travels* with gee-tar and harmonica accompaniment: "Johnny 99" gives an antic-chaotic Sturges treatment to the grim proceedings ("Fist fight broke out in the courtroom/They had to drag Johnny's girl away"), lacking only Eddie Bracken as the hero, Betty Hutton as his gal, William Demarest as Judge Mean John Brown, and a last-minute pardon. The gum-snapping, wisecracking local color of "Open All Night" ("I met Wanda when she was employed/Behind the counter of the Route 60 Bob's Big Boy"), the touches of stir-craziness to "State Trooper," and the flyaway ironies of "Reason to Believe" can take their place alongside Sullivan's travails. While mass murder may have been outside Sturges's purview, the trials of Starkweather and Fugate supplied plenty of material worthy of *The Miracle of Morgan's Creek*'s octuplet-mania, including the prosecutor telling the jury: "Even fourteen-year-old girls must realize they cannot go on eight-day murder sprees."

Manny Farber (writing with W. S. Poster) pinpointed Sturges's moral vs. aesthetic quandary, with well-meaning but wrong-headed admirers like René Clair.

suggesting . . . that Sturges would be considerably improved if he annihilated himself. Similarly, Sigfried Kracauer has scolded him for not being the consistent, socially-minded satirist of the rich, defender of the poor, and portrayer of the evils of modern life. . . . The more popular critics have condemned Sturges for not liking America enough; the advanced critics for liking it too much. He has also been accused of espousing a snob point of view and sentimentally favoring the common man.

This line of thought is taken up later by Farber and Poster:

His pictures at no time evince the slightest interest on his part as to the truth or falsity of his direct representation of society. His neat, contrived plots are unimportant per se and developed chiefly to provide him with the kind of movements and appearances he wants, with crowds of queer, animated individuals, with juxtapositions of unusual actions and faces. These are then organized, as items are in any art that does not boil down to mere sociology, to evoke feelings about society and life which cannot be reduced to doctrine or judged by flea-hopping from the work of art to society in the manner of someone checking a portrait against the original.

With *Nebraska*, Springsteen turns Sturges's world outside-in, inverting the ratio of tragedy to comedy, speed and multiplicity to stasis and abandonment (fabled car songs like "Thunder Road" and "Born to Run" give way to born-to-lose and the road to nowhere), embracing introspection with pensive ardor, working hard to do social justice to his characters, empathizing like an unsullied-by-commerce Sully. At the same time, "Nebraska" itself succeeds because it is far more mis- than philanthropic, establishing a locale where Springsteen can annihilate his "consistent, socially-minded" persona and make music irreducible to doctrine or social efficacy, where he can be autonomous in spite of himself.

Sullivan's Travels concludes, however, with a knee-jerk epiphany that suggests "Reason to Believe" after an overdose of laughing gas. Sully, having successfully concluded his experiment, intact and thinking himself much the wiser, decides to show his gratitude to the downtrodden by passing out cash to the homeless. One of the winos rolls him for his bankroll, knocks him unconscious, and steals his clothes and identification. Sullivan awakes as an amnesiac, gets into a scuffle with a railroad bull, and brains the goon with a fistful of rock. Still befuddled, he's taken before a judge and without so much as a how'd-ya-due process is sentenced to six years on a chain gang. Meantime, the thief has been run over by a train, leaving behind nothing but a basket of remains and the director's I.D. By the time the real Sullivan comes to his senses, no one will believe his cockeyed story: the brute captain locks him in the sweatbox for reading his own obituary. ("What do you think this is, a vaudeville show?") But one Sunday the prisoners are taken to a Negro church, where the (white) convicts are led to the pews in shackles and welcomed by the proper, dignified, careworn black faces of the congregation singing "Go Down, Moses" ("Let my people go"—one of the strangest, most didactic-paradoxic displays of racial solidarity-cum-irony ever devised). Together, they watch the raucous, early Disney cartoon antics of *Playful Pluto*, and everyone from the convicts and the congregation to the preacher, the warder, and finally even the stuck-up Sullivan himself dissolves in convulsive hilarity.

Getting his picture in the paper by confessing to Sullivan's murder, he's recognized and sprung to resume his old life. Though not to make *O Brother, Where Art Thou?* (cries a now-crestfallen studio flack: "But it's had more publicity than the Johnstown flood!"). Sullivan has seen the light and wants to make a comedy after all, because he's learned the moral lesson that laughter is the best medicine: "Didja know it's all some people have. It's not much but it's better than nothing. . . ." What follows is a montage of delirious laughter, the toothless faces of the convicts (does that mean the movie audience being invited to join in grateful merriment is also comprised of captives, prisoners who have nothing but the chains that bind them together?) fading into those of ordinary folk, one momentarily happy family of man united by the need to escape the pain of life. This rationale for escapism may be facile and unctuous, especially presented via a burst of mechanically engineered catharsis, but hysteria notwithstanding, Sturges was right about one thing: there are masses of people who truly have lives to escape from, and they don't necessarily appreciate being lectured about facing "harsh reality" by "rich people and theorists, who are usually rich people."

Mythologizing poverty and desperation—giving it an ennobling, sentimental, quasi-heroic aura—isn't far from "the caricaturing of the poor and needy." The appeal of *The Grapes of Wrath*, first as John Steinbeck's widely hailed novel of 1939 and then John Ford's Big Statement film of 1940, was in the way it mixed up realism, poetry, and gross hokum. Woody Guthrie based his song "Tom Joad" on the movie ("best cussed pitcher I ever seen"), but the novel feels like a massive literary elaboration of Guthrie's music, while the movie is a distillation of his great theme—namely, the displacement of Dust Bowl Okie and Arkie sharecroppers by nature and capital alike, indomitable migrant workers seeking the promised land in California but finding more exploitation and hardship. In *The Grapes of Wrath*, this breeds its own form of mystical socialism, a pantheistic blend of earth-worship, Bible-school Scripture, and union organizing: individuals as components of "the one big soul that belongs to everybody." As Tom Joad, an ordinary fellow driven to violence and flight by a hard, unjust country, Henry Fonda (fresh from playing Young Mr. Lincoln in another rousing cracker-barrel John Ford film) made a stalwart cynic turned idealist. His parting words to Ma reverberate through generations of American social romantics, from Guthrie to Sullivan to Springsteen: "I'll be all around in the dark. I'll be everywhere, wherever you can look. Wherever there's a fight so hungry people can eat, I'll be there. Wherever there's a cop beatin' up a guy, I'll be there. I'll be in the way guys yell when they're mad. I'll be in the way kids laugh when they're hungry and they know supper's ready. And when the people are eatin' the stuff they raise and livin' in the houses they build, I'll be there too."

Dogged belief runs through the story like a river: convoluted in Steinbeck, persuasively simplified in Ford and Guthrie. Springsteen picks up that thread along the riverside of "Reason to Believe," in the voice of an apostate who still has the preacher's calling—even in the face of the absurd, the great river of being runs off into the sea of souls. His former faith in testimonials like "I believe in the faith that could save me" and "I believe in a Promised Land" isn't gone, just dispersed. He tells a joke, or maybe a parable. Man's standing over a dead dog in a ditch. He pokes it with a stick, "like if he stood there long enough/That dog'd get up and run." Second man is up the road a piece, sort of bemused by the ridiculous sight, chuckling at the poor fool. He tells himself he knows better than that; he wouldn't need to poke a dog to know it wasn't going to rise again. Now a sedan pulls up and a young fella jumps out, surveying the whole tableau like he'd found the place he'd been looking for. He says something to the girl in the passenger seat and then he calls to the first guy. Man looks up from the ditch and the shotgun blast pitches him right on top of the dog. Second one still has a "kinda puzzled" smirk on his face when the next shot takes the top of his forehead clean off. That's the funny, chilly thing about "Nebraska": so devoid of insulation and affect and belief as to sound un-American, the ballad of a sub-Misfit whose life is so arbitrary and acts so capricious as to imply a tight-lipped comedy spilling innocent blood on the laugh tracks.

"Blackwatertown"

Engraving in Auguste Marseille Barthélemy,
Syphilis; poème en quatre chants, *Paris:*
Martinon, 1851.

PAUL MULDOON

"Blackwatertown"

AS I RODE OUT THROUGH THAT SWEET-SCENTED VALLEY
THAT RUNS BY THE PRINTWORKS IN BLACKWATERTOWN
I MET A YOUNG MAID WHO WAS PROOFING A GALLEY
WHO WOULD ASK ME TO HELP HER FIND HER WAY DOWN

WHO KNEW THAT MY LOVE WOULD TAKE ME TO THE CLEANERS
WHEN I PUT A FEW PENNIES INTO HER PURSE?
NOW WHEN I LOOK BACK ON THAT SLIGHT MISDEMEANOUR
I SEE I WAS PAYING UP FRONT FOR MY HEARSE

WHEN MUTTON IS LED LIKE A LAMB TO THE ALTAR
THERE'S JUST NO USE CRYING OVER SPILT MILK
THE STORM CLOUDS FILL OUT WHEN THE MERCURY FALTERS
FOR THAT PURSE WAS A PIG'S EAR RATHER THAN SILK

SHE VOWED THAT SUCH MATTERS WERE ALL IMMATERIAL
THAT OUR BAD BEHAVIOUR WAS ALL IN GOOD FUN
BUT FUN HAS A WAY OF BECOMING FUNEREAL
THE HORSES FALL SHORT IN THE NOT-SO-LONG RUN

SO BRING ME TWO PINTOS FOR ONE PAINTED LADY
BRING ME TWO CHESTNUTS FOR HER CHESTNUT HAIR
AND BRING ME TWO BAYS FOR HER DEALINGS SO SHADY
AND BRING ME TWO BLACKS FOR HER BLACK UNDERWEAR

AS I RIDE OUT THROUGH THAT SWEET-SCENTED VALLEY
THAT RUNS BY THE PRINTWORKS IN BLACKWATERTOWN
IF I MEET A YOUNG MAID WHO'S PROOFING A GALLEY
I'LL ASK HER TO HELP ME FIND MY WAY DOWN

GREIL MARCUS

Envoi

Folk music was a terrible embarrassment at the progressive, Quaker-founded grade school I attended in the 1950s. Square dancing! A teacher dressed in floppy jeans and a Pendleton shirt standing on a box calling out "Swing your partner!" and "Do-si-do!" Then the sing-alongs! The sententious, larded, corpse-like ballads about cowboys and laborers and fair maidens, mines and dungeons, sylvan glades and faraway shores! All while we made fun of the one person in our class, a girl, who had had the nerve to force her parents take her to the Auditorium Arena in Oakland to see Elvis Presley. It was 1956; soon her parents would be dead on the highway.

"Dead on the highway"—so much more romantic, more fated, than "killed in an auto accident." It's not language anyone used at the time to tell what had happened; it's the language of the American ballad, which seeks to make death into a story. For it to be a story, the song must make you want to listen; thus it calls upon metaphors from all across the land, reaching back across the Atlantic Ocean, across hundreds of years and uncounted generations, to catch your ear. "Dead on the highway": those words could call back the English highwaymen President Theodore Roosevelt heard when he read John A. Lomax's *Cowboy Songs and Other Frontier Ballads*. "There is something very curious in the reproduction here on this new continent," Roosevelt wrote Lomax in 1910 from Cheyenne, Wyoming, "of essentially the conditions of ballad-growth which obtained in medaeval England; including, by the way, sympathy for the outlaw, Jesse James taking the place of Robin Hood." No, nothing like that would have worked, even if anyone had been sophisticated enough, or stupid enough, to try: to try to make our friend's parents, our school shop teacher and his wife, into outlaws.

But what if someone had tried? In fact these two people were outlaws. Teaching in our school were, among others, conscientious objectors who had spent the Second World War in prison; a strict woman, to her students far more identifiable as a German, if not a Prussian, than a Jew, who had escaped Hitler; and, like our friend's parents, in those days of the Red Scare, people of suspect politics, unemployable elsewhere, working far below their levels of education or training, in this case two Jews from back East who, in Menlo Park, California, seemed almost foreign to their students, speaking in accents that, to our ears, were harsh and strange. The shop teacher would get angry, shouting at the world only minutes after gently guiding a student's hand over a piece of wood. At the disgusting things they showed on television. At the injustice of movie stars making millions when teachers were paid nothing. At—things, no doubt, he knew better than to say, even at a Quaker school.

"Dead on the highway": to say that, to make these two deaths into a ballad, or to weave their deaths into a ballad about someone else—a trucker in the night, a thief on the run, a killer fleeing the police or looking for his next victim, Pretty Boy Floyd or James Dean—would be to do many things. It would make our friend's parents heroic, dramatizing their whole lives as an attempt to escape from enemies too powerful even to name. It would seek to mark their deaths as an event, at once singular and part of a tradition—to raise these people out of the crowd of the anonymous and at the same time join them to a community, even if it were a community of the dead. Or, rather, a community of ghosts, road spirits, watching as the story they among so many others enacted continued, changed, never changed, only made room for more.

I can imagine this now. Maybe others of my classmates could have imagined it at the time: one went on to become the drummer for the Warlocks, who became the Grateful Dead, a one-time jug band who would take their versions of old prison songs like "Viola Lee Blues" into the Fillmore Auditorium in 1966; another, inspired by the thirties troupe of radio cowboy balladeers, founded the country-rock band New Riders of the Purple Sage. Perhaps even the timing would have been right. So many American ballads, those about real, specific deaths, appeared almost immediately, as if it was less that they were about certain deaths than that they had emerged from them: "Omie Wise," murdered in 1807, "Tom Dooley" (if you believe the story so often printed as fact, composed by Tom Dula himself in 1868, in his cell, the day before he was hanged for the murder of Laura Foster two years earlier), "John Henry," dying in his race with the steam drill perhaps a decade after the end of the Civil War, "Stag" Lee Shelton shooting Billy Lyons on Christmas night, 1895, and hearing "Stag-o-lee" again and again even before he went on trial, Frankie Baker shooting her lover Allen Britt on October 15, 1899, and pianist Bill Dooley composing "Frankie and Albert," which would travel the world as "Frankie and Johnny," the very next night ("They say there really was a Frankie and Johnny," said a patron during intermission at the Broadway play of the same name in 2002, "sometime in the 1930s, I think"), Charles Starkweather finding his place in Theodore Roosevelt's gallery long before Bruce Springsteen came along to write a song that, in its way, had already been sung.

We didn't sing about our friend's dead parents—but their deaths, I think, passed into the first folk song I ever heard that carried the sting of death. That's what it's really about, after all: not to lift the dead into a heaven of incorporeality, to make them more than they were, to give them new faces, a swifter carriage, a quicker draw, a greater resolve, a motive no one could question, but to make you feel the world turning, to realize that as someone once walked the earth, he or she then left it, and in a particular way.

I'll say it was one night in 1957. Whenever it was, it was on *The Big Surprise*, one of the quiz shows that sprang up in the wake of the runaway success of *The $64,000 Question* and *Twenty-One*. The Big Surprise was the Big Prize—$100,000—and this was the big night, when a woman always referred to as "a grandmother" would go for it all. Her category was "American Folk Songs."

She was a schoolteacher, I think. Probably she knew that, sometime in the nineteenth century, perhaps as part of the great Irish migrations following the Potato Famine of the late 1840s, a song about a syphilitic, most often known as "The Unfortunate Rake," made it across the Atlantic and began to travel the United States. One version, from before the trip, began with the singer passing "St. James' Hospital"; another is called "Locke Hospital."

> As I was a-walking out by the Locke Hospital
> Cold was the morning and dark was the day
> I spied a young squaddie wrapped up in old linen
> Wrapped up in old linen and cold as the day

The singer calls for a proper funeral ("Over his coffin throw a bunch of white laurels/For he's a young soldier cut down in his prime"), and then the dead man begins to speak, writing his will after the fact, correcting the man who has begun the song ("Get six of me comrades to carry my coffin/Get six of me comrades to carry me on high/And let everyone hold a bunch of white roses/So no one will notice as we pass them by").

The song followed the routes of the country's story, or reenacted that story as the song found it. After the Civil War, among freedmen and women, it became "St. James Infirmary"—which, as the song continued its journeys across another hundred years, along its way (for its own story may be in its infancy), in 1983 became Bob Dylan's "Blind Willie McTell." The singer, looking out the window of the St. James Hotel, and carefully walking the lines of the melody of "The Unfortunate Rake," feels all that the song's first African-American singers took from it rushing back upon him: "See them big plantations burning/Hear the cracking of the whip/Smell that sweet magnolia burning/See the ghosts of slavery ships." As a Negro song there was no happenstance in the story: "I went down to St. James Infirmary," Bobby "Blue" Bland sang in 1960, as horns sagged behind him, "And I heard my baby groan/And I felt so broken-hearted/She used to be my/Very own." But among whites, the song remained a kind of accident, or, more crucially—dramatizing the right of white Americans to public space and the mandated invisibility of black Americans, the rule that they never call attention to themselves, that they pass through white houses or across white streets as if they were not there—a procession.

In "St. James Infirmary," the singer's beloved dies behind the walls; no party carries the corpse through the town. But in "The Streets of

Laredo," everything is public. There is no pathetic syphilitic soldier, "cold as the day": there is a cowboy, shot down, wanting only to get his tale told before he takes his last breath.

In 1999, precisely one hundred years after Frankie Baker shot Allen Britt, the singer Anna Domino and the instrumentalist Michel Delory, recording as Snakefarm, released a collection of American ballads called *Songs from My Funeral*. The songs were remade—felt through—with modern sound effects, shifting them into a dimension where they could be heard as if they had never been played before. Blips, roars, speeded-up tapes, distortions, programmed instruments, and sudden shifts of sonic atmosphere made a milieu where it seemed natural, right, that just as a number turned toward the familiar the bottom might be dropped out of its sound like a trap door opening beneath its characters. Domino's mode was cool, regretful, unhurried, unsurprised by the stories she was telling, the roles she was inhabiting, or the people she became: "Frankie and Johnny," "Tom Dooley," "John Henry," the whore in "House of the Rising Sun," the man and the woman in "St. James Infirmary," the spurned suitor and the murdered girl in "Banks of the Ohio," the cowboy in "The Streets of Laredo." A wah-wah guitar ran the opening theme:

> As I walked out through the streets of Laredo
> As I walked out through Laredo one day
> I spied a young cowboy all dressed in white linen
> Dressed in white linen and cold as the clay

"Sit down beside me and hear my sad story," he says. "I'm shot through the breast and I know I must die." As the song breaks for an instrumental passage, an unnaturally perfect Duane Eddy guitar sound, coming very slowly, plays under Spanish words from a second female voice. "So beat the drum slowly," Domino says, returning to the ballad, her witness now turning urgent, pressing like Johnny Cash as he sang the song in the months before his death in 2003, describing the funeral: "Beat the drum slowly," then "Play the fife LOWLY!" his voice all but expiring in desperation and fear. Domino moves on: "We all loved our comrade," she says, the survival of the word *comrade* queer in the Texas air, "even though he done wrong." She and the rest bear his coffin through the streets, covered with roses—"roses to deaden the clods when they fall."

"What are the words," host Jack Barry asked the woman on *The Big Surprise*, "to 'The Streets of Laredo'?" She might have been in her fifties; to me she looked a hundred years old, with wispy white hair and a small flowered hat. It seemed remarkable she could stand without help. But, standing as she was, she pulled herself up even higher and stood even more firmly as she opened her mouth and, instead of reciting the answer, sang it. She sang the song slowly, as if she in fact did not really remember it, but was trusting each word to take her to the next, relying on the melody—and in her quivering voice, there was no melody anyone but she could hear—to give her the story. And yet, because of her age, or her demeanor, she got it across that, somehow, the story the song was telling was more important than whether she won the money; for as long as the song lasted, she made you forget that anything outside the song existed at all.

That was when, for me, folk music became more than an embarrassment—when old songs became something unfathomable, and undeniable. And, as I recall, if I am not substituting wish for memory, *The Big Surprise* was one of the only big quiz shows that, when the investigations concluded, was found not to have been fixed.

In this book, it is Paul Muldoon who rewrites "The Unfortunate Rake" as "Blackwatertown," and Anna Domino who conducts a séance with Naomi Wise. In their writing, you can hear a moment every contributor to this book seems to have passed through: that moment when he or she realized that the old ballads carried a kind of truth, or, in the art historian T. J. Clark's phrase, a kind of collective vehemence that is its own truth, that could not be found anywhere else. Such old ballads as "Barbara Allen" and "Pretty Polly," or such old ballads as "El Paso" and "Nebraska"—when you play "Nebraska" after "Barbara Allen," you realize that all ballads, regardless of when they might have been made, are old, and draw what power they have from a faith that just as the songs they turn back to seem to have been sung forever, they will be, too.

Notes, Books and Recordings

DAVE MARSH
"Barbara Allen"

"Barbara Allen" is more than three hundred years old. It originated somewhere in Britain. Samuel Pepys believed that it was a "little Scotch song," but England also claims it. Across the Atlantic, nearly one hundred versions of the song have turned up in Virginia alone.

Bradley Kincaid recorded "Barbara Allen" for Gennett Records in 1928, a version most accessible today on the CD compilation *The Rose Grew Round the Briar: Early American Rural Love Songs, Vol. 1.* Yazoo 2030, 1997.

The other versions discussed in this essay, listed in chronological order, are:

John Jacob Niles, "The Ballad of Barberry Allen, Parts I and II." 78 rpm. RCA Red Seal 2019–A&B, 1938.

Merle Travis, "Barbara Allen," on *Folk Songs of the Hills.* 10" EP. Capitol AD 50, 1947. Rereleased on CD with the tracks from two additional early Travis recordings as *Folk Songs of the Hills.* Bear Family BCD 15636, 1994.

John Jacob Niles, "Barb'ry Ellen," on *The Ballads of John Jacob Niles.* LP. Tradition TLP 1046, 1960.

Joan Baez, "Barbara Allen," on *Joan Baez Volume Two.* LP. Vanguard VRS-9094, 1961. Rereleased on CD by Vanguard in 1990.

Jean Ritchie, "Barbara Allen," on *British Traditional Ballads in the Southern Mountains, Volume 1.* LP. Folkways FA 2301, 1961. Version entitled "Barbary Allen," available on CD, *Ballads from Her Appalachian Family Tradition,* Smithsonian Folkways 40145, 2003.

Bob Dylan, "Barbara Allen," on *Gaslight Tapes.* Bootleg CD. Laser 76025. This is one of several unofficial releases of the same material, recorded in October 1962 at the Gaslight Café in New York, and informally known as the Second Gaslight Tape.

Roscoe Holcomb, "Barbara Allen Blues," on *The High Lonesome Sound.* LP. Folkways FA 2368, 1965. Rereleased on CD, Smithsonian Folkways 40104, 1998.

Dolly Parton, "Barbara Allen," on *Heartsongs (Live From Home).* CD. Columbia CB0066123, 1994.

Various artists, *Songcatcher: Music from and Inspired by the Motion Picture.* CD. Vanguard 79586, 2001. Both Emmy Rossum and Emmylou Harris sing versions of the song in the film, although Rossum's is truncated on the soundtrack.

—*SW*

ANN POWERS
"The Water Is Wide"

Debra Allbery, "The Reservoir," 1990, collected in *Walking Distance*,
Pittsburgh: University of Pittsburgh Press, 1991.

Joan Baez, "The Water Is Wide," *Very Early Joan*. LP. Vanguard, 1982, live
recordings from 1960 to 1963, reissued on CD, Vanguard 79446, 1991.

——, "The Water Is Wide," released as bonus track on reissue of *Farewell,
Angelina*. CD. Vanguard 79701-2, 2002.

Bob Dylan, "The Water Is Wide" (with Joan Baez), from *Live 1975—The
Rolling Thunder Revue (the bootleg series, Vol. 5)*. CD. Columbia
C2K87047, 2002.

Jean Ritchie, *Folk Songs of the Southern Appalachians*. New York: Oak
Publications, 1965.

Pete Seeger, *American Favorite Ballads, Volume 2*. LP. Folkways FA 2321,
1959, reissued on CD, Smithsonian Folkways 40151, 2003.

——, The *Incompleat Folksinger*, ed. by Jo Metcalf Schwartz. New York:
Simon & Schuster, 1972.

—Ann Powers

RENNIE SPARKS
"Pretty Polly"

I referred to the following sources:

John Bakeless, *The Journals of Lewis and Clark*. New York: Penguin Group,
1964.

Carol Berkin, *First Generations: Women in Colonial America*. New York:
Farrar, Straus and Giroux, 1996.

Beloit [Wis.] *Daily News*, "The Scenes Are Disturbing," May 13, 1996.

Bruno Bettelheim, *The Uses of Enchantment: The Meaning and Importance
of Fairy Tales*. New York: Vintage Books, 1989.

Ray Allen Billington, *The Far Western Frontier 1830–1860*. New York:
Harper & Row, 1956.

Bodleian Library Broadside Ballads, University of Oxford.
www.bodley.ox.ac.uk/ballads/ballads.html/.

Thomas Bulfinch, *Bulfinch's Mythology* [abridged edition]. New York: Dell Publishing, 1959.

Joseph Campbell, *Occidental Mythology: The Masks of God*. New York: Penguin Books, 1964.

Sylvia Cranston, *HPB: The Extraordinary Life and Influence of Helena Blavatsky, Founder of the Modern Theosophical Movement*. New York: G. P. Putnam's Sons, 1993.

David Crockett, *A Narrative of the Life of David Crockett of the State of Tennessee* [1834]. Knoxville: University of Tennessee Press, 1973.

William Cronon, *Changes in the Land: Indians, Colonists, and the Ecology of New England*. New York: Farrar, Straus and Giroux, 1983.

James Deetz, *The Times of Their Lives: Life, Love, and Death in the Plymouth Colony*. New York: W. H. Freeman, 2000.

Allan W. Eckert, *That Dark and Bloody River*. New York: Bantam Books, 1995.

Phil Edwards, "Real Wizards: The Search for Harry's Ancestors." Internet article accompanying Channel 4 TV show "Real Wizards," originally aired November 2001, United Kingdom.

Paul Ehrlich and Anne Ehrlich, *Extinction*. New York: Random House, 1981.

John Mack Faragher, *Daniel Boone: The Life and Legend of an American Pioneer*. New York: Henry Holt, 1992.

Waverly Fitzgerald, "Celebrating May Day." www.schooloftheseasons.com/mayday.html/.

Robert Graves and Raphael Patai, *Hebrew Myths*. New York: Doubleday, 1964.

———, *Mammon and the Black Goddess*. New York: Doubleday, 1965.

———, *The White Goddess*. New York: Creative Age Press, 1948.

Francis Haines, *The Buffalo*. New York: Thomas Y. Crowell Co., 1970.

Terri Hardin, ed., *A Treasury of American Folklore: Our Customs, Beliefs, and Traditions*. New York: Barnes & Noble Books, 1994.

Paul Hawken, *The Magic of Findhorn*. New York: Harper & Row, 1975.

H. J. Irwin, *An Introduction to Parapsychology*. Jefferson, NC: McFarland & Co., 1994.

Gertrude Jobes, *Dictionary of Mythology, Folklore and Symbols*. Metuchen, NJ: Scarecrow Press, 1961.

John Keel, *The Mothman Prophecies*. New York: Tor Books, 1975.

John Lame Deer and Richard Erdoes, *Lame Deer, Seeker of Visions*. New York: Simon & Schuster, 1972.

G. Malcolm Laws, Jr., *American Ballads from British Broadsides: A Guide for Students and Collectors of Traditional Song*. Philadelphia: American Folklore Society, 1957.

Elliott Leyton, *Compulsive Killers*. New York: New York University Press, 1986.

Barry Lopez, *Of Wolves and Men*. New York: Touchstone, 1978.

Stephen G. Michaud, "To Have and To Kill," *Salon.com*, August 25, 1999.

Jay Robert Nash, *Bloodletters and Badmen*. New York: M. Evans and Co., 1973.

Roderick Nash, *Wilderness and the American Mind*. New Haven: Yale University Press, 1967.

John Jacob Niles, *The Ballad Book of John Jacob Niles*. New York: Dover, 1960.

William M. Osborn, *The Wild Frontier: Atrocities During the American-Indian War from Jamestown Colony to Wounded Knee*. New York: Random House, 2000.

Camille Paglia, *Sexual Personae: Art and Decadence from Nefertiti to Emily Dickinson*. New Haven: Yale University Press, 1990.

Kirkpatrick Sale, *The Conquest of Paradise: Christopher Columbus and the Columbian Legacy*. New York: Alfred A. Knopf, 1990.

A. W. Schorger, *The Passenger Pigeon*. Madison: University of Wisconsin Press, 1955.

Cecil Sharp, *One Hundred English Folksongs*. New York: Dover, 1975.

Paul Shepard, *Nature and Madness*. Athens: University of Georgia Press, 1982.

Kenneth Silverman, *The Life and Times of Cotton Mather*. New York: Harper & Row, 1984.

Richard Slotkin, *Regeneration Through Violence: The Mythology of the American Frontier, 1600–1860*. Middletown, CT: Wesleyan University Press, 1973.

Marion L. Starkey, *The Devil in Massachusetts: A Modern Inquiry into the Salem Witch Trials*. New York: Doubleday, 1969.

Merlin Stone, *Ancient Mirrors of Womanhood: A Treasury of Goddess and Heroine Lore from Around the World*. New York: New Sibylline Books, 1979.

Robert B. Waltz and David G. Engle, eds., *The Traditional Ballad Index*. Fresno: California State University, 2003. www.csufresno.edu/folklore/BalladIndexTOC.html/.

James Wilson, *The Earth Shall Weep: The History of Native Americans*. New York: Atlantic Monthly Press, 1998.

Lorraine Wyman and Howard Brockway, *Lonesome Tunes: Folksongs from the Kentucky Mountains*. New York: H. W. Gray, 1916.

Notes, Books and Recordings

There are many recorded versions of "Pretty Polly," some of which are listed at
www.folkindex.mse.jhu.edu/.

The versions I cite appear on:

Dock Boggs, *Country Blues: Complete Early Recordings*. CD. Revenant 205, 1998.

Pete Steele, *Banjo Tunes and Songs*. LP. Folkways, FS 3828, 1958.

—*Rennie Sparks*

SHARYN McCRUMB

"Pretty Peggy-O"

Olive D. Campbell and Cecil Sharp, *English Folk Songs from the Southern Appalachians*. New York, G. P. Putnam's Sons, 1917.

Chad Mitchell Trio, "Golden Vanity," from *The Chad Mitchell Trio at the Bitter End*. Folk Era CMT3281D, 1997, originally issued 1962 as Kapp 3281. Roger "Jim" McGuinn, later of the Byrds, appears on guitar.

Clancy Brothers with Tommy Makem, *The Rising of the Moon—Irish Songs of Rebellion*. Tradition 1006, 1959; reissued as Rykodisc 1195387, 1998.

Lester Flatt and Earl Scruggs, "Salty Dog Blues," from *Flatt and Scruggs at Carnegie Hall*. LP. Columbia 8845, 1963. Reissued on CD as *Flatt and Scruggs at Carnegie Hall! The Complete Concert*. Koch 379292, 1998.

[Grandmother], "Pop Goes the Weasel," "Wait 'Til the Sun Shines, Nellie."

Kossoy Sisters with Erik Darling, "Down in a Willow Garden" (aka "Rose Connelly"), from *Bowling Green*. Tradition 1065, 1993, originally issued 1956.

MacEdward Leach, ed., *The Ballad Book*. New York: A. S. Barnes, 1955.

"My Bonnie Moorhen." Scotland Guide.
www.siliconglen.com/scotfaq/9_3_19.html.

Marty Robbins, "El Paso." Columbia 41511, 1959. Included on Robbins, *Gunfighter Ballads and Trail Songs*. CD. Columbia/Legacy 65996, 1999, originally issued in 1959, and on *The Essential Marty Robbins: 1951–1982*. CD. Columbia/Legacy C2K 48537, 1991.

Betty Smith, *For My Friends of Song*. LP/cassette. June Appal 0018, 1977.

—*Sharyn McCrumb*

ANNA DOMINO
"Omie Wise"

Naomi Wise was murdered by Jonathan Lewis in the spring of 1807, at Deep River, in Randolph County, North Carolina. There were witnesses and he was soon caught, hungover and repentant, in the nearby town of Guilford. He sobered up, broke out of jail with the help of friends who were later pardoned by the governor, and disappeared for a few years. At some point, a group of citizens got together and hired bounty hunters to go after Lewis and bring him back to stand trial for the murder. He was found in Kentucky and brought back, only to be acquitted for lack of sufficient evidence. Naomi was pregnant when she died and already had two little children by other fathers.

There is a marked penchant in American balladry for tales of the killing of young women by an admirer. Why did they have to die? There is the satisfying pathos of the death of an innocent, but these tales are often of premeditated crimes. A look at the laws of the time helps explain how a pregnant woman could be such a threat as to inspire murder. In the first place, a child without a father was considered legally orphaned and subject to removal to the custody of the state or indentured servitude. By publicly naming a father, a woman not only might keep her child but the man named would be legally obligated to provide support for the first two years of its life. In this way, a pregnant woman could wreak havoc on a young man's prospects. If a woman had means, she could purchase a stand-in father to keep the poverty laws at bay, but if she was poor, she had to throw herself on the mercy of her lover. Following the example set by the state, he often had little mercy to spare for her or the baby.

There are probably hundreds of versions of the song if you include those that go by other titles. I referred to the four versions listed below. Copies of court records and other information gathered by Eleanor Long-Wilgus, and made available to me through Greil Marcus, proved invaluable. Long-Wilgus has done a lot of research into the murder and the times, and has recently published her findings in *Naomi Wise: Creation, Re-Creation, and Continuity in an American Ballad Tradition* (Chapel Hill: Chapel Hill Press, 2003). Besides laying out what little is known of Naomi's history, Long-Wilgus's work led me to Victoria Bynum's *Unruly Women: The Politics of Social and Sexual Control in the Old South* (Chapel Hill: University of North Carolina Press, 1992), a fascinating account of the laws and conventions used to control the economic power in children, as heirs and as labor.

Clarence Ashley, "Naomi Wise." 78 rpm. Columbia 15522-D, 1930. Reissued on CD, *Greenback Dollar: The Music of Clarence "Tom" Ashley, 1929–1933*. County 3520, 2001.

Bob Dylan, "Omie Wise," recorded by Tony Glover on December 22, 1961, in a hotel room, included on a bootleg LP, *Blind Boy Grunt*, and on the 3-CD bootleg, *The Minnesota Tapes*.

G. B. Grayson, "Ommie Wise." 78 rpm. Victor 21625, 1927. This recording was reissued on Harry Smith's influential and now legendary *Anthology of American Folk Music*, first released in 1952 on Folkways and now available on CD, Smithsonian Folkways 40090.

Doc Watson, "Omie Wise." *Doc Watson*. LP. Vanguard 79152, 1964. Reissued on 4-CD set, *Doc Watson: The Vanguard Years*, Vanguard 70055, 1995.

—*Anna Domino*

SARAH VOWELL

"John Brown's Body" and "The Battle Hymn of the Republic"

There is never a shortage of recordings of "The Battle Hymn of the Republic," suited to every purse and political persuasion. In December 2003, Amazon.com showed 524 listings for the song currently in print, ranging from versions adapted to karaoke to a rendition by The Irish Tenors.

My money is firmly on the Grammy-winning recording by the Mormon Tabernacle Choir: *Mormon Tabernacle Choir Greatest Hits: 22 Best-Loved Favorites*. CD. Sony Masterworks 48294, 1992.

"John Brown's Body" came in with a much smaller but still respectable fifty entries on Amazon.com. The range of performers of "John Brown's Body" is narrower but with some surprises: there are versions, now available, by Van Morrison, the offbeat contemporary folk group Thanatos, and the jazz greats John Coltrane and Oscar Peterson, as well as by Odetta, Paul Robeson, Bernice Johnson Reagon, and Pete Seeger. For this piece, I just used Robeson's and Seeger's versions.

On John Brown and the background to both songs, I found a recent public television documentary, now available on video, quite useful: Robert Kenner, *John Brown's Holy War*. WGBH Boston/PBS Home Video, 2000.

The following books are essential reading:

Stephen B. Oates, *To Purge This Land with Blood: A Biography of John Brown.* 1970. Amherst: University of Massachusetts Press, 1984.

Merrill D. Peterson, *John Brown: The Legend Revisited.* Charlottesville and London: University of Virginia Press, 2002.

Gary Williams, *Hungry Heart: The Literary Emergence of Julia Ward Howe.* Amherst: University of Massachusetts Press, 1999.

Edmund Wilson, *Patriotic Gore.* New York: Farrar, Straus and Giroux, 1962.

—*Sarah Vowell*

R. CRUMB

"When You Go A Courtin'"

Lyrics for "When You Go A Courtin'" taken from 78 rpm record by George Wade and Francum Brasswell, Columbia 15515, issued circa 1930; their only record as far as I know; probably recorded somewhere in the South by a Columbia company field-recording team, as was the practice of major record companies in the period 1925–32. These field-recording units captured a wealth of great rural American music, both black and white (not to mention Mexican, Caribbean, etc.), in this period, most of it by performers unknown outside of their own community or region. The Great Depression of the 1930s, plus competition from radio broadcasting, brought this "Golden Age" of field recording pretty much to an end by the mid-thirties, with a few exceptions.

—*R. Crumb*

JOYCE CAROL OATES
"Little Maggie"

"Little Maggie" is older than Blue-Eyed Bill Brandy would have been, although how much older is unclear. A durable Scots ballad, "Maggie Lawder," dates back to the mid-seventeenth century, but there is no similarity between the two. "Little Maggie" most closely resembles another American song, "Darlin' Corey" (sometimes known as "Country Blues," "Hustlin' Gamblers," or "Dig a Hole"), about a female moonshiner who must be awakened in order to elude some approaching revenue officers. As performed by Lester Flatt and Earl Scruggs, "Darlin' Corey" includes lines that are interchangeable with parts of familiar versions of "Little Maggie," including:

> Well the first time I seen darling Corey
> She was sitting on the banks of the sea
> Had a forty-four around her body
> And a banjo on her knee

Given its themes of liquor and thwarted love, and given the Gaelic associations of the nickname "Maggie," it seems a fair guess that the song has Scots-Irish origins, and that it first flourished, in its many versions, in the southern American backcountry of which the mythical Vergennes County, Kentucky, was and is a part.

Most variants of the song tell the same story—of a beautiful, elusive, and somewhat sinister Maggie, who is standing over yonder, drinking and sparking with someone other than the adoring singer. The Stanley Brothers' "Little Maggie," recorded in 1947, is a good representative:

> Over yonder stands little Maggie
> With a dram glass in her hand
> She's drinkin' away her trouble
> And a courting some other man
>
> Oh how can I ever stand it
> To see them two blue eyes
> A shining in the moonlight
> Like two diamonds in the sky
>
> Pretty flowers were made for blooming
> Pretty stars were made to shine

Notes, Books and Recordings

Pretty women were made for loving
Little Maggie was made for mine

Last time I saw little Maggie
She was sitting on the banks of the sea
With a forty-four around her
And a banjo on her knee

I'm a goin' down to the station
With my suitcase in my hand
I'm a goin' to leave this country
I'm a goin' to some far distant land

Go away, go away little Maggie
Go and do the best you can
I'll get me another woman
You can get you another man

The earliest recording of the song, by G. B. Grayson and Henry Whitter, dates from 1929. Grayson—whose 1927 recording of the murder ballad "Ommie Wise" remains the starkest account of a song since covered by scores of singers—was a superb fiddle player and vocalist from Johnson County in eastern Tennessee, and a close friend and collaborator of the celebrated banjo player and singer Clarence Ashley, who hailed from the same county. As early as 1918, Grayson later recalled, the two went on what they called "busting trips" to the West Virginia coalfields, playing for the miners and passing the hat. They also appeared as a duo at a famous Old Fiddlers' Convention in Mountain City, Tennessee, in May 1925. Two years later, at another gathering in Mountain City, Grayson met Henry Whitter, a guitarist, harmonica player, and singer from Fries, Virginia, and the pair had a successful performing and recording career that was cut short when Grayson died in an automobile wreck in 1930. Among Grayson and Whitter's better-known records, aside from "Little Maggie," were versions of "Cluck Old Hen," "Tom Dooley," "The Banks of the Ohio," and "Handsome Molly," since covered by modern performers ranging from the Kingston Trio to Bob Dylan and Mick Jagger.

—SW

CECIL BROWN

"Frankie and Albert"
and
"Frankie and Johnny"

The most important study of "Frankie and Albert" and its hundreds of variations is Bruce Redfern Buckley, "Frankie and Her Men: A Study of the Interrelationships of Popular and Folk Traditions" (Ph.D. dissertation, Indiana University, 1962). Important material also appears in John David, "Tragedy in Ragtime: Black Folktales from St. Louis" (Ph.D. dissertation, St. Louis University, 1978), and James Fuld, *The Book of World-Famous Music: Classical, Popular and Folk* (New York: Crown, 1971). David's dissertation quotes the reporter Dudley L. McClure's interview with Frankie Baker in 1935, which first appeared as "The Real Story of Frankie and Johnnie," in *Daring Detective Tabloid*, June 1935. Richard Clay's reminiscences appear in John Huston, *Frankie and Johnny* (New York: Albert and Charles Boni, 1930). Sigmund Spaeth's original claim that the ballads were based on the Frankie Baker incident came in his *Weep Some More, My Lady* (New York: Doubleday, 1927).

The original news report on the shooting appears in the *St. Louis Republic*, October 16, 1899. Additional evidence about the events, and their subsequent transformation into the various versions of the ballad, appear in the *St. Louis Post-Dispatch*, February 11, 13, and 17, 1942, in connection with Frankie Baker's suit against Republic Pictures. According to the best available information, as reported by John David, Frankie Baker died on January 6, 1952.

Guy Lombardo's version of "Frankie and Johnny" is available on a CD issued in 2002 by Jasmine Music, *Guy Lombardo & His Royal Canadians: Get Out Those Old Records: Fifty of His Many Greatest Hits*, Jasmine Music, JSCD 396.

The other recorded versions of the ballad that are important in connection with my essay are:

Mississippi John Hurt, "Frankie." 78 rpm. OKeh 8560, 1928, reissued on CD, *Mississippi John Hurt 1928 Sessions*. Yazoo 1065, 1990.

Leadbelly (Huddie Ledbetter), "Frankie and Albert," field recording at Louisiana State Penitentiary, Angola, LA, July 1, 1934, issued on CD, *You Don't Know My Mind*. Fabulous FABCD 113, 2002.

—Cecil Brown

SEAN WILENTZ

"Delia"

The surviving evidence about Delia Green and Cooney Houston, and the musical history of the song, have been exhaustively explored by Professor John Garst of the University of Georgia. The most complete summary appears in his unpublished paper, "Delia's Gone—Where Did She Come From, Where Did She Go?" delivered to the International Country Music Conference at Belmont College, Nashville, Tennessee, in 2003, which he kindly made available to me in draft form. Professor Garst's preliminary findings about the case can be found at http://hem.passagen.se/obrecht/ backpages/chords/36_wgw/ballad_of_delia_green.html. The newspaper accounts of the murder and trial, cited in Professor Garst's paper, are in the Savannah *Morning News*, December 26, 1900, March 14, 15, 1901, and the Savannah *Evening Press*, December 26, 1900, and March 14, 1901. Additional information about Houston's white lawyer, Raiford Falligant, appears in Thomas Walker Reed, "History of the University of Georgia," typescript, p. 1791, University of Georgia Archives. It is as yet unclear when Houston obtained Falligant's services.

Musically, "Delia"/"Delia's Gone" has led many mixed-up lives. According to the Library of Congress folklorist Robert Winslow Gordon, the song was sung as early as 1901, to the same tune as "McKinley ('White House Blues')," about the president's assassination. Although that original "Delia" has not been recovered, Professor Garst argues persuasively that internal evidence shows that the two songs were linked. The name of the bard who wrote the first version of the song remains unknown, but that version must have been completed very shortly after the events it described.

The folklorist and sociologist Howard Odum collected the song, under the title "One More Rounder Gone," between 1906 and 1908 in Newton County, Georgia. He published that version in *The Journal of American Folklore* in 1911. In 1928, Robert Gordon traced the song's origins more than halfway across the state to Savannah. That same year, the song collector Newton Ivey White published three variants, obtained between 1915 and 1924 in North Carolina, Georgia, and Alabama. Zora Neale Hurston found another version in Florida; and three more appeared under the title "Delia Holmes" in an article by Chipman Milling published in *The Southern Folklore Quarterly* in 1937. By 1940, there were at least four recorded versions: two field recordings along with Reese Du Pree's "One More

Rounder Gone," released on Okeh Records in 1924, and Jimmy Gordon's "Dehlia," released on Decca Records in 1939.

At some point before 1927, the song migrated to the Bahamas, where the first versions with the refrain, "Delia's gone, one more round, Delia's gone," appeared. The line seems to have been a reworking of "one more rounder gone," possibly lifted from Du Pree's record. Several more Bahamian variants turned up on local field recordings and commercial releases before World War II. Those versions, in turn, did not stay confined to the Caribbean but traveled back to the United States, mingled with the older versions, and emerged transformed once again by American singers. Blind Willie McTell first recorded what appears to be a hybrid, "Delia," for the Library of Congress in 1940.

The song's contemporary history began in 1952, when the Bahamian calypso singer Blind Blake Alphonso Higgs (not to be confused with the American Arthur "Blind" Blake, "the King of the Ragtime Guitar") recorded "Delia Gone" for the small Art Records label. As Professor Garst shows, Higgs's version has been the basis for most of the subsequent American recordings of the song, beginning in the 1950s with renderings by Josh White and Harry Belafonte and continuing into the present. (Before 1952, no American recorded the song under the title "Delia's Gone.") Both of Johnny Cash's recordings of the song bear Higgs's influence, if only indirectly. So does Roger McGuinn's 2002 online version, which McGuinn sings with a calypso lilt. Yet, as Professor Garst also shows, there are important exceptions. Above all, Bob Dylan's "Delia" from 1993, with the refrain, "All the friends I ever had are gone," seems to be a mixture of McTell's adaptation and a "Delia" sung by the Reverend Blind Gary Davis on a live recording from the beginning of the 1970s that was released in 1990.

Over the years, elements of "Frankie and Albert" aka "Frankie and Johnny" have been absorbed into different versions of "Delia." In their 2001 recording of "Delia," for example, Spider John Koerner and Dave Ray rhetorically ask Delia why she didn't run, and if she didn't see "that desperado with his .44 smokeless gun." The smokeless-gun reference appeared in early collected versions of "Frankie and Albert" as well. The borrowings are not surprising, given the similarity of the two situations, and given that the actual killings described took place only a little more than a year apart.

"Delia"/"Delia's Gone" has been recorded so often, under such diverse titles, and by so many different kinds of performers—including Pat Boone, Waylon Jennings, and Sonny Rollins—that any discography must declare itself provisional. The following list is in chronological order.

Reese Du Pree, "One More Rounder Gone." 78 rpm. Okeh 8127, 1924. Reissued on CD, *Male Blues of the Twenties*. Document DOCD-5482.

Booker T. Sapps and Roger Matthews, "Frankie and Albert (Cooney and Delia)." Field recording. 1935. Released on CD, *Field Recordings, Volume 7, Florida, 1935–1936*. Document DOCD-5587.

Blind Jesse Harris, "All the Friends I Got Is Gone." Field recording. 1937. Released on CD, *Field Recordings, Volume 4: Mississippi & Alabama, 1934–1942*. Document DOCD-5578.

Jimmy Gordon, "Delilia." Decca 7592, 1939. Reissued on CD, *Jimmy Gordon, 1934–41*. Story of Blues CD 3510-2.

Blind Willie McTell, "Delia." 1940. Library of Congress field recording, 1940. Issued on CD, *Blind Willie McTell 1940*. Document BDCD-6001.

———, "Little Delia." 1949. Unreleased commercial recording. Issued on CD, *Atlanta Twelve String*. Atlantic 82366.

Blake Alphonso Higgs (Blind Blake), "Delia Gone," *A Third Album of Bahamian Songs by "Blind Blake" and the Royal Victoria Hotel "Calypso" Orchestra*. LP. Art ALP-6, 1952.

Harry Belafonte, "Delia," *Mark Twain and Other Folk Favorites*. LP. RCA Victor. LPM-1022, 1954.

Josh White, "Delia's Gone," *The Story of John Henry & Ballads, Blues and Other Songs*. LP. Elektra EKL 701, 1955.

Paul Clayton, "Delia," *Bloody Ballads*. LP. Riverside RLP 12-615, 1956.

Bob Gibson, "Delia," *Offbeat Folksongs*. LP. Riverside RLP 12-802, 1956.

Harry Belafonte, "Delia's Gone," *Love Is a Gentle Thing*. LP. RCA Victor. RCA LPM-1927, 1959.

The Gateway Singers, "Dehlia's Blues," . . . *On the Lot*. LP. Warner Bros. WS-1295, 1959.

Pat Boone, "Delia Gone." 45 rpm. Dot 16122, 1960. Reissued on CD, *Pat Boone: The Fifties Complete*. Bear Family BCD 15844, 1997.

Bud and Travis, "Delia's Gone," *Bud and Travis*. LP. Liberty LRP 3125, 1960.

Johnny Cash, "Delia's Gone," *The Sound of Johnny Cash*. LP. Columbia CS 8602, 1962.

Casey Anderson, "Delia's Gone," *Casey Anderson "Live" at the Ice*. LP. Atco 33-172, 1963.

Will Holt, "Delia's Gone," *Will Holt Concert*. LP. Stinson SLP 64, 1963.

The Kingston Trio, "(Delia's Gone) One More Round," *The Kingston Trio #16*. LP. Capitol ST-1871, 1963.

Waylon Jennings, "Delia's Gone." 45 rpm. RCA Victor 74-0157, 1969. Also on *The Best of Waylon Jennings*. LP. RCA Victor LSP 4341, 1970. Reissued on CD, RCA, 1990.

Rev. Gary Davis, "Delia," *Delia—Late Concert Recordings, 1970–71*. CD. American Activities UACD103, 1990.

Roy Bookbinder, "Delia," *Travelin' Man*. LP. Adelphi AD 1017, 1972.

Happy Traum, "Delia's Gone," *American Stranger*. LP. Kicking Mule KM 110, 1977.

George Gritzbach, "Delia," *Sweeper*. LP. Kicking Mule SNKF 157, 1978.

Ron Wood, "Delia," *Gimme Some Neck*. LP. CBS JC35702, 1979. Reissued on CD, Sony 35702, 1989.

Al Stewart, "Delia's Gone," *Indian Summer*. LP. Arista A2L 8607, 1981.

Gary Stewart, "Delia," *Battleground*. CD. HighTone, 1990.

Cordelia's Dad, "Delia," *How Can I Sleep?* CD. Okra Records OKCD 33019, 1992. Rereleased by Omnium Recordings OMM 2010, 1996.

Bob Dylan, "Delia," *World Gone Wrong*. CD. Columbia 57590, 1993.

Sonny Rollins, "Delia," *Old Flames*. CD. Milestone MCD-9215-2, 1993.

Johnny Cash, "Delia's Gone," *American Recordings*. CD. American 9 45520-2, 1994.

Paul Lansky, "Delia," *Folk Images*. CD. Bridge 9060, 1995.

Koerner, Ray & Glover, "Deliah's Gone," *One Foot in the Groove*. CD. TimKerr Records TK96CD137, 1996.

Stefan Grossman, "Delia," *Shake That Thing*. CD. Shanachie 97027, 1998.

Peter Stanley, "Delia's Gone," *At the Sidekick*. CD. Talkeetna 25003, 1999.

David Alvin, "Delia," *Public Domain: Songs from the Wild Land*. CD. HighTone HCD 8122, 2000.

Eric Bibb, "Delia 's Gone," *Painting Signs*. CD. EarthBeat 74382, 2001.

Spider John Koerner and Dave Ray, "Delia," *A Nod to Bob: An Artists' Tribute to Bob Dylan on His Sixtieth Birthday*. CD. Red House RHR 154, 2001.

Roger McGuinn, "Delia's Gone," The Folk Den Website. 2002. Available at www.reveries.com/folkden/delia.html.

—SW

DAVID THOMAS
"The Wreck of Old 97"
and
"Dead Man's Curve"

Arizona Wranglers, "Wreck of the 97." 1929. Included on the anthology *Train 45: Railroad Songs of the Early 1900's* (Rounder 1143), a set produced by Norm Cohen and Dick Spottswood and featuring also "Wreck of the 1256" by Curly Fox, Uncle Dave Macon's "Death of John Henry," "Railroad Blues" by Sam McGee, "Pullman Passenger Train" by the Pullman Porters Quartette, and "He Is Coming to Us Dead" by G. B. Grayson and Henry Whitter.

Chris Cutler, "Scale," *Unfiled: Music Under New Technology*, vol. 4, no. 2 (1997): 59–64.

Woody Guthrie, "The Wreck of Old 97," recording date unknown. Originally released on *Woody Guthrie Sings Folk Songs, Vol. 2* (Folkways Records FA 2484), included on Guthrie, *Muleskinner Blues: The Asch Recordings, Vol. 2*. CD. Smithsonian Folkways 40101, 1997.

Jan and Dean, "Dead Man's Curve." 45 rpm. Liberty 55672, 1964. Included on *"Dead Man's Curve"/"New Girl in School."* One Way Records 18684, 1996. The CD includes both this 1964 album and the 1966 Jan and Dean album *Popsicle*.

Katie Letcher Lyle, *Scalded to Death by the Steam: The True Stories of Railroad Disasters and the Songs That Were Written About Them*. Chapel Hill, NC: Algonquin Books, 1991.

—*David Thomas*

Additional thanks to G. Howard Gregory, author of the informative booklet *History of the Wreck of the Old 97*, Appomattox, VA: G. H. Gregory, 1992, for his help in tracking down visual materials.

—*SW*

"Buddy Bolden's Blues"

"Buddy Bolden's Blues" aka "I Thought I Heard Buddy Bolden Say" aka "Funky Butt Blues" has been recorded often but retains a special allure to performers directly connected to New Orleans. Jelly Roll Morton first made the song famous in the late 1920s and 1930s and included it in a series of important sessions arranged by Alan Lomax for the Library of Congress in 1938. The sessions are available on CD, with "Buddy Bolden's Blues" appearing on *Anamule Dance: Jully Roll Morton: The Library of Congress Recordings, Vol. 2*. Rounder CDROUN1092, 1994.

Sidney Bechet, Wynton Marsalis, and Doctor John (Mac Rebennack) are among the better-known artists who have recorded the song. An interesting version, sung by Billie Holiday, appears on the soundtrack of the 1947 Republic Pictures film *New Orleans*. The film's soundtrack is available on a CD issued in 2000 by the small Definitive Classics label (ASIN: B000050HR7), and can be ordered from the better-known online stores as well as the better retail outlets.

In addition to the sources discussed in this essay, anyone interested in learning more about Buddy Bolden and his world will want to read the brilliant fictional evocation by Michael Ondaatje, *Coming Through Slaughter*, first published in 1976 and in print in paperback from Vintage International.

—SW

JON LANGFORD

"The Cuckoo"

Jon Langford's piece is a version of his song "See Willy Fly By," from the Waco Brothers' *Cowboy in Flames* (Bloodshot 015, 1997)—which is itself a version of "The Cuckoo," aka "The Coo Coo," aka "Jack o' Diamonds" ("Gonna build me/Log cabin/On a mountain/So high/So I can see Willy/When he goes/On by"). The earliest known variant, probably dating back a thousand years, is "Sumer Is Icumen In," which Richard Thompson performs on *1000 Years of Popular Music* (Beeswing/www.richardthompsonmusic.com BSW 003, 2003). As "The Cuckoo," the song has been recorded countless times since at least the 1920s—most recently, as of this writing, by Tim Eriksen and Riley

Baugus for the soundtrack album for the film *Cold Mountain* (DMZ/Columbia CK 86843, 2003). Versions drawn on by Langford, which represent all sorts of approaches to the theme, include the Virginia singer and fiddler Kelly Harrell's 1926 "The Cuckoo She's a Fine Bird," a bizarre recording that combines Central European–style gypsy violin with the repeated sound of an actual cuckoo clock (originally released as Victor 3567-3-Vi V-40047), available on Kelly Harrell, *Complete Recorded Works in Chronological Order, Volume 2 (1926–1929)* (Document 8027); the North Carolina singer and banjo player Clarence Ashley's unequaled 1929 "The Coo Coo Bird" (originally released as Columbia 15489D), available on *Greenback Dollar: The Music of Clarence "Tom" Ashley, 1929–1933* (County 3520), and probably best known because of its inclusion by Harry Smith on his 1952 *Anthology of American Folk Music* (Smithsonian Folkways 1997); the blues singer and guitarist John Lee Hooker's 1949 "Jack o' Diamonds," from *The Unknown John Lee Hooker: 1949 Recordings* (Flywright 57, 2000); John Cohen's 1959 field recording of the unaccompanied Mr. & Mrs. Sams's "The Coo Coo," collected on *Mountain Music of Kentucky* (Smithsonian Folkways 40077, an expanded 1996 reissue of a highly influential set originally released in 1960); Bob Dylan's ca. 1962 publishing demo "Cuckoo Is a Pretty Bird," a tough-guy rendition included on various bootlegs, including *Documents of Bob Dylan* (Magic Music 31002); the Virginia singer and banjoist Hobart Smith's fierce "The Coo Coo Bird," originally released on the anthology *Traditional Music at Newport, 1964, Part 1* (Vanguard 79182, 1965), included on *Songcatcher II: The Tradition That Inspired the Movie* (Vanguard 79712-2, 2002); a speechifying 1965 demo "Jack of Diamonds" by the San Francisco old-timey/rock 'n' roll band the Charlatans, collected on *The Amazing Charlatans* (Big Beat WIKD 138, 1996); the San Francisco rock 'n' roll band Big Brother and the Holding Company's fast 1966 "Coo Coo," one of Janis Joplin's most unfettered recordings, originally released as Mainstream 678 in 1967 and included on Janis Joplin, *Janis* (Columbia Legacy C3K 48845, 1993); a very cynical "Cuckoo" by the Los Angeles old-timey/new-age rock 'n' roll band Kaleidoscope, originally released in 1966 on *Kaleidoscope* (Epic BN 26467) and included on Kaleidoscope, *Egyptian Gardens (A Collection)* (Epic/Legacy EK 47723, 1991); an unaccompanied, very archaic "The Cuckoo" by the British folksinger Anne Briggs (instead of the usual American "She sucks the pretty flowers/To keep her voice clear," Briggs—alluding to the fact that the cuckoo lays its eggs in the nests of other birds, and it or the cuckoo nestling often attacks the host bird, its eggs, or the other nestlings, to protect its progeny or itself—sings, "She sucks the little birds' eggs/To keep her voice clear"), originally released in 1971 on *Anne*

Briggs (Topic) and included on Anne Briggs, *A Collection* (Topic 504, 1999); the Irish singer and guitarist Rory Gallagher's solo "The Cuckoo," a passionate home recording from the early 1970s, included on Rory Gallagher, *Wheels within Wheels* (Capo/BM Heritage/Buddha 74465 997872); "Coo Coo," as done by John Snipes and then Dink Roberts, as recorded by Cece Conway in 1974 and collected on the anthology *Black Banjo Songsters of North Carolina and Virginia* (Smithsonian Folkways 9628, 1998); the Brooklyn chamber-music country band Hem's "The Cuckoo" (Dreamworks B0000841-02, 2001, 2002); and the British folk singer Charlotte Greig's "The Cuckoo," from her *Winter Woods* (Harmonium Music 725, 2003).

Jon Langford tips his hat to Sir Dickie Thompson.

—*GM*

PAUL BERMAN
"Volver, Volver"

¡Arriba Huentitán!, containing the classic recording of "Volver, Volver" from the early 1970s, is available in *Vicente Fernández 35 Anniversario*, Vol. 22. Sony Discos, 1990, 2003.

A recent alternative rendition of the song by the duet of Vicente Fernández and his son, Alejandro Fernández, still in the arrangement by Fernando Z. Maldonado, can be heard in *Vicente y Alejandro Fernández en Vivo Juntos por Ultima Vez*. Sony Discos, Sony Music Entertainment Mexico, S.A. de C.V., 2003.

La Fiesta del Mariachi Vargas de Tecalitlán, which contains a useful brochure, no author listed. PolyGram Discos S.A. de C.V., 1994.

My essay cites the following literary works:

Mercedes Díaz Roig, *Romancero tradicional de América*. Mexico City: El Colegio de México, 1990.

"The Spanish Element in Our Nationality," by Walt Whitman, from "November Boughs" in his *Complete Prose Works* (1892). "A Broadway Pageant" from *Leaves of Grass*, Deathbed Edition (1891–92). Both works are included in the Library of America edition of *Whitman: Poetry and Prose*, Justin Kaplan, ed., New York: Literary Classics of the United States, 1982.

Henry Wadsworth Longfellow's "The Bells of San Blas," one of his last poems, written the year of his death, 1882, collected in his posthumous volume *In the Harbor* (1882) and included in the Library of America edition of *Longfellow: Poems and Other Writings*. J. D. McClatchy, ed., New York: Literary Classics of the United States, 2000.

I draw also from Jas Reuter, *La Música popular de México*. Mexico City: Panorama Editorial, S.A., 1992. And I have drawn on the cinemata expertise of Fernanda Solórzano, the film critic of *Letras Libres* magazine in Mexico.

—Paul Berman

JOHN ROCKWELL
"The Foggy, Foggy Dew"

The chief pertinent recording is "The Foggy, Foggy Dew," on Burl Ives, *Wayfaring Stranger*. 10" LP, Stinson SLP 1, 1949. Earlier Ives 78 rpm recordings of the song appeared on the Stinson and Asch labels, both run by the Popular Front folk-song collector and record maker Moe Asch. A 1940 recording of Ives performing the song on CBS Radio appears on Burl Ives, *Poor Wayfaring Stranger*. CD. Pearl 7090, 1996.

—SW

STANLEY CROUCH
"Come Sunday"

The original recording of *Black, Brown and Beige* is available on *The Duke Ellington Carnegie Hall Concerts, January 1943*. CD. Prestige Records 2PCD-34004-2. The 1958 recording with Mahalia Jackson, including the previously unreleased a cappella version of "Come Sunday," appears on the CD of *Black, Brown, and Beige*. Columbia/Legacy CK 065566.

—Stanley Crouch

JAMES MILLER
"El Paso"

Perhaps the most revealing interview with Marty Robbins appears in Alanna Nash, *Behind Closed Doors* (New York: Knopf, 1988), pp. 436–54. Jim Glaser's account of how "El Paso" was composed can be found as a "memo" from Jim Glaser to Norma J, posted in the summer of 2003 at http:/norma100.com/glsrrobns1.html/. Douglas B. Green, *Singing in the Saddle* (Nashville: Vanderbilt & Country Music Foundation, 2002), offers an informed history of the singing cowboy, from the 1930s to the present. A comprehensive overview of Robbins's recording career is offered on *The Essential Marty Robbins: 1951–1982* (Columbia/Legacy C2K 48537), a 2-CD boxed set issued in 1991. All of his Western recordings are collected on *Under Western Skies* (Bear Family BDC 15646 DI, 1995), a 4-CD boxed set that includes many rare and previously unreleased items. The most recent digitally remastered version of the album *Gunfighter Ballads and Trail Songs* appeared in 1999 (Columbia/Legacy CK 65996). Two 1959 television broadcasts featuring Robbins with the Glaser Brothers appear on a DVD, *Marty Robbins at Town Hall Party* (Bear Family BVD 20007 AT, 2003). Robbins performs "El Paso" in *Road to Nashville*, a movie he financed, originally released in 1967, now available on DVD (Rhino R2 972848, 2000). Robbins's most ambitious Western film, *Ballad of a Gunfighter,* was released in 1964 and was reissued on VHS videotape in 1984 (Prism 2351). My quote from John A. Lomax comes from his introduction to *Cowboy Songs and Other Frontier Ballads* (first published in 1910; my edition is New York: Macmillan, 1925). The Mexican Western genre of *ranchera* is discussed in Ramiro Burr, *The Billboard Guide to Tejano and Regional Mexican Music* (New York: Billboard Books, 1999). For the emergence of the noir Western, watch Anthony Mann's *Winchester '73* (1950); any early episode of the TV show *Have Gun Will Travel* (1957–63); Howard Hawks's *Rio Bravo* (1959); and then the masterpiece of the genre, *The Magnificent Seven.* Based on Akiro Kurosawa's *Seven Samurai,* the 1960 John Sturges film depicts a desperate group of Mexican villagers hiring a band of amoral American gunmen for protection against bandits—a borderland setting and nihilistic premise that Sergio Leone would use as a template for his even darker series of Westerns, from *A Fistful of Dollars* (1964) to *Once Upon a Time in the West* (1969).

—*James Miller*

ED WARD

"Trial of Mary Maguire"

Bobby Patterson, "Trial of Mary Maguire." 45 rpm. Jetstar 118, 1969.
Included, with previously unreleased first version, on *Soul Is My Music: The Best of Bobby Patterson*. CD. Sundazed 11105, 2003.

—Ed Ward

ERIC WEISBARD

"Down from Dover"

Skeeter Davis, "Down from Dover," from *Skeeter Sings Dolly*. LP. RCA, 1972.
Reissued as *Skeeter Davis Sings Buddy Holly/Skeeter Sings Dolly*. CD.
Eagle JZO0, 1999.

Whitney Houston, "I Will Always Love You"/"Jesus Loves You." Arista 12490,
1992. Included on the soundtrack album for *The Bodyguard*. CD. Arista
18699, 1992.

Alanna Nash, *Dolly: The Biography*. 1978. Reissued with an additional
chapter, New York: Cooper Square Press, 2003.

Dolly Parton, *Dolly in London*. Columbia TriStar Home Entertainment, 1983.

———, "Down from Dover," originally issued on *The Fairest of Them All*. LP.
RCA Victor LSP 4288, 1970. Included on *The Best of Dolly Parton*. LP.
RCA Victor LSP 4449, and on *The RCA Years: 1967–1986*, CD. RCA
07863, 1993). Rerecorded (with "Mountain Angel") for *Little Sparrow*.
CD. Sugar Hill 3927, 2001.

———, "I Will Always Love You." 45 rpm. RCA Victor 0234, 1974. Included on *I
Will Always Love You: The Essential Dolly Parton*. CD. RCA 2 66533, 1995.
Rereleased on the soundtrack album for *The Best Little Whorehouse in
Texas*, a film that starred Parton and Burt Reynolds. LP. MCA 6122, 1982.

———, "Letter to Heaven," *Hits Made Famous by Country Queens*. LP.
Somerset 19700, 1963. Rerecorded on *Joshua*. LP. RCA Victor 4507, 1971.

———, "Me and Little Andy," *Here You Come Again*. LP. RCA 2544, 1977.

———, *Dolly: My Life and Other Unfinished Business*. New York:
HarperCollins, 1994.

———, with Porter Wagoner, "Jeannie's Afraid of the Dark," *The Best of Porter
Wagoner and Dolly Parton*. LP. RCA Victor LSP 4556, 1971.

Willadeene Parton, *In the Shadow of a Song: The Story of the Parton Family.* New York: Bantam, 1985. Reissued as *Smoky Mountain Memories: Stories from the Hearts of the Parton Family.* Nashville: Rutledge Hill Press, 1996.

Lee Smith, *Fair and Tender Ladies.* New York: G. P. Putnam's Sons, 1988.

Sally Timms and the Drifting Cowgirls, "Down from Dover," on *Butcher's Boy.* T.I.M., 1987; *It Says Here* (live version). Feel Good All Over 7004, 1995; *Somebody's Rocking My Dreamboat.* T.I.M., 1998.

——, with Jon Langford, on *Songs of False Hope and High Values.* Bloodshot 072, 2000.

Ian Watt, *The Rise of the Novel.* Berkeley: University of California, 1965. Reissued 2001.

Thanks to Don Yates, Dave Vorhees, Jake Austen, and Greil Marcus for help obtaining records.

—Eric Weisbard

STEVE ERICKSON

"Sail Away" and "Louisiana 1927"

Randy Newman's "Sail Away" was first heard in 1972 on *Sail Away* (Reprise 2064). His "Louisiana 1927" appeared in 1974 on *Good Old Boys* (Reprise 2193). An early version of "Sail Away," with bombastic, not to say half-looped, percussion and Newman banging his piano is included on the 2002 reissue *Sail Away (Expanded & Remastered)* (Rhino 78244),which ends with what sounds like a tape splice into a samba fade. The 2002 *Good Old Boys (Deluxe Reissue)* (Rhino 73839) follows the original album with a second disc, "Johnny Cutler's Birthday," Newman's original conception for the set: a Birmingham steelworker's autobiography. Newman talks his way through the demo session, setting up each performance: "Louisiana" has a rough piano accompaniment, and a loose, conversational vocal as seemingly artless as the testimony of an eyewitness being interviewed on TV about an accident. Both "Sail Away" and "Louisiana 1927" are included on *Guilty: 30 Years of Randy Newman* (Warner Archives/Reprise/Rhino 75567). In 2003, Newman released new versions of "Sail Away" and "Louisiana 1927" as part of a set of voice-and-piano recordings, *The Randy Newman Songbook Vol. 1* (Nonesuch 79689-2).

—GM

WENDY LESSER

"Lily, Rosemary and the Jack of Hearts"

"Lily, Rosemary and the Jack of Hearts" is from Bob Dylan's *Blood on the Tracks*, LP, Columbia PC 33235, 1975, and, on CD, Columbia CK 33235. His earlier acetate recording of the song appears on a widely distributed bootleg, *New York Sessions*. Given the song's epic length, it is not surprising that few performers other than its composer have tackled it, either in concert or in the studio. Dylan himself appears to have performed it on stage only once, on May 25, 1976, the day after his thirty-fifth birthday, at the very last Rolling Thunder Revue concert in Salt Lake City. Joan Baez included her own concert recording of the song on her double album *At Every Stage* (A&M Records, 1976, since rereleased several times, most recently as part of *The Complete A&M Recordings*). The band Mary Lee's Corvette recorded it on a *Blood on the Tracks* tribute album (Bar None Records, 2002). The Grateful Dead lyricist Robert Hunter—and Dylan's co-writer for "Silvio"—performed "Lily, Rosemary and the Jack of Hearts" during the second of his spring 1997 concert tours. He told audiences that he wanted to test his memory.

There is also a fascinating Galician translation of the song, "Corazón de Pau," performed by the group 7 Lvvas on their 1998 album *Nu*. The complete translated lyrics are posted online at www.iespana.es/7Lvvas/.

—SW

HOWARD HAMPTON

"Nebraska"

Badlands, directed by Terrence Malick, Warner Bros., 1973.
Ninette Beaver with B. K. Ripley and Patrick Trese, *Caril*. Philadelphia and
New York: J. B. Lippincott, 1974.
Chuck Berry, "You Can't Catch Me." 45 rpm. Chess 1645, 1955.
Manny Farber, *Negative Space*. New York: Praeger, 1971.
Robert Frank, *The Americans*, with an introduction by Jack Kerouac. New
York: Grove Press, 1959.
Woody Guthrie, "Tom Joad, Parts 1 & 2," from *Dust Bowl Ballads*. 2 10" LPs.
RCA Victor, P-27 and P-28, 1940.

Bruce Springsteen, *Nebraska*. Columbia, 38358, 1982. Reissued on CD, 1990.
Sullivan's Travels, directed by Preston Sturges. Paramount Pictures, 1941.

—*Howard Hampton*

PAUL MULDOON

"Blackwatertown"

The source I used for this song was a version of "The Unfortunate Rake," a broadside text with the most graphic account of the root of the rake's problem—his contracting syphilis through a sexual dalliance:

> And had she but told me before she disordered me,
> Had she but told me of it in time,
> I might have got pills and salts of white mercury,
> But now I'm cut down in the height of my prime.

I was particularly taken by the instructional verse in this version:

> Get six young soldiers to carry my coffin,
> Six young girls to sing me a song,
> And each of them carry a bunch of green laurel
> So they don't smell me as they bear me along.

This verse is rather famously carried over, and cleaned up, by Francis Henry Maynard in his 1876 version of "The Streets of Laredo," where we meet "six jolly cowboys" and "six pretty maidens." The tune of "The Streets of Laredo" is based on "The Bard of Armagh," which I've known for years in the version sung by my fellow Armaghman, Tommy Makem:

> Oh list to the lays of a poor Irish harper
> And scorn not the strains of his old withered hands
> But remember his fingers they once could move sharper
> To raise up the memory of his dear native land

The "bard" in question was Phelim Brady, a local poet who flourished (if that's the term) in the very early eighteenth century. Vince Gill sings "The

Bard of Armagh" on *Long Journey Home* (Unisphere Records/BMG 099026-68963-2, 1998), segueing into "The Streets of Laredo." A lovely version of "The Streets of Laredo" is sung by Joan Baez on *Very Early Joan* (Vanguard VSD 764467/7, 1982/1991, live recordings from 1960 to 1963), while Tommy Makem sings "The Bard of Armagh" on an album of the same title (GWP ST 2006, 1970). I call my version "Blackwatertown" in honor of a town on the Armagh/Tyrone border near where I was raised.

—*Paul Muldoon*

Contributors

Paul Berman writes on literature and politics for the *New Republic*, the *New York Times*, *Dissent*, and other journals. He is the author of *A Tale of Two Utopias* (1996), *Terror and Liberalism* (2003), and *The Passion of Joschka Fischer* (2004). From 1967 to 1980 he played trombone (and sometimes worked as an arranger and composer) for a variety of soul and big bands in New York, notably the Soul Syndicate with the saxophonist Kenny Blake, and the Uptown Horns with the saxophonist Arno Hecht. He performed regularly with the Jon Paris band, as well as with many other groups, including the Theatre for a New City, the Bob January Band at the Village Gate, with blues musician Buddy Guy and the singer Johnny Maestro. From 1999 to 2002 he played the viola in the Danny Kalb Trio, together with the guitarist, bassist, and singer Bob Jones. His cartoons have appeared in his *Make-Believe Empire*, a children's book, and in the IWW newspaper the *Industrial Worker*.

Cecil Brown was born in North Carolina and educated at Columbia, the University of Chicago, and the University of California at Berkeley, where he received a Ph.D. in anthropology in 1993. He is the author of the novels *The Life and Loves of Mr. Jiveass Nigger* (1970) and *Days without Weather* (1983), the memoir *Coming Up Down Home* (1993), and *Stagolee Shot Billy* (2003).

Stanley Crouch has been an actor, playwright, and educator. Born and raised in Los Angeles, he moved to New York City in 1975 and soon began writing for the *Soho Weekly News* and the *Village Voice*, where he remained a staff writer until 1988. His books include *Notes of a Hanging Judge* (1991), *The All-American Skin Game, or, The Decoy of Race* (1995), the novel *Don't the Moon Look Lonesome* (2000), *The Artificial White Man* (2004), and, with Playthell Benjamin, *Reconsidering the Souls of Black Folk* (2003). He is the recipient of the Jean Stein Award from the American Academy of Arts and Sciences and is a John D. and Catherine T. MacArthur Fellow. His twice-weekly column appears in the *New York Daily News*. He is currently at work on *Kansas City Lightning*, a biography of Charlie Parker.

R. Crumb published his first comic panels, introducing Fritz the Cat, in 1964 in *Help!* After that his work upended the American comic book and, thanks to the depredations of Mr. Natural, Frankie Foont, Angelfood McSpade, and the host of sex-drugs-violence-and-domination-crazed characters running through the pages of *Zap Comix*, *Self-Loathing Comics*, and countless other titles, left behind a landscape of confusion and ruin. He is also the creator of a comix biography of the founding country bluesman Charley Patton; "Jelly Roll Morton's Voodoo Curse"; "That's Life," an account of the journey of a Mississippi blues from its creation to its collection by Northern record fiends; and the card packages *Heroes of the Blues*, *Jazz Greats*, and *Pioneers of Country Music*. Albums by his band R. Crumb and the Cheap Suit Serenaders, devoted to the music of the 1920s and '30s, include *R. Crumb and His Cheap Suit Serenaders* (1974), *Chasin' Rainbows* (1976—the band included Terry Zwigoff, director of the 1995 film *Crumb*), and *Singing in the Bathtub* (1978). He lives in France.

Anna Domino is a singer and songwriter living in Los Angeles. She has released a number of albums in Europe and Japan, including *East and West* (1984), *Anna Domino* (1986), *This Time* (1987), *Coloring in the Edge and the Outline* (1988), and *Mysteries of America* (1990). In 1987 she began working with the multi-instrumentalist and arranger Michel Delory, and their collaboration on music, soundtracks, and performance continues to this day. In 1999 she was drawn back to the traditional songs she had grown up with, and to the challenge of reinterpreting these legends in a new way. This experiment produced a recording of classic American ballads with a contemporary tone, released under the name Snakefarm as *Songs from My Funeral*. Born in Tokyo, Domino has lived in Ann Arbor, Florence, Ottawa, New York, Brussels, and Paris.

Steve Erickson is the author of the novels *Days Between Stations* (1985), *Rubicon Beach* (1986), *Tours of the Black Clock* (1989), *Arc d'X* (1993), *Amnesiascope* (1996), *The Sea Came in at Midnight* (1999), and the forthcoming *Our Ecstatic Days*, as well as two books on American politics and culture, *Leap Year* (1989) and *American Nomad* (1997). Over the years his work has appeared in *Esquire*, *Rolling Stone*, the *New York Times Magazine*, the *Los Angeles Times Magazine*, *Salon.com*, and other publications. He is currently the film critic for *Los Angeles Magazine* and the editor of *Black Clock*, a literary journal published by CalArts, where he teaches writing.

Howard Hampton began writing criticism in 1982 for the *Boston Phoenix*. He has written about music and movies for the *Village Voice, LA Weekly, Artforum, Film Comment*, the *Boston Globe*, and other publications. He continues to work on *Badlands: A Psychogeography of the Reagan Era*, following the lost highway from Bruce Springsteen's *Nebraska* to Missy Elliott's "Pass that Dutch."

Jon Langford is an artist and founding member of the British punk band the Mekons. Born in Newport, South Wales, he now lives in Chicago, where he paints and performs with the Waco Brothers and the Pine Valley Cosmonauts.

Wendy Lesser founded the *Threepenny Review* in 1980 and remains its editor. She is the author of *Life Below the Ground: A Study of the Subterranean in Literature and History* (1987), *His Other Half: Men Looking at Women through Art* (1991), *Pictures at an Execution* (1994), *A Director Calls: Stephen Daldry and the Theater* (1997), *The Amateur* (1999), and *Nothing Remains the Same: Reading and Remembering* (2002), and the editor of *Hiding in Plain Sight*, a *Threepenny Review* anthology (1993). She is a member of the American Academy of Arts and Sciences, a winner of the Morton Dauwen Zabel Award for criticism, a former Regents Lecturer at the University of California at Berkeley, and a former fellow of the Guggenheim Foundation, the American Academy in Berlin, and the National Arts Journalism Program. She lives in Berkeley.

Sharyn McCrumb is best known for her "Ballad" novels, set in the North Carolina/Tennessee mountains, which incorporate traditional Appalachian music into the history and cultural conflicts of the region. At her author appearances she often shares the stage with a bluegrass musician who performs the ballads linked to the novels. Her latest book, *Ghost Riders* (2003), is an account of the Civil War in the Appalachians and its echoes in the area today. Her other novels include *She Walks These Hills* (1996) and *The Rosewood Casket* (1994), which deal with the question of the vanishing wilderness; *The Ballad of Frankie Silver* (1998), the story of the first woman hanged for murder in North Carolina; *The Hangman's Beautiful Daughter* (1992); *If Ever I Return, Pretty Peggy-O* (1995); and *The Songcatcher* (2000). She has been honored with the 2003 Wilma Dykeman Award for Literature, given by the East Tennessee Historical Society; the AWA Award for Outstanding Contribution to Appalachian Literature; the Chafin Award for

Achievement in Southern Literature; the Plattner Award for Short Story; the St. Andrew's College Flora MacDonald Award; and the Sherwood Anderson Short Story Award. She has served as writer in residence at King College in Tennessee and at Shepherd College in West Virginia; in 2001 she was fiction writer in residence at the WICE Conference in Paris. She is a graduate of the University of North Carolina, with an M.A. from Virginia Tech. She lives in the Virginia Blue Ridge.

Dave Marsh's previous work with folk music includes co-editing *Pastures of Plenty* (1990), a collection of writing by Woody Guthrie, and *Louie Louie: The History and Mythology of the World's Most Famous Rock 'n' Roll Song; Including the Full Details of Its Torture and Persecution at the Hands of the Kingsmen, J. Edgar Hoover's F.B.I., and a Cast of Millions; and Introducing, for the First Time Anywhere, the Actual Dirty Lyrics* (1994, reissued in 2004).

James Miller is the author of *Flowers in the Dustbin: The Rise of Rock and Roll, 1947–1977* (1999), winner of the ASCAP–Deems Taylor and Ralph J. Gleason music book awards. The original editor of *The Rolling Stone Illustrated History of Rock & Roll* (1976, 1980) and pop music critic for *Newsweek* in the 1980s, his criticism has also appeared in *Rolling Stone*, where he began writing in 1968, the *New Republic*, and the *New York Times*. His other books include *History and Human Existence: From Marx to Merleau-Ponty* (1979), *Rousseau: Dreamer of Democracy* (1984), *"Democracy Is in the Streets"* (1987), and *The Passion of Michel Foucault* (1993). Currently professor of political science at the New School for Social Research in New York City, he is also the editor of *Daedalus*, the quarterly journal of the American Academy of Arts and Sciences.

Paul Muldoon was born in 1951 in County Armagh, Northern Ireland, and educated in Armagh and at the Queen's University of Belfast. From 1973 to 1986 he worked in Belfast as a radio and television producer for the BBC. Since 1987 he has lived in the United States, where he is now Howard G. B. Clark '21 Professor in the Humanities at Princeton University. In 1999 he was elected professor of poetry at the University of Oxford. His main collections of poetry are *New Weather* (1973), *Mules* (1977), *Why Brownlee Left* (1980), *Quoof* (1983), *Meeting the British* (1987), *Madoc: A Mystery* (1990), *The Annals of Chile* (1994), *Hay* (1998), *Poems 1968–1998* (2001), and *Moy Sand and Gravel* (2002). A fellow of the Royal Society of Literature and the

American Academy of Arts and Sciences, he has won the 1994 T. S. Eliot Prize, a 1996 American Academy of Arts and Letters Award in Literature, the 1997 *Irish Times* Poetry Prize, and the 2003 Pulitzer Prize in poetry.

Joyce Carol Oates, author most recently of *The Faith of a Writer* (2003), *Rape: A Love Story* (2004), and *I Am No One You Know: Stories* (2004), is Roger S. Berlind Professor of Humanities at Princeton University. In 2003 she received the Common Wealth Award for Distinguished Service in Literature.

Ann Powers is a senior curator at the Experience Music Project in Seattle, where she has developed exhibits on subjects ranging from Bob Dylan to disco to live music photography. She is the author of *Weird Like Us: My Bohemian America* (2000) and co-editor, with Evelyn McDonnell, of *Rock She Wrote: Women Write About Rock, Pop and Rap* (1996). She was a pop critic for the *New York Times* during the late 1990s. Currently working on a book with the singer-songwriter Tori Amos, she lives in Seattle with her husband, Eric Weisbard, and daughter Rebecca.

John Rockwell is the senior cultural correspondent of the *New York Times*. Born in Washington, D.C., and raised in San Francisco, he attended Phillips Academy in Andover, Massachusetts; Harvard College; the University of Munich; and the University of California at Berkeley, from which he holds a Ph.D. in German cultural history. He was a critic for the *Oakland Tribune* and the *Los Angeles Times* before joining the *New York Times*, where from 1972 until 1991 he was a classical music critic; from 1974 to 1980, he was also chief rock critic. Between 1992 and 1994 he was based in Paris as European cultural correspondent. In the fall of 1994 he became the first director of the Lincoln Center Festival. He rejoined the *Times* in 1998, serving until 2002 as editor of the Sunday Arts and Leisure section. His books include *All-American Music: Composition in the Late Twentieth Century* (1983), *Sinatra* (1984), and *The Idiots*, a monograph on the Lars von Trier film (2003).

Luc Sante is celebrating his forty-fifth year as a Resident Alien. He is the author of *Low Life* (1991), *Evidence* (1992), *The Factory of Facts* (1998), and *Walker Evans* (2001), and co-editor, with Melissa Holbrook Pierson, of *O.K. You Mugs: Writers on Movie Actors* (1999). He teaches writing and the history of photography at Bard College and lives with his wife and son in Ulster County, New York.

Rennie Sparks, one half of the numinous country duo the Handsome Family, is the author of *Evil*, a collection of short stories (2001). She is at work on a novel concerning the invisible world. To rant, praise, or satisfy nagging curiosity, go to www.handsomefamily.com.

Founder of avant-rock band Pere Ubu, singer **David Thomas** has been rewriting the rules of popular music for more than twenty-eight years. Formed in Cleveland, Ohio, in 1975, Pere Ubu integrated found sound, analog synthesizers, and musique concrète into a hybrid of overdriven midwestern garage rock tempered by abstract sensibilities. Thomas has lectured on "The Geography of Sound in the Magnetic Age" and starred in London's West End in the *Tales of Hoffman*–inspired *Shockheaded Peter*; his rogue opera *Mirror Man* had its American debut in 2003 at the Freud Playhouse at UCLA. He also maintains the improvisational trio David Thomas and two pale boys. He lives in Brighton, England.

Sarah Vowell was born in Oklahoma and grew up in Montana. She is the author of *The Partly Cloudy Patriot* (2002), *Take the Cannoli* (2000), and *Radio On* (1997). She is a contributing editor at the public radio show *This American Life*, and lives in New York City.

Ed Ward wrote almost exclusively about music from 1965 to 1979, for *Crawdaddy!*, *Rolling Stone* (where he was an editor for six months), *Creem*, and other publications. In 1979 he became music columnist for the *Austin American-Statesman*. He is the author of *Michael Bloomfield: The Rise and Fall of an American Guitar Hero* (1983) and co-author of *Rock of Ages: The Rolling Stone History of Rock & Roll* (1986); the latter led to his residency as rock historian for the daily NPR program *Fresh Air*. In 1993, under the delusion that Americans wanted to read about life in Europe, he moved to Berlin, where, until he was hired as a disc jockey for Jazz Radio, he supported himself by selling magazines and tending bar. From 1997 to 2003, he wrote cultural reportage for the *Wall Street Journal*. He now hopes for a reversal of fortune that would enable him to move to France.

Eric Weisbard is senior program director in the education department of the Experience Music Project in Seattle and the organizer of its annual Pop

Conference. A former music editor at the *Village Voice* and senior editor at *Spin*, he is the co-editor of the *Spin Alternative Music Guide* (1995) and editor of *This Is Pop: In Search of the Elusive at Experience Music Project* (2004), a collection drawn from the 2002 EMP Pop Conference. The first ballads he can remember hearing are "The Ballad of Oh Boy" by Allen Sherman and "The Night Chicago Died" by Paper Lace.

Acknowledgments

Bob Weil, our editor at W. W. Norton, understood immediately our intentions for this book, and if they have come to pass it is due to his enthusiasm, prodding, imagination, and hard work. The book is not simply immeasurably better, thanks to Bob; without him, it would not exist at all. His assistant, Brendan Curry, was a stalwart, encouraging, and impeccable help all around. Bob also arranged for us to work with the designer Rubina Yeh, a genius in her craft, whose vision of both a thousand particulars and the book as a whole revealed aspects of the ballad we'd not imagined. To everyone else at Norton, including Drake McFeely (who had the wit to take a chance on our proposal) and our unflappable managing editor, Nancy Palmquist, and production manager, Amanda Morrison, our immense gratitude.

⁂

Two editors and twenty-two authors means a lot of contractual headaches. For undoing all the snags and taking care of business, we are both indebted to Wendy Weil of the Wendy Weil Agency, Inc., and Andrew Wylie of the Wylie Agency.

⁂

The idea for this book was born during an idle chat when Greil Marcus was in residence in the American Studies Program at Princeton as its Anschutz Distinguished Visitor in 2000–2001. The idea really got off the ground two years later, when Greil was back in Princeton as Old Dominion Fellow for the Council of the Humanities. We owe a great debt to the Anschutz Family Foundation, to the Council, and to the Council's director, Anthony Grafton, and executive director, Carol Rigolot, for making possible our collaboration, as we do to Princeton's Society of Fellows in the Liberal Arts, and its director, Leonard Barkan, for facilitating it.

⚜

At Princeton, we also owe a large bow, a tip of the hat, and much more to Judith Ferszt, the program manager in American Studies, for help, advice, and solidarity well beyond the call of duty. Thanks also to Michael Rivera, who saved Sean Wilentz's computer operations from utter destruction, and Michael Gordon, who saved Greil Marcus's from his panic attacks.

⚜

Jeff Rosen of Special Rider Music has been a special friend of this enterprise, and its authors, from start to finish. So has Tony Glover, better known to his many fans as the harmonica virtuoso "Little Sun" Glover.

⚜

Many other friends and loved ones helped enormously—sometimes more than they realized—with comments, readings of drafts, challenges, and quips. At the risk of forgetting anyone important here, we will thank them all personally—except, as ever, the essential Jenny Marcus and Christine Stansell.

⚜

In November 2002, Heather O'Donnell, then of the Princeton Society of Fellows, got us involved in organizing a conference on the American field recordings of the 1920s and 1930s, and we were lucky enough to lure Tony Glover and his bandmates, "Spider" John Koerner and Dave "Snaker" Ray, to provide some of the musical entertainment. Dave was mortally ill, but he insisted on making the show anyway; and he and Tony and John played brilliantly on November 22, in what would be Koerner, Ray, and Glover's final

Acknowledgments

performance. On November 28, Thanksgiving Day, Dave died in Minneapolis. This book is dedicated to his memory—for all he gave us and the world at the end, and for more than forty years of blues, rags, ballads, and hollers before that.

Above all, we want to thank our friends who contributed the essays, stories, comic strip, collage, and ballad that are *The Rose & the Briar*. Each joined in without hesitation, simply (we think) for the love of writing and or visually rendering these songs. Each astounded all over again with their gifts; and each was a trouper during the long haul of production. A salute to you all: Dave Marsh, Ann Powers, Rennie Sparks, Sharyn McCrumb, Anna Domino, Sarah Vowell, R. Crumb, Joyce Carol Oates, Cecil Brown, David Thomas, Luc Sante, Jon Langford, Paul Berman, John Rockwell, Stanley Crouch, James Miller, Ed Ward, Steve Erickson, Eric Weisbard, Wendy Lesser, Howard Hampton, and Paul Muldoon.

—S.W. and G.M.

Index

"ABC" (Jackson 5), 283
Abdnor, John Howard, Jr., 276, 284
Abdnor, John Howard, Sr., 276–79, 283, 284
"Abraham, Martin, and John" (Dion), 283
Adler, Renata, 334
"After the Ball" (Harris), 233, 235
"Ain't It Funky" (Brown), 186
Alexander, Danny, 16–17
Allbery, Debra, 23, 29, 37
"All My Trials," 291
"All Shook Up" (Parton), 302
"All Shook Up" (Presley), 266
"All the Whores Like the Way I Ride" (Bolden), 181
"Alone and Forsaken" (Mekons, Williams), 291
American Ballads and Folk Songs (Lomax), 127
American Recordings (Cash), 150
Americans, The (Frank), 335–36
American Songbag (Sandburg), 22
"Amor de la Calle" (Fernández), 226
Amos, Tori, 239
Anderson, Laurie, 299
Another Side of Bob Dylan (Dylan), 320
"Answer to Little Blossom" (Snow), 293
Arizona Wranglers, 263
Armstrong, Louis, 179–80, 243
Arnold, Eddy, 266
¡Arriba Huentitán! (Fernández), 224–25
Ashley, Clarence, 189–97
"Atlantic City" (Springsteen), 338
Autry, Gene, 262, 263, 264, 267, 270

"Back in the Saddle Again" (Autry), 264
Badlands, 334–35
Baez, Joan, 13–15, 28, 32, 88, 217, 239, 318
Baker, Frankie, 124–45, 154, 351, 353
Baldwin, James, 125

Ballad Book of John Jacob Niles, The (Niles), 10
Ballad of a Gunfighter, 270
Ballads (Ritchie), 13
"Banks of the Ohio" (Domino), 353
"Barbara Allen," 4, 7, 9–17, 354
"Barbara Allen Blues" (Holcomb), 16
"Barbary Allen," 9
"Barbry Allen," 293
"Barbry Ellen," 9
Barry, Jack, 354
"Battle Hymn of the Republic" (Howe), 81, 83–89
Bayas, Arthur, 156
Beatles, 17, 217, 283, 318
"Beautiful Dreamer" (Foster), 312
"Beauty and the Beast," 25
Bechet, Sidney, 183, 243
Beethoven, Ludwig van, 231
Beginning of the End, 186
"Bells of San Blas, The" (Longfellow), 212–13
Beltrán, Lola, 217
Benton, Brook, 282, 283
Berry, Chuck, 266, 337, 338
Best Bluegrass Songbook—Yet! (Bayas and Nemser), 156
Best Loved American Folk Songs (Lomax and Lomax), 261
Best Of Dolly Parton (Parton, 1970), 290, 292
Best Of Dolly Parton (Parton, 1975), 290
Best Of Portor Wagoner and Dolly Parton (Wagoner and Parton), 296
Bibb, Eric, 149
"Big Iron" (Robbins), 267
Big Surprise, The, 351–52, 354
"Billy the Kid" (Robbins), 267
"Bird in a Gilded Cage, A" (Bolden), 181
Birthday Party, 291

Birth of a Nation, The, 309
Bishop, Bridget, 43
Black, Brown and Beige (Ellington), 241, 247–48, 250–51
"Black Is the Color" (Ives), 231
"Blackwatertown" (Muldoon), 347–48
Bland, Bobby "Blue," 352
Blavatsky, Helena, 48
"Blind Willie McTell" (Dylan), 352
Blonde on Blonde (Dylan), 318
Blood on the Tracks (Dylan), 317–18
Blow Up, 310
Bly, Nellie, 126, 128
Bobby Patterson and the Mustangs, 276–81
Bob Wills and his Texas Playboys, 262
Boggs, Dock, 46
Bolden, Buddy, 178–86
"Bold Soldier, The" (Ives), 231
"Bonnie and Clyde" (Gainsbourg), 297
"Bonnie Streets of Fy-vie-O, The," 57–58
Booth, John Wilkes, 310
"Born to Run" (Springsteen), 340
Bouch, Boyd, 128
"Bowery Buck, The" (Turpin), 142
Brady, Diamond Jim, 320
Brahms, Johannes, 231
Brando, Marlon, 335
Braud, Wellman, 183
"Brennan on the Moor" (Ives), 231
"Bridge Over Troubled Water" (Simon), 283
Brightman, Sarah, 239
Bringing It All Back Home (Dylan), 15, 318
"British Literature" (Whitman), 212
Britt, Allen [Albert], 126–45, 154, 351, 353
Britten, Benjamin, 240
"Broadway Pagent, A" (Whitman), 211
Broady, Steve, 163, 165–66
Bronson, Bertrand Harris, 10
"Brother Love's Traveling Salvation Show" (Parton), 302
Brown, James, 186, 282
Brown, John, 83–84, 85
Brown, John, Sgt., 85–86
Browning, Todd, 313
"Buckeye Jim" (Ives), 231
Buckley, Bruce Redfern, 127, 130, 132, 137, 144

Burl Ives Song Book (Ives), 236
Bush, George W., 91, 309
"Butcher Boy, The," 22
Butcher's Boy (Sally Timms and the Drifting Cowgirls), 299
Butte, Montana (Frank), 336
Byrds, 291

Campbell, Joseph, 48
Car Accident—U.S. 66 between Winslow and Flagstaff, Arizona (Frank), 336
Cárdenas, Lázaro, 215, 227
"Careless Love," 26, 27
"Careless Love" (Bolden), 181
Carroll, J., 277
"Carry Me Back to Old Virginny," 84
Carson, Anne, 28
Carter, A. P., 167
Caruso, Enrico, 234
Cash, Johnny, 150–51, 157, 353
Cat on a Hot Tin Roof, 233
Cervantes, Miguel de, 212
"Chas" (Parton), 296
"Chattanooga Shoe Shine Boy" (Foley), 269
Chieftans, 235
Child, Francis, 2, 9
Christgau, Robert, 232, 239, 240
Christian, Arlester, 185
Church, Charlotte, 28, 239
Clark, William, 45
Clarke, James F., 86
Clay, Richard, 130–36
Clinton, George, 186
Coen, Ethan, 312
Coen, Joel, 312
Cohen, Eddie, 152–53, 158
Cohen, Leonard, 291
Coleridge, Samuel Taylor, 4
Collective Soul, 292
"Come All You Fair and Tender Ladies," 22
"Come Sunday" (Jackson and Ellington), 243–57
Conley, Arthur, 185–86
Conniff, Ray, 266
Cooper, Ira, 143–44
Cornish, Willie (William), 179, 182, 183
Cory, Martha, 43

Cowboy Songs and Other Frontier Ballads (Lomax), 263, 349
Creme de Funk (Woods and Quill), 185
Crosses on scene of highway accident—U.S. 91, Idaho (Frank) 236
Crumb, R., 93, 95–98
"Cuckoo, The," 187–97
"Cutthroat Song, The," 269

"Daddy Come and Get Me" (Parton), 296
"Daddy Was an Old Time Preacher Man" (Parton), 302
Dahl, Bill, 275, 277
Darkness on the Edge of Town (Springsteen), 334
Dark Side of the Moon (Pink Floyd), 163
Davis, Miles, 185
Davis, Skeeter, 292, 296
"Dead Man's Curve" (Jan and Dean), 161–74
Dean, Carl, 298–99
Dean, James, 335, 350
"Delia," 149–58
"Delia" (Dylan), 150
"Delia" (McTell), 153, 156–57
"Delia's Gone" (Bibb), 149
"Delia's Gone" (Cash, 1994), 150–51, 157
"Delia's Gone" (Cash, 1962), 150
"Delia's Gone" (Koerner, Ray, and Glover), 157
Delory, Michel, 353
de Paris, Sidney, 183
Department Store—Lincoln, Nebraska (Frank), 336
"Deportee (Plane Wreck at Los Gatos)" (Guthrie), 164
"De un rancho a otro" (Fernández), 222
Diamond, Neil, 302
Diamond Jim, 320
Dido, 239
"Dink's Song" (Lomax), 22
Dinning, Mark, 2
"Do It Again a Little Bit Slower" (Jon and Robin & the In Crowd), 276
Dolly (Nash), 292
Dolly in London (Parton), 294
Dolly: My Life and Other Unfinished Business (Parton), 300–301
Domino, Anna, 353
"Don't Go Way Nobody" (Bolden), 181

Dooley, Bill, 126, 142–44, 351
Doors, 280
Dorsey, Thomas A., 244
Douglas, Malcolm, 31
Douglass, Frederick, 91, 309
"Down from Dover" (Howard), 291
"Down from Dover" (Parton), 290–302
"Down from Dover" (Sinatra and Hazlewood), 296–97
"Down from Dover" (Timms), 291, 299–300
Drive-by Truckers, 299
Dunbar, William, 3
Dunn, Louis, 269
Dusen, Frankie, 184
Duston, Hannah, 44–45
Dyer-Benett, Richard, 232–33, 240
Dyke and the Blazers, 185
Dylan, Bob, 14–15, 16, 32, 150, 156, 238, 239, 280, 292, 317–25, 332, 352

Eagles, 186
"Eastbound Train," 293
Edison, Thomas Alva, 161–62, 164, 167–68, 174
Edmiston, Susan, 14–15
"18 Wheels of Love" (Drive-By Truckers), 299
Eisenhower, Dwight, 164, 174
"El Charro Mexicano" (Negrete), 214
El Cid (Cervantes), 212
Ellington, Duke, 241, 243–57
Ellison, Ralph, 253
"El Paso" (Robbins), 4, 259, 261–71, 354
Emerson, Ralph Waldo, 84, 174
"Empty-Handed Heart" (Zevon), 17
Ephron, Nora, 14–15
Eros the Bittersweet (Carson), 28
Essential Porter Wagoner and Dolly Parton (Parton and Wagoner), 296

Fair and Tender Ladies (Smith), 301
Fairest of Them All, The (Parton), 294, 296
Farber, Manny, 339–40
Father of the Blues (Handy), 132
Faulkner, William, 320
Fear and Whiskey (Mekons), 297
"Female Soldier, The," 25

Ferguson, Bob, 297
Ferlinghetti, Lawrence, 167
Fernández, Alejandro, 224–25
Fernández, Vicente "Chente," 203, 218, 219–28
Fields, James T., 87
"Fight and Scratch" (Parton and Wagoner), 297
"Fitcher's Bird" (Grimm), 41–42, 43
Five Americans, 280
"Flee as a Bird" (Bolden), 181
Floyd, Pretty Boy, 350
Flying Burrito Brothers, 161
Fodor, Nandor, 44
"Foggy, Foggy Dew, The" (Britten), 240
"Foggy, Foggy Dew, The" (Dyer-Bennett) 240
"Foggy, Foggy Dew, The" (Ives), 231–32, 236, 240
"Foggy Dew, The" (McCormack), 235
"Foggy Dew, The" (O'Connor and the Chieftans), 235
Foley, Red, 269
Folk Songs from the Southern Appalachians (Ritchie), 26
Folksongs of North America (Lomax), 236, 237
"Folsom Prison Blues" (Cash), 150
Fonda, Henry, 331, 332, 342
Ford, Henry, 164
Ford, John, 334, 342
"For Dave Glover" (Dylan), 14
Foster, Stephen, 311–12, 313
Fowke, Edith, 33
"Fox, The" (Ives), 231
Frank, Robert, 335–36
"Frankie and Albert" (Dooley), 123, 125–45, 351
"Frankie and Her Men: A Study of the Interrelationships of Popular and Folk Traditions" (Buckley), 127–28
"Frankie and Johnny" (Domino), 353
Frankie and Johnny (film), 140
Frankie and Johnny (Huston) (book), 131
Frankie and Johnny (Huston) (play), 131
"Frankie and Johnny" (Taylor), 123, 125–45, 351
"Frankie Killed Allen" (Dooley), 126
"From One Ranch to Another"

(Fernández), 222
Fugate, Caril Ann, 330–37
Fulks, Robbie, 296
"Funk Bomb" (Brown), 186
Funk Junction (Pleasure), 185
Funky (Gene Ammon's All Stars), 185
"Funky Broadway" (Christian), 185
"Funky Broadway" (Pickett), 185
"Funky Butt" (Bolden), 182–83
"Funky Chicken" (Thomas), 186
"Funky Drummer" (Brown), 186
"Funky Funky Xmas" (New Kids on the Block), 186
"Funky Kingston" (Toots and the Maytals), 186
"Funky Nassau" (Beginning of the End), 186
"Funky New Year" (Eagles), 186
"Funky President" (Brown), 186
"Funky Ride" (OutKast), 186
"Funky Side of Town" (Brown), 186
"Funky Street" (Conley), 185–86

Gainsbourg, Serge, 297
"Gates of Eden" (Dylan), 15
Gene Ammon's All Stars, 185
Gentry, Bobbie, 298
Gershwin, George, 311
"Get Up and Bar the Door," 55
Gilded Palace of Sin, The (Flying Burrito Brothers), 161
"Girl Left Alone" (Parton), 294
Giselle, 236
Glaser, Bobby, 266
Glaser, Jim, 266–67
Glaser Brothers, 266, 269
"Gloryland" (Hall), 88
Goblins, 294
"Go Down Moses," 341
"Go Down Moses" (Bolden), 181
Gone With the Wind, 309
Gonsalves, Paul, 255
Good, Sarah, 44
"Good Man Is Hard to Find, A" (O'Connor), 332
Gordon, Robert Winslow, 127
"Gosport Tragedy, The," 39–42, 46
Grand Funk Railroad, 186
Grapes of Wrath, The (Steinbeck), 87, 336, 342

Grateful Dead, 350
Green, Delia, 149–58
"Green, Green Grass of Home" (Parton
    and Wagoner), 295
Grimm Brothers, 41
*Grove Dictionary of Music and
    Musicians,* 237
Gun Club, 291
Gunfighter Ballads and Trail Songs
    (Robbins), 265, 267
Gunsmoke, 265, 292
Guthrie, Woody, 164, 262, 329, 332, 333,
    336–38, 342

Halgreen, Henry, 85
Hall, Daryl, 88
Hall and Oates, 88
Hamlet, The (Faulkner), 320
Hamm, Charles, 238
Handy, W. C., 132, 142–43
Harris, Charles K., 233
Harris, Emmylou, 14
Have Gun Will Travel, 265, 267
Hawkins, Dale "Susie Q.," 276
Hazlewood, Lee, 296–97
"Heartbreak Hotel" (Presley), 172
"He Done Me Wrong: Death of Bill
    Bailey," 127
"Henry Martin" (Ives), 231
Here You Come Again (Parton), 295
"Here You Come Again" (Parton), 302
High Noon, 267, 268
"Highway Patrolman" (Springsteen),
    338, 339
Holcomb, Roscoe, 16
Holmes, John Clellon, 185
"Home on the Range," 261, 271
Hood, Patterson, 299
Hopper, Edward, 33
Horn, The (Holmes), 185
"Hound Dog" (Presley), 266
"House of the Rising Sun" (Domino), 353
Houston, Moses "Cooney," 149–58
Houston, Whitney, 289
Howard, Rowland S., 299
Howe, Julia Ward, 86–88
Howe, Samuel Gridley, 86
Hugo, Victor, 211, 212
"Hungry Heart" (Springsteen), 16
Hurt, Mississippi John, 125, 128–29, 139

Huston, John, 130–31

"If You See Her, Say Hello" (Dylan), 319
"I Gave My Love a Cherry," 13
"I Get Lonesome by Myself" (Parton and
    Wagoner), 295
"I Have Been to the Mountaintop"
    (King), 87
"I'm Doing This for Your Sake" (Parton),
    296
Incompleat Folksinger, The (Seeger), 30
Indigo Girls, 28
Infante, Pedro, 216, 221, 226, 228, 268
In the Shadow of a Song (Parton), 293
Irving, Washington, 210
"It's All Over Now, Baby Blue" (Dylan),
    15
"It's All Right Ma (I'm Only Bleeding)"
    (Dylan), 15
It Stays Here (Timms), 299–300
"It Was a Very Good Year" (Sinatra), 2
Ives, Burl Icle Ivanhoe, 231–40, 262
"I Want You Back" (Jackson 5), 283
"I Will Always Love You" (Houston), 289
"I will Always Love You" (Parton), 289,
    301
IWW Songbook, The, 88

Jackson, Mahalia, 231, 241, 243–45,
    247–57
Jackson 5, 283
"Jamie Douglas," 22, 26, 31
Jan and Dean, 161–62
"Jeannie's Afraid of the Dark" (Fulks),
    296
"Jeannie's Afraid of the Dark" (Parton
    and Wagoner), 296
Jenkins, James, 85
Jewel, 239
J. Frank Wilson and the Cavaliers, 16
"Jimmy Crack Corn" (Ives), 231
"John Brown's Body," 81, 83–89
"John Henry," 351
"John Henry" (Domino), 353
"Johnny 99" (Springsteen), 338, 339
John Robichaux Orchestra, 178
Johnson, Bunk, 180, 183, 184
Johnson, Jimmy, 179, 180
Johnson, Robert, 164, 167
Jon and Robin & the In Crowd, 276

Jones, J., 277
Jones, Marshall, 12
Jones, Quincy, 185
Jordanaires, 266
José, José, 218
Joshua (Parton), 293–94
"Just Married" (Robbins), 266
"Just the Way I Am" (Parton), 296

Kael, Pauline, 335
Keppard, Freddie, 180
Kern, Jerome, 311
Kerouac, Jack, 164, 174, 335
Kincaid, Bradley, 12, 13, 15
"King Brady," 141

"Lady Isabel and the Elf Knight," 39,
    40–41, 42, 46
Land of Dreams (Newman), 308
Langford, Jon, 299
Las Mujeres de mi general, 216, 221
"Last Kiss," 298
"Last Kiss" (Pearl Jam), 16
Leadbelly, 128, 135
Leaves of Grass (Whitman), 211, 212
Leighton, Bert, 128
Leighton Brothers, 128
Lennardson, Samuel, 45
"Let it Be" (Beatles), 283
"Letter Edged in Black, The," 293
"Letter to Heaven" (Parton), 293–94
Lewis, Frank, 179
Lewis, Jerry Lee, 333, 337
Lewis, Myra Gale, 333, 337
"Light My Fire" (Doors), 280
"Like a Rolling Stone" (Dylan), 280
Lilith Fair, 28
"Lily, Rosemary and the Jack of Hearts"
    (Dylan), 317–25
"Lily of the West" (Dylan), 321
Lincoln, Abraham, 9, 85, 87, 184, 309–13
Lindbergh, Charles, 312
Lipton, Nemser, 156
"Little Bessie," 293
"Little Blossom" (Parton), 293
"Little Brown Dog," 15
"Little Maggie," 99, 101–22
"Little Son Hugh," 293
Little Sparrow (Parton), 292, 295, 298
Live 1975 (Dylan), 32

Lomax, Alan, 2, 22, 30, 135, 183, 231,
    232, 236, 239, 261
Lomax, John A., 2, 30, 127, 135, 261, 263,
    349
Lombardo, Guy, 128
"Lonesome Town" (Howard), 291
"Long and Winding Road, The"
    (Beatles), 283
Long Black Veil (Chieftans), 235
Longfellow, Henry Wadsworth, 210,
    212–13, 228
"Lord Edward," 15
"Louisiana 1927" (Newman), 4, 307–14
"Love in Vain" (Johnson), 167
Lyrical Ballads (Coleridge and
    Wordsworth), 4

McCartney, Paul, 16
McCormack, John, 234–35
"Machine Gun Funk" (Notorious B.I.G.),
    186
McLachlan, Sarah, 239
McTell, Blind Willie, 152–53, 156–57
"Make It Funky" (Brown), 186
Maldonado, Fernando Z., 224–25, 226
Malick, Terrence, 334
"Mama's Got a Baby Called Tee-Na-Na"
    (Bolden), 182
"Mammie" (Parton), 296
"Mansion on the Hill" (Springsteen), 337,
    339
"Many Thousands Gone" (Baldwin), 125
Mariachi Vargas de Tecalitlán, 207, 215,
    227
Marquis, Donald, 184
Marsalis, Wynton, 252
Martin, Grady, 269
Martin, Susannah, 43
"Mary Had a Little Lamb" (Edison), 168
"Maybellene" (Robbins), 266
Maynard, Ken, 263
"Me and Little Andy" (Parton), 295, 302
"Mean Talking Blues" (Guthrie), 332
Mekons, 291, 299
Metacom (King Philip), 44
Mezzrow, Mezz, 185
Michael, George, 186
Miller, Mitch, 266
*Million Seller Hits Made Famous by
    Country Queens* (Parton), 293

Mills, Willie, 152–53
Miracle of Morgan's Creek, The, 339
Moman, Chips, 277–80
"Mood Indigo" (Ellington), 252
Moore, Bob, 269
Mormon Tabernacle Choir, 88
Morton, Jelly Roll, 183, 184, 185, 243
Moseley, Caroline, 24
"Mountain Angel" (Parton), 295
"Mr. Tambourine Man" (Dylan), 15
Muldoon, Paul, 817–10
"Mule Skinner Blues (Blue Yodel No. 8)"
    (Parton), 297
Mumford, Jefferson "Brock," 179
Musik in Geschichte und Gegenwart, 237
"My Blue Ridge Mountain Boy" (Parton),
    297
"My Bucket's Got a Hole in It" (Bolden),
    181
"My Father's House" (Springsteen), 338
"My Old Kentucky Home" (Foster), 311
"My Old Kentucky Home" (Newman),
    313

Nash, Alanna, 292
Natural Born Killers, 337
Nature and Madness (Shepard), 48
Nebraska (Springsteen), 337–38
"Nebraska" (Springsteen), 4, 329–43,
    354
Neff, Mary, 44–45
Negrete, Jorge, 214, 268
"Nelly Was a Lady" (Foster), 311
Nelson, Ricky, 291
New Kids on the Block, 186
Newman, Randy, 4, 307–14
New Orleans Jazzmen, 183
New Riders of the Purple Sage, 350
Nicholas, Albert, 183
Niles, John Jacob, 10–11, 12, 13, 14, 232
Nine to Five, 301
Notorious B.I.G., 186
"Nottemun Town," 15

O Brother, Where Art Thou?, 312
O'Connor, Flannery, 313, 332, 335
O'Connor, Sinéad, 235
"Ode to Billie Joe" (Gentry), 298
"Oh, Pretty Woman" (Orbison), 269
Oklahoma!, 231

"Old Chisholm Trail, The," 261
"O Love Is Teasing," 22, 26
O'Malley, D. J., 263
"Omie Wise," 69, 71–80, 351
"Open All Night" (Springsteen), 338, 339
Orbison, Roy, 269
OutKast, 186
"O Waly Waly," 22, 26, 31
Owens, Buck, 297

Painting Signs (Bibb), 149
Pamela (Richardson), 300
Parrish, Abigail, 43
Parsons, Gram, 291
Parton, Avie Lee, 298
Parton, Dolly, 14, 15, 289–303
Parton, Willadeene, 293, 298
"Party, The" (Parton and Wagoner), 295
Patterson, Bobby, 275–84
Paul, Les, 269
"Payaso" (Solís), 226
Pearl Jam, 16
Pepys, Samuel, 9, 10
Pere Ubu, 335
Pete (Seeger), 31
Phair, Liz, 239
Philip, King (Metacom), 44
Pickett, Wilson, 185
Pink Floyd, 162–63
Pitney, Gene, 312
Pleasants, Henry, 234
Pleasure, King, 185
"Political Science" (Newman), 308
Ponce, Manuel M., 216
Poster, W. S., 339–40
Prescott, William H., 210
"Present Is Dead, The" (Howe), 87
Presley, Elvis, 162, 164, 166, 167, 172, 174,
    266, 302, 349
"Pretty Boy Floyd" (Guthrie), 333
"Pretty Peggy-O," 51–57
"Pretty Polly," 4, 37–49, 354
Proby, P. J., 312
Pruett, Jack H., 269
Pryor [Pryar], Alice, 132, 134–36, 141

Quill, Gene, 185

"Raindrops Keep Fallin' on My Head,"
    283

"Rainy Day Women #12 & 35" (Dylan), 318

"Rainy Night in Georgia" (Benton), 282

Ramsay, Allan, 22

Randy Newman Songbook, Vol 1, The (Newman), 313–14

RCA Years, The (Parton), 292

Really the Blues (Mezzrow), 185

"Reason to Believe" (Springsteen), 338, 339, 340, 342

Reconquista, 212

Red River, 267

"Red River Valley, The," 63

Reeves, Jim, 277

Rennick, Robert M., 25

"Reservoir, The" (Allbery), 23

Richards, Keith, 291

Richardson, Samuel, 300

Rio Bravo, 268–69, 271

Rise of the Novel, The (Watt), 300

Ritchie, Jean, 13–16, 26–27

Robbins, Marty, 4, 259, 261–71

"Robert" (Parton), 296

Robeson, Paul, 231

"Rocket 88" (Turner), 173

Rodgers, Jimmie, 264, 297

Roig, Mercedes Díaz, 213

Romancero tradicional de América (Roig), 213

Room in Brooklyn (Hopper), 33

Roosevelt, Theodore, 349, 351

Rossum, Emmy, 14

Royal Rockers, 276

Russell, William, 183

"Sail Away" (Newman), 307–14

"Sailor's Return, or the Broken Token, The," 25

"St. James Infirmary," 352

"St. James Infirmary" (Domino), 353

"St. Louis Tickle," 182

"St. Louis Woman" (Handy), 132

Sally Timms and the Drifting Cowgirls, 299

"San Angelo" (Robbins), 268, 270

Sandburg, Carl, 22, 231, 236, 237

Santayana, George, 238

Saved (Dylan), 319

"Say, Brothers, Will You Meet Us?," 85

Schubert, Franz, 284

"Second Gaslight Tape" (Dylan), 15

Seeger, Pete, 28, 30, 31, 233, 262

"See Willy Fly By" (Waco Brothers), 187–97

Shakespeare, William, 321

Sharp, Cecil, 24, 30, 31, 231

She Done Him Wrong, 140

Sheen, Martin, 334

Shepard, Paul, 48

Shepherd, Bill, 98

"Shine" (Parton), 292

"Short but Funky" (Too Short), 186

"Silly Love Songs" (McCartney), 16

Sinatra, Frank, 2, 234

Sinatra, Nancy, 296–97

"Singing the Blues" (Robbins), 266

Singleton, Zutty, 183

$64,000 Question, The, 351

Skeeter Sings Dolly (Davis), 292

Sly and the Family Stone, 283

Smith, Harry, 239

Smith, Lee, 301

Smith, Stephen, 183, 184

"Smokestack Lightning," 336

Smokey Mountain Memories (Parton), 293

Snakefarm, 353

Snow, Hank, 293

"Solidarity Forever," 88

Solís, Javier, 226

Solomon, Maynard, 13

Somebody's Rocking My Dreamboat (Timms), 299

Songcatcher, 14

Songs from My Funeral (Snakefarm), 353

Songs of False Hope and High Values (Timms and Langford), 299

"Sonnet 94" (Shakespeare), 321

Sons of the Pioneers, 263–64, 267

Souchon, Edmond "Doc," 184

Soul Is My Music: The Best of Bobby Patterson (Patterson), 275, 277, 282

South Pacific, 231

"Sow Took the Measles, The" (Ives), 231

Spacek, Sissy, 334

"Spanish Element in our Nationality, The" (Whitman), 210

Sprague, Carl T., 263, 267

Springfield, Dusty, 312
Springsteen, Bruce, 4, 16, 329–43, 351
"Stagolee," 141, 144–45, 351
"Stairway to Heaven" (Parton), 292
Starkweather, Charles, 329–37, 351
Starr, Edwin, 283
"Starting in San Francisco"
        (Ferlinghetti), 167
"Statesboro Blues" (McTell), 152–53
"State Trooper" (Springsteen), 338, 339
Steele, Pete, 19
Steinbeck, Carol, 87
Steinbeck, John, 87, 342
"Story of my Life, The" (Robbins), 266
Stowe, Harriet Beecher, 87
Strawberry Roan, The, 263
"Strawberry Roan, The" (Robbins), 263
"Strawberry Roan" (Arizona Wranglers),
        263
"Streets of Laredo, The," 352–53, 354
"Streets of Laredo, The" (Domino), 353
Streisand, Barbra, 28
String Quintet in C Major (D. 956, op.
        posth. 163) (Schubert), 284
Sturges, Preston, 320, 338–42
"Subterranean Homesick Blues" (Dylan),
        280
Sullivan's Travels, 329, 338–42
"Sweet Adeline" (Bolden), 181
"Sweet Betsy from Pike," 63
Sydney, Sylvia, 331

"Tales of the Wayside Inn" (Longfellow),
        212
"Tangled Up in Blue" (Dylan), 319
Tarantino, Quentin, 337
Taylor, James, 239
Taylor, Tell, 128
"T.C.B. or T.Y.A." (Patterson), 277, 282
Tea-Table Miscellany (Ramsay), 22
"Teen Angel" (Dinning), 2
"Teacher Hit Me with a Ruler," 88
"Tell Laura I Love Her" (Peterson), 298
"Tennessee Homesick Blues" (Parton),
        299
Terry, Clark, 249
Tex, Joe, 277, 282, 283
"Thank You (Fallettinme Be Mice Elf
        Agin)" (Sly and the Family Stone),
283
"That's All Right" (Robbins), 266
These Immortal Souls, 291
"They Live by Night," 329
13 Hillbilly Giants (Fulks), 296
Thomas, Rufus, 186
Thoreau, Henry David, 174, 210
"Thunder Road" (Springsteen), 340
Tillman, Cornelius, 179, 180
Timms, Sally, 291, 299–300
"Tom Dooley," 351
"Tom Dooley" (Domino), 353
"Tom Joad" (Guthrie), 329, 333, 342
"Too Funky" (Michael), 186
Too Short, 186
Toots and the Maytals, 186
Traditional Ballad Index, 24
Travis, Merle, 13, 15
Trent, Buck, 297
"Trial of Mary Maguire" (Patterson),
        275–86
Tristan und Isolde (Wagner), 236
Trouble in Paradise (Newman), 308
True Romance, 337
Truth, Sojourner, 86
Tubb, Ernest, 283
Tumbling Tumbleweeds, 264
"Tumbling Tumbleweeds" (Sons of the
        Pioneers), 264, 267
Turner, Ike, 173
Turpin, Tom, 142–43
Twenty-One, 351
"Twenty-third Psalm, The" (Jackson),
        256
"Two Little Babes," 293
"Two Little Orphans" (Parton), 293

Uncle Tom's Cabin (Stowe), 87
"Unfortunate Rake, The," 351–52
Union Boys '44, 233
"Used Cars" (Springsteen), 338, 339
U.S. 30 between Ogallala and North
        Platte, Nebraska (Frank), 336
U.S. 285, New Mexico (Frank), 335
"Utah Carol" (Robbins), 267

Vallee, Rudy, 234
"Vaya con Dios," 269
Vega, Lope de, 212
Villon, François, 3

"Viola Lee Blues," 350
Volume Two (Baez), 13
"Volver, Volver," 203–28
"Volver, Volver" (Fernández), 203, 219–27

Wagner, Richard, 236
Wagoner, Porter, 295–98
"Waillie, Waillie" (Sandburg), 22
"Wait 'Til the Sun Shines, Nellie," 61–62
Walker, Cas, 292, 301
"Walking the Floor Over You" (Tubb), 283
"Walk the Dog" (Anderson), 299
"War" (Starr), 283
Warlocks, 350
Warner, Willie, 179
"Water Is Wide, The," 21–33
Waters, Muddy, 179
Watt, Ian, 300
Wayfaring Stranger, The (Ives), 231
"Wayfaring Stranger, The" (Ives), 231
"Welcome to my World" (Reeves), 277
Wells, Kitty, 293
West, Emma, 151–54, 158
West, Willie, 151–54
Westenra, Hayley, 239
"Wheels" (Flying Burrito Brothers), 161
"When Cockle Shells Turn Silver Bells," 22
"When the Work's All Done This Fall"
(Sprague), 263
"When You Go A Courtin'" (Wade and Brasswell), 93, 96–97
White, Tony Joe, 282–83
"White Sport Coat and a Pink Carnation, A" (Robbins), 266
Whitman, Walt, 174, 210–11, 212, 213, 228
Willard, Patricia, 252
Williams, Hank, 291, 332
Winchester '73, 267
Winkler, Ray, 277, 283
"With God on Our Side" (Dylan), 332
Woode, Jimmy, 256–57
Woods, Phil, 185
Wordsworth, William, 4
World Gone Wrong (Dylan), 150
"Worried Man Blues" (Carter Family), 167
"Wreck of Old 97, The," 161–74
"Wreck on the Highway" (Springsteen), 336

"Yesterday" (Beatles), 17
Yesterdays: Popular Song in America (Hamm), 238
"You Can't Catch Me" (Berry), 338
You Only Live Once, 331, 332
"You're Going to Make Me Lonesome When You Go" (Dylan), 319

Zevon, Warren, 17

About the Editors

Sean Wilentz is the author of *Chants Democratic, The Kingdom of Matthias* (with Paul E. Johnson), and other works of history, including *The Rise of American Democracy: From Jefferson to Lincoln*, which is forthcoming from W. W. Norton & Company in 2005. A contributing editor at *The New Republic*, he writes regularly on politics, books, and the arts for the *New York Times, The American Prospect, Dissent*, and other publications. He is also historian-in-residence at Bob Dylan's official web site, www.bobdylan.com, where some of his essays on American music have first appeared. A distinguished teacher and lecturer, he is Dayton-Stockton Professor of History and director of the Program in American Studies at Princeton University.

Greil Marcus was born in San Francisco in 1945 and attended the University of California at Berkeley, where he was Regents Lecturer in American Studies in 1997. He began writing in 1968 for *Rolling Stone*, and has since been a columnist for the *San Francisco Express-Times, Creem, New West* (later *California*), *Artforum, Salon*, the *New York Times*, and other publications, while also publishing in *Die Zeit, La Nouvelle Revue Française, Granta*, and *Threepenny Review*. He is a member of the editorial board of the journal *Common Knowledge* and from 1992 to 1995 was a member of the Rock Bottom Remainders, the all-author rock 'n' roll band. In 1989, for the Institute of Contemporary Art in Boston, he was co-curator of the exhibition *On the passage of a few people through a rather brief moment of time: The Situationist International, 1957–1972*, and in 1998 of *1948—From the Permanent Collection* at the Whitney Museum of American Art in New York. In 2000 he taught the seminar "Prophecy and the American Voice" at Berkeley and as Anschutz Distinguished Fellow in American Studies at Princeton, and in 2002, as an Old Dominion Fellow of the Council of the Humanities at Princeton, the seminar "Practical Criticism." His books include *Lipstick Traces, The Dustbin of History*, and *The Old, Weird America*. He lives in Berkeley.

An unprecedented collection of songs, both ancient and modern, from *The Rose & The Briar: Death, Love and Liberty in the American Ballad*.

The Rose & The Briar CD contains most of the songs treated in *The Rose & The Briar* book. On this CD, the saga of the American ballad unfolds much as the songs themselves appeared in historical record, from classic recordings dating to the 1920s and 1930s to brand-new recordings, made especially for this collection, of equally traditional tunes, from such modern classics of the ballad form as Marty Robinson's "El Paso," Dolly Parton's "Down From Dover," Randy Newman's "Sail Away," Bob Dylan's 'Lily, Rosemary And The Jack Of Hearts," and Bruce Springsteen's "Nebraska," to The Handsome Family's Recording of Paul Muldoon's "Blackwatertown."

"We envisioned the book version of *The Rose & The Briar* as a stage. Here, on the CD, is one version of the show."

—SEAN WILENTZ AND GREIL MARCUS,
FROM THE LINER NOTES

TRACK LISTING:

1. **Jean Ritchie** *Barbary Allen*
2. **The Coon Creek Girls** *Pretty Polly*
3. **G.B. Grayson** *Ommie Wise*
4. **Snakefarm** *Little Maggie*
5. **Mississippi John Hurt** *Frankie*
6. **Koerner, Ray & Glover** *Deliah's Gone*
7. **John Mellencamp** *Wreck of The Old 97*
8. **Jan & Dean** *Dead Man's Curve*
9. **Jelly Roll Morton** *Buddy Bolden's Blues (I Though I Heard Buddy Bolden Say)*
10. **Clarence Ashley** *The Coo Coo Bird*
11. **Vicente Fernández** *Volver, Volver*
12. **Burl Ives** *The Foggy Foggy Dew*
13. **Duke Ellington And His Orchestra, Featuring Mahalia Jackson** *Black, Brown & Beige Part IV (Come Sunday)*
14. **Marty Robbins** *El Paso*
15. **Bobby Patterson** *Trial of Mary Maguire*
16. **Dolly Parton** *Down From Dover*
17. **Randy Newman** *Sail Away*
18. **Bob Dylan** *Lily, Rosemary And The Jack Of Hearts*
19. **Bruce Springsteen** *Nebraska*
20. **The Handsome Family** *Blackwatertown*